D1365212

Essays,
Letters, and Reviews
by Matthew Arnold

Essays,
Letters, and Reviews
by Matthew Arnold

Collected and Edited
by FRASER NEIMAN

HARVARD UNIVERSITY PRESS
Cambridge, Massachusetts 1960

94044

To Stella

Preface

Essays, Letters, and Reviews by Matthew Arnold is not an anthology of the "beauties" of Arnold. It is a collection of articles by him that time or shifting interests or oversight have made difficult of access to readers of Arnold, frequently even to the scholar. The collection embraces almost Arnold's entire career as a writer of prose, extending from "On the Modern Element in Literature," which he gave as a lecture in 1857, to his essay "Disestablishment in Wales," which appeared in March 1888, the month before his death. By virtue of this span it is representative of his varied styles and of his intellectual development in many of its phases. These essays, though they cannot increase his stature, afford a lively sense of his breadth of interests, his essential modesty, and his lambent humor.

The present volume is, I think, justified by the current state of Arnold scholarship. More than fifty years ago the fifteen-volume Edition de Luxe of *The Works of Matthew Arnold* (London, 1903–1904) was published. The inclusion in the last volume of Thomas B. Smart's *Bibliography of Matthew Arnold* indicated even then the selective nature of what has remained the standard edition. E. J. O'Brien's collection, published as *Essays in Criticism, Third Series* (Boston, 1910), and the Oxford edition of the *Essays of Matthew Arnold* (Oxford, 1914), brought together from their original places of publication certain additional papers. But these books, like Arnold's own volume *Civilization in the United States* (Boston, 1888), of which no part was included in the Edition de Luxe, have long been out of print. The current renewal of popular and scholarly interest in the Victorian period has encouraged the republication of individual essays and of selections like Merle M. Bevington's edition of *England and the Italian Question* (Durham, N. C., 1953) and Kenneth Allott's *Five Uncollected Essays of Matthew Arnold* (Liverpool, 1953). Moreover, textual studies of Arnold's revisions of his prose by the late E. K. Brown, Francis G. Townsend and William E. Buckler have disclosed other inadequacies of the Edition de Luxe, while the critical perspectives of our time have given increased significance to articles like "The Bishop and the Philosopher," which has never been reprinted in its original form.

In addition, the canon of Arnold's prose itself has not been finally established. The limitations of T. B. Smart's bibliography were indicated in Miss Marion Mainwaring's "Notes toward a Matthew Arnold Bibliography," *Modern Philology* (February 1952). R. H. Super has provided a more complete listing of Arnold's public lectures (*Modern Language Notes,* December 1955) than hitherto existed. Unpublished accounts of money received, which Arnold entered in his notebooks or pocket diaries, have made possible the identification recently of several unsigned reviews and articles in the *Pall Mall Gazette,* the *London Review,* and the *Quarterly Review.* Entries in published and unpublished notebooks suggest that a few other articles await detection. To these R. H. Super's "Arnold's Notebooks and Arnold Bibliography," *Modern Philology* (May 1959), affords a guide. The habits of scholarship, and in the end the interests of the "general reader" — the anomalous figure whom Arnold, except in his school reports, almost exclusively addressed — require both the fixing of the canon and, in time, the publication of a definitive edition of his writings that will show the entire scope of his endeavor and that will indicate his often interesting and sometimes extensive textual revisions.

The present volume brings together a number of pieces of Arnold's occasional prose that fall in one of the following categories: (1) articles signed by Arnold that have not been reprinted since their original publication in the nineteenth century, largely in periodicals of the day; (2) articles not collected in the Edition de Luxe of 1903–1904, but which, though gathered into one or more small collections since then, are now either out of print or accessible only in scattered volumes; (3) articles that Arnold contributed anonymously or pseudonymously to various journals and which have been ascribed to him only very recently. In the first category fall essays like "The Nadir of Liberalism" and "The Zenith of Conservatism"; in the second, essays like "Dr. Stanley's Lectures on the Jewish Church"; in the third are the essays assigned to Arnold by Marion Mainwaring in "Notes toward a Matthew Arnold Bibliography," by myself in "Some Newly Attributed Contributions of Matthew Arnold to the *Pall Mall Gazette,*" *Modern Philology* (November 1957), by R. H. Super in "Arnold's Notebooks and Arnold Bibliography," *Modern Philology* (May 1959), in the case of "Ordnance Maps"; and, in the instance of the review of Count de Maistre's *Lettres et opuscules inédits,* by R. H. Super in the article just cited and by me in "Matthew Arnold's Review of the *Lettres et opuscules inédits* by Joseph de Maistre," *Modern Language Notes* (June 1959).

To assemble all the unassembled material, even excluding on grounds of their specialization the frequently interesting school reports, would exceed the limits of a single volume, and would include curiosities like "A Speech at the Distribution of Prizes at Dulwich College" or the Preface to Mary S. Claude's lugubrious stories for children, *Twilight Thoughts* (Boston, 1887), which will scarcely concern anyone other than the historian of Dulwich College or the bibliographer. It is difficult to predict what may be of value to some reader, yet it is questionable whether it would be desirable to reprint, in a selective volume, Arnold's two articles on General Grant, or the one on Arthur Mynors entitled "An Eton Boy," consisting as they do of extract and gloss, united by the barely discernible thread of an idea. On the other hand, the five long reviews of Curtius's five-volume *History of Greece* seem to me to justify more attention, because although they too consist largely of extract and gloss, the device here serves to illuminate Arnold's sense of historical and moral process; and the parallels Arnold perceived between his own age and the century of Pericles reflect his views of society.

An interest in seeing Arnold whole demands that attention be given those several vigorous essays of 1886 to 1888, which reveal his lively concern with topical political matters, namely, the Irish question and Welsh disestablishment. Furthermore, the absence of a biography of Arnold, in accord with his own desire (always excepting Lionel Trilling's study) and the personal reticence in his own work lend value to the topical speeches and addresses he was willing to make in his later years. However, although "The Twice Revised Code," which appeared in *Fraser's Magazine* (March 1862), is the basic statement of Arnold's long continuing protest against the educational reform of 1861, it is excluded here, because its length is far in excess of its general interest and because, like the formal school reports or the survey "Schools" in T. W. Ward's *The Reign of Queen Victoria,* 2 vols. (London, 1887), it is highly technical. But I have chosen to retain Arnold's short letters to the press on this subject, for they present the basic case with brevity and they possess an ardor that gives them a personal quality.

The personality of Arnold is seldom absent from anything he wrote, though in several essays there are admittedly longueurs for the modern reader. There were perhaps stretches of tedium for Arnold, too, for sometimes, as in "Common Schools Abroad," the promise of a brisk beginning declines into rather pedestrian achievement. On the other hand, the force of his conviction or his alert awareness of the follies of the day — from the Mme. Rachel who claimed to make women "beautiful for ever," to the extravagances of ritualism or the popular enthusiasm for the murderer Müller, casts of whom "taken after his execution" were advertised for sale in London — often illuminate his writing. But beyond the matter of personality, these essays, letters, and reviews demonstrate afresh the great range of Arnold's mind, his cosmopolitanism, his habit of seeing in the particular or the local event evidences of the general culture of his time.

The articles are reprinted as they were presented in the source where they first appeared. I have retained in most respects the punctuation of the source, including occasional inconsistencies in the spelling and punctuation of Arnold or his editors. Arnold's own footnotes, indicated by asterisks, have been retained also. However, modern usage with reference to the treatment of the titles of books, articles, and poems, and in the treatment of quotations and quotations within quotations has been followed. Ligatured letters have been replaced by diphthongs. The essays are given in the chronological order of their publication, with the exception of "On the Modern Element in Literature," for in this case publication was delayed almost twelve years. The discussion which precedes each piece is intended to afford some orientation of the article in the canon of Arnold's work, and I have attempted in the endnotes to provide annotations that might clarify Arnold's allusions, but I do not pretend to completeness. Arnold's range of contemporary reference, as of historical and literary, is very great. The pursuit of allusion has often been entertaining, often exasperating, often fruitless. Such results as have been achieved will I hope be useful.

In certain instances I have drawn freely upon my article on Arnold's contributions to the *Pall Mall Gazette*, originally published in *Modern Philology*, and my article on de Maistre's *Lettres et opuscules inédits* in *Modern Language Notes*. I wish to thank the editors of both those magazines for their kind permission to use this material.

For their encouragement in completing this project and for their helpful suggestions or advice I am indebted to Professor Kenneth Allott of the University of Liverpool; the late Professor E. K. Brown; Professor Arthur Kyle Davis of the University of Virginia; Professor Frederic E. Faverty of Northwestern University; Professor William B. Guthrie of the University of Richmond; President H. F. Lowry of the College of Wooster; Miss Marion Mainwaring; Dean Francis E. Mineka of Cornell University; the late Professor Hyder E. Rollins; Professor George J. Ryan of the College of William and Mary; Professor William D. Templeman of the University of Southern California; Sister Thomas Marion of Ithaca, New York; Professor Emeritus Chauncey B. Tinker of Yale University; and Professor Lionel Trilling of Columbia University. For their helpfulness in making freely available to me their resources I wish to thank the staff of the libraries of the Boston Athenaeum, Harvard College, Radcliffe College, The University of Pennsylvania, the College of William and Mary, and Yale University; and the staffs of the Boston Public Library and the Library of Congress. Leisure to prepare this volume would not have been available without the assistance of research funds granted through the University Center in Virginia and the College of William and Mary and through a fellowship from the Fund for the Advancement of Education. I wish also to thank Miss Ann Orlov of the Harvard University Press for her invaluable assistance in preparing the manuscript for the press. I owe a special debt of gratitude to the hospitality of Mr. and Mrs. Thaddeus R. Beal of Cambridge, Massachusetts.

Fraser Neiman

May 19, 1959

Contents

xiv

Essays,
Letters, and Reviews
by Matthew Arnold

On the Modern Element in Literature

Macmillan's Magazine
XIX (February 1869), 304–314

Matthew Arnold delivered his inaugural lecture as Professor of Poetry at Oxford in the Clarendon Building on Saturday afternoon, November 14, 1857. At the election on May 5, 1857, he had defeated by eighty-five votes the Rev. J. E. Bode, the candidate of Christ Church and representative of the High Church party in Oxford. Of the votes cast Bode polled 278 and Arnold 363.[1] According to *The Times*, May 6, 1857, the polling began a few minutes after twelve o'clock "and was carried on with great spirit till 2." Arnold was actively interested in his candidature, having urged at least two of his friends to go down to Oxford to give him a vote.[2]

On May 15 he wrote to his brother Tom, "I think it probable that I shall lecture in English: there is no direction whatever in the Statute as to the language in which the lectures shall be: and the Latin has so died out, even among scholars, that it seems idle to entomb a lecture which, in English, might be stimulating and interesting." [3] Mrs. Humphry Ward also quotes from Arnold's letter to his mother on the occasion of his election: "The income is £130 a year or thereabouts: the duties consist as far as I can learn in assisting to look over the prize compositions, in delivering a Latin oration in praise of founders at every alternate commemoration, and in preparing three Latin lectures on ancient poetry in the course of the year. *These lectures I hope to give in English.*" [4]

Arnold's delay in publishing the address is sufficiently explained by the apologetic note with which he introduced it in *Macmillan's Magazine*. His sense of its manner being no longer congenial to him is confirmed by a recently published letter of Arnold in which he speaks of its "rather high-horse academic style." [5] Professor Buckler also discloses the embarrassment in which the publication of the lecture placed Arnold with his publisher George Smith (1824–1901), or, as he called himself after 1873, George Murray Smith.

First published in *Macmillan's*, the lecture has been reprinted in *Essays in Criticism, Third Series*, ed. E. J. O'Brien (Boston, 1910), in *Essays by Matthew Arnold* (Oxford, 1914) [cited hereafter as The Oxford *Essays*]; and in F. L. Mulhauser, *Matthew Arnold: Selected Poetry and Prose* (New York, 1953). Without the first two paragraphs and most of the preliminary note, it is included in John Bryson, *Matthew Arnold, Poetry and Prose* (Cambridge, Mass., 1954). It also appears in W. E. Houghton and G. R. Stange, *Victorian Poetry and Poetics* (Boston, 1959).

(What follows was delivered as an inaugural lecture in the Poetry Chair at Oxford. It was never printed, but there appeared at the time several comments on it from critics who had either heard it, or heard reports about it. It was meant to be followed and completed by a course of lectures developing the subject entirely, and some of these were given. But the course was broken off because I found my knowledge insufficient for treating in a solid way many portions of the subject chosen. The inaugural lecture, however, treating a portion of the subject where my knowledge was perhaps less insufficient, and where besides my hearers were better able to help themselves out from their own knowledge, is here printed. No one feels the imperfection of this sketchy and generalizing mode of treatment more than I do; and not only is this mode of treatment less to my taste now than it was eleven years ago, but the style too, which is that of the doctor rather than the explorer, is a style which I have long since learnt to abandon. Nevertheless, having written much of late about Hellenism and Hebraism, and Hellenism being to many people almost an empty name compared with Hebraism, I print this lecture with the hope that it may serve, in the absence of other and fuller illustrations, to give some notion of the Hellenic spirit and its works, and of their significance in the history of the evolution of the human spirit in general. M. A.)

It is related in one of those legends which illustrate the history of Buddhism, that a certain disciple once presented himself before his master, Buddha, with the desire to be permitted to undertake a mission of peculiar difficulty. The compassionate teacher represented to him the obstacles to be surmounted and the risks to be run. Pourna — so the disciple was called — insisted, and replied, with equal humility and adroitness, to the successive objections of his adviser. Satisfied at last by his answers of the fitness of his disciple, Buddha accorded to him the desired permission; and dismissed him to his task with these remarkable words, nearly identical with those in which he himself is said to have been admonished by a divinity at the outset of his own career: — "Go then, O Pourna," are his words; "having been delivered, deliver; having been consoled, console; being arrived thyself at the farther bank, enable others to arrive there also."[6]

It was a moral deliverance, eminently, of which the great Oriental reformer spoke; it was a deliverance from the pride, the sloth, the anger, the selfishness, which impair the moral activity of man — a deliverance which is demanded of all individuals and in all ages. But there is another deliverance for the human race, hardly less important, indeed, than the first — for in the enjoyment of both united consists man's true freedom — but demanded far less universally, and even more rarely and imperfectly obtained; a deliverance neglected, apparently hardly conceived, in some ages, while it has been pursued with earnestness in others, which derive from that very pursuit their peculiar character. This deliverance is an intellectual deliverance.

An intellectual deliverance is the peculiar demand of those ages which are called modern; and those nations are said to be imbued with the modern spirit most eminently in which the demand for such a deliverance has been made with most zeal, and satisfied with most completeness. Such a deliverance is emphatically, whether we will or no, the demand of the age in which we ourselves live. All intellectual pursuits our age judges according to their power of helping to satisfy this demand; of all studies it asks, above all, the question, how far they can contribute to this deliverance.

I propose, on this my first occasion of speaking here, to attempt such a general survey of ancient classical literature and history as may afford us the conviction — in presence of the doubts so often expressed of the profitableness, in the present day, of our study of this literature — that, even admitting to their fullest extent the legitimate demands of our age, the literature of ancient Greece is, even for modern times, a mighty agent of intellectual deliverance; even for modern times, therefore, an object of indestructible interest.

But first let us ask ourselves why the demand for an intellectual deliverance arises in such an age as the present, and in what the deliverance itself consists? The demand arises, because our present age has around it a copious and complex present, and behind it a copious and complex past; it arises, because the present age exhibits to the individual man who contemplates it the spectacle of a vast multitude of facts awaiting and inviting his comprehension. The deliverance consists in man's comprehension of this present and past. It begins when our mind begins to enter into possession of the general ideas which are the law of this vast multitude of facts. It is perfect when we have acquired that harmonious acquiescence of mind which we feel in contemplating a grand spectacle that is intelligible to us; when we have lost that impatient irritation of mind which we feel in presence of an immense, moving, confused spectacle which, while it perpetually excites our curiosity, perpetually baffles our comprehension.

This, then, is what distinguishes certain epochs in the history of the human race, and our own amongst the number; — on the one hand, the presence of a significant spectacle to contemplate; on the other hand, the desire to find the true point of view from which to contemplate this spectacle. He who has found that point of view, he who adequately comprehends this spectacle, has risen to the comprehension of his age: he who communicates that point of view to his age, he who interprets to it that spectacle, is one of his age's intellectual deliverers.

The spectacle, the facts, presented for the comprehension of the present age, are indeed immense. The facts consist of the events, the institutions, the sciences, the arts, the literatures, in which human life has manifested itself up to the present time: the spectacle is the collective life of humanity. And everywhere there is connexion, everywhere there is illustration: no single event, no single literature, is adequately comprehended except in its relation to other events, to other literatures. The literature of ancient Greece, the literature of the Christian Middle Age, so long as they are regarded as two isolated literatures, two isolated growths of the human spirit, are not adequately comprehended; and it is adequate comprehension which is the demand of the present age. "We must compare," — the illustrious Chancellor of Cambridge* said the other day to his hearers at Manchester, — "we must compare the works of other ages with those of our own age and country; that, while we feel proud of the immense development of knowledge and power of production which we possess, we may learn humility in contemplating the refinement of feeling and intensity of thought manifested in the works of the older schools." To know how others stand, that we may know how we ourselves stand; and to know how we ourselves stand, that we may correct our mistakes and achieve our deliverance — that is our problem.

But all facts, all the elements of the spectacle before us, have not an equal value — do not merit a like attention: and it is well that they do not, for no man would be adequate to the task of thoroughly mastering them all. Some have more significance for us, others have less; some merit our utmost attention in all their details, others it is sufficient to comprehend in their general character, and then they may be dismissed.

What facts, then, let us ask ourselves, what elements of the spectacle before us, will naturally be most interesting to a highly developed age like our own, to an age making the demand which we have described for an intellectual deliverance by means of the complete intelligence of its own situation? Evidently, the other ages similarly developed, and making the same demand. And what past literature will naturally be most interesting to such an age as our own? Evidently, the literatures which have most successfully solved for *their* ages the problem which occupies ours: the literatures which in their day and for their own nation have adequately comprehended, have adequately represented, the spectacle before them. A significant, a highly-developed, a culminating epoch, on the one hand, — a comprehensive, a commensurate, an adequate literature, on the other, — these will naturally be the objects of deepest interest to our modern age. Such an epoch and such a literature are, in fact, *modern*, in the same sense in which our own age and literature are modern; they are founded upon a rich past and upon an instructive fulness of experience.

* The late Prince Consort.[7]

It may, however, happen that a great epoch is without a perfectly adequate literature; it may happen that a great age, a great nation, has attained a remarkable fulness of political and social development, without intellectually taking the complete measure of itself, without adequately representing that development in its literature. In this case, the *epoch*, the *nation* itself, will still be an object of the greatest interest to us; but the *literature* will be an object of less interest to us: the facts, the material spectacle, are there; but the contemporary view of the facts, the intellectual interpretation, are inferior and inadequate.

It may happen, on the other hand, that great authors, that a powerful literature, are found in an age and nation less great and powerful than themselves; it may happen that a literature, that a man of genius, may arise adequate to the representation of a greater, a more highly developed age than that in which they appear; it may happen that a literature completely interprets its epoch, and yet has something over; that it has a force, a richness, a geniality, a power of view which the materials at its disposition are insufficient adequately to employ. In such a case, the literature will be more interesting to us than the epoch. The interpreting power, the illuminating and revealing intellect, are there; but the spectacle on which they throw their light is not fully worthy of them.

And I shall not, I hope, be thought to magnify too much my office if I add, that it is to the poetical literature of an age that we must, in general, look for the most perfect, the most adequate interpretation of that age, — for the performance of a work which demands the most energetic and harmonious activity of all the powers of the human mind. Because that activity of the whole mind, that genius, as Johnson nobly describes it, "without which judgment is cold and knowledge is inert; that energy which collects, combines, amplifies, and animates," is in poetry at its highest stretch and in its most energetic exertion.[8]

What we seek, therefore, what will most enlighten us, most contribute to our intellectual deliverance, is the union of two things; it is the coexistence, the simultaneous appearance, of a great epoch and a great literature.

Now the culminating age in the life of ancient Greece I call, beyond question, a great epoch; the life of Athens in the fifth century before our era I call one of the highly developed, one of the marking, one of the modern periods in the life of the whole human race. It has been said that the "Athens of Pericles was a vigorous man, at the summit of his bodily strength and mental energy."[9] There was the utmost energy of life there, public and private; the most entire freedom, the most unprejudiced and intelligent observation of human affairs. Let us rapidly examine some of the characteristics which distinguish modern epochs;[10] let us see how far the culminating century of ancient Greece exhibits them; let us compare

it, in respect of them, with a much later, a celebrated century; let us compare it with the age of Elizabeth in our own country.

To begin with what is exterior. One of the most characteristic outward
features of a *modern* age, of an age of advanced civilization, is the ban-
ishment of the ensigns of war and bloodshed from the intercourse of civil
life. Crime still exists, and wars are still carried on; but within the limits
of civil life a circle has been formed within which man can move securely,
and develop the arts of peace uninterruptedly. The private man does not
go forth to his daily occupation prepared to assail the life of his neighbour or to have to defend his own. With the disappearance of the constant
means of offence the occasions of offence diminish; society at last acquires
repose, confidence, and free activity. An important inward characteristic,
again, is the growth of a tolerant spirit; that spirit which is the offspring
of an enlarged knowledge; a spirit patient of the diversities of habits and
opinions. Other characteristics are the multiplication of the conveniences
of life, the formation of taste, the capacity for refined pursuits. And this
leads us to the supreme characteristic of all: the intellectual maturity of
man himself; the tendency to observe facts with a critical spirit; to search
for their law, not to wander among them at random; to judge by the rule
of reason, not by the impulse of prejudice or caprice.

Well, now, with respect to the presence of all these characteristics in
the age of Pericles, we possess the explicit testimony of an immortal work,
— of the history of Thucydides. "The Athenians first," he says — speaking
of the gradual development of Grecian society up to the period when the
Peloponnesian War commenced — "the Athenians first left off the habit of
wearing arms:" [11] that is, this mark of superior civilization had, in the age
of Pericles, become general in Greece, had long been visible at Athens. In
the time of Elizabeth, on the other hand, the wearing of arms was universal in England and throughout Europe. Again, the conveniences, the
ornaments, the luxuries of life, had become common at Athens at the time
of which we are speaking. But there had been an advance even beyond
this; there had been an advance to that perfection, that propriety of taste
which prescribes the excess of ornament, the extravagance of luxury. The
Athenians had given up, Thucydides says, had given up, although not
very long before, an extravagance of dress and an excess of personal
ornament which, in the first flush of newly-discovered luxury, had been
adopted by some of the richer classes. The height of civilization in this
respect seems to have been attained; there was general elegance and
refinement of life, and there was simplicity. What was the case in this
respect in the Elizabethan age? The scholar Casaubon, who settled in
England in the reign of James I., bears evidence to the want here, even
at that time, of conveniences of life which were already to be met with
on the continent of Europe. On the other hand, the taste for fantastic, for

excessive personal adornment, to which the portraits of the time bear testimony, is admirably set forth in the work of a great novelist, who was also a very truthful antiquarian — in the *Kenilworth* of Sir Walter Scott. We all remember the description, in the thirteenth and fourteenth chapters of the second volume of *Kenilworth*, of the barbarous magnificence, the "fierce vanities," of the dress of the period.

Pericles praises the Athenians that they had discovered sources of recreation for the spirit to counterbalance the labours of the body: compare these, compare the pleasures which charmed the whole body of the Athenian people through the yearly round of their festivals with the popular shows and pastimes in *Kenilworth*. "We have freedom," says Pericles, "for individual diversities of opinion and character; we do not take offence at the tastes and habits of our neighbour if they differ from our own." [12] Yes, in Greece, in the Athens of Pericles, there is toleration; but in England, in the England of the sixteenth century? — the Puritans are then in full growth. So that with regard to these characteristics of civilization of a modern spirit which we have hitherto enumerated, the superiority, it will be admitted, rests with the age of Pericles.

Let us pass to what we said was the supreme characteristic of a highly developed, a modern age — the manifestation of a critical spirit, the endeavour after a rational arrangement and appreciation of facts. Let us consider one or two of the passages in the masterly introduction which Thucydides, the contemporary of Pericles, has prefixed to his history. What was his motive in choosing the Peloponnesian War for his subject? Because it was, in his opinion, the most important, the most instructive event which had, up to that time, happened in the history of mankind. What is his effort in the first twenty-three chapters of his history? To place in their correct point of view all the facts which had brought Grecian society to the point at which that dominant event found it; to strip these facts of their exaggeration, to examine them critically. The enterprises undertaken in the early times of Greece were on a much smaller scale than had been commonly supposed. The Greek chiefs were induced to combine in the expedition against Troy, not by their respect for an oath taken by them all when suitors to Helen, but by their respect for the preponderating influence of Agamemnon; the siege of Troy had been protracted not so much by the valour of the besieged as by the inadequate mode of warfare necessitated by the want of funds of the besiegers. No doubt Thucydides' criticism of the Trojan War is not perfect; but observe how in these and many other points he labours to correct popular errors, to assign their true character to facts, complaining, as he does so, of men's habit of *uncritical* reception of current stories. "So little a matter of care to most men," he says, "is the search after truth, and so inclined are they to take up any story which is ready to their hand." [13]

"He himself," he continues, "has endeavoured to give a true picture, and believes that in the main he has done so. For some readers his history may want the charm of the uncritical, half-fabulous narratives of earlier writers; but for such as desire to gain a clear knowledge of the past, and thereby of the future also, which will surely, after the course of human things, represent again hereafter, if not the very image, yet the near resemblance of the past — if such shall judge my work to be profitable, I shall be well content." [14]

What language shall we properly call this? It is *modern* language; it is the language of a thoughtful philosophic man of our own days; it is the language of Burke or Niebuhr assigning the true aim of history. And yet Thucydides is no mere literary man; no isolated thinker, speaking far over the heads of his hearers to a future age — no: he was a man of action, a man of the world, a man of his time. He represents, at its best indeed, but he represents, the general intelligence of his age and nation; of a nation the meanest citizens of which could follow with comprehension the profoundly thoughtful speeches of Pericles.

Let us now turn for a contrast to a historian of the Elizabethan age, also a man of great mark and ability, also a man of action, also a man of the world, Sir Walter Ralegh. Sir Walter Ralegh writes the *History of the World*, as Thucydides has written the *History of the Peloponnesian War;* let us hear his language; let us mark his point of view: let us see what problems occur to him for solution. "Seeing," he says, "that we digress in all the ways of our lives — yea, seeing the life of man is nothing else but digression — I may be the better excused in writing their lives and actions." [15] What are the preliminary facts which he discusses, as Thucydides discusses the Trojan War and the early naval power of Crete, and which are to lead up to his main inquiry? Open the table of contents of his first volume. You will find: — "Of the firmament, and of the waters above the firmament, and whether there be any crystalline Heaven, or any primum mobile." You will then find: — "Of Fate, and that the stars have great influence, and that their operations may diversely be prevented or furthered." Then you come to two entire chapters on the place of Paradise, and on the two chief trees in the garden of Paradise. And in what style, with what power of criticism, does Ralegh treat the subjects so selected? I turn to the 7th section of the third chapter of his first book, which treats "Of their opinion which make Paradise as high as the moon, and of others which make it higher than the middle region of the air." Thus he begins the discussion of this opinion: — "Whereas Beda saith, and as the schoolmen affirm Paradise to be a place altogether removed from the knowledge of men ('locus a cognitione hominum remotissimus'), and Barcephas conceived that Paradise was far in the east, but mounted above the ocean and all the earth, and near the orb of the moon (which opinion, though the schoolmen charge Beda withal, yet Pererius lays it off from Beda and his master Rabanus); and whereas Rupertus in his geography of Paradise doth not much differ from the rest, but finds it seated next or nearest Heaven — " So he states the error, and now for his own criticism of it. "First, such a place cannot be commodious to live in, for being so near the moon it had been too near the sun and other heavenly bodies. Secondly, it must have been too joint a neighbour to the element of fire. Thirdly, the air in that region is so violently moved and carried about with such swiftness as nothing in that place can consist or have abiding. Fourthly," — but what has been quoted is surely enough, and there is no use in continuing.

Which is the ancient here, and which is the modern? Which uses the language of an intelligent man of our own days? which a language wholly obsolete and unfamiliar to us? Which has the rational appreciation and control of his facts? which wanders among them helplessly and without a clue? Is it our own countryman, or is it the Greek? And the language of Ralegh affords a fair sample of the critical power, of the point of view, possessed by the majority of intelligent men of his day; as the language of Thucydides affords us a fair sample of the critical power of the majority of intelligent men in the age of Pericles.

Well, then, in the age of Pericles we have, in spite of its antiquity, a highly-developed, a modern, a deeply interesting epoch. Next comes the question: Is this epoch adequately interpreted by its highest literature? Now, the peculiar characteristic of the highest literature — the poetry — of the fifth century in Greece before the Christian era, is its *adequacy;* the peculiar characteristic of the poetry of Sophocles is its consummate, its unrivalled *adequacy;* that it represents the highly developed human nature of that age — human nature developed in a number of directions, politically, socially, religiously, morally developed — in its completest and most harmonious development in all these directions; while there is shed over this poetry the charm of that noble serenity which always accompanies true insight. If in the body of Athenians of that time there was, as we have said, the utmost energy of mature manhood, public and private; the most entire freedom, the most unprejudiced and intelligent observation of human affairs — in Sophocles there is the same energy, the same maturity, the same freedom, the same intelligent observation; but all these idealized and glorified by the grace and light shed over them from the noblest poetical feeling. And therefore I have ventured to say of Sophocles, that he "saw life steadily, and saw it whole." Well may we understand how Pericles — how the great statesman whose aim was, it has been said, "to realize in Athens the idea which he had conceived of human greatness," [16] and who partly succeeded in his aim — should have been drawn to the great poet whose works are the noblest reflection of his success.

I assert, therefore, though the detailed proof of the assertion must be reserved for other opportunities, that, if the fifth century in Greece before our era is a significant and modern epoch, the poetry of that epoch — the poetry of Pindar, Aeschylus, and Sophocles — is an adequate representation and interpretation of it.

The poetry of Aristophanes is an adequate representation of it also. True, this poetry regards humanity from the comic side; but there is a comic side from which to regard humanity as well as a tragic one; and the distinction of Aristophanes is to have regarded it from the true point of view on the comic side. He too, like Sophocles, regards the human nature of his time in its fullest development; the boldest creations of a riotous imagination are in Aristophanes, as has been justly said,[17] based always upon the foundation of a serious thought: politics, education, social life, literature — all the great modes in which the human life of his day manifested itself — are the subjects of his thoughts, and of his penetrating comment. There is shed, therefore, over his poetry the charm, the vital freshness, which is felt when man and his relations are from any side adequately, and therefore genially, regarded. Here is the true difference between Aristophanes and Menander. There has been preserved an epitome of a comparison by Plutarch between Aristophanes and Menander, in which the grossness of the former, the exquisite truth to life and felicity of observation of the latter, are strongly insisted upon; and the preference of the refined, the learned, the intelligent men of a later period for Menander loudly proclaimed. "What should take a man of refinement to the theatre," asks Plutarch, "except to see one of Menander's plays? When do you see the theatre filled with cultivated persons, except when Menander is acted? and he is the favourite refreshment," he continues, "to the overstrained mind of the laborious philosopher." [18] And every one knows the famous line of tribute to this poet by an enthusiastic admirer in antiquity: — "O Life and Menander, which of you painted the other?" [19] We remember, too, how a great English statesman is said to have declared that there was no lost work of antiquity which he so ardently desired to recover as a play of Menander. Yet Menander has perished, and Aristophanes has survived. And to what is this to be attributed? To the instinct of self-preservation in humanity. The human race has the strongest, the most invincible tendency to *live*, to *develop* itself. It retains, it clings to what fosters its life, what favours its development, to the literature which exhibits it in its vigour; it rejects, it abandons what does not foster its development, the literature which exhibits it arrested and decayed. Now, between the times of Sophocles and Menander a great check had befallen the development of Greece; — the failure of the Athenian expedition to Syracuse, and the consequent termination of the Peloponnesian War in a result unfavourable to Athens. The free expansion of her growth was checked; one of the noblest channels of Athenian life, that of political activity, had begun to narrow and to dry up. That was the true catastrophe of the ancient world; it was then that the oracles of the ancient world should have become silent, and that its gods should have forsaken their temples; for from that date the intellectual and spiritual life of Greece was left without an adequate material basis of political and practical life; and both began inevitably to decay. The opportunity of the ancient world was then lost, never to return; for neither the Macedonian nor the Roman world, which possessed an adequate material basis, possessed, like the Athens of earlier times, an adequate intellect and soul to inform and inspire them; and there was left of the ancient world, when Christianity arrived, of Greece only a head without a body, and of Rome only a body without a soul.

It is Athens after this check, after this diminution of vitality, — it is man with part of his life shorn away, refined and intelligent indeed, but sceptical, frivolous, and dissolute, — which the poetry of Menander represented. The cultivated, the accomplished might applaud the dexterity, the perfection of the representation — might prefer it to the free genial delineation of a more living time with which they were no longer in sympathy. But the instinct of humanity taught it, that in the one poetry there was the seed of life, in the other poetry the seed of death; and it has rescued Aristophanes, while it has left Menander to his fate.

In the flowering period of the life of Greece, therefore, we have a culminating age, one of the flowering periods of the life of the human race: in the poetry of that age we have a literature commensurate with its epoch. It is most perfectly commensurate in the poetry of Pindar, Aeschylus, Sophocles, Aristophanes; these, therefore, will be the supremely interesting objects in this literature; but the stages in literature which led up to this point of perfection, the stages in literature which led downward from it, will be deeply interesting also. A distinguished person,* who has lately been occupying himself with Homer, has remarked that an undue preference is given, in the studies of Oxford, to these poets over Homer. The justification of such a preference, even if we put aside all philological considerations, lies, perhaps, in what I have said. Homer himself is eternally interesting; he is a greater poetical power than even Sophocles or Aeschylus; but his age is less interesting than himself. Aeschylus and Sophocles represent an age as interesting as themselves; the names, indeed, in their dramas are the names of the old heroic world, from which they were far separated; but these names are taken, because

* Mr. Gladstone.[20]

the use of them permits to the poet that free and ideal treatment of his characters which the highest tragedy demands; and into these figures of the old world is poured all the fulness of life and of thought which the new world had accumulated. This new world in its maturity of reason resembles our own; and the advantage over Homer in their greater significance for *us,* which Aeschylus and Sophocles gain by belonging to this new world, more than compensates for their poetical inferiority to him.

Let us now pass to the Roman world. There is no necessity to accumulate proofs that the culminating period of Roman history is to be classed among the leading, the significant, the modern periods of the world. There is universally current, I think, a pretty correct appreciation of the high development of the Rome of Cicero and Augustus; no one doubts that material civilization and the refinements of life were largely diffused in it; no one doubts that cultivation of mind and intelligence were widely diffused in it. Therefore, I will not occupy time by showing that Cicero corresponded with his friends in the style of the most accomplished, the most easy letter-writers of modern times; that Caesar did not write history like Sir Walter Ralegh. The great period of Rome is, perhaps, on the whole, the greatest, the fullest, the most significant period on record; it is certainly a greater, a fuller period than the age of Pericles. It is an infinitely larger school for the men reared in it; the relations of life are immeasurably multiplied, the events which happen are on an immeasurably grander scale. The facts, the spectacle of this Roman world, then, are immense: let us see how far the literature, the interpretation of the facts, has been adequate.

Let us begin with a great poet, a great philosopher, Lucretius. In the case of Thucydides I called attention to the fact that his habit of mind, his mode of dealing with questions, were modern; that they were those of an enlightened, reflecting man among ourselves. Let me call attention to the exhibition in Lucretius of a modern *feeling* not less remarkable than the modern *thought* in Thucydides. The predominance of thought, of reflection, in modern epochs is not without its penalties; in the unsound, in the over-tasked, in the over-sensitive, it has produced the most painful, the most lamentable results; it has produced a state of feeling unknown to less enlightened but perhaps healthier epochs — the feeling of depression, the feeling of *ennui.* Depression and *ennui;* these are the characteristics stamped on how many of the representative works of modern times! they are also the characteristics stamped on the poem of Lucretius. One of the most powerful, the most solemn passages of the work of Lucretius, one of the most powerful, the most solemn passages in the literature of the whole world, is the well-known conclusion of the third book. With masterly touches he exhibits the lassitude, the incurable tedium which pursue men in their amusements; with indignant irony he upbraids them for the cowardice with which they cling to a life which for most is miserable; to a life which contains, for the most fortunate, nothing but the old dull round of the same unsatisfying objects for ever presented. "A man rushes abroad," he says, "because he is sick of being at home; and suddenly comes home again because he finds himself no whit easier abroad. He posts as fast as his horses can take him to his country-seat: when he has got there he hesitates what to do; or he throws himself down moodily to sleep, and seeks forgetfulness in that; or he makes the best of his way back to town again with the same speed as he fled from it. Thus every one flies from himself." What a picture of *ennui!* of the disease of the most modern societies, the most advanced civilizations! "O man," he exclaims again, "the lights of the world, Scipio, Homer, Epicurus, are dead; wilt thou hesitate and fret at dying, whose life is well-nigh dead whilst thou art yet alive; who consumest in sleep the greater part of thy span, and when awake dronest and ceasest not to dream; and carriest about a mind troubled with baseless fear, and canst not find what it is that aileth thee when thou staggerest like a drunken wretch in the press of thy cares, and welterest hither and thither in the unsteady wandering of thy spirit!" And again: "I have nothing more than you have already seen," he makes Nature say to man, "to invent for your amusement; *eadem sunt omnia semper* — all things continue the same for ever." [21]

Yes, Lucretius is modern; but is he adequate? And how can a man adequately interpret the activity of his age when he is not in sympathy with it? Think of the varied, the abundant, the wide spectacle of the Roman life of his day; think of its fulness of occupation, its energy of effort. From these Lucretius withdraws himself, and bids his disciples to withdraw themselves; he bids them to leave the business of the world, and to apply themselves *"naturam cognoscere rerum* — to learn the nature of things"; but there is no peace, no cheerfulness for him either in the world from which he comes, or in the solitude to which he goes. With stern effort, with gloomy despair, he seems to rivet his eyes on the elementary reality, the naked framework of the world, because the world in its fulness and movement is too exciting a spectacle for his discomposed brain. He seems to feel the spectacle of it at once terrifying and alluring; and to deliver himself from it he has to keep perpetually repeating his formula of disenchantment and annihilation. In reading him, you understand the tradition which represents him as having been driven mad by a poison administered as a love-charm by his mistress, and as having composed his great work in the intervals of his madness. Lucretius is, therefore, over-strained, gloom-weighted, morbid; and he who is morbid is no adequate interpreter of his age.

I pass to Virgil; to the poetical name which of all poetical names has perhaps had the most prodigious fortune; the name which for Dante, for the Middle Age, represented the perfection of classical antiquity. The perfection of classical antiquity Virgil does not represent; but far be it from me to add my voice to those which have decried his genius;[22] nothing that I shall say is, or can ever be, inconsistent with a profound, an almost affectionate veneration for him. But with respect to him, as with respect to Lucretius, I shall freely ask the question, *Is he adequate?* Does he represent the epoch in which he lived, the mighty Roman world of his time, as the great poets of the great epoch of Greek life represented theirs, in all its fulness, in all its significance?

From the very form itself of his great poem, the Aeneid, one would be led to augur that this was impossible. The epic form, as a form for representing contemporary or nearly contemporary events, has attained, in the poems of Homer, an unmatched, an immortal success; the epic form as employed by learned poets for the reproduction of the events of a past age has attained a very considerable success. But for *this* purpose, for the poetic treatment of the events of a *past* age, the epic form is a less vital form than the dramatic form. The great poets of the modern period of Greece are accordingly, as we have seen, the *dramatic* poets. The chief of these — Aeschylus, Sophocles, Euripides, Aristophanes — have survived: the distinguished epic poets of the same period — Panyasis, Chœrilus, Antimachus — though praised by the Alexandrian critics, have perished in a common destruction with the undistinguished. And what is the reason of this? It is, that the dramatic form exhibits, above all, *the actions of man as strictly determined by his thoughts and feelings;* it exhibits, therefore, what may be always accessible, always intelligible, always interesting. But the epic form takes a wider range; it represents not only the thought and passion of man, that which is universal and eternal, but also the forms of outward life, the fashion of manners, the aspects of nature, that which is local or transient. To exhibit adequately what is local and transient, only a witness, a contemporary, can suffice. In the *reconstruction,* by learning and antiquarian ingenuity, of the local and transient features of a past age, in their representation by one who is not a witness or contemporary, it is impossible to feel the liveliest kind of interest. What, for instance, is the most interesting portion of the Aeneid, — the portion where Virgil seems to be moving most freely, and therefore to be most animated, most forcible? Precisely that portion which has most a *dramatic* character; the episode of Dido; that portion where locality and manners are nothing — where persons and characters are everything. We might presume beforehand, therefore, that if Virgil, at a time when contemporary epic poetry was no longer possible, had been inspired to represent human life in its fullest significance, he would not have selected the epic form. Accordingly, what is, in fact, the character of the poem, the frame of mind of the poet? Has the poem the depth, the completeness of the poems of Aeschylus or Sophocles, of those adequate and consummate representations of human life? Has the poet the serious cheerfulness of Sophocles, of a man who has mastered the problem of human life, who knows its gravity, and is therefore serious, but who knows that he comprehends it, and is therefore cheerful? Over the whole of the great poem of Virgil, over the whole Aeneid, there rests an ineffable melancholy: not a rigid, a moody gloom, like the melancholy of Lucretius; no, a sweet, a touching sadness, but still a sadness; a melancholy which is at once a source of charm in the poem, and a testimony to its incompleteness. Virgil, as Niebuhr has well said, expressed no affected self-disparagement, but the haunting, the irresistible self-dissatisfaction of his heart, when he desired on his death-bed that his poem might be destroyed.[23] A man of the most delicate genius, the most rich learning, but of weak health, of the most sensitive nature, in a great and overwhelming world; conscious, at heart, of his inadequacy for the thorough spiritual mastery of that world and its interpretation in a work of art; conscious of this inadequacy — the one inadequacy, the one weak place in the mighty Roman nature! This suffering, this graceful-minded, this finely-gifted man is the most beautiful, the most attractive figure in literary history; but he is not the adequate interpreter of the great period of Rome.

We come to Horace: and if Lucretius, if Virgil want cheerfulness, Horace wants seriousness. I go back to what I said of Menander: as with Menander so it is with Horace: the men of taste, the men of cultivation, the men of the world are enchanted with him; he has not a prejudice, not an illusion, not a blunder. True! yet the best men in the best ages have never been thoroughly satisfied with Horace. If human life were complete without faith, without enthusiasm, without energy, Horace, like Menander, would be the perfect interpreter of human life: but it is not; to the best, to the most living sense of humanity, it is not; and because it is not, Horace is inadequate. Pedants are tiresome, men of reflection and enthusiasm are unhappy and morbid; therefore Horace is a sceptical man of the world. Men of action are without ideas, men of the world are frivolous and sceptical; therefore Lucretius is plunged in gloom and in stern sorrow. So hard, nay, so impossible for most men is it to develop themselves in their entireness; to rejoice in the variety, the movement of human life with the children of the world; to be serious over the depth, the significance of human life with the wise! Horace warms himself before the transient fire of human animation and human pleasure while he can, and is only serious when he reflects that the fire must soon go out: —

> Damna tamen celeres reparant coelestia lunae:
> Nos, ubi decidimus —

"For nature there is renovation, but for man there is none!" [24] — it is exquisite, but it is not interpretative and fortifying.

In the Roman world, then, we have found a highly modern, a deeply significant, an interesting period — a period more significant and more interesting, because fuller, than the great period of Greece; but we have not a commensurate literature. In Greece we have seen a highly modern, a most significant and interesting period, although on a scale of less magnitude and importance than the great period of Rome; but then, co-existing with the great epoch of Greece there is what is wanting to that of Rome, a commensurate, an interesting literature.

The intellectual history of our race cannot be clearly understood without applying to other ages, nations, and literatures the same method of inquiry which we have been here imperfectly applying to what is called classical antiquity. But enough has at least been said, perhaps, to establish the absolute, the enduring interest of Greek literature, and, above all, of Greek poetry.

NOTES

[1] *Spectator,* XXX (May 9, 1857), 489; *The Times,* May 6, 1857, p. 12, col. 3.

[2] Kenneth Allott prints a letter to the Rev. William H. Lucas in "Matthew Arnold: Two Unpublished Letters," *Notes and Queries,* CC (1955), 356. Two letters to George Henry Sumner, urging him to go down to vote, are in the manuscript collection of the Boston Public Library.

[3] Mrs. Humphry Ward, *A Writer's Recollections,* 2 vols. (New York, 1918), I, 73.

[4] *Ibid.,* I, 74–75. For a full account of Arnold's professional lectures, see R. H. Super, "Arnold's Oxford Lectures on Poetry," *Modern Language Notes,* LXX (December 1955), 581–584.

[5] William E. Buckler, *Matthew Arnold's Books: Towards a Publishing Diary* (Geneva and Paris, 1958), p. 154.

[6] The legend of Pûrna is recounted in Eugène Bournouf, *Introduction à l'histoire du buddhisme indien* (Paris, 1844), pp. 235–275. The legend is also briefly retold, including the portion that Arnold translates, in Jules Barthélmy Saint-Hilaire, *Du Bouddhisme* (Paris, 1855), pp. 153–154. *Du Bouddhisme,* originally published in the *Journal des Savants,* May 1854–April 1855, uses the spelling Poûrna.

[7] The Prince Consort opened the Manchester Art Treasures Exhibition on May 5, 1857. See Sir Theodore Martin, *The Life of His Royal Highness, The Prince Consort,* 5 vols. (London, 1875–1880), IV, 39, and *The Times,* May 6, 1857, p. 9, col. 5.

[8] Samuel Johnson, "Pope," *Lives of the English Poets,* ed. G. B. Hill, 3 vols. (Oxford, 1905), III, 222.

[9] Although the exact words do not appear in the essay, the analogy between the life of the nation and the life of the individual is the dominant figure in Appendix I of Dr. Thomas Arnold's edition of Thucydides, *The History of the Peloponnesian War,* 3 vols. (Oxford, 1830–1835), I, 633, 637.

[10] Cf. Dr. Thomas Arnold: "In conclusion I must beg to repeat what I have said before, that the period to which the work of Thucydides refers belongs properly to the modern and not to ancient history; and it is this circumstance, over and above the great ability of the historian himself, which makes it so peculiarly deserving of our study." Preface to *The History of the Peloponnesian War,* III, xviii–xix.

[11] Bk. I, ch. 6.

[12] Bk. II, ch. 37.

[13] Bk. I, ch. 20.

[14] *Ibid.*, ch. 22.

[15] *The Works of Sir Walter Ralegh*, 8 vols. (Oxford, 1829), II, lxi.

[16] K. O. Müller, *History of the Literature of Ancient Greece*, 2 vols. in one (London, 1840), I, 278.

[17] *Ibid.*, II, 37. Müller is speaking particularly of the *Ecclesiazusae.*

[18] *Moralia*, 854, B-C.

[19] Aristophanes of Byzantium.

[20] See W. E. Gladstone, "On the Place of Homer in Classical Education and in Historical Inquiry," in *Oxford Essays*, contributed by Members of the University (London, 1857), p. 10.

[21] See Lucretius, *De Rerum Natura*, III, 1060–68, 1034–52, 944–945. The first of these passages is echoed in Arnold's "Obermann Once More," lines 97–104. See also C. B. Tinker and H. F. Lowry, *The Poetry of Matthew Arnold: A Commentary* (London and New York, 1940), pp. 268–270.

[22] See B. G. Niebuhr, *Lectures on the History of Rome*, ed. Leonhard Schmitz, 2 ed., 3 vols. (London, 1849), III, 135–137. Niebuhr proposes, in contrast to the *Georgics:* "His Aeneid, on the other hand, is a complete failure: it is an unhappy idea from beginning to end." See also W. E. Gladstone: "It is perhaps hardly possible to exhaust the topics of censure which may be justly used against the Aeneas of Virgil" in "Homer and His Successors in Epic Poetry," *Quarterly Review*, CI (January 1857), 84.

[23] B. G. Niebuhr, *The History of Rome*, trans. J. C. Hare et al., new ed., 3 vols. (London, 1851), I, 196.

[24] Horace, *Carmina*, IV. vii. 13–14.

The Creweian Orations of 1858 and 1862

Nathaniel Lord Crewe, Bishop of Durham (1633–1722) bequeathed to the University of Oxford an annuity of £ 200 a year to be applied to such public uses in the University as he might direct or the Chancellor, Master, and Scholars might appoint. In default of Lord Crewe's direction, his Chaplain, Richard Gray, attested to the details of a plan expressed by Lord Crewe shortly before his death. Accordingly a decree of Convocation, dated July 2, 1731, directed, among other provisions, that £ 20 each be applied to the Professor of Poetry and the Public Orator for their alternate speeches at the Encaenia.[1]

Matthew Arnold's first term as Professor of Poetry, 1857–1862, was extended, apparently without contest, for a second five years. During his incumbency he delivered the Creweian Oration on June 16, 1858; June 20, 1860; July 2, 1862; June 8, 1864; June 13, 1866. Richard Michell (1805–1877), first Principal of Hertford College, Oxford, served as Public Orator from 1849 until his death and was therefore the alternate throughout this period. Michell's sixteen orations, which are said to have been notable for their excellent Latinity and conservative sentiment, were reverently edited and published by his son, E. B. Michell, *Orationes Creweianae in Memoriam Publicorum Benefactorum Academiae Oxoniensis* (London and Oxford, 1884). E. B. Michell said, "Of the Professors of Poetry none of the biennial speeches have, as far as I am aware, been preserved, with the exception of Bishop Lowth's in 1751." [2] However, at least two of Arnold's orations survive, those of 1858 and 1862.

The 1858 *Oratio Anniversaria* was printed in the same year by T. and G. Shrimpton, Oxford. The title page bore the seal of the university press. The oration of 1862 was printed without indication of place or date. The translations of the orations which are given here were made by Professor George J. Ryan, Chairman of the Department of Ancient Languages at the College of William and Mary.

Anniversary Address in Memory of the Public Benefactors of Oxford University; according to the Decree of the Most Honored Lord and Very Reverend Father, Nathaniel Lord Crewe, Formerly Baron of Stene and Bishop of Durham; Delivered in the Sheldonian Theatre, on the Sixteenth Day before the Kalends of July 1858.

Members of the University, many other things in the ancient customs of this University have changed and are changing daily, yet this single one remains, preserved not so much by usage and habit as by the devoted interest of all and by a kind of common bond, this yearly commemoration of those men whose benefactions we enjoy in this home of learning. And at least in my opinion this custom is so strong that it can have nothing to fear from the greatest changes or from the harshest and most tumultuous disturbances of our old discipline. For I do not doubt that, whatever be the intentions with which men may come to constitute and direct this University, it will always seem to all alike both just and due to profess to our very sources, founders, and originators, our eternal good will. Men will not attribute to them the blame of a changed University as they themselves judge it; they will without doubt assign praise for its foundation, its increase, and its establishment, most wisely for those times. For what is so worthy of admiration as the fact that there should exist, out of an endless number of men, some few who provide not only for their own children but for the whole state; what is so generous, so liberal as to make the resources of learning and knowledge available to all; what is so humane as to wish to share with the largest possible number of men those things which are most excellent, most pleasing, and most characteristic of humanity, and not merely to preserve them for one's own use. Therefore, Members of the University, never let the memory of such men fade. It is certainly such that it can never suffer even from the feebleness and lack of resource of the praiser.

To come now to those things which, since they have changed in the University, may have caused, to those observing cursorily, some concern regarding the continuance of this yearly duty to our founders (a foolish concern indeed but forgivable): these changes are indeed great and such as must appear obvious at first sight to those returning to your present place after a long absence. We have seen some things changed by the intervention of laws; but more changed by the free will of the Colleges themselves; we have seen men admitted to learn in this place without the administered oath; we have seen that large parts of the endowments of certain colleges, reserved till now for a particular and previously chosen type of petitioners, are now open to the striving of all; we have seen that the properties of the Colleges are administered by another and wiser method than formerly; we have seen that some incumbents of grants voluntarily do without their present aid, with no pressure from others, in

Oratio Anniversaria in Memoriam Publicorum Benefactorum Academiae Oxoniensis; ex Instituto Honoratissimi Domini et Patris admodum Reverendi, Nathanielis Domini Crewe, Olim Baronis de Stene, et Episcopi Dunelmensis; Habita in Theatro Sheldoniano XVI Kalendas Julii, A. D. MDCCCLVIII.

Quum multae aliae res, Academici, in veteribus praeclarae hujus Academiae institutis mutatae sint et in dies mutentur, restat hoc unum, non tantum usu ac consuetudine quantum pio omnium studio et communi quâdam religione servatum — solennis eorum, quorum beneficiis in hoc doctrinae domicilio fruimur, con celebratio. Ac meâ quidem sententiâ tale est hoc institutum quod a gravissimis tempestatibus, ab asperrimâ et turbulentissimâ perturbatione disciplinae veteris, nihil possit habere, quod extimescat. Nam quocumque consilio homines ad constituendam moderandamque hanc Academiam accesserint, non dubito quin hoc omnibus pariter aequum ac debitum videatur, erga fontes ipsos et principes atque auctores nostros benevolentiam profiteri sempiternam. His culpam corruptae, prout ipsi judicant, Academiae, non attribuent: laudem fundatae auctaeque, immo vero sapienter, ut temporibus illis, constitutae, sine dubio assignabunt. Quid enim est tam admirabile, quam ex infinitâ multitudine hominum existere aliquos, qui non solum liberis suis prospiciant, sed universae civitati: quid tam liberale, tam munificum, quam opem doctrinae scientiaeque porrigere omnibus: quid tam humanum, quam, quae praestantissima, quae jucundissima, quae maxime propria humanitatis sunt, ea non ad usum suum reservare sed quam potissimum cunctis hominibus communicare velle? Talium igitur virorum, Academici, non unquam evanescet memoria: ea certe est, quae ne quidem ex imbecillitate et tenuitate laudantis aliquid detrimenti possit capere.

Ut vero jam ad illa ipsa veniamus, quae in hâc Academiâ mutata nimis leviter anquirentibus forsitan sollicitudinem aliquam de perpetuitate sollennis hujus erga auctores nostros officii, vanam illam quidem, at tamen ignoscendam, potuissent injicere; magna profecto illa sunt, et quae in oculos redeuntium post longum tempus in hanc sedem vestram necesse est primo statim obtutu incurrant. Vidimus legum interventu nonnulla, plurima liberâ ipsorum Collegiorum voluntate mutari: vidimus cunctos, nullo adhibito sacramento, ad discendum in hoc loco admitti: vidimus pleraque singulorum Collegiorum emolumenta, usque in hunc diem parvo cuidem praescriptoque petentium ordini reservata, nunc omnium certationi ses offerre: vidimus Collegiorum bona aliâ ac prudentiore quam olim ratione administrari: praesenti beneficio possessores sponte suâ, non aliorum impulsu, carere, quo rem communem auctiorem atque ampliorem

order that they may leave the common property greater and increased for those that follow them. We have seen that a new and most excellent curriculum lies open to that study of Nature which they profess who are called physicists; we have seen that the glory of those sciences which were once dark and hidden as it were between humble and narrow walls, now are come to light and have obtained a place worthy of their own usefulness and importance; we have seen finally that admittance to your learning, discipline, and honors is now sought by all gymnasia, by all schools of all classes which were once very far separated from you and differed extremely from your custom and discipline, and that admission is sought by them as eagerly as it is generously granted by you. All these things, new and unaccustomed as they are, happen at once, brought to the University by recent times.

But why do I speak of others? I myself confess, Members of the University, that in as far as my limitations permit, I too have brought some increase to this abundance of novelty and change. Who does not know that they who before me have filled the office which I now hold through your favor (never sufficiently to be praised) have always used the Latin tongue in their lectures? Nor does it escape you not only how much refinement of Philosophy these illustrious men have achieved by doing so, but also what force and fluency of Latin speech they possessed. They had a variety and seriousness of thought joined with richness and conciseness of words. But, Members of the University, just as I lack and shall always lack the genius of these most learned men, so I lack their distinction in Latin speech; and in the performance of this my task I was the first to leave the Latins and to dare to take refuge in my ancestral and native speech.

And I scarcely know whether I shall bring you to approve of this at all, but I do not hesitate to say what I think. For I propose this: that changes of this sort, which have been brought into this University at all times and under every kind of Rector, have never been without a certain fear and blame; but that they have never brought harm to us as long as wisdom and counsel were shown in using and controlling them. Although very many examples abound on every side, I shall mention only a few, and these the most important. For I must seek not so much an abundance of words as the avoidance of boring you.

Indeed you have heard with what contention and quarrel Greek Letters were once introduced among us; yet these afterwards flourished with unbelievable favor; they were able to draw to themselves the minds of all; they attained and to this day hold the principal place among all the studies and arts which we cultivate. At first, however, they were opposed by the art of the dialecticians and their vain quarrel over the word, which held tangled in its nets the men of that age who were more

post se successuris tradant. Vidimus huic studio Naturae, quod profiten-
tur ei, qui Physici vocantur, novum et praeclarissimum patere curriculum:
harum scientiarum gloriam, primum quasi luce carentem, intra humiles
angustosque parietes reconditam, jam tandem in lucem prodire, habita-
tionem suâ utilitate et magnitudine dignissimam consequi. Vidimus
denique omnibus gymnasiis, omnibus omnium ordinum scholis, longis-
sime a vobis olim disjunctorum, a vestro more et disciplinâ abhorrentium
quam maxime, aditum ad doctrinam, disciplinam, honores vestros, nunc
quaeri: nec quaeri ab illis tam vehementer, quam a robis liberaliter con-
cedi. Haec omnia statim occurrent, quae nova et inusitata huic Academiae
recentissimum tempus protulit.

Quid autem de aliis loquor? Ego quidem ipse, Academici, nonnihil me
incrementi, quantum fert tenuitas mea, huic novitatis mutationisque
copiae attulisse fateor. Quis ignorat, eos, qui ante me explêrunt id munus
quod insigni vestro et nunquam satis laudando favore nunc teneo, semper Latino sermone in disserendo usos esse? Neque enim vos fugit quan-
tam in eo officio viri clarissimi elaboraverint, non solum philosophandi
subtilitatem, sed etiam Latine dicendi vim atque copiam. Erat quidem
illis varietas gravitasque sententiarum summâ ubertate atque concinnitate
verborum conjuncta. Ego vero doctissimorum horum virorum, Academici,
ut ingenio, sic item Latinae eloquentiae laude, careo et semper carebo: qui
primus in obeundo isto munere Latinos reliquerim, ad patrium nativum-
que sermonem ausus sim confugere.

Atque haud scio an minus vobis hoc sim probaturus: equidem non
dubitabo, quod sentio, dicere. Ita enim statuo: hujusmodi mutationes
omni tempore, omni genere rectorum, in hanc Academiam importatas
esse, nunquam sine timore quodam et vituperatione: nihil unquam, quoties sapientia atque consilium in accommodandis temperandisque iis fuerit
adhibitum, detrimenti nobis eas attulisse. Cujus rei quum plurima exem-
pla ab omni parte abundent, perpauca tantum proponam gravissima.
Mihi enim non tam orationis conquirenda copia est, quam vestra satietas
refugienda.

Et quidem audivistis inter quantum discrimen certamenque fuerint
olim apud nos introductae Graecae literae: quae post incredibili favore
floruerunt, omnium potuerunt animos ad se allicere: principatum inter
cuncta studia artesque, quas hic colimus, consecutae sunt et in hunc diem
tenent. Primo autem obstabat eis Dialecticorum ars atque inanis verbi
controversia, quae laqueis tenebat irretitos homines illius aevi, conten-
tionis cupidiores quam veritatis: nihil docentes praeter ineptas argutias
et vanissimam disputationum interrogationumque volubilitatem. Etenim

desirous of disputation than of truth, teaching nothing but empty subtleties and a most foolish facility of disputes and questionings. Indeed when Erasmus, a man most learned in Greek Letters, came to Oxford from Holland with the hope of inaugurating and fostering these studies, he found some, like Colet and Grocyn, who were greatly delighted with Greek literature; but he saw it excluded by most men almost with one voice and barred from the schools of this University. Wolsey revived these fading studies, and though they had been neglected and thrust as it were into a most unworthy status, he raised them to the highest peak of dignity; he was a man of noble generosity, of great and inspired mind, a man who should be honored by us always and especially today. But what of the illustrious Savile, who was the first to loosen the rigid and very narrow limits within which the Mathematicians were then expounding their rich study, that Savile who showed to masters the advantages of the art and to learners its rewards, and who by his valiant teaching and discussions aroused the minds of his hearers toward that learning? [3] Have we not heard that it was the lot of this Savile to achieve his excellent goals only with a certain envy and blame? There were those who would call home their sons from this University lest they be harmed by the pestilential corruption of that new and accursed teaching. Now there is almost no young man, desirous of commendation, who does not think that he should strive for these studies with every effort.

And this is what I have had to say about studies. I shall come now to changes of laws and customs. Who does not admit what considered kindness Laud showed to us and our common interest by changing so many and such serious things in the constitution of this University? Would that there had been in him such judgment in directing the mind of his King toward sound counsels as there was zeal in him for aiding this University! He found among us a kind of confused complexity of laws, some of which he removed, some he restored to their former condition, but the greater part he revised and adapted to his own times. This excellent service the University experienced only with much common talk and resentment; he refused to bear the administering hand of a curator.

What shall I say about my own neglect and abandonment of the Latin tongue? I shall seek an example from the ancient and almost hidden beginnings of our University; I shall name Alfred, that leader of ours as some say and founder according to Grimbaldus,[4] Alfred who professed here a knowledge of divine matters with the greatest praise of his time, I shall say that Alfred decreed to use no longer the language of the Saxons but to make use of the Latin language for writing laws and edicts. At that time the illustrious king approved this language for the same reason for which I have now been led to abandon it. For he wished to use that form of writing which then was the most intelligible; he dismissed that which

quum Erasmus, vir Graecarum literarum peritissimus, ex Batavia venisset Oxoniam excitandi eam doctrinam et promovendi spe, nonnullos invenit, ut Coletum Grocynumque, quos magnopere delectabant Graecae literae: a plurimis vero unâ paene voce eas repelli, atque excludi a scholis hujus Academiae vidit. Quae studia languentia refecit Wolseius, neglecta et tanquam in indignum locum detrusa ad summum dignitatis fastigium extulit: vir regiae liberalitatis, magni elatique animi; quum omnibus temporibus, tum praecipue hodierno die apud nos celebrandus. Quid? nonne accepimus, summo illo viro Savilio, qui arctos perangustosque limites intra quos referti disciplinam suam Mathematici tunc traderent, primus relaxavit — qui emolumenta exposuit magistris hujus artis, paremia discentibus — ipse docendo ac disputando fortiter animos audientium ad eam doctrinam excitavit — huic non sine invidiâ quâdam et reprehensione contigisse, ut praeclara sua consilia perficeret. Erant qui filios suos ab hâc Academiâ revocarent ad domum, ne pestiferâ novae nefandaeque istius doctrinae corruptelâ nocerentur. Nunc nemo fere laudis cupidus adolescens non sibi ad haec studia ardore omni enitendum putat.

Et de studiis quidem haec sunt illa quae habui dicenda: veniam ad legum institutorumque mutationes. Quis non confitetur, Laudius, qui in constituendâ hâc Academiâ tot tantaque immutavit, quam perspectâ fuerit erga nos nostramque rem communem benevolentiâ? Utinam in eo talis mens ad impellendum in bona consilia sui regis animum fuisset, quale studium ad hanc Academiam adjuvandam fuit. Invenit apud nos mixtam quamdam et indigestam legum multitudinem, quarum nonnihil sustulit, aliquid in integrum restituit, maximam quidem partem refecit, accommodavitque suis temporibus. Quod praeclarum acutissimi viri beneficium non sine magno rumore atque indignatione admisit Academia. Voluit enim a confusione illâ legum institutorumque, quâ tum laborabat, liberari: adjutricem curantis manum noluit perferre.

Quid dicam de Latino sermone a me neglecto derelictoque? Repetam ab incunabulis nostrae Academiae veteribus ac paene abditis exemplum: dicam Alfredum, principem illum nostrum, ut quidam ferunt, atque auctorem, suasu Grimbaldi, qui tunc temporis rerum divinarum scientiam summâ laude hic profitebatur, decrevisse, Saxonum litteris non amplius uti, usurpare Latinam scripturam ad leges auctoritatesque perscribendas. Probavit eo tempore hanc linguam rex egregius eâdem ex causâ, quâ equidem nunc, ut eam derelinquam, adductus sum. Voluit enim eâ formâ scribendi uti, quae tum clarissima fuit: missam fecit eam, quae obscurior ac difficilior. Sed antiqua haec sunt; ad recentiora veniamus. Adhibebo

was more obscure and difficult. But these are ancient things; let us come to things more recent. I submit therefore the decree of the most valiant and wise Queen Elizabeth, by which the Latin tongue is excluded from those places and times in which unlearned men meet with the learned. You, however, members of the University, have recently called unlearned and uncultivated men to this your training school of the country as it were, this workshop of study; you prepare yourselves to charm rude and rustic minds with the refined allurements of your learning; you are to bring to violent natures lacking any curb, the sweet reasonableness and good sense of your restraint.

Therefore do not think that any changes happen in your affairs which your vigilance cannot happily moderate and control. Continue therefore as you are doing, and apply yourselves to that study in which you are occupied; moreover know that in so doing, you offer not a diminishing or forgetfulness of the glory of our founders but rather its enlargement and perpetuity. Moreover, if there is any dignity in learning, and it is very great, if there is any sweetness and delight in leisure, what do you think of those who generally turn to action before learning, whom labor itself exhausts in the city, in the field, in daily business before they can conjecture anything about leisure — what fine and great cultivators of learning and leisure do you think they will be? This you must not fear: that respect for your simplicity of life may be curtailed or cut off. For my part, as often as I return from the excitement of public intercourse to this most pleasant leisure as though to a harbor, I must needs feel with what strength this respect is implanted in my mind; and how deeply rooted in me is the care that I not only may not be slow in paying to our founders the duty of a grateful spirit, but also that I may seem more worthy of the honor by which you have recalled me to this most beautiful and most pleasant seat. And so I promise you this and will ever fulfil it: that I shall neglect absolutely nothing by which your studies and the glory of our founders may seem able in any way to be aided; and that to this end I shall devote my whole life, that I may be judged sufficiently grateful to those guides, leaders, and authors of this my honor.

Anniversary Address in Memory of the Public Benefactors of Oxford University; according to the Decree of the Most Honored Lord and Very Reverend Father, Nathaniel Lord Crewe, Formerly Baron of Stene and Bishop of Durham; Delivered in the Sheldonian Theatre, on the Sixth Day before the Nones of July 1862.[5]

In this kind of oration we are accustomed at the beginning to praise our founders and then pass to commemorating particulars worthy of note

igitur fortissimae sapientissimaeque reginae, Elizabethae, decretum, quo excluditur Latinus sermo ab iis locis temporibusque, in quibus indocti homines cum doctis congregentur. Vos autem, Academici, egregiâ liberalitate homines indoctos atque incultos in hunc vestrum totius patriae quasi ludum atque officinam cognoscendi nuper vocavistis: paratis vos ad deleniendos rudes agrestesque animos exquisitis vestrae doctrinae blanditiis: ingeniis vehementibus et fraeno carentibus salubritatem atque sanitatem moderationis vestrae estis allaturi.

Quamobrem nolite existimare, ullas accidisse commutationes rerum vestrarum, quas non possit feliciter temperare atque gubernare vigilantia vestra. Pergite igitur, ut facitis, atque in id studium, in quo estis, incumbite: immo vero scitote, vos haec agendo auctorum nostrorum gloriae non imminutionem oblivionemque, sed potius amplificationem atque aeternitatem parare. Etenim si ulla sit, sicut est permagna, in doctrinâ dignitas, in otio suavitas delectatioque, quid censetis, qui ante ad agendum quam ad cognoscendum plerumque accedunt; quos in urbe, quos in agro, quos in diuturnis negotiis labor ipse solet prius conficere, quam possint aliquid de otio suspicari — quales illos et quantos doctrinae otiique vestri cultores futuros? Illud igitur non verendum est, ne circumcidatur aut amputetur reverentia amplitudinis vestrae. Equidem, quoties ab exercitatione et consuetudine populari et publicâ in amoenissimum hoc otium, tanquam in portum, confugio, sentiam necesse est, quantâ vi infixa sit animo meo haec reverentia: hæc cura quam pænitus sit insita, ut, quum auctoribus nostris non sim tardus in persolvendo grati animi officio, tum vobis dignissimus eo honore videar, quo me in pulcherrimam jucundissimamque hanc sedem revocâstis. Itaque hoc vobis polliceor semperque praestabo, nihil me omnino praetermissurum quo vestra studia, atque auctorum nostrorum gloria, ullo modo adjuvari posse videantur: illuc transferendam meam totam vitam esse, ut erga duces ipsos et principes atque auctores honoris mei satis gratus judicarer.

Oratio Anniversaria in Memoriam Publicorum Benefactorum Academiae Oxoniensis; ex Instituto Honoratissimi Domini et Patris admodum Reverendi, Nathanielis Domini Crewe, Olim Baronis de Stene et Episcopi Dunelmensis; Habita in Theatro Sheldoniano VI Nonas Julii, A. D. MDCCCLXII.

Quum in hoc genere orationum, Academici, initio dicendi laudare soleamus auctores nostros, deinde ad singula commemoranda, quae intra

which have happened to us within the limit of a year; because of this I ask this day that you permit me, speaking as I am in the midst of new and unusual matters, to depart a little from the usual subject and manner. For the affairs in which we are engaged are of such importance that they fill and occupy the minds of us all, that they cut short the greatest part of my speech, that they so block up all its approaches that I cannot go abroad and treat of many things in the accustomed manner. Therefore our founders will forgive me if I am distracted a little from their praise and honor; you also will excuse me especially since you also are certainly strongly moved by those very thoughts by which my mind is held; I fear that this your assembly, and I see how disturbed it is, may not bear a varied discourse.

Indeed there are two things, members of the University, which are missing to us today; two things which no one could perceive without grief are lacking during these days, denied to our hope and expectation. We have seen most excellent men presented with our citizenship; we have seen them elected to the most honorable rank; we have approved with the greatest shouts of applause the honor conferred upon them. Nevertheless, two men we miss; two upon whom we cannot confer the honor already promised and due to them. I seem with my eyes to behold our PRINCE whom I used to see two years ago sitting in those very seats; I seem to call him forth though absent and to address him again in my speech.[6] You remember his countenance, his appearance, his words; you remember his charm of manner; you recall this high-born youth, how great his modesty, his humanity, his friendliness. We were wishing to summon him to us, to receive him in hospitality, to present him with full citizenship, educated as he was by the studies and discipline of two universities, informed by well known travels and commended by all whom he visited, for his innate, gentle kindness. Yea more, led by false hope we were promising ourselves certain greater and finer things; that our Prince would not come alone to us, that he would have his honored father as comrade of his coming. With what acclaim would we have received him! with what joy would we have shown him our Museum completed and finished in every detail (for he was most eager in all the studies cultivated there). Alas for the unbelievable changes in human affairs! Alas for our vain confidence! Dead is that illustrious man, known to us even in absence for the renown of his intellect, though not known by his presence itself; his most lamentable death has saddened everything, public and private, the most distinguished as well as the humble, the country and the city, our business affairs and our pleasures. But this grief is too heavy and too wide-spread for me to dwell upon it longer; I return now to ourselves and matters of our University.

The arrival of our Prince indeed seems not so much to be removed

finem unius anni digna notatu nobis evenerint, transire; quaso a vobis, ut
in hoc die mihi hanc detis veniam, ut me inter novas et inusitatas res
dicentem patiamini aliquantulum de usitado spatio curriculoque deflec-
tere. Res enim, quibus intersumus eâ sunt magnitudine ut impleant oc-
cupentque animos omnium; ut mihi maximam partem praecidant orationis, omnesque aditus hujus ita intercludant, ut eminere foras, et ad
multa, quae extra sunt, solito suo more aspirare, non possit. Quare ig-
noscent mihi auctores nostri, si paullum a laudatione ac celebratione
eorum hodie distrahar; ignoscetis etiam vos, praesertim quum et illis ipsis
cogitationibus, quibus mea mens teneatur, certe vos quoque vehementer
sitis commoti; et haec vestra frequentia, quae quam perturbata sit video,
vereor ne orationem variam non facile sustineat.

Et duo quidem sunt, Academici, quae a nobis in hoc die desiderantur;
duo, quae inter has ferias nobis deesse, votis atque exspectationique
nostrae negari, nemo sine luctu quodam senserit. Vidimus praeclarissimos
homines civitate nostrâ donari; vidimus in amplissimum ordinem cooptari;
delatum iis honorem summo clamore et plausu comprobavimus. Duos
tamen desideramus, quibus desponsum jam et destinatum honorem
deferre non possumus. Videor oculis aspicere PRINCIPEM nostrum, quem
duobus abhinc annis in istis subselliis sedentem intuebar; videor absentem
evocare, et sermone meo iterum compellare. Meministis ejus vultum,
habitum, voces; meministis morum jucunditatem; Juvenis summo loco
natus quantâ fuerit modestiâ, quantâ humanitate, quantâ comitate, re-
cordamini. Hunc studiis et disciplina duarum Academiarum institutum,
nobili peregrinatione informatum, opinioni omnium quos inviserat hominum naturali ac suavissimâ benignitate commendatum, revocare ad nos,
excipere hospitio, plenâ civitate donare, cupiebamus. Quinetiam nobis
majora quaedam atque praeclariora, falsâ spe inducti, olim policebamur;
fore, ut non solus veniret ad nos Princeps noster; fore, ut Patrem honora-
tissimum adventûs sui haberet comitem. Hunc quantâ admiratione ex-
cepissemus! huic quanto gaudio Museum nostrum (omnium enim quae
ibi coluntur scientiarum flagrabat studio) perfectum atque ex omni parte
absolutum ostendissemus! o incredibiles humanarum rerum mutationes!
O cassam fiduciam nostram! Exstinctus est ille Vir, famâ ingenii et laude
virtutum nobis iam absentibus notus, ipsâ praesentiâ non notus; omnia
publica ac privata, primores, plebem, rus, urbem, negotia, voluptates,
luctuosissimo suo funere contristavit. Sed hic dolor gravior et latior est,
quam ut eum longius pertractare velim; ad nos nostraeque Academiae res
revertor.

Et quidem Principis nostri adventus non tam ex spe conatuque nostro

from our hope and effort as to be put off to another time. But would that
we could enjoy the same comfort in the absence also of another man.[7] I
speak of our Earl CANNING whose proffered citizenship with you has been
taken away from him with his life itself. If he had appeared in this your
gathering of men who love their country well, a man renowned for his
service to his country, with what zeal would you have greeted him, with
what outcry would you have approved his service! His early youth was
devoted and with great fruit to those disciplines and arts in which young
men are instructed among you for entering public life, for honor, glory,
and dignity; when he left you he stood forth in the state a great man and
an excellent citizen; he held the highest offices; he attained outstanding
praise for his labor and diligence. Afterwards he set out for Asia; he
held and administered great power in India. That horrible and wicked
war broke out. He undertook and finished it in such a way that he seemed
to seek nothing but peace. He defeated most cruel enemies; he stamped
out the smoking remnants of a most terrible conspiracy. And indeed in
this victory the great and admirable virtue of the man shone forth. For
the salvation of the enemy he offered himself to the bitterest conflicts, to
the great and daily attacks of very angry men. By his gentleness and mercy
he softened the inhumanity and harshness of his own citizens who demanded an inhuman and eternal war against a most inhuman enemy. By
his kindness and clemency he averted from us the grave reputation of
cruelty. When he had performed glorious labors, when he had been
broken by so many and great cares and vigilance, when, touched by
domestic sorrow, he had returned after seven years to his country, his
friends and to the congratulations of the whole state, untimely death
overtook him. He had completed scarcely fifty years; he was not able
to put a gentle conclusion to the active story of his life. In his very death
he addresses us with a loud voice and exhorts all of us whose age is still
firm or not far advanced: that our industry should be carried to our last
breath; that nothing should be left to chance, nothing conceded to sloth;
that we must not give in to our health, we must repair its weaknesses
with labor; that we must conquer the weakness and frailty of our body
with great strength and severity of mind.

But why do I speak of severity? You have received today a man to
whom all severity is foreign; I speak of Viscount PALMERSTON; who even
in old age itself reconciles labor and strength of mind with the most
delightful ease and gentleness.[8] Since his old age is not only not weak and
inactive but on the contrary ever industrious, contriving and striving after
something, he nevertheless denies that it ought to be either hard or
austere. And so in all his life he is gentle and in this sweetness of human
feeling, with which even now we are all delighted, he is accustomed to
deal most pleasantly with all; he lives easily with the lazy, strongly with

prorsus tolli, quam ad aliud tempus differri videtur. Atque utinam nos in alterius quoque viri absentiâ eodem hoc solatio uti possemus! De Vice-Comite de CANNING loquor; cui oblata vestra civitas pariter cum vitâ ipsâ detracta est. Hic in vestro concursu hominum patriae amantissimorum si comparuisset, vir praeclaro in rempublicam beneficio nobilitatus, quanto studio salutâssetis, quanto illud clamore approbâssetis! Cujus prima aetas magno cum fructu dedita disciplinis fuit iisque artibus, quibus apud vos instruuntur juvenes ad capessendam republicam, ad honorem, gloriam, dignitatem; quum autem a vobis discessisset, in civitate suumus vir et optimus civis exstitit; amplissimos magistratus gessit; egregiam laudem laboris et diligentiae est consecutus. Postea in Asiam profectus est; maximum in Indos tenuit et gessit imperium. Exarsit Asiaticum illud bellum horribile ac nefarium. Quod ita suscepit, ita confecit, ut a se nihil aliud nisi pax quaesita videretur. Profligavit crudelissimos hostes; fumantes formidolosissimae conjurationis relliquias exstinxit. Quâ quidem in victoriâ virtus hominis enituit egregia ac admirabilis. Se pro hostium salute in acerrimas dimicationes, atque in magnos iratissimorum hominum quotidianos impetus objecit. Immanitatem et duritatem suorum civium, qui inhumanissimis hostibus inhumanum ac sempiternum bellum indicebant, lenitate ac misericoridâ mitigavit; mansuetudine et clementiâ suâ gravem a nobis crudelitatis famam reppulit. Quem gloriosis laboribus perfunctum, tot tantisque curis ac vigiliis fractum, domestico luctu afflictum post septem annos patriae, amicis, gratulationi universae civitatis tandem redditum, immatura mors oppressit. Vix quinquaginta complevit annos; actuosae aetatis fabulae clausulam lenem imponere non potuit. Qui nos quoque omnes, Academici, quibus jam constans aetas sit, vel nondum multo inclinata, in morte ipsâ compellat, ac magnâ voce hortatur: usque ad extremum spiritum esse provehendam industriam; nihil fortunae relinquendum esse, nihil ignaviae concedendum; resistendum etiam valetudini esse, ejusque vitia labore compensanda; imbecillitatem ac fragilitatem corporis magnâ animi contentione atque severitate esse vincendas.

Sed quid ego loquor de severitate? Adscivistis hodie Virum, cui omnia severa aliena sunt; Vice-Comitem de PALMERSTON dico; qui in ipsâ quidem senectute laborem animique contentionem cum suavissimâ facilitate ac lenitate conciliat. Cui quum senectus non modo languida atque iners non sit, verum etiam sit operosa et semper agens aliquid et moliens, negat is tamen, eandem aut duram aut austeram esse debere. Quare in omni vitâ mitis est, et in hâc suavitate humanitatis, quâ prope jam delectamur omnes, versari perjucunde solet; cum remissis facile, cum laboriosis fortiter, cum senibus prudenter, cum juventute comiter vivit: inest naturae ejus et consuetudini tantum delectationis, quantum auctoritatis. Multum valet dignitate, multum ingenio, multum sententiâ; valet etiam plus humanitate et morum jucunditate. Quam felicissimam et amoenissimam

the troublesome, wisely with the old, and kindly with the young. There is in his nature and manner as much pleasure as there is power. He is great in character, in mind and in his spoken word; he is even greater in the charm and delight of his manner. What a most happy and pleasant old age, infused with a certain marvellous delight and pleasure; neither has any sadness enervated it nor any sickness stricken or afflicted it. In Cicero's work that famous old man M. Cato says this: that he is afraid that an orator may become weak in old age for he has need not only of mind but also of body and strength. But from this opinion he would withdraw if he heard this man. Whatever strength youths can have in speaking, whatever strength of passion, force of mind, all this you will find in this old man. Better, the same Cato says, that the greatest states have been weakened by the young, but have been sustained and restored by the old. Would you say that our Empire was better sustained by any one than by this one? With him safe all our affairs are strong, but with him lost no one can predict what will happen. Let us therefore pay our respect to this illustrious and honored elder with most joyful hearts; in greeting him, in praising him, let us banish all gloom and sadness. Not because there is need that our University solicit the favor of great and powerful men, but because in honoring the virtue of this man we admire those faculties of nature, we approach those fountains of industry and courage by which all the affairs of our University have their origin, are nourished, and are preserved forever.

Notes

[1] The Encaenia, or commemoration exercises, remained traditionally unruly in Arnold's time. Arnold himself was aware that on these occasions no one listened (see his letter to George Smith in Buckler, *Matthew Arnold's Books*, p. 65). *The Times* reported on one occasion that "The Creweian oration, as it is termed from its founder, was read by Mr. Matthew Arnold; but, unfortunately, he was unable to make himself heard" (June 17, 1858, p. 12, col. 4). On another occasion *The Times* described Commemoration Day as "a sort of festival of misrule at the University, when the usual order of things is reversed, and a degree of licence is allowed which could not be tolerated at other times" (July 3, 1862, p. 8, cols. 5–6). In 1866 they wrote that "The Creweian oration was . . . short and to the point, containing a touching eulogy of the late John Keble, a former Poetry Professor, but the impatience of the undergraduates allowed little of it to be heard, except by those in the immediate vicinity of the professor [Arnold]" (June 14, 1866, p. 14, col. 4).

[2] P. 175. E. B. Michell observed, with some severity, in connection with his father's orations, "When, however, it is remembered that the tumult was not only unseemly and vexatious in itself, but also consisted in great part of gratuitous abuse, heaped with impunity upon the speakers, it will be seen how great a command of good temper, and how complete an absence of personal vanity, were required to enable the Orator to continue his thankless and disagreeable task" (pp. 105–106, n. 1).

[3] Sir Henry Savile (1549–1622), Warden of Merton. See Anthony à Wood, *The History and Antiquities of the University of Oxford*, ed. John Gutch, 2 vols. (Oxford, 1792–1796), II, 335.

[4] St. Grimbald (820?–903). See Anthony à Wood, I, 21.

senectutem, mirâ quâdam delectatione et voluptate perfusam, nec tristitia ulla enervavit, nec infirmitas perculit afflixitque. Apud Ciceronem M. Cato ille senex haec dicit: metuere se, ne orator languescat senectute; esse enim munus ejus non ingenii solum sed laterum etiam et virium. De quâ sententiâ certe, si hunc audiret, recederet. Quicquid enim potest esse adolescentibus in dicendo vis, ardoris, impetûs animi, id omne in hoc seni repperietis. Melius idem Cato, maximas respublicas ab adolescentibus labefactas, a senibus sustentatas et restitutas esse. Num enim imperium nostrum ab ullo potius sustentari dicetis, quam ab hoc uno? quo salvo, firma nostra sint omnia; quo amisso, nemo possit praedicere, quid sit eventurum. Hunc igitur clarum et honoratum Senem laetissimo studio colamus; in hoc salutando, laudando, omnem maerorem tristitiamque deponamus. Non quia Academiae nostrae opus sit magnorum potentiumque hominum favorem aucupari: sed in colendâ hujus virtute, eas naturae facultates admiramur, eos industriae et fortitudinis fontes adimus, a quibus Academiae quoque nostrae omnia sua et gignant, et alantur, et in perpetuum conserventur.

---

[5] Arnold wrote to his mother, June 28, 1862: "Your letter, a truly delightful one, shall not go without an answer this week, although I am much pressed by my Latin speech. I have not written a word of it, and it has to be spoken on Wednesday. The subject is very good — the postponement of the Prince of Wales's degree owing to his father's death, Lord Canning's degree prevented by his death, and, finally, Lord Palmerston receiving his degree. Such good matter as this will enable one to leap over all the tiresome topics which generally have to be treated in a Creweian, and to go straight to what is interesting. I hear, however, that there will be a great row; both the Vice-Chancellor and the Public Orator write me this, so probably it does not matter much what I say, as I shall not be heard. However, I cannot compose without doing as well as I can, even if I know the composition will never obtain publicity," *Letters of Matthew Arnold, 1848–1888*, ed. G. W. E. Russell, 2 vols. (London, 1895), I, 171–172. [Hereafter cited as *Letters.*]

[6] Edward, Prince of Wales (1841–1910), was present at the Oxford Commemoration on June 20, 1860, when Arnold gave his second Creweian Oration. He had been educated for three months in 1859 under the direction of Dr. Lyon Playfair of the University of Edinburgh prior to his entry as an undergraduate at Oxford. His father, the Prince Consort, died in 1861.

[7] Charles John Canning, Earl Canning (1812–1862), died June 17. He entered Christ Church, Oxford, in 1828 and took his degree with a first in classics and a second in mathematics in 1832. Governor-General of India from 1856 to 1862, he gained the originally unpopular nickname of "Clemency Canning." Lady Canning died of jungle fever in 1861.

[8] Henry John Temple, third Viscount Palmerston (1784–1865), who attended St. John's College, Cambridge, received the honorary degree of D.C.L. from the University of Oxford at the present exercises.

The "Principle of Examination"

Daily News (London)
March 25, 1862, p. 6, col. 1

Arnold was appointed one of Her Majesty's Inspectors of Schools in 1851. In 1861 Robert Lowe (1811–1892), afterwards Viscount Sherbrooke, who was then Vice-President of the Education Department, and Ralph Lingen (1819–1905), afterwards Lord Lingen, who was the Permanent Secretary of the Education Department, accepted the proposals of the Newcastle Commission for an improved basis for payment to instructors in the elementary schools, and going beyond the recommendations of the Commission produced the so-called Revised Code. Two principles were involved. The first concerned administrative handling of funds. The second principle was formulated in the phrase "Payment by results." It proposed to make payment of grants to schools dependent upon individual examination of the pupils in reading, writing, and arithmetic, together with the inspector's report, instead of, as formerly, upon the inspector's report alone.

The Revised Code aroused immediate opposition when it was announced in July 1861. Sir James Phillips Kay-Shuttleworth (1804–1877) presented his vigorous protest in his *Letter to Earl Granville on the Revised Code* (London 1861). On November 13 Arnold wrote to his mother: "I am taking one or two of the spare days left me to begin either my lecture or my article on the Code. I do not quite know whether I will not put off the latter till January's *Fraser*. Shuttleworth has just published a most important pamphlet, and it is said that the Dean of Hereford, Dawes, is preparing an answer. . . . Shuttleworth's pamphlet is most effective. . . . It sells like wild-fire." [1] Arnold's long, unsigned article "The Twice-Revised Code" appeared in *Fraser's Magazine* for March 1862. "I think you will find my article lively," he wrote to his mother on February 26, 1862, "and presenting the subject in its *essence*, free from those details with which it is generally encumbered, and which make 'outsiders' so afraid of it." [2]

Arnold took pleasure in the response to his article. Lady de Rothschild, he wrote, was making Disraeli read it; Shuttleworth asked Arnold to procure permission from the editor of *Fraser's* to reprint it for distribution to the Members of Parliament; and "whether they get it from this article or not," he observed that Lord Derby and Samuel Wilberforce, the Bishop of Oxford, were coming around to his view on the State's interest in primary schools as a "civilising agent." Yet though it was designed for the general reader, "The Twice Revised Code" is warmed to life only by an occasional breath of irony.

Arnold's own history of the Revised Code is given in the unreprinted article "Schools," which he contributed to T. H. Ward's *The Reign of Queen Victoria,* 2 vols. (London, 1887). The issue has recently been surveyed with better perspective in W. F. Connell, *The Educational Thought and Influence of Matthew Arnold* (London, 1950).

The following pseudonymous letter was printed on the day that the House of Commons went into committee of the whole House on the issue. "The 'Principle of Examination' " states Arnold's essential position on the Revised Code. It is in a fine vein of irony, and it introduces one of Arnold's several public masks — "A Lover of Light" — from behind which his opinions might issue as another voice to influence public opinion.

To the Editor of the *Daily News.*

Sir, — You are, I believe, opposed to State interference with religion or education. But, when the State does interfere with these matters, you have no wish, I am sure, that it should regulate them unwisely rather than wisely. I think, therefore, that your candour will permit me to point out how the partisans of the Revised Code are attempting, by a false use of the admitted value of the principle of examination, to recommend a measure which, as I believe, regulates popular education unwisely.

The principle of examination is, it is said, an excellent thing. There is no such test as the examination test. Lord Overstone got on slowly under a teacher who did not apply it to him, and fast under the late Bishop of London who did.[3] Where there is any shrinking, on a school's part, from this test, there must be something unsound in that school; a school's soundness is proved by its being willing to submit to it.

And why should not the State, it is asked, carry out in practice here this principle of individual examination? It carries it out already in Ireland.

The value of the principle of examination, for certain purposes, no one denies. No doubt it is a good thing for the scholar to be examined. No doubt Lord Overstone got on better the more Bishop Blomfield examined him. But the question is — Is it a good thing to make the scholar's success in his examination the sole measure of the payment of those who educate him? If Lord Overstone's father had proposed to Bishop Blomfield to make his son's performance in examination at the end of the year the basis for fixing what he should pay for that year's schooling, and proposed this before the Bishop could know the admirable talents which Lord Overstone, under his care, was to develop, would the excellent tutor have "willingly submitted"? If he did not submit, ought he to have submitted? Would his "shrinking" from this test have implied that there was "something unsound" even in that tuition which has made Lord Overstone what we see him? Would the Bishop have deserved all the depreciatory sarcasm of Mr. Lowe, all the exquisite *amenities* of the *Times,* for shrinking from it?

For this is all that the managers of schools are doing. These ravenous sharks, these importunate beggars, these interested filchers of public money, these bad citizens who have subscribed nine millions of their own money to educate the people, are doing no more than this. "Examine our scholars as much as you will," they say; "the more of them the better; all of them if you can. Whether the State should undertake such a task is not a question for us to settle; it is a question of administration and public expense; it is a question for Government and the House of Commons. But the more our scholars are examined, the better for them, and the better we shall be pleased. Only — since we educate a great number of children, of the most various circumstances, the most various attainments — do not make in any school, infant school or juvenile school either, each scholar's success in reaching, under examination, a certain standard, the sole basis of your payments to us. If you do, you will seriously embarrass us. The circumstances of our scholars, the backwardness of their civilisation, must for some time prevent their reaching that standard in numbers sufficient from heavy loss. You are premature by at least twenty years in fixing that standard."

But in Ireland the State examines every child. Let us see what the State really does in Ireland. It is an official regulation that the Inspector shall examine every child. So much the better for the school. But if the children fail to reach a certain standard, does the Irish School lose its grants? It does not.

This, then, is not the "principle of examination" of the Revised Code. This is examination used as a stimulus, not as a machine for measuring payment.

In Dublin, in a school filled with children of poor weavers of the Liberty, every child, we will say, is examined by the Inspector. Great numbers of them fail to come up to the standard of the Revised Code. Yet progress is being made with them, much good is being done to them, they are far better where they are than in the streets. Accordingly, their school receives its grant notwithstanding the examination failure.

In London, in a school filled with the children (not infants) of poor weavers of Spitalfields, every child will under the Revised Code be examined by the Inspector. Great numbers of them will fail: so backward are they, so long neglected, so physically feeble. Yet most of the good they get, they get from that school. But now the "principle of examination" is to become a reality. There is to be no "shrinking." It is to be "no work no pay." The grant will sink to nothing, and the school managers will be left to enjoy perfect "liberty of action."

The opponents of the Revised Code value the "principle of examination" as much as Lord Overstone. It is this false use of it which they deprecate. — I am, &c.,

A LOVER OF LIGHT

Notes

[1] *Letters,* I, 150.

[2] *Ibid.,* 159.

[3] Samuel Jones Loyd (1796–1883) was the only son of a Welsh dissenting minister who had given up the ministry for a partnership in his father-in-law's bank, Jones's Manchester Bank, which later merged with the London and Westminster Bank. Educated at Eton, Samuel Loyd studied classics for a year under Bishop Charles James Blomfield (1786–1857) before matriculating at Trinity College, Cambridge. Loyd was a banking authority. He was chairman of the Irish Famine Committee in 1847, and was a leading promoter of the Great Exhibition of 1851. He was created Baron Overstone of Overstone and Fotheringay in 1860. He received the degree of D.C.L. from the University of Oxford in 1864, on the occasion of one of Arnold's Creweian orations. Lord Overstone supported the Revised Code in the House of Lords on March 20, 1862. His speech was reported together with lengthy editorial comment in *The Times,* March 21, 1862.

Ordnance Maps

London Review
V (December 6, 1862), 491–492

The *London Review and Weekly Journal of Politics, Literature, Art and Society* began publication July 7, 1860. Its editor was Charles Mackay (1814–1889), who had recently terminated his editorship of the *Illustrated London News.* Arnold had a brief association with the magazine, for his carefully kept accounts acknowledge the receipt of eleven guineas from the *London Review* in the course of 1862 and 1863. Professor R. H. Super has shown that a part of this sum was in payment for "Ordnance Maps," a title that Arnold in 1862 marked in his notebooks as a completed project.[1] The other contributions for which he received payment remain to be determined.

The notice which newspapers attract to a subject is vivid, but it is transient. To-day's topic is not yesterday's, and will not be to-morrow's; Folly has to be shot flying, and is soon out of the reach of danger. No one talks now of the Salisbury scandals; no one gives an ill-natured thought to that wise old Canon, who, no doubt, as he looks at his son-in-law in his stall, and opens his newspaper without finding his own name in it, thanks God that he held his tongue, and waited for the sure deliverance of time. A fortnight hence nobody will ask the etymology of *reindeer;* and Colonel Burnaby, now (they say) ill from the annoyance which his attainments in philology have brought upon him, will be going about as usual with his *Johnson* in his carpet-bag, well and cheerful as if nothing had happened.[2]

Before a similar oblivion quite covers the Ordnance Surveyors and Sir Henry James — household words as the *Times* made them a few weeks ago, — we want to recall attention to them for one moment. It is just possible, though not, we fear, very probable, that they may be now setting themselves in silence to amend the errors with which they have been reproached. In that case it would be a pity they should not know that in what they have hitherto heard about their errors they have by no means heard the worst of themselves.[3]

The Ordnance Surveyors have been reproached with letting the nomenclature of their maps become obsolete; the names of places are left (it is said) just as they stood forty or fifty years ago; new railways, new roads, new churches, new groups of houses are not marked in. And this in the maps of a country which changes so fast as England! There is much truth in this charge; but it is not the charge which a real lover of maps would be disposed to press most warmly. The imperfect nomenclature of the older Ordnance maps is no doubt a grievance, but the worn out condition of their plates is a far worse one. The writing of an old map is inaccurate, but its shading is a great deal more than inaccurate. The dark shading is all blurred, and the fine shading is all gone.

By its shading a good map becomes, to the lover of maps, almost a picture; it shows him all the relief and configuration of a country. He can trace, in those finely graduated lines, mountain and valley, slope and plain, open ground and woodland, in all their endless variety. It is by the completeness and beauty of their shading that modern maps distinguish themselves from ancient most advantageously. But the Ordnance sheet of Oxford or Cheltenham which one buys at the present day is, in its shading, little superior to the country map of a hundred years ago. It cannot be denied that the Ordnance Surveyors have done a good deal to amend the obsolete nomenclature of their maps. To amend their effaced shading they have done nothing. They have, indeed, in some of the most worn of their sheets, attempted a little detestable patching here and there; but the remedy is worse than the disease. A lover of maps would in general be only too happy if he could obtain the unworn sheet of thirty years ago, with all its imperfections of writing, in exchange for the indistinct catalogue of names which he now buys under the title of an Ordnance sheet. Names he can put in or correct for himself, but he cannot restore shading. He is therefore not very grateful to the Ordnance Surveyors for doing the former for him, so long as they neglect to do the latter. They give him, indeed, in the sheets already mentioned of Oxford and Cheltenham, the Great Western and the London and North Western Railways; but where, he sorrowfully asks, is the Cumnor hill country on the right bank of the Thames, as the original map gave it? Where is Bredon Hill, with all its beautiful staging from the plain to its summit? As they were in the Roman maps of Britain — absent.

As is usual in England, the defects of the Ordnance Survey are at once attributed to its being a Government work, and it is proposed to cure them by leaving the map of England to be made by private enterprise. A more absurd proposition it would be hard to conceive. What English private enterprise produces in the way of map-making one has only to walk down the Strand to see. The truth is, map-making is by no means an English specialty; the taste of our general public for maps, as for cooking, is not yet cultivated enough to demand a very superior article; it is satisfied with less than what in several other countries is demanded. Not only are the Government maps in England inferior to the maps made in Germany or Switzerland, but our private enterprise-maps are inferior to them in still greater degree. Nothing was more noticeable for any map-lover

who went and came between London and Paris during the Italian war
of 1859, than the difference between the maps of the seat of war exposed
for sale in the shops of the two capitals. No doubt the best and most
expensive foreign map of North Italy might be bought in London as well
as in Paris; but the maps manufactured in London to meet the common
home demand were daubs which in Paris would have been unsaleable.
Mr. Stanford is a most intelligent and enterprising map-seller — much the
best, probably, now that Mr. Arrowsmith has become somnolent, to be
found in London; but his shop is not yet that of Andriveau or of Artaria.[4]
A sheet of the English Ordnance Survey can be obtained at Andriveau's;
but a sheet of the map of France by the *état-major* could not a year or
two ago be obtained in London without sending to Paris expressly for it;
and we greatly doubt whether it is obtainable here at this moment.

Neither on the Continent nor in England, however, would the ordinary
public demand ensure a supply of maps of first-rate excellence. As a
mere matter of trade, a Swiss publisher would not think it worth his while
to go to the expense of preparing such maps as the Dufour map of
Switzerland,[5] or a Viennese tradesman such maps as we have just seen in
the Austrian department of the International Exhibition. A tradesman's
business is simply to make money, and he can make it with less risk by
publishing inferior maps to these. But a government is not a tradesman;
and the governments of civilized European countries have very properly
thought it their business to get first-rate maps made of the countries under
their rule, whether the making should prove a good trade speculation or
no. To perform this duty, governments have at their disposal in the
scientific branches of their armies an instrument superior to any which
private enterprise can employ. The English government could not well
shirk the duty of providing a map of England; but, in discharging this
duty, it has been hampered as only an English government is hampered,
and it has shown an irresolution such as only an English executive can
display. The history of our Ordnance Survey and of the Select Commit-
tees which have kindly undertaken to be its nursing fathers, is the satire
of administration under a Parliamentary Government. But it was a folly
of the late Mr. Joseph Hume (and with all his usefulness he had many)
which made the deterioration of the English Ordnance map a necessity.[6]
He procured the reduction of its price to 2s. for a full sheet, and to 6d. for
a quarter sheet. Even the general public were willing to get good maps
when they were to be given away at this rate; and the demand which
followed wore out the plates. Modern science has supplied the Ordnance
Surveyors with means by which, for their new sheets, the wear and tear
of incessant engraving can be avoided. It will be long before electrotyped
maps equal for beauty and clearness the best engraved ones; still, the

preservation of the new plates has been rendered possible. But, meanwhile, the old plates are spoilt.

The whole matter lies in a nutshell. It is the duty of a Government to provide a good map of its country, and to keep that map in good order; but it is not its duty to provide cheap maps for the million. If, however, it chooses to assume this latter duty, it cannot thereby get rid of the former. If the English government thinks itself bound to sell its map of Oxfordshire at sixpence a sheet, it is bound to renew the plates as fast as the great demand caused by this low price wears them out. If this cannot be done by reason of the expense, that proves that the price of the Ordnance maps is at present fixed too low. For a Government's first and indispensable duty in the way of map-making is (we cannot repeat it too often), to provide a *good* map of its country, not to provide a *cheap* one. The cheapness or dearness is a secondary consideration for it; the first consideration is excellence. When an excellent map has been once secured, then let private enterprise bring this out on a reduced scale, and let Mr. Stanford sell the performances of private enterprise as cheap as he will. To compete in the sale of cheap maps with Mr. Stanford, is no part of a Government's business.

To this day the Ordnance Surveyors seem unable to comprehend this. Sir Henry James, reproached with the imperfection of his maps, talks to us about new means of multiplying impressions of them. Let him clearly understand what is expected of him. It is expected that he shall have a first-rate map of England on the one-inch scale (which is very nearly the scale adopted in other European countries), producible at the demand of an English or foreign purchaser; and that, if he is precluded by his present conditions of price from having this, he should, instead of writing letters to the *Times* about photo-zincography, address an urgent representation to his official superior, the War Minister, and get those conditions altered.[7] His map of Cumberland (if it is ever going to appear) will even then, probably, be inferior to the Dufour map of Lucerne just published; but at any rate he will no longer be compelled to offer to a foreigner, who asks for our Government map of Kent or Devonshire, a production discreditable to the English nation and Government, and hardly superior to the old French map of Cassini.[8]

Notes

[1] R. H. Super, "Arnold's Notebooks and Arnold Bibliography," *Modern Philology*, LVI (May 1959), 268–269. See also *The Note-Books of Matthew Arnold*, ed. H. F. Lowry et al. (London and New York, 1952), p. 568. [Hereafter cited as *Note-Books*.]

[2] Lt. Col. Edwyn S. Burnaby of the Grenadier Guards and Captain Randolph Stewart of the Black Watch Regiment bet on the spelling of *reindeer*, the name Colonel Burnaby proposed to rename Palm Oil, a race horse in which he had an

interest. He supported his spelling *raindeer* by reference to Dr. Johnson's dictionary. Captain Stewart was accused subsequently of having proposed the bet with Mr. R. Ten Broeck on terms that he was bound to win. Vice-Admiral H. J. Rous, steward of the Jockey Club, let the story out to the *Morning Post.* The affair was the occasion of extensive editorials in the London *Times* on November 6, p. 6, cols. 4–5, and November 13, 1862, p. 8, cols. 3–5, as well as of several explanatory letters to *The Times* from the parties concerned. The issue was one of orthography rather than, as Arnold suggests, etymology.

Of the Salisbury scandals I have discovered nothing.

[3] Sir Henry James (1803–1877) was director-general of the ordnance survey, an appointment he received in 1854. The poor quality of the maps issued in 1862 was the subject of widespread comment, eliciting from *The Times* leading articles on September 22 and 24, 1862.

[4] Edward Stanford was a map dealer at Charing Cross.

Aaron Arrowsmith (1750–1823) was the head of a family of cartographers. He established his business in London in 1790, where his brother Samuel and his son Aaron carried on the business until 1839.

Gabriel Gustave Andriveau-Goujon (b. 1808), Parisian map dealer. His most famous map, "Plan de Paris et des communes environnantes," was esteemed from 1834 to 1855, when it was shown in the Exposition Universelle of that year.

Artaria was the name of a Viennese publishing house founded in 1760. Originally publishers of music, the concern widened its interest to include the printing of maps under the direction of Augusto Artaria (1806–1893).

[5] Guillaume Henri Dufour (1787–1875), Swiss general and cartographer. The 25 maps of the *Topographische Karte der Schweiz* were published between 1832 and 1864.

[6] Joseph Hume (1777–1855), a leader of the radical party and M.P. for various constituencies, was especially interested in financial policy, advocating retrenchment and tirelessly exposing extravagance.

[7] Sir Henry James sponsored the introduction in 1859 of photozincography at the ordnance survey office. His book *Photozincography* was published in 1860. In 1862 he addressed letters to *The Times* (September 22, p. 7, col. 3; October 9, p. 11, col. 1; and November 4, p. 10, col. 6) with reference to the development of a similar process by J. W. Osborne.

[8] Comte Jacques Dominique de Cassini (1747–1845), director of the Paris Observatory, completed in 1793 the great *Carte de France* begun by his father César-François Cassini de Thury.

The Bishop and the Philosopher

Macmillan's Magazine
VII (January 1863), 241–256

"The Bishop and the Philosopher" has never been reprinted in its original form, although the latter half is familiar to readers of the essay "Spinoza and the Bible" which is printed in Arnold's *Essays in Criticism* [First Series], 2 ed. (London, 1869).

Arnold explained his intention in a letter to his mother, November 19, 1862: "I think, *apropos* of Colenso, of doing what will be rather an interesting thing — I am going to write an article called 'The Bishop and the Philosopher,' contrasting Colenso and Co.'s jejeune and technical manner of dealing with Biblical controversy with that of Spinoza in his famous treatise on the *Interpretation of Scripture,* with a view of showing how, the heresy on both sides being equal, Spinoza broaches his in that most edifying and pious spirit by which alone the treatment of such matters can be made fruitful, while Colenso and the English Essayists, from their narrowness and want of power, more than from any other cause, do not." [1] "The article," he added, "will be in *Fraser* or *Macmillan* — I don't know which."

Arnold wrote a second article about Spinoza for the London *Times* (see the letter of April 17, 1863, to his mother). [2] No trace of it appears in *The Times* between April and December 1863. However, he wrote on November 19, 1863, "I am not quite pleased with my *Times* Spinoza as an article for *Macmillan;* it has too much of the brassiness and smartness of a *Times* article in it." [3] The *"Times* Spinoza," nevertheless, is most probably "A Word More about Spinoza," *Macmillan's Magazine* (December 1863). It was reprinted as "Spinoza" in the *Essays in Criticism* [First Series], 1 ed. (London, 1865) and combined with the latter half of "The Bishop and the Philosopher" to form "Spinoza and the Bible" in the 1869 and subsequent editions of *Essays in Criticism* [First Series].

Controversial in manner, enlivened by Arnold's gay irony, "The Bishop and the Philosopher" is far more vivacious than the magisterial "Spinoza and the Bible," and it reflects far better the mood that animated him while he composed it. He explained in a note on "The Function of Criticism at the Present Time," (*Essays in Criticism* [First Series],) that his dislike of controversy prevented him from reprinting his essays critical of Dr. Colenso's book on the Pentateuch, but he declared, nevertheless, his "sincere impenitence for having written them." [4]

"Der Engländer ist eigentlich ohne Intelligenz," said Goethe; by which he meant, not that the Englishman was stupid, but that he occupied

himself little with the *rationale* of things.[5] He meant that an Englishman held and uttered any given opinion as something isolated, without perceiving its relation to other ideas, or its due place in the general world of thought; without, therefore, having any notion of its absolute value. He meant, in short, that he was uncritical.

Heedless of what may be said about him, the Englishman is generally content to pursue his own way, producing, indeed, little in the sphere of criticism, but producing from time to time in the sphere of pure creation masterpieces which attest his intellectual power and extort admiration from his detractors. Occasionally, however, he quits this safe course. Occasionally, the uncritical spirit of our race determines to perform a great public act of self-humiliation. Such an act it has recently accomplished. It has just sent forth as its scapegoat into the wilderness, amidst a titter from educated Europe, the Bishop of Natal.[6]

The Bishop's book on the Pentateuch has been judged from a theological point of view by members of his own profession; and critics too, who were not members of that profession, have judged it from the same point of view. From the theological point of view I do not presume to judge it. But a work of this kind has to justify itself before another tribunal besides an ecclesiastical one; it is liable to be called up for judgment, not only before a Court of Arches, but before the Republic of Letters. It is as a humble citizen of that republic that I wish to say a few words about the Bishop of Natal's book. But what, it may be asked, has literary criticism to do with books on religious matters? That is what I will in the first instance try to show.

Literary criticism's most important function is to try books as to the influence which they are calculated to have upon the general culture of single nations or of the world at large. Of this culture literary criticism is the appointed guardian, and on this culture all literary works may be conceived as in some way or other operating. All these works have a special professional criticism to undergo: theological works that of theologians, historical works that of historians, philosophical works that of philosophers, and in this case each kind of work is tried by a separate standard. But they have also a general literary criticism to undergo, and this tries them all, as I have said, by one standard — their effect upon general culture. Every one is not a theologian, a historian, or a philosopher, but every one is interested in the advance of the general culture of his nation or of mankind. A criticism therefore which, abandoning a thousand special questions which may be raised about any book, tries it solely in respect of its influence upon this culture, brings it thereby within the sphere of every one's interest. This is why literary criticism has exercised so much power. The chief sources of intellectual influence in Europe, during the last century and a half, have been its three chief critics — Voltaire, Lessing, Goethe. The chief sources of intellectual influence in England, during the same period, have been its chief organs of criticism — Addison, Johnson, the first Edinburgh Reviewers.

Religious books come within the jurisdiction of literary criticism so far as they affect general culture. Undoubtedly they do affect this in the highest degree: they affect it whether they appeal to the reason, or to the heart and feelings only; whether they enlighten directly, or, by softening and purifying, prepare the way for enlightenment. So far as by any book on religious matters, the raw are humanised or the cultivated are advanced to a yet higher culture, so far that book is a subject for literary criticism. But, undoubtedly, the direct promotion of culture by intellectual power is the main interest of literary criticism, not the indirect promotion of this culture by edification. As soon, therefore, as a religious work has satisfied it that it pursues no other end than edification, *and that it really does pursue* this, literary criticism dismisses it without further question. Religious books, such as are sold daily all round us by thousands and tens of thousands, of no literary merit whatever, which do not pretend to enlighten intellectually, which only profess to edify, and do in some way fulfil their profession, literary criticism thus dismisses with respect, without a syllable of disparaging remark. Even a work like that of M. Hengstenberg on the Pentateuch, which makes higher claims without fulfilling them, literary criticism may dismiss without censure, because it is honestly written for purposes of edification.[7] Over works, therefore, which treat of religious matters, literary criticism will only in certain cases linger long. One case is, when, through such works, though their object be solely or mainly general edification, there shines an ethereal light, the presence of a gifted nature; for this entitles the *Imitation*, the *Spiritual Works* of Fénelon, the *Pilgrim's Progress*, the *Christian Year*, to rank with the works which inform, not with those which edify simply; and it is with works which inform that the main business of literary criticism lies. And even over works which cannot take this high rank, but which are yet freshened, as they pursue their aim of edification, with airs from the true poetical sky — such as the "Mother's Last Words" of Mrs. Sewell — [8] literary criticism will be tempted to linger; it will, at least, salute them in passing, and say: "There, too, is a breath of Arcadia!"

This is one case; another is, when a work on religious matters entirely foregoes the task of edifying the uninstructed, and pursues solely that of informing the instructed, of raising the intellectual life of these to a yet higher stage. Such an attempt to advance the highest culture of Europe, of course powerfully interests a criticism whose especial concern is with that culture. There is a third and last case. It is, when a work on religious matters is neither edifying nor informing; when it is neither good for the many nor yet for the few. A Hebrew moralist, in the *Ethics of the Fathers*, says: "Every dispute that is instituted for God's sake will in the end be established; but that which is not for God's sake will not be established." [9] What may be considered as a dispute for God's sake? Literary criticism regards a religious book, which tends to edify the multitude, as a dispute for God's sake; it regards a religious book which tends to inform the instructed, as a dispute for God's sake; but a religious book which tends neither to edify the multitude nor to inform the instructed, it refuses to regard as a dispute for God's sake; it classes it, in the language of the moralist just cited, not with the speaking of Hillel and Shamai, but with the gainsaying of Korah.[10] It is bound, if the book has notoriety enough to give it importance, to pass censure on it.

According to these principles, literary criticism has to try the book of the Bishop of Natal, which all England is now reading. It has to try it in respect of the influence which it is naturally calculated to exercise on the culture of England or Europe; and it asks: "Does this book tend to advance that culture, either by edifying the little-instructed, or by further informing the much-instructed?"

Does it tend to edify the little-instructed — the great majority? Perhaps it will be said that this book professes not to edify the little-instructed, but to enlighten them; and that a religious book which attempts to enlighten the little-instructed by sweeping away their prejudices, attempts a good work and is justifiable before criticism, exactly as much as a book which attempts to enlighten on these matters the much-instructed. No doubt, to say this is to say what seems quite in accordance with modern notions; the *Times* tells us day after day how the general public is the organ of all truth, and individual genius the organ of all error; nay, we have got so far, it says, that the superior men of former days, if they could live again now, would abandon the futile business of running counter to the opinions of the many, of persisting in opinions of their own: they would sit at the feet of the general public, and learn from its lips what they ought to say. And, no doubt, this doctrine holds out, both for the superior man and the general public, a prospect in a high degree tempting; the former is to get more pudding than formerly, and the latter more praise. But it is a doctrine which no criticism that has not a direct interest in promulgating it can ever seriously entertain. The highly-instructed few, and not the scantily-instructed many, will ever be the organ to the human race of knowledge and truth. Knowledge and truth, in the full sense of the words, are not attainable by the great mass of the human race at all. The great mass of the human race have to be softened and humanised through their heart and imagination, before any soil can be found in them where knowledge may strike living roots. Until the softening and humanising process is very far advanced, intellectual demonstrations are uninforming for them; and, if they impede the working of influences which

advance this softening and humanising process, they are even noxious;
they retard their development, they impair the culture of the world. All
the great teachers, divine and human, who have ever appeared, have
united in proclaiming this. "Remember the covenant of the Highest, and
wink at ignorance," says the Son of Sirach.[11] "Unto you," said Christ to a
few disciples, "it is given to know the mysteries of the kingdom of heaven,
but to them (the multitude) it is not given." [12] "My words," said Pindar,
"have a sound only for the wise." [13] Plato interdicted the entry of his
school of philosophy to all who had not first undergone the discipline of a
severe science. "The vast majority," said Spinoza, "have neither capacity
nor leisure to follow speculations." "The few (those who can have a
saving knowledge) can never mean the many," says, in one of his noblest
sermons, Dr. Newman.[14] Old moral ideas leaven and humanise the multitude: new intellectual ideas filter slowly down to them from the thinking
few; and only when they reach them in this manner do they adjust themselves to their practice without convulsing it. It was not by the intellectual truth of its propositions concerning purgatory, or prayer for the dead,
or the human nature of the Virgin Mary, that the Reformation touched
and advanced the multitude: it was by the moral truth of its protest
against the sale of indulgences, and the scandalous lives of many of the
clergy.

Human culture is not, therefore, advanced by a religious book conveying intellectual demonstrations to the many, unless they be conveyed in
such a way as to edify them. Now, that the intellectual demonstrations of
the Bishop of Natal's book are not in themselves of a nature to edify the
general reader, that is, to serve his religious feeling, the Bishop himself
seems well aware. He expresses alarm and misgivings at what he is about,
for this very reason, that he is conscious how, by shaking the belief of
the many in the Inspiration of Scripture, he may be shaking their religious
life — working, that is, not to their edification. He talks of "the sharp
pang of that decisive stroke which is to sever their connexion with the
ordinary view of the Mosaic story for ever." Again: "I tremble," he says,
"at the results of my own inquiry — the momentous results" (he elsewhere
calls them) "to which it leads." And again: "I cannot but feel, that having
thus been impelled to take an active part in showing the groundlessness
of that notion of Scripture Inspiration which so many have long regarded
as the very foundation of their faith and hope, a demand may be made
upon me for something to supply the loss, for something *to fill up the
aching void* which will undoubtedly be felt at first." Even if he had not
been himself conscious of the probable operation of his book, there were
plenty of voices to tell him beforehand what it would be. He himself
quotes these words of Mr. Cook: "One thing with the Englishman is fixed
and certain; — a narrative purporting to be one of positive facts, which

is wholly, or in any considerable portion, untrue, can have no connexion with the Divine, and cannot have any beneficial influence on mankind" *(der Engländer ist eigentlich ohne Intelligenz).*[15] He quotes Mr. Burgon as expressing the common belief of English Christians when he says: "Every verse of the Bible, every word of it, every syllable of it, every letter of it, is the direct utterance of the Most High." [16] And so, too, since the publication of the Bishop of Natal's book, a preacher in the Oxford University pulpit has declared, that if the historical credit of a single verse of the Bible be shaken, all belief in the Bible is gone.[17]

But indeed, without looking at all to these momentous results of his demonstrations, the Bishop would probably have no difficulty in admitting that these demonstrations can have in themselves nothing edifying. He is an excellent arithmetician, and has published an admirable Manual of Arithmetic;[18] and his book is really nothing but a series of problems in this his favourite science, the solution to each of which is to be the *reductio ad absurdum* of that Book of the Pentateuch which supplied its terms. The Bishop talks of the "multitude of operatives" whose spiritual condition we must care for: he allows that to the pious operative his proceedings must give a terrible shock; but will the impious operative be softened or converted by them? He cannot seriously think so; for softening and converting are positive processes, and his arithmetical process is a purely negative one. It is even ruthlessly negative; for it delights in nothing so much as in triumphing over attempts which may be made to explain or attenuate the difficulties of the Bible narrative. Such an attempt Dr. Stanley has made with respect to the history of the sojourn of the Israelites in the wilderness; the quotations on this matter from Dr. Stanley's *Sinai and Palestine* are the refreshing spots of the Bishop of Natal's volume, but he cites them only to refute them.[19] In a similar spirit he deals with M. Hengstenberg. M. Hengstenberg is, in general, only too well contented to remain with his head under water, raking about in the sand and mud of the letter for the pearl which will never be found there; but occasionally a mortal commentator must come up to breathe. M. Hengstenberg has hardly time to gasp out a rational explanation of any passage, before the remorseless Bishop pushes him under water again.

So we must look for the edifying part of the Bishop of Natal's work elsewhere than in his arithmetical demonstrations. And I am bound to say, that such a part the Bishop does attempt to supply. He feels, as I have said, that the work he has been accomplishing is not in itself edifying to the common English reader, that it will leave such a reader with an "aching void" in his bosom; and this void he undoubtedly attempts to fill. And how does he fill it? "I would venture to refer him," he says, "to my lately published Commentary on the Epistle to the Romans . . . which I would humbly hope by God's mercy may minister in some measure to the comfort and support of troubled minds under present circumstances." He candidly adds, however, that this Commentary was written "when I had no idea whatever of holding my present views." So as a further support he offers "the third and sixth chapters of Exodus" (that Exodus on which he has just been inflicting such severe blows), "the noble words of Cicero preserved by Lactantius" in the eighth section of the sixth book of his *Divine Institutions,* "the great truths revealed to the Sikh Gooroos," as these truths are set forth in Cunningham's *History of the Sikhs,* pp. 355, 356, and lastly a Hindoo prayer, to be found in the *Journal of the Asiatic Society of Bengal,* vol. vi. pp. 487, 750, 756, beginning "Whatever Rám willeth." He finds the simple everyday Englishman going into church, he buries him and the sacred fabric under an avalanche of rule-of-three sums; and when the poor man crawls from under the ruins, bruised, bleeding, and bewildered, and begs for a little spiritual consolation, the Bishop "refers him" to his own Commentary on the Romans, two chapters of Exodus, a fragment of Cicero, a revelation to the Sikh Gooroos, and an invocation of Rám. This good Samaritan sets his battered brother on his own beast (the Commentary), and for oil and wine pours into his wounds the Hindoo prayer, the passage of Cicero, and the rest of it.

Literary criticism cannot accept this edification as sufficient. The Bishop of Natal must be considered to have failed to edify the little-instructed, to advance the lower culture of his nation. It is demanded of him, therefore, that he shall have informed the much-instructed, that he shall have advanced the higher culture of his nation or of Europe.

Literary criticism does not require him to edify this; it is enough if he informs it. We may dismiss the Commentary on the Romans and the truths revealed to the Sikh Gooroos from our consideration, for the Bishop himself has told us that it is the weak vessel, the little-instructed, whom he refers to these. There remain his arithmetical demonstrations. And, indeed, he himself seems to rely for his justification upon the informing influence which these are calculated to exercise upon the higher culture of his nation; for he speaks of the "more highly educated classes of society," and of the "intelligent operative" (that favourite character of modern disquisition) — those, that is, who have either read much or thought much — as the special objects of his solicitude. Now, on the higher culture of his nation, what informing influence can the Bishop of Natal's arithmetical demonstrations exercise? I have already said what these are: they are a series of problems, the solution of each of which is meant to be the *reductio ad absurdum* of that Book of the Pentateuch which supplied its terms. This being so, it must be said that the Bishop of Natal gives us a great deal too many of them. For his purpose a smaller number of problems and a more stringent method of stating them would have sufficed. It would then have been possible within the compass of a single page to put all the information which the Bishop's book aspires to convey to the mind of Europe. For example: if we take the Book of Genesis, and the account of the family of Judah there related — "*Allowing 20 as the marriageable age, how many years are required for the production of 3 generations?*" The answer to that sum disposes (on the Bishop's plan) of the Book of Genesis. Again, as to the account in the Book of Exodus of the Israelites dwelling in tents — "*Allowing 10 persons for each tent (and a Zulu hut in Natal contains on an average only 3½) how many tents would 2,000,000 persons require?*" The parenthesis in that problem is hardly worthy of such a master of arithmetical statement as Dr. Colenso; but, with or without the parenthesis, the problem, when answered, disposes of the Book of Exodus. Again, as to the account in Leviticus of the provision made for the priests: "*If three priests have to eat 264 pigeons a day, how many must each priest eat?*" That disposes of Leviticus. Take Numbers, and the total of firstborns there given, as compared with the number of male adults: "*If of 900,000 males, 22,273 are firstborns, how many boys must there be in each family?*" That disposes of Numbers. For Deuteronomy, take the number of lambs slain at the Sanctuary, as compared with the space for slaying them: "*In an area of 1,692 square yards, how many lambs per minute can 150,000 persons kill in two hours?*" Certainly not *1,250*, the number required; and the Book of Deuteronomy, therefore, shares the fate of its predecessors. *Omnes eodem cogimur.*[20]

Even a giant need not waste his strength. The Bishop of Natal has, indeed, other resources in his conflict with the Pentateuch, if these are insufficient; he has the overcrowding of the Tabernacle doorway, and the little difficulty about the Danites; but he need not have troubled himself to produce them. All he designed to do for the higher culture of his nation has been done without them. It is useless to slay the slain.

Such are the Bishop of Natal's exploits in the field of biblical criticism. The theological critic will regard them from his own point of view; the literary critic asks only in what way can they be informing to the higher culture of England or Europe? This higher culture knew very well already that contradictions were pointed out in the Pentateuch narrative; it had heard already all that the Bishop of Natal tells us as to the "impossibility of regarding the Mosaic story as a true narrative of actual historical matters of fact;" of this impossibility, of which the Bishop of Natal "had not the most distant idea" two years ago, it had long since read expositions, if not so elaborate as his, at least as convincing. That which the higher culture of Europe wanted to know is, —*What then?* What follows from all this? What change is it, if true, to produce in the relations of mankind to the Christian religion? If the old theory of Scripture Inspiration is to be abandoned, what place is the Bible henceforth to hold among books?

What is the new Christianity to be like? How are Governments to deal with national Churches founded to maintain a very different conception of Christianity? It is these questions which the higher culture of Europe now addresses to those who profess to enlighten it in the field of free religious speculation, and it is intellectually informed only so far as these questions are answered. It is these questions which freethinkers who really speak to the higher culture of their nation or of Europe — men such as Hegel was in Germany, such as M. Renan now is in France — attempt to answer; and therefore, unorthodox though such writers may be, literary criticism listens to them with respectful interest. And it is these questions which the Bishop of Natal never touches with one of his fingers.

I will make what I mean yet clearer by a contrast. At this very moment is announced* the first English translation of a foreign work which treats of the same matter as the Bishop of Natal's work — the interpretation of Scripture — and, like the Bishop of Natal's work, treats of it in an unorthodox way. I mean a work signed by a great name — to most English readers the name of a great heretic, and nothing more — the *Tractatus Theologico-Politicus* of Spinoza. It is not easy to give a summary of this book as of the book of the Bishop of Natal. Still, with the aim of showing how free religious speculation may be conducted so as to be informing to the much-instructed, even though it be not edifying to the little-instructed, I will attempt the task.

The little-instructed Spinoza's work could not unsettle, for it was inaccessible to them. It was written in Latin, the language of the instructed few — the language in which Coleridge desired that all novel speculations about religion should be written. Spinoza even expressly declares that he writes for the instructed few only, and that his book is not designed for the many — *reliquis hunc tractatum commendare non studeo*. Not only the multitude, but all of a higher culture than the multitude who yet share the passions of the multitude, he intreats not to read his book: they will only, he says, do harm to others, and no good to themselves. So sincere was this author's desire to be simply useful, his indifference to mere notoriety, that when it was proposed to publish a Dutch translation of his work, and thus bring it within the reach of a wider public, he requested that the project might be abandoned. Such a publication could effect no benefit, he said, and it might injure the cause which he had at heart.

He was moved to write, not by admiration at the magnitude of his own sudden discoveries, not by desire for notoriety, not by a transport of excitement, not because he "had launched his bark on the flood and was carried along by the waters;" but because, grave as was the task to be

* The book has since been published.[21]

attempted, and slight as was the hope of succeeding, the end seemed to him worth all the labour and all the risk. "I fear that I have taken this work in hand too late in the day; for matters are nearly come to that pass that men are incapable, on these subjects, of having their errors cleared away, so saturated with prejudices are their minds. Still, I will persevere, and continue to make what effort I can; for the case, after all, is not quite hopeless." For the instructed few he was convinced that his work might prove truly informing — *his hoc opus perquam utile fore confido.*

Addressing these, he tells them how, struck with the contrast between the precepts of Christianity and the common practice of Christians, he had sought the cause of this contrast and found it in their erroneous conception of their own religion. The comments of men had been foisted into the Christian religion: the pure teaching of God had been lost sight of. He had determined to go again to the Bible, to read it over and over with a perfectly unprejudiced mind, and to accept nothing as its teaching which it did not clearly teach. He began by constructing a method, or set of conditions indispensable for the adequate interpretation of Scripture. These conditions are such, he points out, that a perfectly adequate interpretation of Scripture is now impossible: for example, to understand any Prophet thoroughly, we ought to know the life, character, and pursuits of that Prophet, under what circumstances his book was composed, and in what state and through what hands it has come down to us; and, in general, most of this we cannot know. Still, the main sense of the Books of Scripture may be clearly seized by us. Himself a Jew with all the learning of his nation, and a man of the highest natural powers, he had in the difficult task of seizing this sense every aid which special knowledge or preeminent faculties could supply.

In what then, he asks, does Scripture, interpreted by its own aid, and not by the aid of Rabbinical traditions or Greek philosophy, allege its own divinity to consist? In a revelation given by God to the Prophets. Now all knowledge is a Divine revelation; but prophecy, as represented in Scripture, is one of which the laws of human nature, considered in themselves alone, cannot be the cause. Therefore nothing must be asserted about it, except what is clearly declared by the Prophets themselves; for they are our only source of knowledge on a matter which does not fall within the scope of our ordinary knowing faculties. But ignorant people, not knowing the Hebrew genius and phraseology, and not attending to the circumstances of the speaker, often imagine the Prophets to assert things which they do not.

The Prophets clearly declare themselves to have received the revelation of God through the means of words and images — not, as Christ, through immediate communication of the mind with the mind of God. Therefore the Prophets excelled other men by the power and vividness of their representing and imagining faculty, not by the perfection of their mind. This is why they perceived almost everything through figures, and express themselves so variously, and so improperly, concerning the nature of God. Moses imagined that God could be seen, and attributed to Him the passions of anger and jealousy; Micaiah imagined Him sitting on a throne, with the host of heaven on his right and left hand; Daniel as an old man, with a white garment and white hair; Ezekiel as a fire; the disciples of Christ thought they saw the Spirit of God in the form of a dove; the Apostles, in the form of fiery tongues.

Whence, then, could the Prophets be certain of the truth of a revelation which they received through the imagination, and not by a mental process? — for only an idea can carry the sense of its own certainty along with it, not an imagination. To make them certain of the truth of what was revealed to them, a reasoning process came in; they had to rely on the testimony of a sign, and (above all) on the testimony of their own conscience, that they were good men, and spoke for God's sake. Either testimony was incomplete without the other. Even the good prophet needed for his message the confirmation of a sign; but the bad prophet, the utterer of an immoral doctrine, had no certainty for his doctrine, no truth in it, even though he confirmed it by a sign. This, the testimony of a good conscience, was, therefore, the prophet's grand source of certitude. Even this, however, was only a moral certitude, not a mathematical; for no man can be perfectly sure of his own goodness.

The power of imagining, the power of feeling what goodness is, and the habit of practising goodness, were therefore the sole essential qualifications of a true prophet. But for the purpose of the message, the revelation, which God designed him to convey, these qualifications were enough. The sum and substance of this revelation was simply: *Believe in God, and lead a good life.* To be the organ of this revelation, did not make a man more learned; it left his scientific knowledge as it found it. This explains the contradictory and speculatively false opinions about God, and the laws of Nature, which the Patriarchs, the Prophets, the Apostles entertained. Abraham and the Patriarchs knew God only as *El Sadai*, the Power which gives to every man that which suffices him; Moses knew Him as *Jehovah*, a self-existent being, but imagined Him with the passions of a man. Samuel imagined that God could not repent of His sentences; Jeremiah, that He could. Joshua, on a day of great victory, the ground being white with hail, seeing the daylight last longer than usual, and imaginatively seizing this as a special sign of the help divinely promised to him, declared that the sun was standing still. To be obeyers of God themselves, and inspired leaders of others to obedience and good life, did not make Abraham and Moses metaphysicians, or Joshua a natural philosopher. His revelation no more changed the speculative opinions of each prophet, than it changed his temperament or style. The wrathful Elisha required the natural sedative of music, before he could be the messenger of good fortune to Jehoram. The high-bred Isaiah and Nahum have the style proper to their condition, and the rustic Ezekiel and Amos the style proper to theirs. We are not therefore bound to pay heed to the speculative opinions of this or that prophet, for in uttering these he spoke as a mere man: only in exhorting his hearers to obey God and lead a good life was he the organ of a Divine revelation.

To know and love God is the highest blessedness of man, and of all men alike; to this all mankind are called, and not any one nation in particular. The Divine Law, properly so named, is the method of life for attaining this height of human blessedness: this law is universal, written in the heart, and one for all mankind. Human law is the method of life for attaining and preserving temporal security and prosperity; this law is dictated by a lawgiver, and every nation has its own. In the case of the Jews, this law was dictated, by revelation, through the Prophets; its fundamental precept was to obey God and to keep His commandments, and it is therefore, in a secondary sense, called Divine; but it was, nevertheless, framed in respect of temporal things only. Even the truly moral and divine precept of this law, to practise for God's sake justice and mercy towards one's neighbour, meant for the Hebrew of the Old Testament his Hebrew neighbour only, and had respect to the concord and stability of the Hebrew Commonwealth. The Jews were to obey God and to keep His commandments, that they might continue long in the land given to them, and that it might be well with them there. Their election was a temporal one, and lasted only so long as their State. It is now over; and the only election the Jews now have is that of the *pious,* the *remnant,* which takes place, and has always taken place, in every other nation also. Scripture itself teaches that there is a universal divine law, that this is common to all nations alike, and is the law which truly confers eternal blessedness. Solomon, the wisest of the Jews, knew this law, as the few wisest men in all nations have ever known it; but for the mass of the Jews, as for the mass of mankind everywhere, this law was hidden, and they had no notion of its moral action — its *vera vita* which conducts to eternal blessedness — except so far as this action was enjoined upon them by the prescriptions of their temporal law. When the ruin of their State brought with it the ruin of their temporal law, they would have lost altogether their only clue to eternal blessedness. Christ came when that fabric of the Jewish state, for the sake of which the Jewish Law existed, was about to fall; and He proclaimed the universal Divine Law. A certain moral action is prescribed by this law, as a certain moral action was prescribed by the Jewish Law; but he who truly conceives the universal Divine Law conceives God's decrees adequately as eternal truths, and for him moral action has liberty and self-knowledge; while the Prophets of the Jewish Law inadequately conceived God's decrees as mere rules and commands, and for them moral action had no liberty and no self-knowledge. Christ, who beheld the decrees of God as God himself beholds them — as eternal truths — proclaimed the love of God and the love of our neighbour as *commands* only because of the ignorance of the multitude: to those to whom it was "given to know the mysteries of the kingdom of God," He announced them, as He himself perceived them, as eternal truths. And the Apostles, like Christ, spoke to many of their hearers "as unto carnal not spiritual;" presented to them, that is, the love of God and their neighbour as a Divine command authenticated by the life and death of Christ, not as an eternal idea of reason carrying its own warrant along with it. The presentation of it as this latter their hearers "were not able to bear." The Apostles, moreover, though they preached and confirmed their doctrine by signs as prophets, wrote their Epistles, not as prophets, but as doctors and reasoners. The essentials of their doctrine, indeed, they took not from reason, but, like the Prophets, from fact and revelation; they preached belief in God and goodness of life as a catholic religion, existing by virtue of the Passion of Christ, as the Prophets had preached belief in God and goodness of life as a national religion existing by virtue of the Mosaic Covenant; but while the Prophets announced their message in a form purely dogmatical, the Apostles developed theirs with the forms of reasoning and argumentation according to each apostle's ability and way of thinking, and as they might best commend their message to their hearers; and for their reasonings they themselves claim no Divine authority, submitting them to the judgment of their hearers. Thus each apostle built essential religion on a non-essential foundation of his own, and, as St. Paul says, avoided building on the foundations of another apostle, which might be quite different from his own. Hence the discrepancies between the doctrine of one apostle and another — between that of St. Paul, for example, and that of St. James; but these discrepancies are in the nonessentials not given to them by revelation, and not in essentials. Human Churches, seizing these discrepant nonessentials as essentials, one maintaining one of them, another another, have filled the world with unprofitable disputes, have "turned the Church into an academy, and religion into a science, or rather a wrangling," and have fallen into endless schism.

What, then, are the essentials of Religion according both to the Old and to the New Testament? Very few and very simple. The precept to love God and our neighbour. The precepts of the first chapter of Isaiah: "Wash you, make you clean; put away the evil of your doings from before mine eyes; cease to do evil; learn to do well; seek judgment; relieve the oppressed; judge the fatherless; plead for the widow." The precepts of the Sermon on the Mount, which add to the foregoing the injunction that we should cease to do evil and learn to do well, not to our brethren and fellow-citizens only, but to all mankind. It is by following these precepts that belief in God is to be shown; if we believe in Him we shall keep His commandment; and this is His commandment, that we love one another. It is because it contains these precepts that the Bible is properly called the Word of God, in spite of its containing much that is mere history, and, like all history, is sometimes true, sometimes false; in spite of its containing much that is mere reasoning, and, like all reasoning, is sometimes sound, sometimes hollow. These precepts are also the precepts of the universal Divine Law written in our hearts; and it is only by this that the Divinity of Scripture is established; — by its containing, namely, precepts identical with those of this inly-written and self-proving law. This law was in the world, as St. John says, before the doctrine of Moses or the doctrine of Christ. And what need was there, then, for these doctrines? Because the world at large "knew not" this original Divine Law, in which precepts are ideas, and the belief in God the knowledge and contemplation of Him. Reason gives us this law, Reason tells us that it leads to eternal blessedness, and that those who follow it have no need of any other. But Reason could not have told us that the moral action of the universal Divine Law — followed not from a sense of its intrinsic goodness, truth, and necessity, but simply in proof of obedience (for both the Old and New Testament are but one long discipline of obedience), simply because it is so commanded by Moses in virtue of the Covenant, simply because it is so commanded by Christ in virtue of His life and passion — can lead to eternal blessedness, which means, for Reason, eternal knowledge. Reason could not have told us this, and this is what the Bible tells us. This is that "thing which had been kept secret since the foundation of the world." It is thus that by means of the foolishness of the world God confounds the wise, and with things that are not brings to nought things that are. Of the truth of the promise thus made to obedience without knowledge, we can have no mathematical certainty; for we can have a mathematical certainty only of things deduced by Reason from elements which she in herself possesses. But we can have a moral certainty of it; a certainty such as the Prophets had themselves, arising out of the goodness and pureness of those to whom this revelation has been made, and rendered possible for us by its contradicting no principles of Reason. It is a great comfort to believe it; because "as it is only the very small minority who can pursue a virtuous life by the sole guidance of reason, we should, unless we had this testimony of Scripture, be in doubt respecting the salvation of nearly the whole human race."

It follows from this that Philosophy has her own independent sphere, and Theology hers, and that neither has the right to invade and try to subdue the other. Theology demands perfect obedience, Philosophy perfect knowledge: the obedience demanded by Theology and the knowledge demanded by Philosophy are alike saving. As speculative opinions about God, Theology requires only such as are indispensable to the reality of this obedience; the belief that God is, that He is a rewarder of them that seek Him, and that the proof of seeking Him is a good life. These are the fundamentals of Faith, and they are so clear and simple that none of the inaccuracies provable in the Bible narrative the least affect them, and they have indubitably come to us uncorrupted. He who holds them may make, as the Patriarchs and Prophets did, other speculations about God most erroneous, and yet their faith is complete and saving. Nay, beyond these fundamentals, speculative opinions are pious or impious, not as they are true or false, but as they confirm or shake the believer in the practice of obedience. The truest speculative opinion about the nature of God is impious if it makes its holder rebellious; the falsest speculative opinion is pious if it makes him obedient. Governments should never render themselves the tools of ecclesiastical ambition by promulgating as fundamentals of the national Church's faith more than these, and should concede the fullest liberty of speculation.

But the multitude, which respects only what astonishes, terrifies, and overwhelms it, by no means takes this simple view of its own religion. To the multitude Religion seems venerable only when it is subversive of Reason, confirmed by miracles, conveyed in documents materially sacred and infallible, and dooming to damnation all without its pale. But this religion of the multitude is not the religion which a true interpretation of Scripture finds in Scripture. Reason tells us that a miracle — understanding by a miracle a breach of the laws of Nature — is impossible, and that to think it possible is to dishonour God; for the laws of Nature are the laws of God, and to say that God violates the laws of Nature is to say that He violates His own nature. Reason sees, too, that miracles can never attain their professed object, — that of bringing us to a higher knowledge of God; since our knowledge of God is raised only by perfecting and clearing our conceptions, and the alleged design of miracles is to baffle them. But neither does Scripture anywhere assert, as a general truth, that miracles are possible. Indeed, it asserts the contrary; for Jeremiah declares that Nature follows an invariable order. Scripture, however, like Nature herself, does not lay down speculative propositions (*Scriptura definitiones non tradit, ut nec etiam Natura*). It relates matters in such an order and with such phraseology as a speaker (often not perfectly instructed himself) who wanted to impress his hearers with a lively sense of God's greatness and goodness would naturally employ; as Moses, for instance, relates to the Israelites the passage of the Red Sea without any mention of the East Wind which attended it, and which is brought accidentally to our knowledge in another place. So that to know exactly what Scripture means in the relation of each seeming miracle, we ought to know (besides the tropes and phrases of the Hebrew language) the circumstances, and also — since every one is swayed in his manner of presenting facts by his own preconceived opinions, and we have seen what those of the prophets were — the preconceived opinions of each speaker. But this mode of interpreting Scripture is fatal to the vulgar notion of its verbal inspiration, of a sanctity and absolute truth in all the words and sentences of which it is composed. This vulgar notion is, indeed, a palpable error. It is demonstrable from the internal testimony of the Scriptures themselves, that the Books from the first of the Pentateuch to the last of Kings were put together, after the first Destruction of Jerusalem, by a compiler (probably Ezra) who designed to relate the history of the Jewish people from its origin to that destruction: it is demonstrable, moreover, that the compiler did not put his last hand to the work, but left it, with its extracts from various and conflicting sources sometimes unreconciled — left it with error of text and unsettled readings. The prophetic books are mere fragments of the Prophets, collected by the Rabbins where they could find them, and inserted in the Canon according to their discretion. They, at first, proposed to admit neither the Book of Proverbs nor the Book of Ecclesiastes into the Canon, and only admitted them because there were found in them passages which commended the Law of Moses. Ezekiel also they had determined to exclude; but one of their number remodelled him, so as to procure his admission. The Books of Ezra, Nehemiah, Esther, and Daniel are the work of a single author, and were not written till after Judas Maccabeus had restored the worship of the Temple. The Book of Psalms was collected and arranged at the same time. Before this time, there was no Canon of the Sacred Writings, and the great synagogue, by which the Canon was fixed, was first convened after the Macedonian conquest of Asia. Of that Synagogue none of the prophets were members; the learned men who composed it were guided by their own fallible judgment. In like manner the uninspired judgment of human councils determined the Canon of the New Testament.

Such, reduced to the briefest and plainest terms possible, stripped of the developments and proofs with which he delivers it, and divested of the metaphysical language in which much of it is clothed by him, is the doctrine of Spinoza's treatise on the interpretation of Scripture. Certainly it is not the doctrine of any of the old Churches of Christendom; of the Church of Rome, or the Church of Constantinople, or the Church of England. But Spinoza was not a member, still less a minister, of any one of these Churches. When he made a profession of faith widely different from that of any of them, he had not vowed to minister the doctrine of one of them "as that Church had received the same." When he claimed for Churchmen the widest latitude of speculation in religious matters, he was inviting Governments to construct a new Church; he was not holding office in an old Church under articles expressly promulgated to check "disputations, altercations, or questions." The Bishop of Natal cries out, that orders in the Church of England without full liberty of speculation are an intolerable yoke. But he is thus crying out for a new Church of England, which is not that in which he has voluntarily taken office. He forgets that the clergy of a Church with formularies like those of the Church of England, exist in virtue of their relinquishing in religious matters full liberty of speculation. Liberal potentates of the English Church who so loudly sound the praises of freedom of inquiry, forget it also. It may be time for the State to institute, as its national clergy, a corporation enjoying the most absolute freedom of inquiry; but that corporation will not be the present clergy of the Church of England. Coleridge maintained that the whole body of men of letters or science formed the true clergy of a modern nation, and ought to participate in the endowments of the National Church. That is a beautiful theory; but it has not hitherto been cordially welcomed by the clergy of the Church of England. It has not hitherto been put in practice by the State. Is it to be put in practice for the future? To any eminent layman of letters, who presents himself on the other side the river with the exterminating Five Problems, the passage of Cicero, and the prayer to Rám as his credentials, will the gates of Lambeth fly open?

Literary criticism, however, must not blame the Bishop of Natal because his personal position is false, nor praise Spinoza because his personal position is sound. But, as it must deny to the Bishop's book the right of existing, when it can justify its existence neither by edifying the many nor informing the few, it must concede that right to Spinoza's for the sake of its unquestionably philosophic scope. Many and many are the propositions in Spinoza's work, which, brought by him to us out of the sphere of his unaccepted philosophy, and presented with all the calm inflexibility of his manner, are startling, repellent, questionable. Criticism may take many and many objections to the facts and arguments of his treatise. But, by the whole scope and drift of its argument, by the spirit in which the subject is throughout treated, his work undeniably becomes interesting and stimulating to the general culture of Europe. There are alleged contradictions in Scripture; and the question which the general culture of Europe, informed of this, asks with real interest is, as I have said, — *What then?* To this question Spinoza returns an answer, and the Bishop of Natal returns none. The Bishop of Natal keeps going round for ever within the barren sphere of these contradictions themselves; he treats them as if they were supremely interesting in themselves, as if we had never heard of them before, and could never hear enough of them now. Spinoza touches these verbal matters with all possible brevity, and presses on to the more important. It is enough for him to give us what is indispensably necessary of them. He points out that Moses could never have written, "And the Canaanite was then in the land," because the Canaanite was in the land still at the death of Moses. He points out that Moses could never have written, "There arose not a prophet since in Israel like unto Moses." He points out how such a passage as "These are the kings that reigned in Edom before *there reigned any king over the children of Israel,*" clearly indicates an author writing not before the times of the Kings. He points out how the account of Og's iron bedstead — "Only Og the king of Bashan remained of the remnant of giants; behold, his bedstead was a bedstead of iron; is it not in Rabbath of the children of Ammon?" — probably indicates an author writing after David had taken Rabbath, and found there "abundance of spoil," amongst it this iron bedstead, the gigantic relic of another age. He points out how the language of this passage, and of such a passage as that in the Book of Samuel — "Beforetime in Israel, when a man went to inquire of God, thus he spake: Come and let us go to the seer; for he that is now called Prophet was aforetime called seer" — is certainly the language of a writer describing events of a long-past age, and not the language of a contemporary. But he devotes to all this no more space than is absolutely necessary. He, too, like the Bishop of Natal, touches on the family of Judah; but he devotes one page to this topic, and the Bishop of Natal devotes thirteen. To the sums in Ezra — with which the Bishop of Natal, "should God, in His providence, call him to continue the work," will assuredly fill folios — Spinoza devotes barely a page. He is anxious to escape from the region of these verbal matters, which to the Bishop of Natal are a sort of intellectual land of Beulah, into a higher region; he apologizes for lingering over them so long: *non est cur circa haec diu detinear: nolo taediosâ lectione lectorem detinere.* For him the interesting question is, not whether the fanatical devotee of the letter is to continue, for a longer or for a shorter time, to believe that Moses sate in the land of Moab writing the description of his own death, but what he is to believe when he does not believe this. Is he to take for the guidance of his life a great gloss put upon the Bible by theologians, who "not content with going mad themselves with Plato and Aristotle, want to make Christ and the Prophets go mad with them too," — or the Bible itself? Is he to be presented by his National Church with metaphysical formularies for his creed, or with the real fundamentals of Christianity? If with the former, religion will never produce its due fruits. A few elect will still be saved; but the vast majority of mankind will remain without grace and without good works, hateful and hating one another. Therefore he calls urgently upon Governments to make the National Church what it should be. This is the conclusion of the whole matter for him; a fervent appeal to the State, to save us from the untoward generation of metaphysical Article-makers. And therefore, anticipating Mr. Gladstone, he called his book *The Church in Its Relations with the State.*[22]

Thus Spinoza attempts to answer the crucial question, "*What then?*" and by the attempt, successful or unsuccessful, he interests the higher culture of Europe. The Bishop of Natal does not interest this, neither yet does he edify the unlearned. His book, therefore, satisfies neither of the two conditions, one of which literary criticism has a right to impose on all religious books: *Edify the uninstructed*, it has a right to say to them, *or inform the instructed*. Fulfilling neither of these conditions, the Bishop of Natal's book cannot justify itself for existing. When, in 1861, he heard for the first time that the old theory of the verbal inspiration of Scripture was untenable, he should instead of proclaiming this news (if this was all he could proclaim) in an octavo volume, have remembered that excellent saying of the Wise Man: "If thou hast heard a word, let it die with thee; and behold, it will not burst thee."

These two conditions, which the Bishop of Natal's book entirely fails to fulfil, another well-known religious book also — that book which made so much noise two years ago, the volume of *Essays and Reviews* — fails, it seems to me, to fulfil satisfactorily.[23] Treating religious subjects and written by clergymen, the compositions in that volume have in general, to the eye of literary criticism, this great fault — that they tend neither to edify the many, nor to inform the few. There is but one of them — that by Mr. Pattison on the "Tendencies of Religious Thought in England" — which offers to the higher culture of Europe matter new and instructive. There are some of them which make one, as one reads, instinctively recur to a saying which was a great favourite — so that Hebrew moralist whom I have already quoted tells us — with Judah Ben-Tamar: "The impudent are for Gehinnan, and the modest for Paradise." [24] But even Dr. Temple's Essay on the "Education of the World," perfectly free from all faults of tone or taste, has this fault — that while it offers nothing edifying to the uninstructed, it offers to the instructed nothing which they could not have found in a far more perfect shape in the works of Lessing. Mr. Jowett's Essay, again, contains nothing which is not given, with greater convincingness of statement and far greater fulness of consequence in Spinoza's seventh chapter, which treats of the Interpretation of Scripture.[25] The doctrines of his Essay, as mere doctrine, are neither milk for babes nor strong meat for men; the weak among his readers will be troubled by them; the strong would be more informed by seeing them handled as acquired elements for further speculation by freer exponents of the speculative thought of Europe, than by seeing them hesitatingly exhibited as novelties. In spite of this, however, Mr. Jowett's

Essay has one quality which, at the tribunal of literary criticism, is sufficient to justify it — a quality which communicates to all works where it
is present an indefinable charm, and which is always, for the higher sort
of minds, edifying; — it has *unction*. From a clergyman's essay on a
religious subject theological criticism may have a right to demand more
than this; literary criticism has not. For a court of literature it is enough
that the somewhat pale stream of Mr. Jowett's speculation is gilded by
the heavenly alchemy of this glow.

Unction Spinoza's work has not; that name does not precisely fit any
quality which it exhibits. But he is instructive and suggestive even to the
most instructed thinker; and to give him full right of citizenship in the
Republic of Letters this is enough. And yet, so all-important in the
sphere of religious thought is the power of edification, that in this sphere
a great fame like Spinoza's can never be founded without it. A court of
literature can never be very severe to Voltaire: with that inimitable wit
and clear sense of his, he can never write a page in which the fullest
head may not find something suggestive: still because, with all his wit
and clear sense, he handles religious ideas wholly without the power of
edification, his fame as a great man is equivocal. Strauss treated the question of Scripture Miracles with an acuteness and fulness which even to
the most informed minds is instructive; but because he treated it wholly
without the power of edification, his fame as a serious thinker is equivocal.[26] But in Spinoza there is not a trace either of Voltaire's passion for
mere mockery or of Strauss's passion for mere demolition. His whole soul
was filled with desire of the love and knowledge of God, and of that only.
Philosophy always proclaims herself on the way to the *summum bonum;*
but too often on the road she seems to forget her destination, and suffers
her hearers to forget it also. Spinoza never forgets his destination: "The
love of God is man's highest happiness and blessedness, and the final end
and aim of all human action; — The supreme reward for keeping God's
Word is that Word itself — namely, to know Him and with free will and
pure and constant heart love Him:" these sentences are the keynote to
all he produced, and were the inspiration of all his labours. This is why
he turns so sternly upon the worshippers of the letter, — the editors of the
Masora, the editor of the *Record* — because their doctrine imperils our
love and knowledge of God.[27] "What!" he cries, "our knowledge of God
to depend upon these perishable things, which Moses can dash to the
ground and break to pieces like the first tables of stone, or of which the
originals can be lost like the original book of the Covenant, like the original book of the Law of God, like the book of the Wars of God! . . .
which can come to us confused, imperfect, miswritten by copyists, tampered with by doctors! And you accuse others of impiety! It is you who
are impious, to believe that God would commit the treasure of the true

record of Himself to any substance less enduring than the heart!" And his life was not unworthy of this elevated strain. A philosopher who professed that knowledge was its own reward — a devotee who professed that the love of God was its own reward, this philosopher and this devotee believed in what he said! Spinoza led a life the most spotless, perhaps, to be found among the lives of philosophers; he lived simple, studious, even-tempered, kind; declining honours, declining riches, declining notoriety. He was poor, and his admirer, Simon de Vries, sent him two thousand florins — he refused them: the same friend left him his fortune — he returned it to the heir. He was asked to dedicate one of his works to the magnificent patron of letters in his century, Louis the Fourteenth; he declined. His great work, his *Ethics,* published after his death, he gave injunctions to his friends to publish anonymously, for fear that he should give his name to a school. Truth, he thought, should bear no man's name. And, finally, "Unless," he said, "I had known that my writings would in the end advance the cause of true religion, I would have suppressed them — *tacuissem.*" It was in this spirit that he lived; and this spirit gives to all he writes not exactly unction — I have already said so, — but a kind of sacred solemnity. Not of the same order as the Saints, he yet follows the same service: *Doubtless Thou art our Father, though Abraham be ignorant of us, and Israel acknowledge us not.*

Therefore he has been, in a certain sphere, edifying, and has inspired in many powerful minds an interest and an admiration such as no other philosopher has inspired since Plato. The lonely precursor of German philosophy, he still shines when the light of his successors is fading away: they had celebrity, Spinoza has fame. Not because his peculiar system of philosophy has had more adherents than theirs; on the contrary, it has had fewer. But schools of philosophy arise and fall; their bands of adherents inevitably dwindle; no master can long persuade a large body of disciples that they give to themselves just the same account of the world as he does; it is only the very young and the very enthusiastic who can think themselves sure that they possess the whole mind of Plato, or Spinoza, or Hegel at all. The very mature and the very sober can even hardly believe that these philosophers possessed it themselves enough to put it all into their works, and to let us know entirely how the world seemed to them. What a remarkable philosopher really does for human thought, is to throw into circulation a certain number of new and striking ideas and expressions, and to stimulate with them the thought and imagination of his century or of after-times. So Spinoza has made his distinction between adequate and inadequate ideas a current notion for educated Europe. So Hegel seized a single pregnant sentence of Heracleitus, and cast it, with a thousand striking applications, into the world of modern thought. But to do this is only enough to make a philosopher noteworthy; it is not enough to make him great. To be great, he must have something in him which can influence character, which is edifying; he must, in short have a noble and lofty character himself, a character — to recur to that much-criticised expression of mine — *in the grand style.* This is what Spinoza had; and because he had it, he stands out from the multitude of philosophers, and has been able to inspire in powerful minds a feeling which the most remarkable philosophers, without this grandiose character, could not inspire. "There is no possible view of life but Spinoza's," said Lessing.[28] Goethe has told us how he was calmed and edified by him in his youth, and how he again went to him for support in his maturity.[29] Heine, the man (in spite of his faults) of truest genius that Germany has produced since Goethe — a man with faults, as I have said, immense faults, the greatest of them being that he could reverence so little — reverenced Spinoza. Hegel's influence ran off him like water: "I have seen Hegel," he cries, "seated with his doleful air of a hatching hen upon his unhappy eggs, and I have heard his dismal clucking. — How easily one can cheat oneself into thinking that one understands everything, when one has learnt only how to construct dialectical formulas!" [30] But of Spinoza, Heine said: "His life was a copy of the life of his Divine kinsman, Jesus Christ." [31]

Still, the *Tractatus Theologico-Politicus* was deemed by Spinoza himself a work not suitable to the general public, and here is Mr. Trübner offering it to the general public in a translation! But a little reflection will show that Mr. Trübner is not therefore to be too hastily blamed. Times are changed since Spinoza wrote: the reserve which he recommended and practised is being repudiated by all the world. Speculation is to be made popular, all reticence is to be abandoned, every difficulty is to be canvassed publicly, every doubt is to be proclaimed; information which, to have any value at all, must have it as part of a series not yet complete, is to be flung broadcast, in the crudest shape, amidst the undisciplined, ignorant, passionate, captious multitude.

> Audax omnia perpeti
> Gens humana ruit per vetitum nefas: [32]

and in that adventurous march the English branch of the race of Japhet is, it seems, to be headed by its clergy in full canonicals. If so it is to be, so be it. But, if this is to be so, the Editor of the *Record* himself, instead of deprecating the diffusion of Spinoza's writings, ought rather to welcome it. He would prefer, of course, that we should all be even as he himself is; that we should all think the same thing as that which he himself thinks. This desire, although all might not consent to join in it, is legitimate and natural. But its realisation is impossible; heresy is here, it is pouring in on all sides of him. If we must have heresy, he himself will admit that we may as well have the informing along with the barren. The author of the *Tractatus Theologico-Politicus* is not more unorthodox than the author of the *Pentateuch Critically Examined,* and he is far more edifying. If the English clergy must err, let them learn from this outcast of Israel to err nobly! Along with the weak trifling of the Bishop of Natal, let it be lawful to cast into the huge caldron, out of which the new world is to be born, the strong thought of Spinoza!

Notes

[1] *Letters,* I, 176.

[2] *Ibid.,* 190.

[3] *Ibid.,* 208.

[4] *The Works of Matthew Arnold,* Edition de Luxe, 15 vols. (London, 1903–1904), III, 31, n. 1. [Hereafter cited as *Works.*]

[5] "Alle Engländer sind als solch ohne eigentliche Reflexion" (February 24, 1825), in Ernst Beutler, ed., Johann P. Eckermann, *Gespräche mit Goethe,* in Johann Wolfgang Goethe, *Gedenkausgabe der Werke, Briefe und Gësprache* (Zürich, 1948), XXIV, 148. Arnold repeated the misquotation in the address to the Ipswich Working Men's College, "Ecce Convertimur ad Gentes," *Fortnightly Review,* February 1879.

[6] John William Colenso (1814–1883) was appointed to the new bishopric of Natal in 1853. A collection of *Village Sermons,* 2 ed. (1854) dedicated to his friend Frederick Denison Maurice (1805–1872), had suggested heterodoxical tendencies before his consecration. His *Commentary on St. Paul's Epistle to the Romans* (1861), which was prompted by his task of interpreting the Bible to Zulu youths, elicited cries of heresy from Bishop Gray of Capetown, but his commentary *The Pentateuch and the Book of Joshua Critically Examined,* 7 parts (1862–1879), excited all England, and cost him Maurice's friendship. Arnold's article is damaging to the sincerity and intrepidness of the Bishop, though its declared object was not to disparage Colenso, but to goad "the uncritical spirit of our race."

[7] Ernst Wilhelm Hengstenberg (1802–1869), Lutheran theologian and Professor of Theology at the University of Berlin, was the author of *Beiträge zum Einleitung in das Alte Testament* (1831–1839), translated as *Dissertations on the Genuineness of the Pentateuch* (Edinburgh, 1847) and *Dissertations on the Genuineness of Daniel and the Integrity of Zechariah* (Edinburgh, 1848).

[8] Mary Wright Sewell (1797–1884) is said to have begun her career as an authoress with *Walks with Mamma,* in words of one syllable. Her *Homely Ballads,* printed privately in 1858, reached a 40th thousand in 1889. The ballad "Mother's Last Words" (1860) "had an unprecedented sale of 1,088,000 copies" (*Dictionary of National Biography*). [Hereafter cited as the *DNB.*]

[9] Chapter V, verse 24, *Sayings of the Jewish Fathers Comprising pirque Aboth,* ed. Charles Taylor, 2 ed. (Cambridge, Eng., 1897), p. 93.

[10] Chapter V, verse 25, *ibid.,* pp. 93–94.

[11] Ecclesiasticus, 28:7.

[12] Matthew, 13:11.

[13] Adapted from *Olympian Ode,* ii, 83–85.

[14] John Henry Newman, "Sermon XVIII. Many Called. Few Chosen," *Parochial and Plain Sermons,* new ed., 8 vols. (London, 1873–1877), V, 268.

[15] Frederick Charles Cook (1810–1899), "Ideology and Subscription," *Aids to Faith,* ed. William Thomson, Archbishop of York (London, 1861), p. 146. Quoted in Colenso, *The Pentateuch and the Book of Joshua Critically Examined,* 6 ed. (London, 1873), I, xviii n.

[16] John William Burgon (1813–1888), *Inspiration and Interpretation* (Oxford and London, 1861), p. xxxvi. Quoted in Colenso, I, xx.

¹⁷ Perhaps the Rev. Edward Garbett, who took this position in a sermon at the University of Oxford, November 16, 1862, and who is cited by Colenso, II, x.

¹⁸ Colenso, while a tutor in mathematics at Harrow, published in 1841, *The Elements of Algebra, Designed for the Use of Schools,* and while a tutor at St. John's College, Cambridge, published in 1843, *Arithmetic, Designed for the Use of Schools.*

¹⁹ Arthur Penrhyn Stanley (1815–1881), Dean of Westminster and biographer of Dr. Thomas Arnold. His *Sinai and Palestine, in Connection with Their History* was published in London in 1851.

²⁰ Horace, *Carmina,* II. iii. 25.

²¹ Spinoza's Tractatus Theologico-Politicus, translated and edited by R. Willis, was published in 1862.

²² William Ewart Gladstone (1809–1898), *The State in Its Relations with the Church* (London, 1838).

²³ The seven contributors to *Essays and Reviews* (London, 1860), which represented a liberal interpretation of the Bible, were the Rev. Henry Bristow Wilson, C. W. Goodwin, Benjamin Jowett, Mark Pattison, Baden Powell, Frederick Temple, and Rowland Williams.

²⁴ *Sayings of the Jewish Fathers,* p. 96.

²⁵ "The Interpretation of Scripture."

²⁶ David Friedrich Strauss (1808–1874). The *Life of Jesus,* originally published in 1835, was translated by Marian Evans (i.e., George Eliot) and published in 1840.

²⁷ The Masora is a collection of critical notes on the Biblical text. The *Record,* founded in 1818, was an Anglican paper. It was edited from 1854 to 1867 by Edward Garbett (1817–1887).

²⁸ Friedrich Heinrich Jacobi, "Über die Lehre des Spinoza," *Werke,* 6 vols. (Leipzig, 1812–1825), IV, 55.

²⁹ Eckermann, *Gespräche mit Goethe* (February 28, 1831), p. 468.

³⁰ "Geständnisse," in *Heinrich Heines Sämtliche Werke,* Insel-Ausgabe, 10 vols. (Leipzig, 1910–1915), X, 171.

³¹ "Zur Geschichte der Religion und Philosophie in Deutschland," *ibid.,* VII, 255.

³² Horace, *Carmina,* I. iii. 25–26.

Dr. Stanley's Lectures on the Jewish Church

Macmillan's Magazine
VI (February 1863), 327–336

The first of Arthur Penrhyn Stanley's three volumes of *Lectures on the History of the Jewish Church* appeared in 1863. Arnold's review, if that may be called a review which uses the book only as a point of departure, was printed in *Macmillan's Magazine* a month after "The Bishop and the Philosopher," of which it forms a continuation. The argument of the opening paragraph almost presupposes acquaintance with the theme of the article on Colenso and Spinoza. Early in January 1863, writing to his mother about the public reaction to that essay, Arnold said, "I shall probably write something for *Macmillan,* to remove the misrepresentation of my doctrine about edifying the many." [1] In the review of Stanley's *Lectures* he attempts this clarification, and in so doing introduces for the first time that Protean, yet important, term in his thinking, the *Zeitgeist.* Despite its importance for understanding Arnold's intellectual development this essay has been reprinted only in the Oxford *Essays.*

Dean Stanley (1815–1881) was at the time Regius Professor of Eclesiastical History in the University of Oxford and Canon of Christ Church.

Here is a book on religious matters, which, meant for all the world to read, fulfils the indispensable duty of edifying at the same time that it informs. Here is a clergyman, who, looking at the Bible, sees its contents in their right proportion, and gives to each matter its due prominence. Here is an inquirer, who, treating Scripture history with a perfectly free spirit, — falsifying nothing, sophisticating nothing — treats it so that his freedom leaves the sacred power of that history inviolate. Who that had been reproached with denying to an honest clergyman freedom to speak the truth, who that had been misrepresented as wishing to make religious truth the property of an aristocratic few, while to the multitude is thrown the sop of any convenient fiction, could desire a better opportunity than Dr. Stanley's book affords for showing what, in religious matters, is the true freedom of a religious speaker, and what the true demand and true right of his hearers? [2]

His hearers are the many; those who prosecute the religious life, or those who need to prosecute it. All these come to him with certain demands in virtue of certain needs. There remain a few of mankind who do not come to him with these demands, or acknowledge these needs. Mr. Maurice (whom I name with gratitude and respect) says, in a remarkable letter, that I thus assert them to be without these needs.[3] By no means: that is a matter which literary criticism does not try. But it sees that a very few of mankind aspire after a life which is not the life after which the vast majority aspire, and to help them to which the vast majority seek the aid of religion. It sees that the ideal life — the *summum bonum* for a born thinker, for a philosopher like Parmenides, or Spinoza, or Hegel — is an eternal series of intellectual acts. It sees that this life treats all things, religion included, with entire freedom as subject-matter for thought, as elements in a vast movement of speculation. The few who live this life stand apart, and have an existence separate from that of the mass of mankind; they address an imaginary audience of their mates; the region which they inhabit is the laboratory wherein are fashioned the new intellectual ideas which, from time to time, take their place in the world. Are these few justified, in the sight of God, in so living? That is a question which literary criticism must not attempt to answer. But such is the worth of intellect, such the benefit which it procures for man, that criticism, itself the creation of intellect, cannot but recognize this purely intellectual life, when really followed, as justified so far as the jurisdiction of criticism extends, and even admirable. Those they regard as really following it, who show the power of mind to animate and carry forward the intellectual movement in which it consists. No doubt, many boast of living this life, or inhabiting this purely intellectual region, who cannot really breathe its air: they vainly profess themselves able to live by thought alone, and to dispense with religion: the life of the many, and not the life of the few, would have been the right one for them. They follow the life of the few at their own peril. No doubt the rich and the great, unsoftened by suffering, hardened by enjoyment, craving after novelty, imagining that they see a distinction in the freedom of mind with which the born thinker treats all things, and believing that all distinctions naturally belong to them, have in every age been prone to treat religion as something which the multitude wanted, but they themselves did not — to affect freethinking as a kind of aristocratic privilege; while, in fact, for any real mental or moral life at all, their frivolity entirely disqualified them. They, too, profess the life of the few at their own peril. But the few do really remain, whose life, whose ideal, whose demand, is thought, and thought only: to the communications (however bold) of these few with one another through the ages, criticism assigns the right of passing freely.

But the world of the few — the world of speculative life — is not the world of the many, the world of religious life; the thoughts of the former cannot properly be transferred to the latter, cannot be called true in the latter, except on certain conditions. It is not for literary criticism to set forth adequately the religious life; yet what, even as criticism, it sees of this life, it may say. Religious life resides not in an incessant movement of ideas, but in a feeling which attaches itself to certain fixed objects. The religious life of Christendom has thus attached itself to the acts, and words, and death of Christ, as recorded in the Gospels and expounded in the Epistles of the New Testament; and to the main histories, the prophecies and the hymns of the Old Testament. In relation to these objects, it has adopted certain intellectual ideas; such are, ideas respecting the being of God, the laws of nature, the freedom of human will, the character of prophecy, the character of inspiration. But its essence, the essence of Christian life, consists in the ardour, the love, the self-renouncement, the ineffable aspiration with which it throws itself upon the objects of its attachment themselves, not in the intellectual ideas which it holds in relation to them. These ideas belong to another sphere, the sphere of speculative life, of intellect, of pure thought; transplanted into the sphere of religious life, they have no meaning in them, no vitality, no truth, unless they adjust themselves to the conditions of that life, unless they allow it to pursue its course freely. The moment this is forgotten, the moment in the sphere of the religious life undue prominence is given to the intellectual ideas which are here but accessories, the moment the first place is not given to the emotion which is here the principal, that moment the essence of the religious life is violated: confusion and falsehood are introduced into its sphere. And, if not only is undue prominence in this sphere given to intellectual ideas, but these ideas are so presented as in themselves violently to jar with the religious feeling, then the confusion is a thousand times worse confounded, the falsehood a thousand times more glaring.

"The earth moves," said Galileo, speaking as a philosopher in the sphere of pure thought, in which ideas have an absolute value; and he said the truth; he was a great thinker because he perceived this truth; he was a great man because he asserted it in spite of persecution. It was the theologians, insisting upon transplanting his idea into the world of theology, and placing it in a false connexion there, who were guilty of folly. But if Galileo himself, quitting the sphere of mathematics, coming into the sphere of religion, had placed this thesis of his in juxtaposition with the Book of Joshua, had applied it so as to impair the value of the Book of Joshua for the religious life of Christendom, to make that book regarded as a tissue of fictions, for which no blame indeed attached to Joshua, because he never meant it for anything else, — then Galileo would have himself placed his idea in a false connexion, and would have deserved censure: his *"the earth moves"* in spite of its absolute truth, would have become a falsehood. Spinoza, again, speaking as a pure thinker to pure thinkers, not concerning himself whether what he said impaired or confirmed the power and virtue of the Bible for the actual reli-

gious life of Christendom, but pursuing a speculative demonstration, said: "The Bible contains much that is mere history, and, like all history, sometimes true, sometimes false." But we must bear in mind that Spinoza did not promulgate this thesis in immediate connexion with the religious life of his times, but as a speculative idea: he uttered it not as a religious teacher, but as an independent philosopher; and he left it, as Galileo left his, to filter down gradually (if true) into the common thought of mankind, and to adjust itself, through other agency than his, to their religious life. The Bishop of Natal does not speak as an independent philosopher, as a pure thinker; if he did, and if he spoke with power in this capacity, literary criticism would, I have already said, have no right to condemn him. But he speaks actually and avowedly, as by virtue of his office he was almost inevitably constrained to speak, as a religious teacher to the religious world. Well, then, any intellectual idea which, speaking in this capacity, he promulgates, he is bound to place in its right connexion with the religious life, he is bound to make harmonise with that life, he is bound not to magnify to the detriment of that life: else, in the sphere of that life, it is false. He takes an intellectual idea, we will say, which is true; the idea that Mr. Burgon's proposition, "Every letter of the Bible is the direct utterance of the Most High," is false.[4] And how does he apply this idea in connexion with the religious life? He gives to it the most excessive, the most exaggerated prominence; so much so, that hardly in one page out of twenty does he suffer his reader to recollect that the religious life exists out of connexion with this idea, that it is, in truth, wholly independent of it. And by way of adjusting this idea to the feeling of the religious reader of the Bible, he puts it thus: — "In writing the story of the Exodus from the ancient legends of his people, the Scripture writer may have had no more consciousness of doing wrong, or of practising historical deception, than Homer had, or any of the early Roman annalists." Theological criticism censures this language as unorthodox, irreverent: literary criticism censures it as *false*. Its employer precisely does what I have imagined Galileo doing: he misemploys a true idea so as to deprive it of all truth. It is a thousand times truer to say that the Book of Exodus is a sacred book, an inspired history, than to say that it is a fiction, not culpable, because no deception was intended, because its author worked in the same free poetic spirit as the creator of the Isle of Calypso and the Garden of Alcinous.

It is one of the hardest tasks in the world to make new intellectual ideas harmonise truly with the religious life, to place them in their right light for that life. The moments in which such a change is accomplished are epochs in religious history; the men through whose instrumentality it is accomplished are great religious reformers. The greatness of these men does not consist in their having these new ideas, in their originating them. The ideas are in the world; they come originally from the sphere of pure thought; they are put into circulation by the spirit of the time. The greatness of a religious reformer consists in his reconciling them with the religious life, in his starting this life upon a fresh period in company with them. No such religious reformer for the present age has yet shown himself. Till he appears, the true religious teacher is he who, not yet reconciling all things, at least esteems things still in their due order, and makes his hearers so esteem them; who, shutting his mind against no ideas brought by the spirit of his time, sets these ideas, in the sphere of the religious life, in their right prominence, and still puts that first which is first; who, under the pressure of new thoughts, keeps the centre of the religious life where it should be. The best distinction of Dr. Stanley's lectures is that in them he shows himself such a teacher. Others will praise them, and deservedly praise them, for their eloquence, their varied information; for enabling us to give such form and substance to our impressions from Bible history. To me they seem admirable, chiefly by the clear perception which they exhibit of a religious teacher's true business in dealing with the Bible. Dr. Stanley speaks of the Bible to the religious world, and he speaks of it so as to maintain the sense of the divine virtue of the Bible unimpaired, so as to bring out this sense more fully. He speaks of the deliverance of the Israelites out of the land of Egypt. He does not dilate upon the difficulty of understanding how the Israelites should have departed "harnessed;" [5] but he points out how they are "the only nation in ancient or modern times, which, throwing off the yoke of slavery, claims no merit, no victory of its own: There is no Marathon, no Regillus, no Tours, no Morgarten. All is from above, nothing from themselves." [6] He mentions the difficulty of "conceiving the migration of a whole nation under such circumstances" as those of the Israelites, the proposal "to reduce the numbers of the text from 600,000 to 600 armed men;" [7] he mentions the difficulty of determining the exact place of the passage of the Red Sea; but he quickly dismisses these considerations to fix the mind on the essential features of this great deliverance" [8] — on the Almighty, "through the dark and terrible night, with the enemy pressing close behind and the driving seas on either side, leading his people like sheep by the hands of Moses and Aaron;" [9] his people, carrying with them from that night "the abiding impression that this deliverance — the first and greatest in their history — was effected not by their own power, but by the power of God." [10] He tells the reader how, "with regard to all the topographical details of the Israelite journey, we are still in the condition of discoverers;" [11] but, instead of impressing upon him as an inference from this that the Bible narrative is a creation such as the Iliad and Odyssey, he reminds him, with truth, how "suspense as to the exact details of form and locality is the most fitting approach for the consideration of the presence of Him who has made darkness his secret place, his pavilion round about Him with dark water, and thick clouds to cover them." [12] Everywhere Dr. Stanley thus seeks to give its due prominence to that for which the religious life really values the Bible. If "the Jewish religion is characterised in an eminent degree by the dimness of its conception of a future life," Dr. Stanley does not find here, like Warburton, matter for a baffling contrast between Jewish and pagan religion, but he finds fresh proof of the grand edifying fact of Jewish history, "the consciousness of the living, actual presence of God himself — a truth, in the limited conceptions of this youthful nation, too vast to admit of any rival truth, however precious." [13] He speaks of the call of Samuel. What he finds to dwell on in this call is not the exact nature of the voice that called Samuel, on which Spinoza speculates so curiously; it is the image of "childlike, devoted, continuous goodness," which Samuel's childhood brings before us;[14] the type which Samuel offers "of holiness, of growth, of a new creation without conversion." [15] He speaks of the Prophets, and he avows that "the Bible recognises 'revelation' and 'inspiration' outside the circle of the chosen people;" but he makes it his business not to reduce, in virtue of this avowal, the greatness and significance of Hebrew prophecy, but to set that greatness and significance in clearer light than ever. To the greatness and significance of what he calls "the negative side" of that prophecy — its attacks on the falsehoods and superstitions which endeavoured to take the place of God — he does due justice; but he reserves the chief prominence for its "positive side — the assertion of the spirituality, the morality of God, His justice, His goodness, His love." [16] Everywhere he keeps in mind the purpose for which the religious life seeks the Bible — to be enlarged and strengthened, not to be straitened and perplexed. He seizes a truth of criticism when he says that the Bible narrative, whatever inaccuracies of numbers the Oriental tendency to amplification may have introduced into it, remains a "substantially historical" work — not a work like Homer's poems; but to this proposition, which, merely so stated, is a truth of criticism and nothing more, he assigns no undue prominence: he knows that a mere truth of criticism is not, as such, a truth for the religious life.

Dr. Stanley thus gives a lesson not only to the Bishop of Natal, but to the Bishop of Natal's adversaries. Many of these adversaries themselves exactly repeat the Bishop's error in this, that they give a wholly undue prominence, in connexion with the religious life, to certain intellectual propositions, on which the essence and vitality of the religious life in no way depends. The Bishop devotes a volume to the exhibition of such propositions, and he is censurable because, addressing the religious world, he exhibits his propositions so as to confuse the religious life by them, not to strengthen it. He seems to have so confused it in many of his hearers that they, like himself, have forgotten in what it really consists. Puzzled by the Bishop's sums, terrified at the conclusion he draws from them, they, in their bewilderment, seek for safety in attacking the sums themselves, instead of putting them on one side as irrelevant, and rejecting the conclusion deduced from them as untrue. "Here is a Bishop," many of Dr. Stanley's brethren are now crying in all parts of England — "here is a Bishop who has learnt among the Zulus that only a certain number of people can stand in a doorway at once, and that no man can eat eighty-eight pigeons a day, and who tells us, as a consequence, that the Pentateuch is all fiction, which, however, the author may very likely have composed without meaning to do wrong, and as a work of poetry, like Homer's." "Well," one can imagine Dr. Stanley answering them, "you cannot think that!" "No," they reply; "and yet the Bishop's sums puzzle us, and we want them disproved. And powerful answers, we know, are preparing. An adversary worthy of the Bishop will soon appear, —

Exoriare aliquis nostris ex ossibus ultor! [17]

He, when he comes, will make mincemeat of the Bishop's calculations. Those great truths, so necessary to our salvation, which the Bishop assails, will at his hands receive all the strengthening they deserve. He will prove to demonstration that any number of persons can stand in the same doorway at once, and that one man can eat eighty-eight pigeons a day with ease." "Compose yourselves," says Dr. Stanley: "he cannot prove this." "What," cry his terrified interlocutors, "he cannot! In that case we may as well shut up our Bibles, and read Homer and the first books of Livy!" "Compose yourselves," says Dr. Stanley again: "it is not so. Even if the Bishop's sums are right, they do not prove that the Bible narrative is to be classed with the Iliad and the Legends of Rome. Even if you prove them wrong, your success does not bring you a step nearer to that which you go to the Bible to seek. Carry your achievements of this kind to the Statistical Society, to the Geographical Society, to the Ethnological Society. They have no vital interest for the religious reader of the Bible. The heart of the Bible is not there."

Just because Dr. Stanley has comprehended this, and, in a book addressed to the religious world makes us feel that he has comprehended it, his book is excellent and salutary. I praise it for the very reason for which some critics find fault with it — for not giving prominence, in speaking of the Bible, to matters with which the real virtue of the Bible is not bound up. "The book," a critic complains, "contains no solution of the difficulties which the history of the period traversed presents in the Bible. The oracle is dumb in the very places where many would wish it to speak. This must lessen Dr. Stanley's influence in the cause of Biblical science. The present time needs bold men, prepared to give utterance to their deepest thoughts." [18] And which are a man's deepest thoughts I should like to know: his thoughts whether it was 215 years, or 430, or 1,000 that the Israelites sojourned in Egypt, — which question the critic complains of Dr. Stanley for saying that it is needless to discuss in detail, — or his thoughts on the moral lesson to be drawn from the story of the Israelites' deliverance? And which is the true science of the Bible — that which helps men to follow the cardinal injunction of the Bible, to be "transformed by the renewing of their mind, that they may prove what is that good, and acceptable, and perfect will of God" — or that which helps them to "settle the vexed question of the precise time when the Book of Deuteronomy assumed its present form"? — that which elaborates an octavo volume on the arithmetical difficulties of the Bible, with the conclusion that the Bible is as unhistorical as Homer's poetry, or that which makes us feel that "these difficulties melt away before the simple pathos and lofty spirit of the Bible itself"? Such critics as this critic of Dr. Stanley are those who commend the Bishop of Natal for "speaking the truth," who say that "liberals of every shade of opinion" are indignant with me for rebuking him. Ah! these liberals! — the power for good they have had, and lost: the power for good they will yet again have, and yet again lose! Eternal bondsmen of phrases and catchwords, will they never arrive at the heart of any matter, but always keep muttering round it their silly shibboleths like an incantation? There is truth of science and truth of religion: truth of science does not become truth of religion until it is made to harmonise with it. Applied as the laws of nature are applied in the *Essays and Reviews,* applied as arithmetical calculations are applied in the Bishop of Natal's work, truths of science, even supposing them to be such, lose their truth, and the utterer of them is not a "fearless speaker of truth," but, at best, a blunderer. "Allowing two feet in width for each full-grown man, nine men could just have stood in front of the Tabernacle." "A priest could not have eaten, daily, eighty-eight pigeons for his own portion, 'in the most holy place.' " And as a conclusion from all this: "In writing the story of the Exodus from the ancient legends of his people, the Scripture-writer may have had no more consciousness of doing wrong, or of practising historical deception, than Homer had, or any of the early Roman annalists." Heaven and earth, what a gospel! Is it this which a "fearless speaker of truth" must "burst" if he cannot utter? Is this a message which it is woe to him if he does not preach? — this a testimony which he is straitened till he can deliver?

I am told that the Bishop of Natal explains to those who do not know it, that the Pentateuch is not to be read as an authentic history, but as a narrative full of divine instruction in morals and religion: I wish to lay aside all ridicule, into which literary criticism too readily falls, while I express my unfeigned conviction that in his own heart the Bishop of

Natal honestly believes this, and that he originally meant to convey this to his readers. But I censure his book because it entirely fails to convey this. I censure it, because while it impresses strongly on the reader that "the Pentateuch is not to be read as an authentic narrative," it so entirely fails to make him feel that it is "a narrative full of divine instruction in morals and religion." I censure it, because, addressed to the religious world, it puts the non-essential part of the Bible so prominent, and the essential so much in the background, and, having established this false proportion, holds such language about the Bible in consequence of it, that, instead of serving the religious life, it confuses it. I do not blame the Bishop of Natal's doctrine for its novelty or heterodoxy — literary criticism takes no account of a doctrine's novelty or heterodoxy: I said expressly that Mr. Jowett's Essay was, for literary criticism, justified by its unction; I said that the Bishop of Natal's book was censurable, because, proclaiming what it did, *it proclaimed no more;* because, not taking rank as a book of pure speculation, inevitably taking rank as a religious book for the religious world, for the great majority of mankind, it treated its subject unedifyingly. Address what doctrine you like to the religious world, be as unorthodox as you will, literary criticism has no authority to blame you: only, if your doctrine is evidently not adapted to the needs of the religious life, — if, as you present it, it tends to confound that life rather than to strengthen it, literary criticism has the right to check you; for it at once perceives that your doctrine, as you present it, is false. Was it, nevertheless, your duty to put forth that doctrine, since you believed it to be true? The honoured authority of the Archbishop of Dublin is invoked to decide that it was. Which duty comes first for a man — the duty of proclaiming an inadequate idea, or the duty of making an inadequate idea adequate? But this difficult question we need not resolve: it is enough that, if it is a man's duty to announce even his inadequate ideas, it is the duty of criticism to tell him that they are inadequate.

But, again, it is said that the Bishop of Natal's book will, in the end, have a good effect, by loosening the superstitious attachment with which the mass of the English religious world clings to the letter of the Bible, and that it deserves from criticism indulgence on this ground. I cannot tell what may, in the end, be the effect of the Bishop of Natal's book upon the religious life of this country. Its natural immediate effect may be seen by any one who will take the trouble of looking at a newspaper called *Public Opinion,* in which the Bishop's book is the theme of a great continuous correspondence. There, week after week, the critical genius of our nation discovers itself in captivating nudity; and there, in the letters of a terrible athlete of Reason, who signs himself "Eagle-Eye," the natural immediate effect of the Bishop's book may be observed. Its natural ulti-mate effect would be, I think, to continue, in another form, the excessive care of the English religious world for that which is not of the real essence of the Bible: as this world has for years been prone to say, "We are the salt of the earth, because we believe that every syllable and letter of the Bible is the direct utterance of the Most High," so it would naturally, after imbibing the Bishop of Natal's influence, be inclined to say, "We are the salt of the earth, because we believe that the Pentateuch is unhistorical." Whether they believe the one or the other, what they should learn to say is: "We are unprofitable servants; the religious life is beyond." But, at all events, literary criticism, which is the guardian of literary truth, must judge books according to their intrinsic merit and proximate natural effect, not according to their possible utility and remote contingent effect. If the Bishop of Natal's demonstrations ever produce a salutary effect upon the religious life of England, it will be after some one else, or he himself, has supplied the now missing power of edification: for literary criticism his book, as it at present stands, must always remain a censurable production.

The situation of a clergyman, active-minded as well as pious, is, I freely admit, at the present moment one of great difficulty. Intellectual ideas are not the essence of the religious life; still the religious life connects itself, as I have said, with certain intellectual ideas, and all intellectual ideas follow a development independent of the religious life. Goethe remarks somewhere how the *Zeit-Geist*, as he calls it, the Time-Spirit, irresistibly changes the ideas current in the world.[19] When he was young, he says, the Time-Spirit had made every one disbelieve in the existence of a single Homer: when he was old, it was bearing every one to a belief in it. Intellectual ideas, which the majority of men take from the age in which they live, are the dominion of this Time-Spirit; not moral and spiritual life, which is original in each individual. In the Articles of the Church of England are exhibited the intellectual ideas with which the religious life of that Church, at the time of the Reformation, and almost to the present day, connected itself. They are the intellectual ideas of the English Reformers and of their time; they are liable to development and change. Insensibly the Time-Spirit brings to men's minds a consciousness that certain of these ideas have undergone such development, such change. For the laity, to whom the religious life of their National Church is the great matter, and who owe to that Church only the general adhesion of citizens to the Government under which they are born, this consciousness is not irksome as it is for the clergy, who, as ministers of the Church, undertake to become organs of the intellectual ideas of its formularies. As this consciousness becomes more and more distinct, it becomes more and more irksome. One can almost fix the last period in which a clergyman, very speculative by the habit of his mind, or very sensible to the whispers of the Time-Spirit, can sincerely feel himself free and at ease in his position of a minister of the Church of England. The moment inevitably arrives when such a man feels himself in a false position. It is natural that he should try to defend his position, that he should long prefer defending his position to confessing it untenable, and demanding to have it changed. Still, in his own heart, he cannot but be dissatisfied with it. It is not good for him, not good for his usefulness, to be left in it. The sermons of Tauler and Wesley were not preached by men hampered by the consciousness of an unsound position. Even when a clergyman, charged full with modern ideas, manages by a miracle of address to go over the very ground most dangerous to him without professional ruin, and even to exhibit unction as he goes along, there is no reason to exult at the feat: he would probably have exhibited more unction still if he had not had to exhibit it upon the tight-rope. The time at last comes for the State, the collective nation, to intervene. Some reconstruction of the English Church, a reconstruction hardly less important than that which took place at the Reformation, is fast becoming inevitable. It will be a delicate, a most difficult task; and the reconstruction of the Protestant Churches of Germany offers an example of what is to be avoided rather than of what is to be followed.

Still, so divine, so indestructible is the power of Christianity — so immense the power of transformation afforded to it by its sublime maxim, "The letter killeth, but the spirit giveth life," that it will assuredly ever be able to adapt itself to new conditions, and, in connexion with intellectual ideas changed or developed, to enter upon successive stages of progress. It will even survive the handling of "liberals of every shade of opinion." But it will not do this by losing its essence, by becoming such a Christianity as these liberals imagine, the *Christianity not Mysterious* of Toland;[20] a Christianity consisting of half-a-dozen intellectual propositions, and half-a-dozen moral rules deduced from them. It will do it by retaining the religious life in all its depth and fulness in connexion with new intellectual ideas; and the latter will never have meaning for it until they have been harmonised with the former, and the religious teacher who presents the latter to it, without harmonising them with the former, will never have fulfilled his mission. The religious life existed in the Church of the Middle Ages, as it exists in the Churches of Protestantism; nay, what monument of that life have the Protestant Churches produced, which for its most essential qualities, its tenderness, its spirituality, its ineffable yearning, is comparable to the *Imitation*. The critical ideas of the sixteenth century broke up the Church of the Middle Ages, resting on the basis of a priesthood with supernatural power of interpreting the Bible. But Luther was a great religious reformer, not because he made himself the organ of these ideas, themselves negative, not because he shattered the idol of a mediatory priest-hood, but because he reconciled these ideas with the religious life, because he made the religious life feel that a positive and fruitful conclusion was to be drawn from them, — the conclusion that each man must "work out his own salvation with fear and trembling." Protestantism has formed the notion that every syllable and letter of the Bible is the direct utterance of the Most High. The critical ideas of our century are forcing Protestantism away from this proposition, untrue like the proposition that the Pope is infallible: but the religious reformer is not he who rivets our minds upon the untruth of this proposition, who bewilders the religious life by insisting on the intellectual blunder of which it has been guilty in entertaining it; he is the man who makes us feel the future which undoubtedly exists for the religious life in the absence of it.

Makes us feel, not the multitude only. I am reproached with wishing to make free-thinking an aristocratic privilege, while a false religion is thrown to the multitude to keep it quiet; and in this country — where the multitude is in the first place, particularly averse to being called the multitude, and in the second, by its natural spirit of honesty particularly averse to all underhand, selfish scheming — such an imputation is readily snatched up, and carries much odium with it. I will not seek to remove that odium by any flattery, by saying that I think we are all one enlightened public together. No, there *is* a multitude, a multitude made up out of all ranks: probably in no country — so much has our national life been carried on by means of parties, and so inevitably does party-spirit, in regarding all things, put the consideration of their intrinsic reason and truth second, and not first — is the multitude more unintelligent, more narrow-minded, and more passionate than in this. Perhaps in no country in the world is so much nonsense so firmly believed. But those on whose behalf I demand from a religious speaker edification are more than this multitude; and their cause and that of the multitude are one. They are all those who acknowledge the need of the religious life. The few whom literary criticism regards as exempt from all concern with edification, are far fewer than is commonly supposed. Those whose life is all in thought, and to whom, therefore, literary criticism concedes the right of treating religion with absolute freedom, as pure matter for thought, are not a great class, but a few individuals. Let them think in peace, these sublime solitaries: they have a right to their liberty: Churches will never concede it to them: literary criticism will never deny it to them. From his austere isolation a born thinker like Spinoza cries with warning solemnity to the would-be thinker, what from his austere isolation a born artist like Michael Angelo, cries to the would-be artist — "Canst thou drink of the cup that I drink of?" Those who persist in the thinker's life, are far fewer even than those who persist in the artist's. Of the educated minority, far the greatest number retain their demand upon the religious life. They share, indeed, the culture of their time, they are curious to know the new ideas of their time; their own culture is advanced, in so far as those ideas are novel, striking, and just. This course they follow, whether they feel or not (what is certainly true), that this satisfaction of their curiosity, this culture of theirs, is not without its dangers to the religious life. Thus they go on being informed, gathering intellectual ideas at their own peril, minding, as Marcus Aurelius reproached himself with too long minding, "life less than notion." But the moment they enter the sphere of religion, they too ask and need to be edified, not informed only. They inevitably, such is the law of the religious life, take the same attitude as the least-instructed. The religious voice that speaks to them must have the tone of the spiritual world: the intellectual ideas presented to them must be made to blend with the religious life.

The world may not see this, but cannot a clergyman see it? Cannot he see that, speaking to the religious life, he may honestly be silent about matters which he cannot yet use to edification, and of which, therefore, the religious life does not want to hear? Does he not see that he is even bound to take account of the circumstances of his hearers, and that information which is only fruitless to the religious life of some of his hearers, may be worse than fruitless, confounding, to the religious life of others of them? Certainly, Christianity has not two doctrines, one for the few, another for the many; but as certainly, Christ adapted His teaching to the different stages of growth in His hearers, and for all of them adapted it to the needs of the religious life. He came to preach moral and spiritual truths; and for His purpose moral genius was of more avail than intellectual genius, St. Peter than Solomon. But the speculative few who stood outside of his teaching were not the Pharisees and the Sadducees. The Pharisees were the narrow-minded, cruel-hearted religious professors of that day; the Sadducees were the "liberals of every shade of opinion." And who, then, were the thinking few of that time? — a student or two at Athens or Alexandria. That was the hour of the religious sense of the East: but the hour of the thought of the West, of Greek thought, was also to come. The religious sense had to ally itself with this, to make certain conditions with it, to be in certain ways inevitably modified by it. Now is the hour of the thought of the West. This thought has its apostles on every side, and we hear far more of its conquests than of the conquests of the religious sense. Still the religious life maintains its indefeasible claims, and in its own sphere inexorably refuses to be satisfied with the new thought, to admit it to be of any truth and significance, until it has harmonised it with itself, until it has imparted to it its own divine power of refreshing souls. Some day the religious life will have harmonised all the new thought with itself, will be able to use it freely: but it cannot use it yet. And who has not rejoiced to be able, between the old idea, tenable no longer, which once connected itself with certain religious words, and the new idea, which has not yet connected itself with them, to rest for awhile in the healing virtue and beauty of the words themselves? The old popular notion of perpetual special interventions of Providence in the concerns of man is weak and erroneous; yet who has yet found, to define Providence for the religious life, words so adequate as the words of Isaiah — "In all their affliction he was afflicted, and the angel of his presence saved them; and he bare them and carried them all the days of old"? [21] The old popular notion of an incensed God appeased in His wrath against the helpless race of mankind by a bloody sacrifice, is barbarous and false; but what intellectual definition of the death of Christ has yet succeeded in placing it, for the religious life, in so true an aspect as the sublime ejaculation of the Litany: "O Lamb of God, that takest away the sins of the world, have mercy upon us!"

And you are masters in Israel, and know not these things; and you require a voice from the world of literature to tell them to you! Those who ask nothing better than to remain silent on such topics, who have to quit their own sphere to speak of them, who cannot touch them without being reminded that they survive those who touched them with far different power, you compel, in the mere interest of letters, of intelligence, of general culture, to proclaim truths which it was your function to have made familiar. And, when you have thus forced the very stones to cry out, and the dumb to speak, you call them singular because they know these truths, and arrogant because they declare them!

Notes

[1] *Letters,* I, 180.

[2] See "Mr. Matthew Arnold on the Aristocratic Creed," *Spectator,* December 27, 1862, pp. 1438–39.

[3] F. D. Maurice, "Spinoza and Professor Arnold," *Spectator,* January 3, 1863, pp. 1472–74.

[4] Colenso, *The Pentateuch and the Book of Joshua Critically Examined,* I, 6.

[5] *Ibid.,* 48–53.

[6] *Lectures on the History of the Jewish Church* (London, 1863), I, 131.

[7] *Ibid.,* 137.

[8] *Ibid.,* 140.

[9] *Ibid.,* 143.

[10] *Ibid.,* 144.

[11] *Ibid.,* 150–151. Arnold has adapted the text here.

[12] *Ibid.,* 151–152.

[13] *Ibid.,* 173.

[14] *Ibid.,* 451.

[15] *Ibid.,* 456.

[16] *Ibid.,* 455–456.

[17] Vergil, *Aeneid,* IV, 625.

[18] *Athenaeum,* January 17, 1863, p. 84.

[19] "Homer noch einmal" (1827), *Goethes Sämtliche Werke,* Jubiläums-Ausgabe, 40 vols. (Stuttgart and Berlin, 1902–1907), XXXVIII, 78. For a discussion of the concept see Fraser Neiman, "The Zeitgeist of Matthew Arnold," *PMLA,* LXXII (December 1957), 977–996.

[20] John Toland (1670–1722) published *Christianity not Mysterious* in 1696.

[21] Isaiah 63:9.

Dante and Beatrice

Fraser's Magazine
LXVII (May 1863), 665–669

In a letter to his mother dated February 4, 1863, Arnold mentioned an article on Dante as one of six he hoped to have printed before summer. A month later he wrote, apparently with reference to "Dante and Beatrice," "I have to get ready an old lecture, which I am going to give to Froude for Fraser." [1] The lecture was presumably "The Modern Element in Dante," which Arnold delivered at Oxford on March 29, 1862, as part of the series on "The Modern Element in Literature." The section of the lecture that he now printed in *Fraser's Magazine* would have been more timely in March 1862, for Theodore Martin's translation, with introduction and notes, *The Vita Nuova of Dante* (London, 1862) had then only just been published, and Arnold's article is in effect a discussion of the introduction to Martin's book.[2]

"Dante and Beatrice" was reprinted first in O'Brien's book *Essays in Criticism; Third Series,* and again in the Oxford *Essays.* In *The Poetry of Matthew Arnold: a Commentary* Tinker and Lowry point out the interest that this brief essay holds as expressing Arnold's appreciation of the delicate relation existing between fact and the free use of fact permitted to the artist.[3]

Those critics who allegorize the *Divine Comedy,* who exaggerate, or, rather, who mistake the supersensual element in Dante's work, who reduce to nothing the sensible and human element, are hardly worth refuting. They know nothing of the necessary laws under which poetic genius works, of the inevitable conditions under which the creations of poetry are produced. But, in their turn, those other critics err hardly less widely, who exaggerate, or, rather, who mistake the human and real element in Dante's poem; who see, in such a passion as that of Dante for Beatrice, an affection belonging to the sphere of actual domestic life, fitted to sustain the wear and tear of our ordinary daily existence. Into the error of these second critics an accomplished recent translator of Dante, Mr. Theodore Martin, seems to me to have fallen.[4] He has ever present to his mind, when he speaks of the Beatrice whom Dante adored, Wordsworth's picture of —

> The perfect woman, nobly planned
> To warn, to comfort, and command;
> And yet a spirit still, and bright
> With something of an angel light.[5]

He is ever quoting these lines in connexion with Dante's Beatrice; ever assimilating to this picture Beatrice as Dante conceived her; ever attributing to Dante's passion a character identical with that of the affection which Wordsworth, in the poem from which these lines are taken, meant to portray. The affection here portrayed by Wordsworth is, I grant, a substantial human affection, inhabiting the domain of real life, at the same time that it is poetical and beautiful. But in order to give this flesh-and-blood character to Dante's passion for Beatrice, what a task has Mr. Martin to perform! how much is he obliged to imagine! how much to shut his eyes to, or to disbelieve! Not perceiving that the vital impulse of Dante's soul is towards reverie and spiritual vision; that the task Dante sets himself is not the task of reconciling poetry and reality, of giving to each its due part, of supplementing the one by the other; but the task of sacrificing the world to the spirit, of making the spirit all in all, of effacing the world in presence of the spirit — Mr. Martin seeks to find a Dante admirable and complete in the life of the world as well as in the life of the spirit; and when he cannot find him, he invents him. Dante saw the world, and used in his poetry what he had seen; for he was a born artist. But he was essentially aloof from the world, and not complete in the life of the world; for he was a born spiritualist and solitary. Keeping in our minds this, his double character, we may seize the exact truth as to his relations with Beatrice, and steer a right course between the error of those who deliteralize them too much, on the one hand, and that of those who literalize them too much, on the other.

The *Divine Comedy,* I have already said, is no allegory, and Beatrice no mere personification of theology. Mr. Martin is quite right in saying that Beatrice is the Beatrice whom men turned round to gaze at in the streets of Florence; that she is no "allegorical phantom," no "fiction purely ideal." He is quite right in saying that Dante "worships no phantoms," that his passion for Beatrice was a real passion, and that his love-poetry does not deal "in the attributes of celestial charms." He was an artist — one of the greatest of artists; and art abhors what is vague, hollow, and impalpable.

Enough to make this fully manifest we have in the *Vita Nuova.* Dante there records how, a boy of ten, he first saw Beatrice, a girl of nine, dressed in crimson; how, a second time, he saw her, nine years later, passing along the street, dressed in white, between two ladies older than herself, and how she saluted him. He records how afterwards she once denied him her salutation; he records the profound impression which, at her father's death, the grief and beauty of Beatrice made on all those who visited her; he records his meeting with her at a party after her marriage, his emotion, and how some ladies present, observing his emotion, "made a mock of him to that most gentle being;" he records her death, and how, a year afterwards, some gentlemen found him, on the anniversary of her death, "sketching an angel on his tablets." He tells us how, a little later, he had a vision of the dead Beatrice "arrayed in the same crimson robe in which she had originally appeared to my eyes, and she seemed as youthful as on the day I saw her first." He mentions how, one day, the sight of some pilgrims passing along a particular street in Florence brought to his mind the thought that perhaps these pilgrims, coming from a far country, had never even heard the name of her who filled his thought so entirely. And even in the *Divine Comedy*, composed many years afterwards, and treating of the glorified Beatrice only, one distinct trait of the earthly Beatrice is still preserved — her smile; the *santo riso* of the *Purgatory*, the *dolce riso* of the *Paradise*.

Yes, undoubtedly there was a real Beatrice, whom Dante had seen living and moving before him, and for whom he had felt a passion. This basis of fact and reality he took from the life of the outward world: this basis was indispensable to him, for he was an artist.

But this basis was enough for him as an artist: to have seen Beatrice two or three times, to have spoken to her two or three times, to have felt her beauty, her charm; to have had the emotion of her marriage, her death — this was enough. Art requires a basis of fact, but it also desires to treat this basis of fact with the utmost freedom; and this desire for the freest handling of its object is even thwarted when its object is too near, and too real. To have had his relations with Beatrice more positive, intimate, and prolonged, to have had an affection for her into which there entered more of the life of this world, would have even somewhat impeded, one may say, Dante's free use of these relations for the purpose of art. And the artist nature in him was in little danger of being thus impeded; for he was a born solitary.

Thus the conditions of art do not make it necessary that Dante's relations with Beatrice should have been more close and real than the *Vita Nuova* represents them; and the conditions of Dante's own nature do not make it probable. Not the less do such admirers of the poet as Mr. Martin — misconceiving the essential characteristic of chivalrous passion in general, and of Dante's divinization of Beatrice in particular, misled by imagining this "worship for woman," as they call it, to be something which it was not, something involving modern relations in social life between the two sexes — insist upon making out of Dante's adoration of Beatrice a substantial modern love-story, and of arranging Dante's real life so as to turn it into the proper sort of real life for a "worshipper of woman" to lead. The few real incidents of Dante's passion, enumerated in the *Vita Nuova,* sufficient to give to his great poem the basis which it required, are far too scanty to give to such a love-story as this the basis which it requires; therefore they must be developed and amplified. Beatrice was a living woman, and Dante had seen her; but she must become

> The creature not too bright and good
> For human nature's daily food,

of Wordsworth's poem: she must become "pure flesh and blood — beautiful, yet substantial," and "moulded of that noble humanity wherewith Heaven blesses, not unfrequently, our common earth." Dante had saluted Beatrice, had spoken to her; but this is not enough: he has surely omitted to "record particulars:" it is "scarcely credible that he should not have found an opportunity of directly declaring his attachment;" for "in position, education, and appearance he was a man worth any woman," and his face "at that time of his life must have been eminently engaging." Therefore "it seems strange that his love should not have found its issue in marriage;" for "he loved Beatrice as a man loves, and with the passion that naturally perseveres to the possession of its mistress."

However, his love did *not* find its issue in marriage. Beatrice married Messer Simone dei Bardi, to whom, says Mr. Martin, "her hand had been, perhaps lightly or to please her parents, pledged, in ignorance of the deep and noble passion which she had inspired in the young poet's heart." But she certainly could not "have been insensible to his profound tenderness and passion;" although whether "she knew of it before her marriage," and whether "she, either then or afterwards, gave it her countenance and approval, and returned it in any way, and in what degree" — questions which, Mr. Martin says, "naturally suggest themselves" — are, he confesses, questions for solving which "the materials are most scanty and unsatisfactory." "Unquestionably," he adds, "it startles and grieves us to find Beatrice taking part with her friends 'in laughing at Dante when he was overcome at first meeting her after her marriage.' But there may," he thinks, "have been causes for this — causes for which, in justice to her, allowance must be made, even as we see that Dante made it." Then, again, as to Messer Simone dei Bardi's feelings about this attachment of Dante to his wife. "It is true," says Mr. Martin, "that we have no direct information on this point;" but "the love of Dante was of an order too pure and noble to occasion distrust, even if the purity of Beatrice had not placed her above suspicion;" but Dante "did what only a great and manly nature could have done — he triumphed over his pain; he uttered no complaint; his regrets were buried within his own heart." "At the same time," Mr. Martin thinks, "it is contrary to human nature that a love unfed by any tokens of favour should retain all its original force; and without wrong either to Beatrice or Dante, we may conclude that an understanding was come to between them, which in some measure soothed his heart, if it did not satisfy it." And "sooner or later, before Beatrice died, we cannot doubt that there came a day when words passed between them which helped to reconcile Dante to the doom that severed her from his side during her all too brief sojourn on earth, when the pent-up heart of the poet swept down the barriers within which it had so long struggled, and he

> Caught up the whole of love, and utter'd it,
> Then bade adieu for ever,

if not to her, yet to all those words which it was no longer meet should be spoken to another's wife."

But Dante married, as well as Beatrice; and so Dante's married life has to be *arranged* also. "It is," says Mr. Martin, "only those who have observed little of human nature, or of their own hearts, who will think that Dante's marriage with Gemma Donati argues against the depth of sincerity of his first love. Why should he not have sought the solace and the support of a generous woman's nature, who, knowing all the truth, was yet content with such affection as he was able to bring to a second love? Nor was that necessarily small. Ardent and affectionate as his nature was, the sympathies of such a woman must have elicited from him a satisfactory response; while, at the same time, without prejudice to the wife's claim on his regard, he might entertain his heavenward dream of the departed Beatrice." The tradition is, however, that Dante did not live happily with his wife; and some have thought that he means to cast a disparaging reflection on his marriage in a passage of the *Purgatory*. I need not say that this sort of thing would never do for Mr. Martin's hero — that hero who can do nothing "inconsistent with the purest respect to her who had been the wedded wife of another, on the one hand, or with his regard for the mother of his children, on the other." Accordingly, "are we to assume," Mr. Martin cries, "that the woman who gave herself to him in the full knowledge that she was not the bride of his imagination, was not regarded by him with the esteem which her devotion was calculated to inspire." It is quite impossible. "Dante was a true-hearted gentleman, and could never have spoken slightingly of her on whose breast he had found comfort amid many a sorrow, and who had borne to him a numerous progeny — the last a Beatrice." Donna Gemma was a "generous and devoted woman," and she and Dante "thoroughly understood each other."

All this has, as applied to real personages, the grave defect of being entirely of Mr. Martin's own imagining. But it has a still graver defect, I think, as applied to Dante, in being so singularly inappropriate to its object. The grand, impracticable Solitary, with keen senses and ardent passions — for nature had made him an artist, and art must be, as Milton says, "sensuous and impassioned" [6] — but with an irresistible bent to the inward life, the life of imagination, vision, and ecstacy; with an inherent impatience of the outward life, the life of distraction, jostling, mutual concession; this man "of a humour which made him hard to get on with," says Petrarch; "melancholy and pensive," says Boccaccio; "by nature abstracted and taciturn, seldom speaking unless he was questioned, and often so absorbed in his own reflections that he did not hear the questions which were put to him;" who could not live with the Florentines, who could not live with Gemma Donati, who could not live with Can Grande della Scala; this lover of Beatrice, but of Beatrice a vision of his youth, hardly at all in contact with him in actual life, vanished from him soon, with whom his imagination could deal freely, whom he could divinize into a fit object for the spiritual longing which filled him — this Dante is transformed, in Mr. Martin's hands, into the hero of a sentimental, but strictly virtuous, novel! To make out Dante to have been eminent for a wise, complete conduct of his outward life, seems to me as unimportant as it is impossible. I can quite believe the tradition which represents him as not having lived happily with his wife, and attributes her not having joined him in exile to this cause. I can even believe, without difficulty, an assertion of Boccaccio which excites Mr. Martin's indignation, that Dante's conduct, even in mature life, was at times exceedingly irregular. We know how the followers of the spiritual life tend to be antinomian in what belongs to the outward life: they do not attach much importance to such irregularity themselves; it is their fault, as complete men, that they do not; it is the fault of the spiritual life, as a complete life, that it allows this tendency: by dint of despising the outward life, it loses the control of this life, and of itself when in contact with it. My present business, however, is not to praise or blame Dante's practical conduct of his life, but to make clear his peculiar mental and spiritual constitution .This, I say, disposed him to absorb himself in the inner life, wholly to humble and efface before this the outward life. We may see this in the passage of the *Purgatory* where he makes Beatrice reprove him for his backsliding after she, his visible symbol of spiritual perfection, had vanished from his eyes.

"For a while" — she says of him to the "pious substances," the angels — "for a while with my countenance I upheld him; showing to him my youthful eyes, with me I led him, turned towards the right way.

"Soon as I came on the threshold of my second age, and changed my life, this man took himself from me and gave himself to others.

"When that I had mounted from flesh to spirit, and beauty and spirit were increased unto me, I was to him less dear and less acceptable.

"He turned his steps to go in a way not true, pursuing after false images of good, which fulfil nothing of the promises which they give.

"Neither availed it me that I obtained inspirations to be granted me, whereby, both in dream and otherwise, I called him back; so little heed paid he to them.

"So deep he fell, that, for his salvation all means came short, except to show him the people of perdition.

"The high decree of God would be broken, could Lethe be passed, and that so fair aliment tasted, without some scot paid of repentance, which pours forth tears." [7]

Here, indeed, and in a somewhat similar passage of the next canto, Mr. Martin thinks that the "obvious allusion" is to certain moral short-comings, occasional slips, of which (though he treats Boccaccio's imputation as monstrous and incredible) "Dante, with his strong and ardent passions, having, like meaner men, to fight the perennial conflict between flesh and spirit," had sometimes, he supposes, been guilty. An Italian commentator gives at least as true an interpretation of these passages when he says that "in them Dante makes Beatrice, as the representative of theology, lament that he should have left the study of divinity — in which, by the grace of Heaven, he might have attained admirable proficiency — to immerse himself in civil affairs with the parties of Florence." But the real truth is, that all the life of the world, its pleasures, its business, its parties, its politics, all is alike hollow and miserable to Dante in comparison with the inward life, the ecstacy of the divine vision; every way which does not lead straight towards this is for him a *via non vera;* every good thing but this is for him a false image of good, fulfilling none of the promises which it gives; for the excellency of the knowledge of this he counts all things but loss. Beatrice leads him to this; herself symbolises for him the ineffable beauty and purity for which he longs. Even to Dante at twenty-one, when he yet sees the living Beatrice with his eyes, she already symbolises this for him, she is already not the "creature not too bright and good" of Wordsworth, but a spirit far more than a woman; to Dante at twenty-five composing the *Vita Nuova* she is still more a spirit; to Dante at fifty, when his character has taken its bent, when his genius is come to its perfection, when he is composing his immortal poem, she is a spirit altogether.

Notes

[1] *Letters,* I, 185.

[2] Martin's *The Vita Nuova of Dante* was reviewed in the *Athenaeum* for February 8, 1862.

[3] P. 156.

⁴ Sir Theodore Martin (1816–1909), lawyer and man of letters, was a frequent contributor to *Tait's* and *Fraser's* magazines. In collaboration with W. E. Aytoun he published *The Book of Ballads* (1845), under his pen name "Bon Gaultier," and he became, at the suggestion of Sir Arthur Helps (1813–1875), the official biographer of the Prince Consort. See page 18, note 7. His wife was the actress Helen Faucit.

⁵ "She Was a Phantom of Delight," lines 27–30.

⁶ Milton's phrase is "simple, sensuous, and passionate." See "Of Education" in *The Works of John Milton*, ed. F. A. Patterson et al., 20 vols. (New York, 1931–1940), IV, 286.

⁷ *Purgatorio*, XXX, 121–145.

Preface to the First Edition of Essays in Criticism [First Series]

Macmillan and Co.
(London, 1865), vii–xix

The original preface to the first series of *Essays in Criticism* has regrettably been neglected. The shorter preface to the second edition has become standard since its publication in 1869; it has, moreover, been misleadingly dated 1865, as in the Edition de Luxe of Arnold's works. This is unfortunate because few other essays exhibit so engagingly Arnold's enjoyment of the fray and his youthful exuberance. He very justly said to his mother, "The Preface will make you laugh." [1]

Arnold was correcting proofs for *Essays in Criticism* in December 1864.[2] The book appeared early in 1865, introduced by a lively rejoinder to James Fitzjames Stephen's attack, "Mr. Arnold and His Countrymen," [3] and to Ichabod Charles Wright's public *Letter to the Dean of Canterbury*. With reference to Stephen's article Arnold wrote to his mother: "So from anything like a direct answer, or direct controversy, I shall religiously abstain; but here and there I shall take an opportunity of putting back this and that matter into its true light, if I think he has pulled them out of it;" and of the other article he observed: "Mr. Wright, the translator of Homer, has printed a letter of attack upon my Homer lectures, but it is of no consequence." [4] Despite these assertions Arnold was not slow to engage in the controversy, and at the top of his form. Not long after the publication of *Essays in Criticism* Arnold reflected, in a letter to Lady Anthony de Rothschild, "I think if I republish the book I shall leave out some of the preface and notes, as being too much of mere temporary matter." [5] Arnold made the deletions in 1869, but in doing so he left out much of the laughter.

Several of the Essays which are here collected and reprinted have had the good or the bad fortune to be much criticised at the time of their first appearance. I am not now going to inflict upon the reader a reply to those criticisms; for one or two explanations which are desirable I shall elsewhere, perhaps, be able some day to find an opportunity; but indeed, it is not in my nature, — some of my critics would rather say, not in my power, — to dispute on behalf of any opinion, even my own, very obstinately. To try and approach Truth on one side after another, not to strive or cry, not to persist in pressing forward, on any one side, with violence and self-will, — it is only thus, it seems to me, that mortals may hope to gain any vision of the mysterious Goddess, whom we shall never see except in outline, but only thus even in outline. He who will do nothing but fight impetuously towards her on his own, one, favourite, particular line, is inevitably destined to run his head into the folds of the black robe in which she is wrapped.

I am very sensible that this way of thinking leaves me under great disadvantages in addressing a public composed from a people "the most logical," says the *Saturday Review*, "in the whole world." [6] But the truth is, I have never been able to hit it off happily with the logicians, and it would be mere affectation in me to give myself the airs of doing so. They imagine truth something to be proved, I something to be seen; they something to be manufactured, I as something to be found. I have a profound respect for intuitions, and a very lukewarm respect for the elaborate machine-work of my friends the logicians. I have always thought that all which was worth much in this elaborate machine-work of theirs came from an intuition, to which they gave a grand name of their own. How did they come by this intuition? Ah, if they could tell us that. But no; they set their machine in motion, and build up a fine showy edifice, glittering and unsubstantial like a pyramid of eggs; and then they say: "Come and look at our pyramid." And what does one find it? Of all that heap of eggs, the one poor little fresh egg, the original intuition, has got hidden away far out of sight and forgotten. And all the other eggs are addled.

So it is not to build rival pyramids against my logical enemies that I write this preface, but to prevent a misunderstanding, of which certain phrases that some of them use make me apprehensive. Mr. Wright, one of the many translators of Homer, has just published a Letter to the Dean of Canterbury, complaining of some remarks of mine, uttered now a long while ago, on his version of the Iliad.[7] One cannot be always studying one's own works, and I was really under the impression, till I saw Mr. Wright's complaint, that I had spoken of him with all respect. The reader may judge of my astonishment, therefore, at finding, from Mr. Wright's pamphlet, that I had "declared with much solemnity that there is not any proper reason for his existing." That I never said; but, on looking back at my Lectures on translating Homer, I find that I did say, not that Mr. Wright, but that Mr. Wright's version of the Iliad, repeating in the main the merits and defects of Cowper's version, as Mr. Sotheby's repeated those of Pope's version, had, if I might be pardoned for saying so, no proper reason for existing. Elsewhere I expressly spoke of the merit of his version; but I confess that the phrase, qualified as I have shown, about its want of a proper reason for existing, I used. Well, the phrase had, perhaps, too much vivacity: alas! vivacity is one of those faults which advancing years will only too certainly cure; that, however, is no real excuse; we have all of us a right to exist, we and our works; an unpopular author should be the last person to call in question this right. So I gladly withdraw the offending phrase, and I am sorry for having used it; Mr. Wright, however, will allow me to observe that he has taken an ample revenge. He has held me up before the public as "condemned by my own umpire;" as "rebutted," and "with an extinguisher put upon me" by Mr. Tennyson's remarkable pentameter,

"When did a frog coarser croak upon our Helicon?" [8]

(till I read Mr. Wright I had no notion, I protest, that this exquisite stroke of pleasantry was aimed at me); he has exhibited me as "condemned by myself, refuted by myself," and, finally, my hexameters having been rejected by all the world, "somewhat crest-fallen." And he has himself made game of me, in this forlorn condition, by parodying those unlucky hexameters. So that now, I should think, he must be quite happy.

Partly, no doubt, from being crest-fallen, but partly, too, from sincere contrition for that fault of over-vivacity which I have acknowledged, I will not raise a finger in self-defence against Mr. Wright's blows. I will not even ask him, — what it almost irresistibly rises to my lips to ask him when I see he writes from Mapperly, — if he can tell me what has become of that poor girl, Wragg? [9] She has been tried, I suppose: I know how merciful a view judges and juries are apt to take of these cases, so I cannot but hope she has got off. But what I should so like to ask is, whether the impression the poor thing made was, in general, satisfactory: did she come up to the right standard as a member of "the best breed in the whole world?" were her life-experiences an edifying testimony to "our unrivalled happiness?" did she find Mr. Roebuck's speech a comfort to her in her prison? But I must stop; or my kind monitor, the *Guardian*, whose own gravity is so profound that the frivolous are sometimes apt to give it a heavier name, will be putting a harsh construction upon my innocent thirst for knowledge, and again taxing me with the unpardonable crime of being amusing.

Amusing — good heavens! We shall none of us be amusing much longer. Mr. Wright would perhaps be more indulgent to my vivacity if he considered this. It is but the last sparkle of flame before we are all in the dark; the last glimpse of colour before we all go into drab. Who that reads the *Examiner* does not know that representative man, that Ajax of liberalism, one of our modern leaders of thought, who signs himself "Presbyter Anglicanus?" [10] For my part, I have good cause to know him; terribly severe he was with me two years ago, when he thought I had spoken with levity of that favourite pontiff of the Philistines, the Bishop of Natal. But his masterpiece was the other day. Mr. Disraeli, in the course of his lively speech at Oxford, talked of "nebulous professors, who, if they could only succeed in obtaining a perpetual study of their writings, would go far to realise that eternity of punishment which they object to." [11] Presbyter Anglicanus says "it would be childish to affect ignorance" that this was aimed at Mr. Maurice. If it was, who can doubt that Mr. Maurice himself, full of culture and urbanity as he is, would be the first to pronounce it a very smart saying, and to laugh at it good-humouredly? But only listen to Mr. Maurice's champion: —

"This passage must fill all sober-minded men with astonishment and dismay; they will regard it as one of the most ominous signs of the time. This contemptible joke, which betrays a spirit of ribald profanity not easily surpassed, excited from the Bishop, the clergy, and laity present, not an indignant rebuke, but 'continued laughter.' Such was the assembly of Englishmen and Christians, who could listen in uproarious merriment to a Parliamentary leader while he asserted that the vilest iniquity would be well compensated by a forced perusal of the writings of Frederick Denison Maurice!" [12]

And, for fear this trumpet-blast should not be carried far enough by the *Examiner*, its author, if I am not greatly mistaken, blew it also, under a different name, in half a dozen of the daily newspapers. As Wordsworth asks: —

> . . . . the happiest mood
> Of that man's mind, what can it be? [13]

was he really born of human parents, or of Hyrcanian tigers? If the former, surely to some of his remote ancestors, at any rate, — in far distant ages, I mean, long before the birth of Puritanism, — some conception of a joke must, at one moment or other of their lives, have been conveyed. But there is the coming east wind! there is the tone of the future! — I hope it is grave enough for even the *Guardian*; — the earnest prosaic, practical, austerely literal future! Yes, the world will soon be the Philistines'; and then, with every voice, not of thunder, silenced, and the whole earth filled and ennobled every morning by the magnificent roaring of the young lions of the *Daily Telegraph*, we shall all yawn in one another's faces with the dismallest, the most unimpeachable gravity. No more vivacity then! my hexameters, and dogmatism, and scoffs at the Divorce Court, will all have been put down; I shall be quite crest-fallen. But does Mr. Wright imagine that there will be any more place, in that world, for his heroic blank verse Homer than for my paradoxes? If he does, he deceives himself, and knows little of the Palatine Library of the future. A plain edifice, like the British College of Health enlarged: [14] inside, a light, bleak room, with a few statues; Dagon in the centre, with our English Caabah, or Palladium of enlightenment, the hare's stomach; [15] around, a few leading friends of humanity or fathers of British philosophy; — Goliath, the great Bentham, Presbyter Anglicanus, our intellectual deliverer Mr. James

Clay[16] and . . . yes! with the embarrassed air of a late convert, the editor of the *Saturday Review*.[17] Many a shrewd nip has he in the old days given to the Philistines, this editor; many a bad half-hour has he made them pass; but in his old age he has mended his courses, and declares that his heart has always been in the right place, and that he is at bottom, however appearances may have been against him, staunch for Goliath and "the most logical nation in the whole world." Then, for the book-shelves. There will be found on them a monograph by Mr. Lowe on the literature of the ancient Scythians, to revenge them for the iniquitous neglect with which the Greeks treated them;[18] there will be Demosthenes, because he was like Mr. Spurgeon;[19] but, else, from all the lumber of antiquity they will be free. Everything they contain will be modern, intelligible, improving; *Joyce's Scientific Dialogues, Old Humphrey, Bentham's Deontology, Little Dorrit, Mangnall's Questions, The Wide Wide World, D'Iffanger's Speeches, Beecher's Sermons;*[20] — a library, in short, the fruit of a happy marriage between the profound philosophic reflection of Mr. Clay, and the healthy natural taste of Inspector Tanner.[21]

But I return to my design in writing this Preface. That design was, after apologizing to Mr. Wright for my vivacity of five years ago, to beg him and others to let me bear my own burdens, without saddling the great and famous University, to which I have the honour to belong, with any portion of them. What I mean to deprecate is such phrases as, "his professional assault," "his assertions issued *ex cathedrâ*," "the sanction of his name as the representative of poetry," and so on.[22] Proud as I am of my connection with the University of Oxford, I can truly say, that, knowing how unpopular a task one is undertaking when one tries to pull out a few more stops in that powerful, but at present somewhat narrow-toned organ, the modern Englishman, I have always sought to stand by myself, and to compromise others as little as possible. Besides this, my native modesty is such, that I have always been shy of assuming the honourable style of Professor, because this is a title I share with so many distinguished men, — Professor Pepper, Professor Anderson, Professor Frickel, and others, — who adorn it, I feel, much more than I do.[23] These eminent men, however, belonging to a hierarchy of which Urania, the Goddess of Science herself, is the sole head, cannot well by any vivacity or unpopularity of theirs compromise themselves with their superiors; because with their Goddess they are not likely, until they are translated to the stars, to come into contact. I, on the other hand, have my humble place in a hierarchy whose seat is on earth; and I serve under an illustrious Chancellor who translates Homer, and calls his Professor's leaning towards hexameters "a pestilent heresy." [24] Nevertheless, that cannot keep me from admiring the performance of my severe chief; I admire its freshness, its manliness, its simplicity; although, perhaps, if one looks for the charm of

94044

Homer, for his play of a divine light . . . Professor Pepper must go on, I cannot.

My position is, therefore, one of great delicacy; but it is not from any selfish motives that I prefer to stand alone, and to concentrate on myself, as a plain citizen of the republic of letters, and not as an office-bearer in a hierarchy, the whole responsibility for all I write; it is much more out of genuine devotion to the University of Oxford, for which I feel, and always must feel, the fondest, the most reverential attachment. In an epoch of dissolution and transformation, such as that on which we are now entered, habits, ties, and associations are inevitably broken up, the action of individuals becomes more distinct, the short-comings, errors, heats, disputes, which necessarily attend individual action, are brought into greater prominence. Who would not gladly keep clear, from all these passing clouds, an august institution which was there before they arose, and which will be there when they have blown over?

It is true, the *Saturday Review* maintains that our epoch of transformation is finished; that we have found our philosophy; that the British nation has searched all anchorages for the spirit, and has finally anchored itself, in the fulness of perfected knowledge, to Benthamism. This idea at first made a great impression on me; not only because it is so consoling in itself, but also because it explained a phenomenon which in the summer of last year had, I confess, a good deal troubled me. At that time my avocations led me to travel almost daily on one of the Great Eastern lines, — the Woodford Branch. Every one knows that Müller perpetrated his detestable act on the North London Railway, close by.[25] The English middle class, of which I am myself a feeble unit, travel on the Woodford Branch in large numbers. Well, the demoralisation of our class, — which (the newspapers are constantly saying it, so I may repeat it without vanity) has done all the great things which have ever been done in England, — the demoralisation, I say, of our class, caused by the Bow tragedy, was something bewildering. Myself a transcendentalist (as the *Saturday Review* knows), I escaped the infection; and, day after day, I used to ply my agitated fellow-travellers with all the consolations which my transcendentalism, and my turn for the French, would naturally suggest to me.[26] I reminded them how Caesar refused to take precautions against assassination, because life was not worth having at the price of an ignoble solicitude for it. I reminded them what insignificant atoms we all are in the life of the world. "Suppose the worst to happen," I said, addressing a portly jeweler from Cheapside; "Suppose even yourself to be the victim; *il n'y a pas d'homme nécessaire*.[27] We should miss you for a day or two upon the Woodford Branch; but the great mundane movement would still go on: the gravel walks of your villa would still be rolled; dividends would still be paid at the Bank; omnibuses would still run; there would still be the old crush at the corner of Fenchurch Street." All was of no avail. Nothing could moderate, in the bosom of the great English middle class, their passionate, absorbing, almost blood-thirsty clinging to life. At the moment I thought this over-concern a little unworthy; but the *Saturday Review* suggests a touching explanation of it. What I took for the ignoble clinging to life of a comfortable worldling, was, perhaps, only the ardent longing of a faithful Benthamite, traversing an age still dimmed by the last mists of transcendentalism, to be spared long enough to see his religion in the full and final blaze of its triumph. This respectable man, — whom I imagined to be going up to London to buy shares, or to attend an Exeter Hall meeting, or to hear Mr. D'Iffanger speak, or to see Mr. Spurgeon, with his well-known reverence for every authentic *Thus saith the Lord*, turn his other cheek to the amiable Dean of Ripon, — was, perhaps, in real truth on a pious pilgrimage, to obtain, from Mr. Bentham's executors, a sacred bone of his great, dissected Master.[28]

And yet, after all, I cannot but think that the *Saturday Review* has here, for once, fallen a victim to an idea, — a beautiful but deluding idea, — and that the British nation has not yet, so entirely as the reviewer seems to imagine, found the last work of its philosophy. No; we are all seekers still; seekers often make mistakes, and I wish mine to redound to my own discredit only, and not to touch Oxford. Beautiful city! so venerable, so lovely, so unravaged by the fierce intellectual life of our century, so serene!

"There are our young barbarians, all at play." [29]

And yet, steeped in sentiment as she lies, spreading her gardens to the moonlight, and whispering from her towers the last enchantments of the Middle Age, who will deny that Oxford, by her ineffable charm, keeps ever calling us near to the true goal of all of us, to the ideal, to perfection, — to beauty, in a word, which is only truth seen from another side? — nearer, perhaps, than all the science of Tübingen. Adorable dreamer, whose heart has been so romantic! who hast given thyself so prodigally, given thyself to sides and to heroes not mine, only never to the Philistines! home of lost causes, and forsaken beliefs, and unpopular names, and impossible loyalties! what example could ever so inspire us to keep down the Philistine in ourselves, what teacher could ever so save us from that bondage to which we are all prone, that bondage which Goethe, in those incomparable lines on the death of Schiller, makes it his friend's highest praise (and nobly did Schiller deserve the praise) to have left miles out of sight behind him; — the bondage of *was uns alle bändigt,* DAS GEMEINE! [30] She will forgive me, even if I have unwittingly drawn upon her a shot or two aimed at her unworthy son, for she is generous, and the cause in which I fight is, after all, hers. Apparitions of a day, what is our puny warfare against the Philistines, compared with the warfare which this Queen of Romance has been waging against them for centuries, and will wage after we are gone?

Notes

[1] *Letters*, I, 246.

[2] *Ibid.*, 243.

[3] *Saturday Review*, XVIII (December 3, 1864), 683–685. Stephen's article is a reply to Arnold's "The Function of Criticism at the Present Time," *National Review*, n.s. I (November 1864), 230–251. Stephen said of Arnold, "He is always using a moral smelling-bottle, like those beloved countrymen, who, at foreign *tables d'hote*, delight to hold forth on the vulgarity of 'those English'" [p. 685].

[4] *Letters*, I, 243.

[5] *Ibid.*, 253.

[6] "Mr. Arnold and His Countrymen," p. 684.

[7] Ichabod Charles Wright (1795–1871), one-time fellow of Magdalen College, Oxford, banker, and translator of Dante's *Divine Comedy* (1833–1840), issued in 1859 the first volume of his *The Iliad of Homer, Translated into English Blank Verse*. Arnold spoke of it in depreciatory terms in his *Lectures on Translating Homer* (1861). Wright replied with *A Letter to the Dean of Canterbury, on The Homeric Lectures of Matthew Arnold, Esq.* (London, 1864).

[8] *Ibid.*, 15–16. Wright appears to have been quite arbitrary in suggesting that Tennyson directed against Arnold the first of his three "Attempts at Classic Metres in Quantity," *Cornhill Magazine*, VIII (December 1863), 707–708.

[9] See, of course, Arnold's ironic discussion of Wragg in "The Function of Criticism at the Present Time."

[10] Joseph Hemington Harris was the author of *Auricular Confession Not the Rule of the Church of England* (London, 1852) and *Sir Morton Peto's Burial Bill: a Few Plain Words to My Brother Churchmen* (London, 1862). He contributed to the *Examiner* (London) in 1863 and 1864 several letters to the editor on the Colenso controversy, and on December 3, 1864, "Mr. Disraeli at Oxford," to which Arnold alludes below.

[11] Disraeli's speech "Church Policy" delivered November 25, 1864, in the Sheldonian Theatre, Oxford, at a meeting to aid the Oxford Diocesan Society for the Augmentation of Small Benefices, was published in *The Times* on November 25, 1864. It was reprinted in *Church and Queen. Five Speeches Delivered by the Rt. Hon. B. Disraeli, M.P., 1860–1864* (London, 1865). The reference to "nebulous professors" is said to be to F. D. Maurice. See W. F. Monypenny and G. E. Buckle, *The Life of Benjamin Disraeli, Earl of Beaconsfield*, 6 vols. (New York, 1910–1920), IV, 372, n. 3.

[12] "Mr. Disraeli at Oxford," p. 773.

[13] "The tenderest mood/ Of that Man's mind, what can it be?" "Sonnet: 1801," beginning "I grieved for Buonaparté," lines 2–3.

[14] The name of the offices of James Morison (1770–1840), whence issued Morison's Pills. See also Arnold on the British College of Health, "the grand name without the grand thing," in "The Function of Criticism at the Present Time."

[15] J. W. Colenso wrote to Theophilus Chepstone, June 2, 1863: "An old gentleman writes to me that he has just seen Professor Hitzig, of Heidelberg, probably the best Hebraist in Europe, who said to him: 'Your Bishops are making themselves the laughter of all Europe. Every Hebraist knows that the animal mentioned in Leviticus is really the hare. The word is derived from the Arabic, and has the same meaning in both languages. Every physicist knows that it does not chew the cud. But most of all is it ridiculous to assume that there are no physical errors in the Pentateuch.' My *hare* has been running a pretty round since I last wrote, and done excellent service in the cause of truth, — the matter being perfectly within the grasp of every old hunting

squire. The following epigram has been going the round of the Clubs, and may amuse you:

> 'The Bishops all have sworn to shed their blood,
> To prove 'tis true the Hare doth chew the cud;
> Of Bishops, Doctors, and Divines, beware!
> Weak is the faith that hangs upon a Hair!' "

Sir George William Cox, *The Life of John William Colenso, D.D., Bishop of Natal,* 2 vols. (London, 1888), I, 239–240.

[16] James Clay, M.P. for Hull, said to his constituents, "I confess though I am no follower of Mr. Spurgeon, that there is something about him, in the rapid and natural movements of his thoughts, and the practical fervour of his address which reminds me of Demosthenes," "Mr. Clay on the Classics," *Saturday Review,* XVIII (November 12, 1864), 594.

[17] John Douglas Cook (1808?–1868).

[18] In a speech at Nottingham, Robert Lowe (1811–1892) had recently said that the object of education was knowledge instead of mental training. The speech was described in the *Spectator* as exhibiting "The ideas of a Dissenting minister expressed in the style of an Oxford Don." See "Mr. Lowe's Last Effort," *Spectator,* November 5, 1864, pp. 1262–63.

[19] Charles Haddon Spurgeon (1834–1892), the popular Baptist preacher, was continuously for Arnold the very type of evangelical Philistine. He came to his London pulpit in 1853, and from 1855 until the completion in 1861 of the Metropolitan Tabernacle, conducted his successful revivalist activities at Exeter Hall.

[20] *Scientific Dialogues for Young People* (1807) by Jeremiah Joyce (1763–1816) enjoyed long popularity. A member of the Society for Constitutional Information and the London Corresponding Society, Joyce was imprisoned in 1794, together with Thomas Hardy and John Horne Tooke, on a charge of high treason.

Old Humphrey was the pen name of George Mogridge (1787–1854). He was a japanner by trade and the author of religious tracts, ballads, tales, and religious books for children. The forty-four works published under the pseudonym Old Humphrey include *Thoughts for the Thoughtful* (1841), *Pithy Papers on Singular Subjects* (1846), *Half Hours with Old Humphrey* (1849), and *Characters for Children* (1853). After 1867 his works were issued by the Religious Tract Society.

The *Deontology, or the Science of Morality* of Jeremy Bentham (1748–1832) was arranged for publication in 1834 by his friend John Bowring (1792–1872), founder and editor of the *Westminster Review.*

Little Dorrit by Charles Dickens (1812–1870) appeared in 1856–57.

Richmal Mangnall (1769–1820), schoolmistress, was the author of *Historical and Miscellaneous Questions for the Use of Young People* (Stockport, 1800).

The Wide, Wide World (1850) was the most popular book by the American novelist Susan Bogert Warner (1819–1885). It was published under her pen name "Elizabeth Wetherell." Thirteen American editions were issued within two years.

Henry Ward Beecher (1813–1887), Congregational minister and anti-slavery spokesman, visited England in 1863. In the Preface to *Culture and Anarchy* Arnold cites him as an example of the provincial in religion.

Of *D'Iffanger's Speeches* I have found nothing.

[21] Inspector Tanner of the London Metropolitan Police Force was in charge of returning to London for trial in October 1864 the celebrated murderer Franz Müller (see note 25 below). *The Times* reported, "Once or twice during the trial Müller bowed across the court to Inspector Tanner, for whose kindly and considerate treatment of him at New York and during the voyage he had often expressed himself grateful. The fact is Mr. Tanner discharged a responsible duty with commendable humanity, but still without ever losing sight of the paramount object, of bringing the fugitive from justice back to this country for trial." *The Times,* November 3, 1864, p. 9, col. 4.

[22] Wright, *A Letter to the Dean of Canterbury,* pp. 6 and 12. Wright wrote "his professorial assault."

[23] John Henry Pepper (1821–1900) was an honorary director of the London Polytechnic Institution, a popular lecturer on scientific subjects, and the author of several books including *The Boys' Play-Book of Science*, 2 ed. (London, 1860) and *The True History of the Ghost, and All about Metempsychosis* (London, 1890). He had gained recent celebrity as having improved Henry Dircks's invention for producing theatrical ghost effects. See "The Patent Ghost," *Spectator*, May 9, 1863, pp. 1976–77.

Professor Anderson, conjuror, advertised himself as "The Great Wizard of the North." His show, advertised as "Professor Anderson's World of Magic," was a popular attraction at Great St. James's Hall, London, late in 1864.

Professor Frickel is no doubt Wiljalba Frikell (1818–1903), author of *W. F.'s Lessons in Magic* (London, [1858]) and *The Secret Out; or, One Thousand Tricks with Cards, and Other Recreations* (New York, [c. 1859]).

[24] Edward George Geoffrey Smith Stanley, 14th Earl of Derby (1799–1869), succeeded the Duke of Wellington as Chancellor of the University of Oxford in 1852. See his translation *The Iliad of Homer Rendered into English Blank Verse*, 2 vols. (London, 1864), I, vi. *The Times* announced, "we have no hesitation in saying that it is by far the best representation of Homer's *Iliad* in the English language" (December 3, 1864, p. 7, col. 6).

[25] Franz Müller (1830–1864) was a German tailor and murderer. His victim was Thomas Briggs who was murdered and robbed on Saturday evening, July 9, 1864, and whose body was found on the rails near Hackney-wick Station. "Murder in a First-Class Carriage on the North London Railway," *The Times*, July 11, 1864, p. 9, cols. 1–2. Müller left London for New York July 14. On July 19 Inspector Tanner and Sgt. Clarke were sent by an Admiralty steamer to apprehend him. He was returned to London where his very popular trial began October 27, 1864.

[26] J. F. Stephen, "Mr. Matthew Arnold and His Countrymen," p. 683–684. Stephen charged, "His self-imposed mission is to give good advice to the English people as to their manifold faults, especially as to their one great fault of being altogether inferior, in an intellectual and artistic point of view, to the French. He is so warm upon this subject that he has taught himself to write a dialect as like French as pure English can be."

[27] Lewis Gates says that the exact phrase is attributed to Napoleon, but he also cites a parallel in Chateaubriand, in his *Selections from the Prose Writings of Matthew Arnold* (New York, 1897), p. 317.

[28] William Goode (1801–1868) was the Dean of Ripon. Charles Haddon Spurgeon's Sermon on Baptismal Regeneration enjoyed a circulation of some 300,000 copies as well as inviting severe assault. Sister Thomas Marion of Ithaca, New York, notes in the British Museum Catalogue the formidable title, *Let Us Hear the Church. The Dean of Ripon's Letter on Mr. Spurgeon's Sermons; with Some Reviews of the Christian Observer, Furnishing Answers to the Query — What Do the Ancient and Modern Reformers Say to Mr. Spurgeon's Charges?* (London and Edinburgh, 1864). The *Saturday Review*, incidentally, savagely commented on Spurgeon's sermon on baptismal regeneration in an article called "The Anabaptist Caliban," September 17, 1864.

Sister Thomas Marion informs me that Spurgeon's motto was *Cedo nulli* — "I yield to none" — and suggests that this may explain Arnold's left-handed expression about "turning the other cheek."

Jeremy Bentham (1748–1832) bequeathed his body for dissection. His skeleton "clothed in Bentham's usual attire" is in University College, London (*DNB*).

[29] Byron, *Childe Harold*, Canto IV, cxli. Byron wrote "were."

[30] "Epilog zu Schillers Glocke," *Goethes Sämtliche Werke*, I, 283.

Three Letters on Education

Pall Mall Gazette
December 11, 1865, p. 4
December 22, 1865, p. 3
January 17, 1866, pp. 2–3

Arnold's association with the *Pall Mall Gazette,* which continued for almost twenty years, began with these three letters on education addressed to the editor, then Frederick Greenwood (1830–1909).[1] The proprietor of the paper was George Murray Smith of Smith, Elder, and Company, Arnold's publishers. The association was a lucrative one. Arnold appears to have been paid at the rate of two guineas a column, though some discrepancies seem to exist, whether the contribution was signed or unsigned, whether it was book review, miscellaneous article, or letter to the editor.[2] In the case of these letters Arnold resumed the pseudonym "A Lover of Light" that he had employed in his letter to the editor of the *Daily News* in March 1862, "The 'Principle of Examination.'"

The three letters on education, arguing in favor of state action, were precipitated by a number of items that had appeared in *The Times*. Under the heading "Oxford Diocesan Training College" *The Times* reported, on December 5, 1865, a meeting held the previous day for the distribution of prizes at Culham Training School. On the same day *The Times* carried a complacent editorial praising the Training School as evidence of the "happy effects" of limiting government aid to education. The writer said, "We were fast developing a colossal system of official education after the model of Continental countries, which would soon have left no place for that local diversity and independent energy which in every other instance are such vital characteristics of our national life. . . . In short, it is daily becoming more evident that we must rely to a far larger extent than we have yet done upon the voluntary system in education." [3] The discussion, thus begun continued in a letter to the editor from R. R. W. Lingen[4] and in a letter from the Rev. T. Ridgway, the Principal of Culham College.[5] These articles form the background for Arnold's letters.

EDUCATION AND THE STATE [I]

To the Editor of the *Pall Mall Gazette.*

Sir, — The recent meeting at the Culham Training School and the comments of the *Times* upon it, Mr. Lingen's letter and the Culham rejoinder, afford a happy opportunity for placing in a point of view where they are intelligible and interesting to all the world the policy of the Revised Code, and that policy's inevitable results.

The Culham speakers say that by the storm of the Revised Code they were suddenly deprived of resources which were absolutely necessary to the maintenance of their students. They were thrown upon themselves, and appealed to those who, like themselves, "felt the importance of the Church education of the people of the land," who "desired to see all classes of the people well trained in Church principles." Their appeal was successful. They are getting, in consequence, "schools far more independent of any Government influence than they had ever been before." The action of Government upon the whole educational system of the country has been, they say, eminently hostile. The tendency of the action of the Government towards the Church of England has been eminently hostile. But whatever the intention of what has been done, they believe it will turn out for good. The desire "to have all classes of the people well trained in Church principles" stands a much better chance of being gratified than it did before the Revised Code.

The *Times* is enchanted. You are wrong it says (and says truly enough) to the Culham speakers, in supposing that the recent proceedings of the Privy Council were animated by any spirit either of hostility or friendship, whether to the Established Church or to other religious bodies. The plain tendency of those proceedings is simply *to restrict the aid of the State in the work of education;* and that not merely in matters of religion, but in every particular. The policy that dictated them is a general policy of limiting the pecuniary aid of the Government. But it is precisely in this general view of the question that the policy of the last two or three years is to be regarded with so much satisfaction. You have easily supplied the resources which Government withdrew. You have got, or are getting, independent schools. When aid comes to schools from the State, its application is necessarily fettered by restrictions; when it comes from the noblemen and gentlemen of the diocese, it can be applied exactly as the donors please. There can, we should think, be little doubt that the latter is the more desirable method; for this method gives us schools supported by spontaneous effort instead of State agency.

And Mr. Lingen confirms, if it wanted confirming, the interpretation put by the *Times* on Mr. Lowe's policy in his educational reform. "Such meetings as the one at Culham," says Mr. Lingen, "afford satisfactory evidence that their lordships' hope of more active local support to these institutions will be fulfilled." He, too, is well pleased, the *Times* is well pleased, the Culham speakers are not ill pleased — they, at any rate, smile through their tears — and who, then, has any reason to be ill pleased? Only the *corpus vile,* on which all our educational machinery is to operate; "the people of the land," as the Bishop of Oxford calls it.

For what are, in truth, the "trammels" which State aid imposes, and from which the Duke of Marlborough, the Bishop of Oxford, and the *Times* are so eager to deliver schools? They are these, as compendiously exhibited in M. Guizot's education law, in one clause, worthy to stand as a model to legislators wishing to impose "trammels" of this kind: "Le voeu des parents sera consulté et suivi en tout ce qui concerne l'éducation religieuse de leurs enfants." [6] These are the "trammels." The parent is to determine whether his child shall be brought up a Protestant or a Catholic, a Churchman or a Dissenter. But such trammels the "noblemen and gentlemen of the diocese" desirous to have "all classes of the people well trained in Church principles" find very objectionable. A clause imposing them, a *conscience* clause, "involves a principle," says the Duke of Marlborough, "to which no clergymen of the Church of England can conscientiously agree." Such a clause the State, if it aids schools, must sooner or later enforce. But if the aid to schools comes from the noblemen and gentlemen of the diocese, why then of course "it can be applied exactly as the owners please." Trammels which prevent "all classes of the people from being well trained in Church principles" can be dispensed with. "There can be little doubt," as the *Times* says, "that the latter is the more desirable method."

The Privy Council Office wishes, of course, to discharge its paramount duty of justice, and to have a conscience clause. If it had continued to take an increasing part in the establishment of schools, this conscience clause must sooner or later have become the rule of the elementary schools of this country. One would think, therefore, that the Privy Council Office should sedulously have pursued its work of intervention; the "people of the land" would have been great gainers. They would have been able, for instance, to educate their children, without necessarily, if Dissenters, paying to the noblemen and gentlemen of the diocese the admission fee of a sound training in Church principles. But no; here Mr. Lowe stepped in. It is right, no doubt, for the State, if it aids schools, to be just; but it is still more right for the State not to aid schools at all. The particular policy of giving to the people of the land schools with the protection of the conscience clause must yield to the general policy of limiting the pecuniary aid of the Government. So the grand thing for the Privy Council Office is to cut the schools adrift, and to leave them to the noblemen and gentlemen of the diocese. Mr. Lowe and the *Times* may be a little sorry that these donors, exercising their indisputable right of applying their aid exactly as they please, should think that to let a Dissenter's child attend school without learning the Church catechism "involves a principle to which no clergyman of the Church of England can conscientiously agree." But then they are very glad "to have restricted the aid of the State in the work of education, and that not merely in matters of religion but in every particular." And "it is in this general view of the questions that the policy of the last two or three years is to be regarded with so much satisfaction."

So our elementary schools are to go as fast as possible to the noblemen and gentry of the diocese, "who have the great interests of the Church and of Church education at heart." And we are all to be very glad of it. The State may still, in any cases where it offers aid, propose to protect religious liberty by a conscience clause. But very soon, as soon as the policy of the Revised Code shall have borne its full fruits, the nobility, clergy, and gentry of the diocese will give the State this answer: — "Why trouble us with your talk of a conscience clause? *The school question is taken out of your hands.*" And Mr. Lingen will have to be charmed with this "satisfactory evidence that their lordships' hopes of more active local support to these institutions have been fulfilled."

For the professors of some better liberalism than the sterile liberalism of the past, with its pedantic application of certain maxims of political economy in the wrong place, this school question is one of the most vital questions of the future. The notion that to establish elementary schools for the "people of the land" is the State's duty — that it has no right to hand over this duty to the "noblemen and gentry of the diocese" — that the people suffers in its liberty, its self-respect, its education, when the State's duty is so handed over — this notion suits the prejudices and preponderance of some persons very ill, and therefore they would gladly extinguish it if they could. But it is sound; and therefore, in spite of hostility, it will live. It will thrive, it will strengthen. Tons of regulation claptrap about the "colossal official education of continental countries," about "the local diversity and independent energy which are such vital characteristics of our national life," will not be able to crush it. —

Your obedient servant,
A LOVER OF LIGHT

EDUCATION AND THE STATE [II]

To the Editor of the *Pall Mall Gazette*.

Sir,—This subject is of such capital importance that you will allow me to return to it for one moment after your leading article of last night.[7]

You say that I am misled by the fallacy — a very common one — that a thing or person called the State probably lives in Downing-street, or its neighbourhood, and is burdened with duties of the utmost importance towards the nation (which is another person living elsewhere), among them that of providing for the education of the people at large, and protecting them against the bigotry of the clergy and the nobility and gentry. But this State, you say, is a mere phantom. The State is only a collective

name for the inhabitants of the country. The State means Parliament: the
bishops and the nobility constitute one House of Parliament, and the
gentry have a good deal to do with the other; so that the State turns out
to be, in fact, a mere *alias* for the very people who manage the matter
as it is.

It could not possibly be better put. And yet, let me ask you, do you
see no meaning in these lines of Wither, quoted by Coleridge? —

> Let not your King and Parliament in one,
> Much less apart, mistake themselves for that
> Which is most worthy to be thought upon,
> Nor think they are essentially the State.
> But let them know there is *a deeper life*
> *Which they but represent;*
> *That there's on earth a yet auguster thing,*
> *Veil'd though it be, than Parliament and King.*[8]

Do we not all desire, or at least are we not ashamed not to profess to
desire, that the collective action of the community should aim at expressing the better reason of the community, and should aim at something
higher than everyday practice, deformed by stupidity and passions, of
the common run of all of us who compose it? Is not Parliament on any
but the coarsest theory of delegation meant to try and give effect to this
better reason? Are not the nobility, clergy and gentry, if, as you say, they
pretty much constitute Parliament, bound to be, as constituting Parliament, something more than a simple *alias* for themselves as private
managers of schools?

This, you will say, is mere transcendental talk, and concerns the State
in the idea. We have to do with the State in practice. Well, I think I can
show you in this very matter of education that the State in practice has a
sense of the duty of being something more than an *alias* for the very
persons who manage education as it is, a sense of the duty of interposing
between the people at large and bigotry, of serving as the organ of that
"deeper life" of which Wither speaks. Mr. G. Shaw Lefevre has lately
published in the *Fortnightly Review* an account of the conscience clause
dispute between the Privy Council Office and the clergy.[9] In one or
two points Mr. Lefevre's information seems not quite perfect, but on the
whole his sketch of the dispute is excellent — most clear, temperate, and
trustworthy. He quotes Lord Granville's evidence, given before a Parliamentary Committee last session, as to the reasons which had prevented
him from bringing the conscience clause dispute before Parliament. Lord
Granville says: — "I think that if I were to lay before the House of Commons a conscience clause now, exactly in the shape which it is, with rather
a difficult and wavering rule as to the number of Dissenters, the first
question of the House of Commons would be, 'Why are any number of

Dissenters to be forced either to violate their religious feelings or to be excluded from the benefit of the education which is partly supported by the State?' I believe that our conscience clause does not go far enough now to satisfy the House of Commons." Lord Granville's ground for such forbearance is, that "it is very desirable that the Privy Council should be on good terms with the Church of England;" and undoubtedly it is one of the strongest traditions and instincts of an aristocratic Government like ours to deal tenderly with a powerful kindred and conservative order like the clergy: but surely here is proof that Parliament, that the State, has an impulse prompting it to protect the people of the land against the exorbitant pretensions of the "noblemen and gentlemen of the diocese" to have them all "well trained in Church principles;" prompting it to be something more than a mere *alias* for the squires and clergy who manage education as it is. And why, then, should you fix yourself in the disheartening conviction that, whatever may be the duties of the State in this matter, its chance of fulfilling them is very remote indeed!

Remote it is, and will be, if we are to wait for the poor to agitate before the State fulfils those duties to them. No civilization is possible on such terms. You say that you wish for a system like that of the common schools of the United States; but show me, anywhere, such a system owing its origin to the clamour and agitation of the poor who need it. Such a system must owe its first establishment to the intelligence and patriotism of the educated class; it educates the poor to prize it, to be no longer "neutral and indifferent;" they will defend it, they will not demand it. I do not deny that the actual oppressiveness of our present system may easily be exaggerated, nor that, in a measure the education given by it humanizes, civilizes, and does good; but have you enough considered how humanizing and civilizing a thing in itself is the contact with reason and justice? how much more service instruction conjoined with these is likely to do the poor than instruction divorced from them? how much better is its hope of rescuing the poor from always "remaining much as they are"? —

Your obedient servant,

A Lover of Light

Dec. 21, 1865.

THE MANSION-HOUSE MEETING

To the Editor of the *Pall Mall Gazette.*

Sir, — The Mansion-House meeting on Middle Class Education has been held.[10] The plan of Mr. Rogers and his friends for furthering this education has been announced; the subscription list has been made public. Any one who doubted that Englishmen were wonderful people at a subscription will have found out his mistake. Any one who doubted whether they were equally wonderful people at organizing on the wisest plan a great public service will perhaps retain his doubts still.

Let us in the amplest manner do homage to the liberality which the subscribers have shown. Let us declare, with the *Times,* that "there is something admirable in the facility with which large sums of money can be raised in this metropolis." Let us boast ourselves, with the *Star,* that "there is probably no other city in Europe in which, upon private application, thirty-three gentlemen would have subscribed a thousand pounds each to any object of this kind." [11] And then, having duly rejoiced, let us ask how the end for which all this money is given is really being served.

The end is to provide schools for the middle class, in London first, afterwards in the suburbs. The *Star* hopes "that the provinces may follow the example of London, and that a movement which is now metropolitan may prove general throughout Great Britain." And evidently from the language of Mr. Freshfield and other speakers at the meeting, the promoters of the scheme have the development of it in view.[12] The middle-class children, for whom these schools are meant, are "the children of clerks, of tradesmen, and other persons in the same rank of life, for whom no adequate system of education exists." Mr. Gassiott put the income of the sort of London clerk that wants these schools at from £200 to £300 a year;[13] let us say, taking the country through, they are meant for the children of people with from £100 to £300 a year. The proposed schools are to be day schools, and the yearly charge for a boy's education is not to exceed £4.

In London and all over the country there are numerous charitable endowments, many of which, it is thought, might be made available for middle-class education. Some of these endowments do not easily at present find proper recipients, and have an unappropriated balance. Mr. Rogers and his friends went to the Charity Commissioners. They were told that all proceedings in connection with ancient charities were so embarrassing that the Commissioners could not provide them any immediate support. They went to the court of Chancery, and were told the same thing. Mr. Rogers and his friends, the *Times* tells us, never contemplated seeking the assistance of Parliament, so as to compel a diversion of these surplus revenues, they only wished to invite the trustees to help them. When they found that even this invitation would be attended with difficulties, they came to what the *Times* calls the very wise conclusion to throw themselves upon private liberality. Hence the subscription and the plan of operations now announced.

Now, Mr. Rogers and his friends give their money and service, and merit due honour; and we are all ready to cry out triumphantly that now the thing is started, and that it is thus we manage these things in England. But let us look what this mode of managing these things really comes to. We are all agreed that middle-class education wants mending. But we have a favourite catchword that the State must not meddle with these things. So a philanthropist like Mr. Rogers, who sees that there is a great want to be met, comes forward. He takes to him a number of City gentlemen, whose clerks cry out that their children's schooling, if good, is very dear; if cheap, is very bad. They call meetings, raise money, and come forth with a programme. They define the middle class in their own way, they fix the school charge in their own way, they arrange the plan of studies in their own way. It is left to them to do, and they do it. Now I wish to speak with the greatest respect of Mr. Rogers and his coadjutors; their intentions are excellent, their liberality is great; Mr. Rogers has had great experience of schools for the poor, and the City gentlemen have had great experience of the wants of their clerks. But it is no disrespect to say to them, that for fixing, in general, the bounds of middle-class education, its cost, and its plan of studies, they are hardly an adequate body. Well, but see how the thing goes on. They get a splendid subscription; they begin a big school in Finsbury; and then they go to Government for a charter and for facilities for getting at the funds of charitable endowments. "What can be more proper?" cries the Government. "God forbid that we should have to deal with middle-class education ourselves; we hate meddling; our Education Department hates it more than any of us; these excellent people are in the field; this is individual enterprise and self-reliance as the country likes to see it; by all means let them have a charter." It is clear that the people who gave the money and started the scheme have the right to manage it. So of course Mr. Rogers and his shower of aldermen are the Corporation by the new charter. Their functions are pretty much those of the Superior Council of Public Instruction in France. This Council consists of the Minister of Public Instruction and of eminent representatives of the different religious communions, of the law, of the Institute, and of education, public and private. Our Council will be Mr. Rogers and his aldermen, who will settle what schools are wanted, what the scholars are to pay, and what learn. No public establishment of middle-class education will be attempted, no stringent scheme for applying charitable endowments to school purposes authorized; but "facilities" will be given for dealing with trustees; a certain number of schools will be built, a good many trustees will be negotiated with, and a good many charities pecked at. Meanwhile to all plans for reforming middle-class education the answer will be found: "These good people are in the field; let them alone, and the thing will work itself right in the end."

Mr. Rogers' corporation will hardly, however, be strong enough for

dealing with the whole country, when the provinces, as the *Star* anticipates, follow the example of the metropolis. As we hate every sort of
centralization, we shall be proud of this, not sorry for it. Other philanthropists will come forward, other aldermen will join them, other subscription lists will be opened, other councils will be constituted; and we
shall have about the country several centres of volunteers, without much
unity of plan or coherence of operation, working away to collect subscriptions, negotiate with trustees, peck at charities, and potter at middle-
class education in general. And the question will be hung up for a great
many years to come.

It is singular that Mr. Tite, who at the Mansion-House meeting quoted
Erasmus's blame of the plan of entrusting the management of a school
to a trading company, did not reflect that what was blamed by the clearest
intelligence then in Europe was likely to be blamable, and that Dean
Colet's piece of claptrap was really no answer.[14] Sooner or later we shall
all learn, even we English people, that there is an appointed sphere for
public function as well as for private, and that this sphere is a good deal
wider than we think. We are very proud of our hospitals. They are excellent, undoubtedly, but entirely insufficient. In other words, for adequately
fulfilling a public service like that of hospitals, private effort has not, and
cannot have, the necessary powers. Have the admirers of our voluntary
system of hospitals ever heard what is the difference in the number of
hospital beds here and in Paris? And how in London do we make up for
the short supply of hospital beds that our voluntary system gives us? By
the workhouse hospitals. The voluntary system is in the field; it does
enough to keep up appearances, to prevent our being forced to organize
a public system; and the horrors of that miserable makeshift, the workhouse hospital, are the price we pay. So it threatens to be with middle-
class education. Schemes, excellent, benevolent schemes, like that of Mr.
Rogers and his aldermen, will keep up appearances, and we shall be able
to flatter ourselves that the work is being done. A few good schools will
probably be established; so much is gain. But an adequate supply of
good schools for the middle class, a proper distribution of them through
the country, a thorough use of funds available for them, a right regulation of their studies, a due esteem of their importance, a due status for
their teachers, a due security for those who use them, we shall never get
in this way. We shall, in fact, be further off from it than ever; we shall be
perpetuating all our present makeshifts. And this we have to set against
the gain which a new school in Finsbury and half a dozen new schools
elsewhere will bring us. —

Your obedient servant,

A Lover of Light

Notes

[1] See J. W. Robertson Scott, *The Story of the Pall Mall Gazette* (London, 1950), p. 149.

[2] See Marion Mainwaring, "Notes toward a Matthew Arnold Bibliography," *Modern Philology*, XLIX (February 1952), 189–194, and Fraser Neiman, "Some Newly Attributed Contributions of Matthew Arnold to the *Pall Mall Gazette*," *Modern Philology*, LV (November 1957), 84–87.

[3] *The Times*, December 5, 1865, p. 9, col. 1.

[4] *Ibid.*, December 7, 1865, p. 9, col. 5.

[5] *Ibid.*, December 9, 1865, p. 5, col. 6.

[6] Quoted in Matthew Arnold, *The Popular Education of France* (London, 1861), pp. 52, 160–161.

[7] "Popular Education," *Pall Mall Gazette*, December 20, 1865, pp. 1–2. The author of this article said of Arnold: "His letter appears to us to be a very good specimen of one of the numerous fallacies which prevent people from appreciating the bearings of such questions. The fallacy is that a thing or person called the State lives probably in Downing-street or its neighbourhood, and is burdened with duties of the utmost importance towards the nation (which is another person living elsewhere), and provided with the powers necessary for discharging the duties, and with the knowledge necessary to direct these powers. It is the duty of the State to provide for the education of the people at large, and to protect them against the bigotry of the clergy and the nobility and gentry."

[8] S. T. Coleridge, *On the Constitution of the Church and State according to the Idea of Each*, in *The Complete Works of Samuel Taylor Coleridge*, ed. W. G. T. Shedd, 7 vols. (New York, 1854), VI, 90.

[9] "The Conscience Clause," *Fortnightly Review*, III (December 1, 1865), 165–180. The conscience clause is explained by G. Shaw Lefevre on page 167. "The persons authorized to manage the school shall be bound to make such orders as shall provide for admitting to the benefits of the school the children of parents not in communion with the Church of England as by law established, but such orders shall be confined to the exemption of such children, if their parents desire it, from attendance at the public worship, and from instruction in the doctrine or formularies of the said Church or denomination, and shall not otherwise interfere with the religious teaching of the scholars as fixed by these presents, and shall not authorize any other religious instruction to be given in the school."

[10] *The Times* published on November 18, 1864 (p. 6, cols. 3–5), an editorial on the announcement of a Royal Commission to inquire into Middle Class Education. A meeting of the Royal Commission on January 12, 1866, was reported in *The Times* on January 13 ("Middle Class Education in the City," p. 6, cols. 4–6), and on the same day *The Times* carried an editorial on the subject (pp. 8–9).

Mr. Rogers is the Rev. William Rogers, rector of Bishopsgate. At the time of writing the sum subscribed was between £30,000 and £40,000.

[11] *Morning Star* (London), January 13, 1866, p. 4, col. 3.

[12] Charles Kaye Freshfield (b. 1812) was M.P. for Dover.

[13] John Peter Gassiott (1797–1877), scientific writer, became the chairman of Kew Observatory.

[14] Mr. Tite, M.P., is quoted in *The Times* (January 13, 1866, p. 6, col. 5) as saying: "Dean Collett, the founder of St. Paul's School, was right when he said to Erasmus, who, while his guest, had expressed his surprise at the management of the school being intrusted to a trading company, 'I know of nothing more perpetual than a trading company in the city of London, nor any body of men more likely to be honest.'"

The Eisteddfod

The Times
September 6, 1866, p. 5, col. 6

One manifestation of the resurgent nationalistic feeling in Wales in the early nineteenth century was the revival of the Eisteddfod, or congress of Welsh bards. The modern custom of annual meetings began with the Eisteddfod at Carmarthen in 1819. The congress at Llangollen in 1858 added the revival of druidic vestments and ancient ceremonies. Understandably Sir Hugh Owen (1804–1881), the Welsh philanthropist and nationalist, was warmed by Arnold's sympathetic lectures on Celtic literature which he delivered at Oxford, beginning December 6, 1865, and which were published in the *Cornhill Magazine* in March, April, May, and July 1866. Sir Hugh Owen invited Arnold to speak at the national Eisteddfod at Chester on September 4, 1866. He declined to attend, but he sent to Owen the brief letter printed here. This reply to Owen was printed in the *Pall Mall Gazette* on September 5, 1866, and in *The Times* the next day. The *Gazette* found Arnold continuously newsworthy; *The Times*, having printed the letter, made it the subject of adverse editorial comment two days later.

In the introduction to *On the Study of Celtic Literature* (London, 1867) Arnold included a large part of this letter to Owen.[1]

A representation to the University of Oxford from the Eisteddfodd, urging the importance of establishing a chair of Celtic at Oxford, could not, I think, but have weight with the University. Your gathering acquires more interest every year. Let me venture to say that you have to avoid two dangers in order to work all the good which your friends could desire. You have to avoid the danger of giving offence to practical men by retarding the spread of the English language in the Principality. I believe that to preserve and honour the Welsh language and literature is quite compatible with not thwarting or delaying for a single hour the introduction, so undeniably useful, of a knowledge of English throughout all classes in Wales. You have to avoid again, the danger of alienating men of science by a blind, partial, and uncritical treatment of your national antiquities. Mr. Stephens's excellent book, *The Literature of the Cymry*, shows how perfectly Welshmen can avoid this danger if they will.[2] When I see the enthusiasm these Eisteddfodds can awaken in your whole people, and then think of the tastes, the literature, the amusements of our own lower and middle classes, I am filled with admiration for you. It is a consoling thought, and one which history allows us to entertain, that races disinherited of political success may yet leave their mark on the world's progress, and contribute powerfully to the civilization of mankind. We in England have come to that point when the continued advance and greatness of our nation is threatened by one cause, and one cause above all; far more than by the helplessness of an aristocracy whose day is fast coming to an end, far more than by the rawness of a lower class whose day is only just beginning, we are imperilled by what I call the "Philistinism" of our middle class. On the side of beauty and taste, vulgarity; on the side of morals and feeling, coarseness; on the side of mind and spirit, unintelligence — this is Philistinism. Now, then, is the moment for the greater delicacy and spirituality of the Celtic peoples who are blended with us, if it be but wisely directed, to make itself felt, prized, and honoured. In a certain measure the children of Taliesin and Ossian have now an opportunity for renewing the famous feat of the Greeks, and conquering their conquerors. No service England can render the Celts by giving you a share in her many good qualities can surpass what the Celts can at this moment do for England by communicating to us some of theirs.

Notes

[1] In 1885 Arnold attended the Eisteddfod at Aberdare. He appears to have addressed the audience very briefly, alluding to his letter of 1866 to Sir Hugh Owen as expressing his sympathy with the Eisteddfodau. See *The Times*, August 28, 1885, p. 6, col. 2.

[2] Thomas Stephens (1821–1875), a chemist at Merthyr Tydfil, published *The Literature of the Kymry* (Llandovery and London, 1849).

Stein plus Hardenberg

Pall Mall Gazette
November 13, 1866, p. 3

"Stein plus Hardenberg" was omitted from *Friendship's Garland* (London, 1871), to which it clearly belongs, when Arnold collected under that title the delightful series of satirical letters he contributed to the *Pall Mall Gazette* between 1866 and 1870. On November 8, 1866, "Prussian Tenant Right," which became Letter VI of *Friendship's Garland,* was carried in the *Gazette.* A reader, who signed himself "An Irish Squire," responded to Arnold's letter with the following one addressed to the editor and published under the heading "Stein in Ireland" in the *Gazette,* November 13, 1866, page 3:

Sir, — As I clearly perceive that "geist" is the thing at the present day, I diligently study the wit and wisdom of Arminius as communicated to the world by Mr. Matthew Arnold in your columns, and of course I did not omit to pay special attention to his expounding of tenant-right in Prussia and the doings of the great Stein.

Two matters, however, puzzle me, which no doubt one or other of those "geistreich" gentlemen will readily explain if you will kindly allow them an opportunity of knowing my wishes. The first of these may be called historical; the other practical. The first is this: if the Prussian landlord owned the land and could eject the tenant, how the latter could be said to have a tenant-right? We all know that the Irish tenant, though in the same position as respects his landlord, has a tenant-right; but then he acquired this by resort to the "ultima ratio regum," viz., by private war and shooting his landlord or his landlord's agent. This, as all Irish tenants are notoriously descendents of Kings, is no doubt quite right; but did the Prussian tenant acquire his right in the same way? Or if not, how otherwise? As soon as the "geist" party form a Ministry, no doubt we shall have a measure similar to Stein's enacted for Ireland first and England after-wards. Now I should like to know whether my little property is Ritter-gut or Bauern-gut. I have always been very proud of my ancient family, and though most of the dirty acres have slipped through our fingers, I still hold by the tenure of presenting the King with a lighted turf to light his pipe when he hunts in the Bogs of Allen. Shall I, then, be Steined and my neighbour Tim Mullooly (whose grandfather kept a shebeen shop and father was a middleman on my ancestral acres, and made so much money that the greater part of them now belong to him) be left un-Steined?

Again, if my rich uncle should leave me some money, shall I be allowed to buy up any bauern-güter, or must Tim Mullooly buy them without my being allowed to compete? Must I and Lord Clanricarde be made junkers (whether we will or not) — too noble to be able to buy dirty little bauern-güter? Will a junker be allowed to dejunkerize himself and become a snob? Shall I be able to get Tim Mullooly made a junker, and so prevent him from buying up bauern-güter? That would be some consolation.

Anyhow I'm puzzled, and I hope those gentlemen will enlighten me. — Your most obedient servant,

  Ballyomadhaun, Bog of Allen.   An Irish Squire.

P.S. — I have another neighbour who turned off all his tenants and now farms all his property, about 3,000 acres. He can't be Steined, I suppose?

In his turn Arnold replied to the "Irish Squire" with "Stein plus Harden-berg," but he chose to leave the letter buried in the files of the *Pall Mall Gazette.* Two reasons perhaps justified the decision. First, as Mr. Peter Smith of Ashtead, Surrey, suggests to me, Arnold may have rejected it from *Friend-ship's Garland* because its point depends too much on the letter of the "Irish Squire." Second, Arnold may have become aware before 1871 that his climactic reference to Prince Karl August von Hardenberg (1750–1822) was invalid, and the force of the paper consequently lost, since the so-called Mémoires of Hardenberg were known to be a forgery.

To the Editor of the *Pall Mall Gazette.*

Sir, — Like so many intellectual Germans at present in this metropolis, and indeed like so many famous professors of "Geist" in all ages, Arminius is often sadly short of ready money, and at such times, when neither his fine old Westphalian family nor (which for my own part I value more) his many-sided culture can save him from the low intrusions of the British tradesman, and more particularly of his tobacconist, he is apt to be more or less what I may call in hiding, and very hard to get hold of. I wanted to get hold of him because I was not at all satisfied, and I could see the British public was not at all satisfied, about the quality and condition of those Prussian tenants he made capital out of; and his bold assertion that they were tenants whom the landlord could turn out struck, I found, some of our best-informed public writers with astonishment as a regular thumper. So coming upon him by a lucky chance at the corner of Leices-ter-square to-day, I button-holed him at once; and, "Arminius," says I, "that was rather too cool of you about the Prussian tenants being people the landlord could turn out, or people the least bit in the world like Irish tenants. Why, when the thing comes to be looked into, it appears they were regular copy-holders, and could sell and bequeath their holdings." "Oh," says Arminius, with his disagreeable grin, "you have got as far as the *erb-pachter,* have you? [1] It is something new for your great nation to attend to anything that concerns us wretched unwashed foreigners. Pursue your studies, my dear friend, *macte novâ virtute;* [2] you will arrive at the *zeit-pachter* in time. Good morning, I am in an immense hurry."

"Stop, Arminius," said I, firmly; "that respectable man coming out of Messers. Bickers and Bush's is *not* your tobacconist. Give me at least chapter and verse for the measure of Stein's which conferred possession on any tenant not a copyholder. And as I understand your noble but obscure language very imperfectly, be good enough to speak English." "In the first place," says Arminius, roughly, "when we Germans talk of Stein's reforms, we mean the whole batch of reforms from 1807 to 1811, because Stein was the originator of the whole movement; and this you, who have been in Germany, ought to have known. Stein led off by abolishing serfage, but Napoleon had Stein turned out in 1808, and our agrarian law, as we call it, dates from Hardenberg's Ministry in 1811. Hardenberg always said that this measure of his was concerted with Stein, and had Stein's approval; and, whether it was so or not, Stein gets the credit of it with the nation. By this measure a *zeit-pachter*, a tenant for a term of years, a tenant who could not leave his holding to his sons, a tenant whom his landlord could turn out the moment his term expired, a tenant with a tenant-right as hard to define, as much reposing on sentiment and custom, as any Irish tenant's tenant-right, got half his holding in absolute property, free from all feudal services, in return for giving up at once the other half to his landlord." "It really sounds," I answered, "too shocking to be lightly believed. I shall look it up, Arminius, I assure you, and so will my countrymen." "Do so," says Arminius, sternly; "the longer you look at it the less you'll like it, I fancy. If you want the precise date of our agrarian law, it is the 14th of September, 1811. And now don't bore me any longer."

"Just one thing before you go, Arminius," I pleaded. "An Irish squire has been writing to me for information about his own position under legislation like Stein's applied to Ireland, and about Lord Clanricarde's position, and the position of a man called Tim Mullooly, and I don't know what all." [3] "I remember," says Arminius, with a grim smile breaking over his face; "that was not a bad joke about Tim Mullooly. If I recollect right, Tim Mullooly was an old *leibeigener* of your friend's or of Lord Clanricarde's, and now that the star of junkerdom is setting, they want to make a junker of poor Tim, who had emancipated himself and was beginning to hold up his head in the world. They should have thought of that sooner. Tell your squire," continued Arminius, his tone relaxing more and more as he went on, "tell that ex-proprietor of poor Tim Mullooly, tell that bloodsucker, that his best plan now is to ponder night and day Hardenberg's 'Reflections on the Prussian Land Reforms,' and to exhort his brother squires round the bog of Allen to do the same. They will find them in a book called *Mémoires tirés des papiers d'un homme d'Etat*, under the year 1810 or 1811. [4] Hardenberg's papers are still locked up in the Berlin archives, but extracts from them are said to have been surreptitiously made, and to have got into this French book, and these reflections are among them." And so saying, Arminius darted up Rupert-street.

The Irish squire asked me so many questions to which I could make no answer that I thought the least I could do was to send him these reflections of Hardenberg's to serve instead. So to the British Museum I went, and, after rummaging in the *Mémoires* through 1810 and 1811, these were the only reflections I could find. They seem to me to be merely adding insult to injury; but I send them to you, Sir, for transmission to the Irish squire, because Arminius wished it. I send them in the original, because I suppose the squire can make them out with his dictionary as well as I: —

Quelques unes de ces réformes portaient atteinte au principe de la propriété; mais les circonstances ou l'on se trouvait furent generalement senties. Aussi les riches subirent-ils leurs pertes avec resignation, tandis qu'on satisfaisait le plus grand nombre des sujets prussiens.[5]

Grub-street, Saturday Evening

Your humble servant,
Matthew Arnold

Notes

[1] *Erb-pächter* designates a hereditary tenant or copyholder; *Zeit-pächter*, a lease-holder.

[2] Vergil, *Aeneid*, IX, 641.

[3] Hubert George De-Burgh-Canning, second Marquess of Clanricarde (1832–1916), was a notorious absentee landlord, to whom Arnold makes several references in his articles dealing with Home Rule. In his obituary in *The Times*, April 14, 1916 (p. 11, col. 4), it is said "The story of Lord Clanricarde's estates in County Galway is an epitome of the whole Irish Land law." He served as Liberal M.P. for Galway from 1867 to 1871; after 1874 he entered the House of Lords as Baron Somerhill.

[4] The so-called *Mémoires* of Hardenberg are stated by J. R. Seeley to be a well-known forgery, and he deplored their use by historians in his own time, by Alphonse de Beauchamp, Alexander Schubert, Count d'Allonville and others — *Life and Times of Stein, or Germany and Prussia in the Napoleonic Age*, 3 vols. (Cambridge, 1878–1879), III, 480–481.

[5] *Mémoires tirés des papiers d'un homme d'état sur les causes secrètes qui ont déterminé la politique des cabinets dans les guerres de la révolution*, 13 vols. (Paris, 1831–1838), XI, 122–23. Arnold has abridged the text.

Theodore Parker

Pall Mall Gazette
August 24, 1867, pp. 11–12

The Note-Books of Matthew Arnold show that he hoped to write on Theodore Parker for the *Pall Mall Gazette* in 1865. In 1866 he still planned to read "Parker. Selections;" but in 1867 both the notation "Parker's Selections" in the list of intended reading and the notation "Th. Parker. & review him," a project for July, are canceled as if completed.[1] The review appeared the next month. It is probably the first book review that Arnold contributed to the *Pall Mall Gazette* and it was unsigned in accordance with the policy of the *Gazette*.

Arnold discouraged bibliographers from ascribing to him unsigned reviews, for on February 22, 1868, when writing to his mother concerning Robert Buchanan, he said: "Buchanan probably credits me with some of the severe reviews which have appeared of his verses, as doctrines of mine appear up and down in them. I am sorry for this, and wish it could be known that I never write anonymous criticism." [2] Perhaps Arnold only meant that he never wrote anonymous criticism of the living, for he had reviewed in the previous summer *Selections from Theodore Parker's Unpublished Sermons* (London: Trübner, 1865).

The full title of the book that he reviews here is *Lessons from the World of Matter and the World of Man by Theodore Parker. Selected from Notes of Unpublished Sermons,* by Rufus Leighton; edited by Frances Power Cobbe. The short title *Selections from Theodore Parker's Sermons* is the title on the spine.

Hardly the barest record of Theodore Parker appears in any biographical dictionary of importance. The *Nouvelle Biographie Générale* devotes less than half a page to him, and thus sums up his history: — Malgré le talent qu'il déploya, la variété de sa prédication et la nouveauté de ses idées, il ne réussit pas à attirer à lui beaucoup de partisans, et en fut toujours réduit à la bizarre position d'un novateur sans disciple, d'un prêtre sans église, et d'un politique sans parti." [3]

Mr. Moncure Conway, an American preacher now resident in London, who has known personally almost all the chief contemporary writers and thinkers of New England, and whose accounts of them are always to be read with interest, has published in the last number of the *Fortnightly Review* a notice of Theodore Parker. His estimate of Parker's career is very different from the estimate of the French biographer. The young men who gathered round Parker formed, says Mr. Conway, "the largest and most important congregation that has ever existed in America." [4] And yet the future which Mr. Conway prophesies for Parkerism, as he calls it, is so splendid as even to throw this bright beginning into the shade. "Theodore Parker has founded a many-gated temple, with a dome wide and lofty enough to include all earnest minds — a study, possibly of the American Church."

These are strong words; but it is undoubtedly true that Theodore Parker's action, considerable in his lifetime, has greatly increased since his death in 1860, and that it bids fair to increase yet more. A volume of selections from notes of his sermons, which was not long ago published in this country, with Miss Cobbe for its editor, affords to the English public the means of acquainting itself with the thoughts, and of determining for itself the position, of this remarkable man, whose name is daily more and more claiming our attention.

It has often been remarked that American literature has no original individuality of its own, but draws its whole life from English literature. American authors are English authors of more or less merit, whose birth has happened to be in America, but who are fed on English books, follow the literary movement of England, and reproduce English thought. Germany and France, the most active centres, for these many years past, of intellectual life, act upon America only through England. This has been so, but it is ceasing to be so, and will soon be so no longer. An American author will write, as an American citizen lives, under the influences of American life and opinion. Parker wrote and preached so; he was not an English Unitarian writing and preaching in America but still governed by the religious thought and tradition of the mother country; he was an American Unitarian moving with the movement of American life and determined by its influences. He is thus a new and original type. The basis of his nature is indeed still that of the Englishman's nature, the Englishman of the middle class, the English Puritan; but this basis is modified by the daily pressure of American circumstance, and not hedged round, and kept in an artificial conformity with the Puritanism of the old country.

Theodore Parker's word has therefore the force, the exuberant hope, the boldness, the expansiveness of America herself, and here is its originality.

> Man advances continually. No man is full-grown. Jesus will not be called good; his ideal haunts him and shames his actual. The cat and dog and ox kind are first moored by Providence in the same harbour; the fleet of animals rides at anchor all their life; but mankind looses from port and sails the sea with God, driven by every wind, voyaging to other shores and continually new. "Nothing venture, nothing have." [5]

That is Puritanism in Boston, Massachusetts, instead of Boston, Lincolnshire, and Puritanism freely drinking in the inspiration of its new sphere.

It has the hope of the new world in it, unclogged by "the heavy and the weary weight" of the old. Again: —

> The mind of New England runs through the schoolhouse, and then jumps over the ditch of poverty, where lie Spain, Italy, Portugal, Ireland, and many another country that never took its start by the run in the schoolhouse; and so failed to leap the ditch and there lies to perish.[6]
>
> I once knew a hard-working man, a farmer and mechanic, who in the winter nights rose a great while before day and out of the darkness coaxed him at least two hours of hard study; and then, when the morning peeped over the eastern hills, he yoked his oxen and went forth to his daily work, or in his shop he laboured all day long; and when the night came he read aloud some simple book to his family, but when they were snugly laid away in their sleep the great-minded mechanic took to his hard study anew; and so, year out and year in, he went on, neither rich nor much honoured, loudly entreated by daily work, and yet he probably had a happiness in his heart and mind which the whole country might have been proud to share.[7]

Puritanism on our side the Atlantic, in presence of all our ignorance, poverty, and misery, naturally deals in no such frank and cheerful spirit with our actual life, but busies itself with the life to come. It is Parker's merit that to a different social medium from ours he did not transfer our religious routine, but allowed the schooling, the plenty, the wholesome social condition of New England, to invigorate his preaching, and to drench it, in the happiest way, in matter.

Thus daring to be himself, to be open to the influences round him, and to touch life with courage and frankness, he often reaches a strain of genuine strength, genuine eloquence: —

> In human action there is always more virtue of every kind than vice; more industry than idleness, more thrift than spendthrift, more temperance than intemperance, more wisdom than folly. Even the American politician does not tell so many lies as he tells truths. Sincerity is more common than hypocrisy; no nation is ever affected; the mass of men are in real earnest. In all the world mankind never put up a single gravestone to evil, as such. No man will ever write on his father's tomb, "He was an eminent slavetrader." Mr. Mason's sons will not write on his tombstone, "Author of the Fugitive Slave Bill." No miserable minister who for the meanest fee shall stand in some pulpit and preach funeral eulogies on such wicked men, will praise them for deeds of this kind; he will try to varnish them over, and say they were mistakes.[8]

Certainly, the Puritan preacher who, instead of the old story about justification and hell-fire, gives us such new and lively strokes as this, is an apparition of great interest and importance. Probably Mr. Conway is right in thinking that this apparition will greatly sway the development of religion in America, and that Theodore Parker has founded "a study of the American Church." The sincerity and nobleness of his life and character, joined to the originality, insight, and eloquence of his teaching, are well fitted to make of Parker such a founder. But whether a Church with Theodore Parker for its founder will be a "many-gated temple, with a dome wide and lofty enough to include all earnest minds," is more doubtful. Parker, born an American, is as a preacher and writer a genuine American voice, not an echo of English pulpits and books; that is much. In the same way, Mr. Walt Whitman, born an American, is as a poet a genuine American voice, not an echo of English poetry; that, too, is much. But the admirers of Theodore Parker or of Mr. Walt Whitman easily make more of it than it is worth. At this time of day it is not enough to be an American voice, or an English voice, or a French voice; for a real spiritual lead it is necessary to be a European voice. When American intellect has not only broken, as it is breaking, the leading strings of England, but has also learnt to assimilate independently the intellect of France and Germany and the ancient world as well as of England, then, and not till then, may the spiritual construction of an American be "a many-gated temple, with a dome wide and lofty enough to include all earnest minds." That the spiritual construction reared by Theodore Parker is not of this supreme order, its very style quickly indicates to any one who has much tact for these matters. Sureness of beauty the style has none; it is continually breaking into the flaws and weaknesses from which the style of master-founders is free. "Blue-eyed Lyra is mine; mine is the many coloured morning; and the ring which marries day and night, its beauty is my own," [9] — that is a sort of dithyramb which may well fill us with misgiving. It is soon matched by Parker's cry on a comet: "This hairy stranger is far inferior to the mind that shall calculate its orbit;" [10] or by his homage to youth: "I love to look on these young faces, and see the firstlings of the young man's beard;" [11] or by his pleasures of memory: "He is a blessed boy again, his early home lingering in his venerable memory for all his mortal life, the glad remembrance of brother and sister, the beautiful affection of uncles and aunts, who seemed a special providence of love watching over him, and dropping their balmy offerings into his expectant hand!" [12]

These are outward and superficial indications of inadequacy — not inadequacy in any disrespectful use of the word, but inadequacy in view of such eminence as Mr. Conway and others of Parker's great admirers claim for him. A deeper indication is his Theism: —

You know that all change and disappointment was foreseen, was provided for, is part of the heavenly mechanism of life; that the Great Director of the world cast his parts wisely, knows how it will turn out. . . . This is the first of all rights, our unalienable right to the infinite providence of the perfect God. . . . God is perfect Cause of all, creating all from a perfect motive, for a perfect purpose, as a perfect means. He has the perfect justice to will the

best, perfect wisdom to devise the best, and perfect power to achieve the best.
. . . The defeats of life, poverty, shame, sickness, death — all that is little; the
good God foreknew it, provided for it all, and will round it all at last into a
globe of infinite satisfaction. . . . The most obvious justice shows that if a
man has suffered wrongfully, he ought to have some compensation in the next
life; a deeper justice shows that if he has sinned he ought to have a chance to
retrieve his wrong. . . . Continually there are sorrows for which the earth has
no recompense. The compensation, the joy, must come in the eternal world.
I know not how; the fact I am sure of. That one and one make two is not
clearer to me. I am not more certain of my own existence. It follows from God's
infinity.[13]

It was hardly worth while crying out so contemptuously against the
"popular theology," to retain as the cardinal points of one's creed dogmas
which have as little scientific substance as the dogmas of ordinary Cal-
vinism. The man who would "found a many-gated temple to include all
earnest minds" must henceforth build under the inevitable condition that
he brings in nothing which the scientific intellect cannot accept. The
idea that the world is in a course of development, of *becoming*, towards
a perfection infinitely greater than we now can even conceive, the idea of
a *tendance à l'ordre* present in the universe "groaning and travailing in
pain together," this the scientific intellect may accept, and may willingly
let the religious instincts and the language of religion gather around it.
But the idea of a "Great Director," or "Wise Engineer," to use Parker's
language, who has set this movement a-going on a fore-known plan, and
who sits *outside* of it watching its operation, this the scientific intellect
can at the present time no more admit than the idea of a God who turns
himself into a sacrificial wafer or who foredooms a large proportion of the
human race to hell.

Mr. Walt Whitman, who has been already mentioned above, relates
that a wounded soldier whom he attended in hospital during the late war
in America asked him "if he enjoyed religion." Mr. Walt Whitman answered, "Perhaps not, my dear, in the way you mean; and yet, maybe, it is
the same thing." Miss Cobbe, a fervent disciple of Parker, believes that Pan-
theism and Positivism are threatening us with an "awful desolation," that
Christianity is doomed, and that in Parker's Theism is our only hope.[14] Let
her be of good cheer. Man, according to Goethe's wise epigram, "calls the
best he knows, *God;*" [15] the God of the Pantheist, the Positivist, and the
Theist is alike the best that each of them knows; and each of them, if the
others ask him whether he enjoys religion may well reply with Mr. Walt
Whitman, "Perhaps not, my dear, in the way you mean; and yet, maybe, it
is the same thing." The reply will have truth in it; but, nevertheless, the
manner in which a man translates and expresses to us the best he knows
must determine his claim to spiritual leadership of the order. Far as

Theodore Parker had outgrown the popular, ghastly theology, as he is fond of calling it, of Puritanism, his basis was Puritan; and the defects of Puritanism — its want of full and harmonious development, its excessive development on one special side — are the defects of Parker, defects which inevitably exclude him from the rank, which his disciples claim for him, of a teacher of the first order.

Short of this claim, which is apt to be set up and allowed far too easily, Theodore Parker has a right to our warm and unstinted respect and admiration. The questions which he says the controlling men of the principal churches of Boston never ask about a minister — "Is the man able? Has he talents large enough, and genius for religion? Has he the morality to make us better? Has he the piety to charm us in our sorrows, to beguile us from our sins? Has he courage, justice, wisdom, love, and religion enough to make us better men, the church better, the city a better town, and the nation a better state?" — all these questions, which the controlling men of the principal churches anywhere, and not in Boston only, are not prompt to ask, are to be answered, if asked about Theodore Parker, with a cordial and admiring "Yes!"

Notes

[1] *Note-Books*, pp. 577, 579, 581.
[2] *Letters*, I, 389.
[3] (Paris, 1865), XXXIX, 225.
[4] Moncure D. Conway, "Theodore Parker," *Fortnightly Review*, VIII (August 1, 1867), 152.
[5] *Lessons from the World of Matter*, p. 227.
[6] *Ibid.*, p. 167.
[7] *Ibid.*, p. 169.
[8] *Ibid.*, p. 212–213. Arnold has here made a pastiche of sentences.
[9] *Ibid.*, p. 19.
[10] *Ibid.*, p. 43.
[11] *Ibid.*, p. 51.
[12] *Ibid.*, p. 150.
[13] *Ibid.*, pp. 276, 278, 296, 297, 303, 321, 327, 328.
[14] *Ibid.*, p. x.
[15] "Gott, Gemüt, und Welt," *Goethes Sämtliche Werke*, IV, 4.

Curtius's History of Greece

Pall Mall Gazette
October 12, 1868, pp. 9–10
April 28, 1871, pp. 10–11
June 4, 1872, pp. 11–12
July 22, 1872, pp. 11–12
March 25, 1876, p. 12

The five volumes of Adolphus William Ward's translation of *The History of Greece* by Ernst Curtius (1814–1896) were published between 1868 and 1873. Arnold reviewed the successive volumes individually in the *Pall Mall Gazette*. On some occasions a considerable interval of time elapsed between the publication of the volume and the review of it.

Arnold's feeling for the continuity of history and his wide acquaintance with the historians of the nineteenth century qualified him for the work. Like his father, Arnold saw a parallelism between the Athens of the age of Pericles and his own time. He had expressed the idea when he wrote "On the Modern Element in Literature;" he returned to emphasize the parallels in these reviews. Frequent and extensive though the use of quotation may be, Arnold employs it to enforce the themes that he continuously develops: the importance of clear ideas, the praise of solidity and method, of strenuousness and seriousness, of "fixity." At times in these papers Arnold writes with the force of a political propagandist, occasionally straining the text to support his message.

A NEW HISTORY OF GREECE

It is now forty years since Goethe, who was not apt to flatter his countrymen, remarked how high was the rank of modern Germany among the nations of Europe in every department of science and learning. A foreigner might then have been tempted to reply that it was unlucky the Germans could do everything but write. Full of science and learning they undoubtedly were, but they seemed unable to communicate their acquisitions in a readable way. But the grounds for this reproach are now disappearing. Book after book now appears in Germany, which is not only full of information, but also eminently well written. Above all is this the case with the recent productions of Germans in the department of Greek and Roman history. It was necessary, no doubt, to work for a long time among the materials of the science of classical antiquity before it became possible to get a firm grasp upon them, to combine them for a general result such as the composition of history, and to use them towards this result with facility and power. It is because Germany has with such indefatigable industry and interest mastered the multifarious materials, supplied not only by Greece and Rome, but by the cognate and parent East also, out of which the history of the Greeks and Romans has to be made up — it is because of the number of good heads busying themselves, in Germany, with these matters, and the medium of clear ideas and sound information thus created there for those who write on them, that productions such as the histories of Dr. Mommsen and Dr. Curtius have now become possible. These two historians write so firmly and currently because of the near and full relation in which they stand with their subject-matter, a nearness and fulness which Englishmen generally reserve for their relations with topics of the day, such as election prospects, the Abergele accident,[1] or the progress of Ritualism.[2] While, therefore, the valuable History of Dr. Thirlwall [3] seems to move in an atmosphere somewhat far off and shadowy, and while round the monumental work of Mr. Grote[4] there seems to hang a certain air of the isolated scholar's study, an air of tentative labour and still continuing research, Dr. Mommsen[5] and Dr. Curtius write Greek or Roman history with the same confidence and animation with which the *Times* discusses the Wesleyan Conference[6] or Mdme. Rachel's trial.[7] In revenge, the German newspapers are apt to treat topics of the day with a want of briskness and of all living sense of reality which nearly equals what most Englishmen feel in touching the philological and historical sciences.

Dr. Mommsen's history smacks even a little too much, perhaps, of the leading article; it is somewhat too pamphleteering, too trenchant, too charged with likes and dislikes. The soberness of history is better maintained in the history of Dr. Curtius, which is now before us. But with the soberness there is a living hold upon his subject-matter, which communicates itself to the reader, and makes the reading of the history in the highest degree fruitful and impressive. To enable the student to *orienter* himself, as the French say — to find his bearings — in the region of history with which he busies himself, is the most real service which a historical work can render him. Particularly this is so in the history of the Greek and Roman world; of the Greek world above all, where the single facts have each and all been the objects of such voluminous research, and where yet to see them in their connection and to comprehend the general result from them is so important.

There can be no thorough knowledge of the Greek people without knowing the original works which they have left. He who has read again and again what is left to us of Pindar will have a more living sense of the Greek world as it was in the first fifty years of the fifth century before Christ than he who has read the most voluminous modern history of that period. But he who has read Dr. Curtius will learn a thousand times more from his Pindar, and will read, as the Germans say, *between the lines*. A work on the scale of Mr. Grote's, on the other hand, is, from its very fulness, of much less service as a readily grasped presentation of the development of the Greek world in its vital characteristics and essential connection, and as a clue to the student seeking to know this development, where alone it can really be known, in the original documents. Much more does a work like Mr. Grote's *History of Greece,* or a work like Sismondi's *History of France,*⁸ seem to afford the means of dispensing with the study of the original documents, and to supply enough of them to give the reader an adequate notion of what they all come to. Yet this history cannot, as has been said, really do; and the semblance of its doing so is, and must be, in real truth, illusory. Sometimes, however, the region of history to be surveyed is such that, the length of human life and the compass of human faculties being what they are, the partial and inadequate knowledge to be gathered from a modern historian is all that it is worth our while to try for. It is the felicity of Gibbon that his immortal work has for its field a region of this nature. Gibbon is a classic, not because the later Empire can be really or adequately known from his History, but because with admirable learning and skill he gives account of a period which we do not most of us care to study in its original documents, or to know more of than he gives us.

But there are other portions of the life of humanity which deserve studying in quite another fashion; and Greek history is emphatically one of them. For these periods the student can hardly wish for anything better in the shape of a modern history than a history on the scale and with the character of that of Dr. Curtius, to serve as a guide and centre of reference in that large study of the original documents which he will still feel impelled to make. Mr. Ward has as yet published but the first volume of his translation, and that volume is not quite coextensive with the first volume of Dr. Curtius; but we hope that he will impose it as a strict rule on himself and his publisher not to let the whole work swell beyond four volumes, the number fixed, we believe, by Dr. Curtius, and wisely fixed, as his utmost limit.

Taking the one volume which has been made accessible to English readers, we shall, perhaps, best give a notion of its merits if we select three or four of the main points of interest to the student of the Greek world and its development — points which have afforded matter for infinite disquisition, which meet the student perpetually in reading the Greek authors, and on which it is of the greatest importance to him to have clear ideas — and see how Dr. Curtius deals with them. "The science of origins," as the French call it, we have most of us had occasion in the course of our training to employ in regard to ancient Greece and its people. The contact of the Greeks with the Phoenicians, the relations of Asiatic with European Greece, the Dorian migration, the question who were the Pelasgians,

the Minyans, the Achaeans, the Ionians; these are points of historical research which every schoolboy is constantly finding himself invited to
elucidate. Clear conceptions about them are very needful for a right understanding of the most commonly read Greek authors; yet how few of us
who have had recourse, we will not say to our common books of reference
only, but even to authorities of the most eminent merit and learning, such
as, for example, Mr. Fynes Clinton and his essays, printed in the first
volume of the *Fasti Hellenici*, have come away with conceptions which
can with any truth at all be called clear? [9] Let us see how the case stands
with us after having recourse to Dr. Curtius.

First, then, as to the Phoenicians, and the origin of the traditions of
Greek contact with them. We shall use Dr. Curtius's own words, though
we must perforce abridge and condense: —

> Pressed in a narrow strip of land between mountains and water, it was
> by sea alone that the Phoenicians could extend themselves. Their ships went
> forth to bring home gain of every kind; above all, to import the materials for
> the manufactories flourishing in their populous towns — Byblus, Sidon, Tyre.
> The discoveries made by individuals on a lucky voyage were used by mercantile
> societies in possession of means sufficient to organize settlements, and to secure
> to the business thus commenced a lasting importance. Whilst in civilized coun-
> tries the right of settlement had to be purchased dearly and under oppressive
> conditions, the rocks on the Greek coasts, hitherto a place of rest only for
> swarms of quails, were to be had for nothing, and yet yielded manifold profits.
> Sea and shore thus came into the hands of the strangers, who on the one hand
> terrified the natives by craft and force, and again ever continued to attract them
> anew to commercial intercourse. The myth of Helen contains reminiscences of
> a time when the island of Cranae, with its sanctuary of Aphrodite, lay like a
> foreign territory close by the coast of Laconia, a Phoenician emporium, where
> the foreigners safely stowed away the women and the rest of the gain and loot
> carried off by them. So close and so constantly extending a contact with the
> foreign traders could not remain without its effect on the natives. At the market-
> fairs held on the shore, they had to come to an agreement with them about
> the objects of trade; about numbers, weights, and measures. Thus a series of
> the most important inventions, which had been gradually matured in the East,
> came, as rearranged by the practical Phoenicians, to the knowledge of the
> natives, who wondered, observed, and learnt; their slumbering powers were
> awakened, and the spell unbound which had kept men fettered in their monoto-
> nous conditions of life. The motion of the mind begins, and with it Greek
> history draws its first breath.[10]

The Phoenicians were, as time went on, pushed out by a branch of
the more gifted and energetic Greek people, whom they left in possession
of their civilization. And what branch of this people first and chiefly received the fruitful boon and communicated it to the rest? The Ionians,
says Dr. Curtius, of the coast of Asia Minor — Ionians who were the orig-

inal possessors of this widespread name, as well as of the characteristics which have become for us the distinguishing characteristics of the Greek genius and people: —

Among all the Greeks, the inhabitants of this thickly peopled coast, by virtue of their special natural endowment and of the exceedingly happy conditions of their land and climate, were the first to secure for themselves the civilization of the Phoenicians. Sagaciously they contrived to learn their arts from them, while the Pelasgian people remained inert. Thus they became known to the nations of the East before any of the rest of the Greeks. The common name of Greeks in the whole East was no other than that which this maritime race of Greek descent gave to itself — that of the Iaones or Ionians, a name subsequently domesticated by the Phoenicians in various dialectic forms, such as Javan with the Hebrews, Iuna or Iauna with the Persians, Uinim with the Egyptians. After the Ionians had learnt navigation and become the masters of their own sea, they sailed in the track of the Phoenicians, as Thucydides so aptly expresses it in reference to Sicily. Especially they settled at the mouths of the streams, where these were of a kind to afford their vessels a safe entrance and a voyage a short way into the interior of the land. The routes of the island sea were opened, and now, in a more and more rapid succession of landings, the Greeks of the East came to the Greeks of the west. From their original habitations, as well as from other regions where they had taken up their abode, an innate impulse of kinmanship led them on across the passage to European Hellas. Here land and air must have met them with the pleasantest of greetings; here they were eager to domesticate themselves, to introduce all the arts and inventions which they had gradually appropriated during a lively intercourse with other nations, and to awaken the natives to a higher phase of life.[11]

That important contact of Hellas with the East, accordingly, of which, in the traditions about the Greek gods, and about personages like Cadmus and Aegyptus, we have such indelible traces, was properly a contact with a *Greek* East, and with Ionic Greeks, who, having absorbed and transformed Phoenician or Egyptian civilization, and coming to Hellas from the other side of the sea, not from the coast of Asia Minor only, but from many a settlement in non-Hellenic lands to which their adventurous genius had led them, "easily came to be called Phoenicians and Egyptians." [12]

And as Cadmus and Aegyptus were not Phoenicians and Egyptians, but Greeks, Greeks awakened and transformed by contact with older civilizations, so Pelasgus and the primitive dwellers on the soil of Hellas were Greeks too, but Greeks not yet fully born, not yet awakened.

There exist no Pelasgian myths, no Pelasgian gods, to be contrasted with the Greek. The first genuine Hellene known to us, the Homeric Achilles, prays to the Pelasgian Zeus; and Dodona, at all times considered the primitive seat of the Pelasgi, was also the most ancient Hellas in Europe. But for all this Pelasgi and Hellenes are by no means identical or merely different names for one idea. Such a view is proved untenable by the manifest fact that from the Hellenes sprang entirely new currents of life. The Pelasgian times lie in the background — a vast period of monotony; impulse and motion are first communicated by Hellen and his sons, and with their arrival history commences. Accordingly, we must interpret them to signify tribes which, endowed with special gifts, and animated by special powers of action, issue forth from the mass of a great people.[13]

The action of one brilliant branch of Hellen's descendants, the maritime Ionians, we have already noticed. This first breaks the monotony of the Pelasgian age; "everywhere with the combination of Pelasgians and Ionians commenced, as by an electric contact, the current of historic life." [14] But in contrast with the action of the mobile Ionians arises presently that of other descendants of Hellen, the firm and stedfast mountaineers of northern Greece. This action develops itself from the land, as that of the Ionians develops itself from the sea. The Minyans, so famous in Greek poetry, the first dwellers in northern Greece, "with whom a perceptible movement of the Pelasgian tribes beyond the sea — in other words, a Greek history in Europe — begins," [15] are in communication with Asiatic Ionia, and with Ionian settlements in Greece itself, and receive their impulse from thence. The same influence appears in the Achaeans. "Achaeans are everywhere settled on the coast, and are always regarded as particularly near relations of the Ionians." [15] The Achaeans, however, in Phthiotis develop much of the strong spirit and tenacity which was the secret, afterwards, of the success of the Dorian mountaineers; "they called forth a more independent development in European Greece than the older tribes had succeeded in producing," [17] and Dr. Curtius therefore styles the Achaean Achilles "the first Hellene." [18] But the true centre of an independent development for European Greece was in the Dorian highlanders, who came down from the roots of Olympus to the district between Parnassus and Oeta. Their subsequent history may almost be described as the history of Greece without Attica; but the traits which gave them this splendid fortune are thus marked by Dr. Curtius: —

Above all other Greek tribes the Dorians possessed an innate tendency towards the establishment, preservation, and spread of fixed systems. While the maritime Greeks in their continual voyages made a home of every coast, the tribes participating in the Thessalian Amphictyony, of which the Dorians were the representatives, were the first who learnt to regard a territory within fixed limits as their common country, and to love, honour, and defend it as their fatherland. With the wandering forth of the Dorians, the strength of the highland tribes came forth from the North to assert its claim to take part in the national history. They had been outstripped by centuries by the tribes of the coasts and islands, but now made their appearance among the latter with a doubly impressive vigour of healthy nature. Their wishes and powers turned towards practical life, towards the performance of fixed tasks, towards serious and purposed action. The changes and new formations arising from their expeditions of conquest endured through the whole course of Greek history. And for this reason the ancient historical writers began the historic times, in contradistinction to the Heroic pre-historic age, with the first deeds of the Dorians.[19]

We hope that by these extracts the reader may gain some notion of what we mean, when we praise Dr. Curtius for having laid firm hold on the main points in the development of the Greek people, and treated them with living clearness and freshness. This seems to us the essential merit for a history of Greece to possess. There are, no doubt, several points where the conclusions reached by Dr. Curtius may be open to dispute. But, in our view of the matter, a reader of Greek history suffers no great loss in having to regard his author's conclusions, on certain points, as provisional; his great loss is in having the essential points indistinctly marked for him, and discussed without living force and freshness.

Mr. Ward's translation has some roughnesses and some misprints, but on the whole it seems to us a production eminently *kernhaft,* as the Germans say, and thus to suit its original, of which it reproduces the mingled freshness and solidity. Clearness, solidity, method, firm and orderly progression — it is of these qualities that the book of Dr. Curtius gives us a sense; and this sense is by Mr. Ward's translation retained, whereas many a more elegant English version of such an original would in all probability have clean lost it.

CURTIUS'S *HISTORY OF GREECE* [I]

We are in arrear with Mr. Ward's translation of this important History of Greece by Dr. Curtius. Since we called attention to the first volume, not only has the second volume appeared, but the third also. The work, however, is one which from the permanent interest of its subject can afford to wait, and from the solidity and thoughtfulness of its execution gains by being well considered. We will not even now attempt to review the second and third volumes together, but will confine ourselves to the second volume, allowing the third, which certainly requires a separate notice, to wait for this yet a little longer.

As to the translation, it has the merit of keeping, in a remarkable degree, the solidity and fulness of significance of the work itself. It is not carefully printed, and the list of errata at the end of the volume needs to be lengthened considerably. The translation is not particularly elegant, and sometimes its English is not only inelegant but inaccurate. "The naval force of the enemy was nothing less than annihilated" (p. 293) means the very contrary of what Mr. Ward intends it to mean. It is not allowable to say in English "the dynasty which *was befriended with* the Lydians," or to say that Herodotus was not "blind *against* the praiseworthy characteristics of the enemy." The word *frostig* has its own rights in German, but an English writer who says that in Aeschylus certain "allusions were not the result of impure and frosty secondary designs obscuring the pure effect of poetry," expresses himself neither perspicuously nor gracefully. These are blemishes which Mr. Ward would do well to remove; but in general his rendering, though it wants grace, has the great merit of retaining the substantialness, the fulness of meaning, and the serious forward stride of the style of his author.

His author sometimes, in matters where a delicate touch is required, has too much of the hardness of the schoolman, and makes us desire the tact of the man of imagination or even of the man of the world. Yet the impression he leaves is on the whole scarcely less agreeable than it is satisfying, from his thorough command over the rich abundance of materials which, with German honesty, he has collected from every side for his work, and from the natural unostentatious way in which he uses them. How simple and yet how instructive, how unlike the vagueness and coldness with which in the old histories of Greece Greek topography is presented to us, is this mention of Paros and Naxos, the two chief and closely connected islands of the Cyclades: —

Paros may be distinguished even in the distance by her mountains, which rise in forms of such grandeur that they seemingly intend to announce the costly treasure they contain — an inexhaustible supply of the fairest marble. Paros is, moreover, of great importance for navigation, on account of the abundance of springs on her shores and the deep bays of her harbours. In this respect she forms the natural complement of the larger contiguous island. For Naxos rises out of the sea, rounded off on all sides without deeper inlets; and her wide circumference and strong position mark her out as the chief among the neighbouring islands, while at the same time nature has blessed her with manifold products, so that the ancients were at times wont to call her the Lesser Sicily. From the broad summit of the Naxian mountains more than twenty islands are visible, lying at their feet, and to the east the view extends as far as the massive ranges of Asia.[20]

In connection with the populousness of ancient Hellas and the importance of her islands now so insignificant, here, again, is information just of the kind to be useful and to stand clear in the memory. The birthplace of the poet Simonides, the island of Ceos, off the southern promontory of Attica, contained at the time of the Persian war, says Dr. Curtius, —

On an entirely mountainous area of about nine square miles four towns, every one of which possessed a harbour, a legislation, and a coinage of its own. To this, the most flourishing period of Greek population, belongs the careful

system of building at all possible points, the vestiges of which astonish the
traveller to this day, when he beholds how once upon a time every little spot
was put to its particular use, every difficulty of settlement and intercourse overcome, and every part of the country pervaded by human life and activity. On
rocky crags, whence in the present day lonely herds of goats derive a scanty
sustenance, are found the remains of towns, surrounded by strong walls, and
supplied with cisterns and aqueducts, while the surrounding heights are
graduated off in artificial terraces up to their summit, for the purpose of obtaining space for the culture of corn and fruit trees.[21]

The same definiteness marks the statements of Dr. Curtius on that
most important and interesting point in the life of Hellenic communities
— slavery: —

By the side of the civic society existed a slave population of very considerable numbers in mercantile and manufacturing cities such as Corinth and
Aegina. Here its numbers must have amounted to as many as ten times those
of the free inhabitants. Even in Attica they must be assumed to have prepon-
derated over the freemen in a proportion of at least four to one.[22]

Dr. Curtius points out very well how it was that, in general, the multitude of slaves constituted no political danger for a Greek State, but in
recollection of Mr. Lucraft's confession to his colleagues of the School
Board, that he often found it difficult to make both ends meet,[23] there
is an especial interest for us in the following: —

Without the slaves the Attic democracy would have been an impossibility,
for they alone enabled the poor, as well as the rich, to take a daily part in
public affairs. For only a very small minority were poor enough to have to get
through life without the help of slaves; and we find Attic families complaining
of being forced to the most painful retrenchment if they were not able to keep
more than seven slaves.[24]

Easily may it have been, therefore, that "the contrast between rich and
poor was altogether neither excessive nor irremovable." The seven slaves
would just make all the difference to Mr. Lucraft; with them, the contrast
between him and Lord Westminster need not, perhaps, be excessive and
irremovable; without them, it can hardly help being so.

Thus far we have tried to illustrate the fulness and yet definiteness of
our author's way of writing history; its strenuousness and seriousness are
not less praiseworthy. Take this summing up of the career of the Spartan
Cleomenes, that "remarkable man, whose naturally grand character had
degenerated into criminal selfishness and indomitable ferocity": —

We find Cleomenes recalled and reinstated in all his honours; but what
manner of man does he return home? Brutalized by his restless wanderings,
distracted by evil passions and the torments of an unsatisfied ambition, bur-

dened with the load of his guilt, and spiritually and physically ruined by sensual excesses. This state of mind ended in raving madness. It was necessary to bind the Spartan king and set his own helots as guards over him, till at last he died the most awful of deaths from his own hand.[25]

But the crowning merit of Dr. Curtius as an historian of Greece lies, according to our judgment, in his power of exhibiting Greek history in its essential connection and vital development. Here he seems to us superior to Mr. Grote; although in describing the course and incidents of political struggles, he is inferior to the English politician, and as a narrator of military actions he shows no special talent for lively and picturesque writing. But as an historian who makes us see the tying of the thread which a people's life and fortunes follow does more than any one else to make us really apprehend history, and retain it in our minds as a lasting possession. A merit of this kind signalizes Dr. Curtius in his second volume no less than in his first, and what space we have yet left shall be employed in showing it.

As the contact with Asia quickened into life the old Pelasgian world, and made it Hellenic, so the formative impulse to this Hellenic world after it had come into being was given by Delphi. Hardy and serious tribes from the mountains of north-western Greece crossed Pindus, and at the foot of Olympus formed a first federation, or Amphictyony, of which the sanctuary of Tempe was the centre, and the Apolline worship the sanction. Moving thence southward to the foot of Parnassus, they there established a second federation, under the guardianship of the same religion, with the already founded Delphi for its sanctuary. Moving again southward, and conquering Peloponnesus, they established there no new sanctuary; but Delphi, its priesthood, and its religion, retained their hold upon them. The combinations which grew out of the Dorian conquest of Peloponnesus were all drawn towards Delphi as an Amphictyonic sanctuary, the one common centre of national Hellenic life. Thither turned the Ionic Athenians, no less than the Doric Spartans. The Apolline worship had come over the sea from Asia, and the Apolline priesthoods, whose strength was now concentrated at Delphi, owed their original ascendency over the rude tribes of Hellas to the possession of an older and higher culture. To retain and secure their ascendency as guides and arbitrators among the tribes of Hellas as they grew in civilization, the Delphian priesthood kept up and extended in every possible way its own communication with places and priesthoods beyond the sea, and the friendly meetings of the Hellenic communities at religious and festive solemnities. To the Apolline religion and to Delphi were due, therefore, the Hellenic festivals with their Amphictyonic and national character; to these festivals were due road-making and bridge-making, safe conducts and peace, interchange of ideas between the communities of Hellas, and

commerce. To the same religion and its priesthood were due the introduction of chronology, records, writing, and history; from the practice of
depositing treasures in the sanctuary for safe-keeping and management
by the priesthood came finance-institutions and banking; from the priesthood's carefully maintained communications with the outer world came
mapping and geography, colonization and missions, foreign culture and
its religious ideas. Finally, from the religious action of Delphi there
proceeded a most powerful influence on Hellenic poetry, architecture,
and the plastic arts.

Hellenic development, as such, was therefore a result of the influence
of Delphi. At Delphi, Dorians and Ionians, Spartans and Athenians, were
Hellenes. Delphic, Doric, and Ionic often occur as interchangeable terms,
because the grave differences of race were comparatively merged in the
common character impressed from Delphi. At the time of the Persian wars,
when the brilliant historic period of Hellas begins, the living influence of
Delphi had ceased. Federation under the religious shadow of its temple
had disappeared; first, Sparta had become preponderant, and had
wrapped herself up in her Peloponnesian interests; then Athens had
arisen as a great State to balance Sparta; Delphi had had to trim between
them, bribes had discredited its sanctity, seriousness and vital power had
left it. Delphi had come to be little more than a name, and what continued to exist there was merely a number of forms. But European Greece
had grown into existence, and grown into existence under Delphi's influence; Athens, Sparta, Corinth had taken their bent; what they were to
become they in the main were, and they owed it to Delphi.

An Apolline character belongs, as Dr. Curtius points out, to every
state of illumination and elevation of the human soul, and Apollo is thus
the great awakener and sustainer of genius and intellect. Why was the
destiny of Sparta so superior to that of the tribes of grave and sturdy
mountaineers left behind in northwestern Greece — tribes with much the
same original basis of mind, soul, and character as the Spartans? Because
Sparta had been in contact with the inspiring and mind-awakening influence of Delphi, so that there were moments when the intellectual
development of Hellas seemed bidding fair to find for itself a centre in
a Dorian State; and to this quickening of the Doric genius by Delphi the
Dorism of Greek lyric poetry is an abiding witness.

But the Hellas of Hellas is Athens, and it is for enabling us to see the
nature and consequences of Delphian influence upon Athens that Dr.
Curtius so deserves our gratitude. Athens was Ionian: why was she not
like Asiatic Ionia, which could found nothing, which had not character
and energy enough to balance the love of change and the love of pleasure?
In Ionia no city engaged in the enduring and heroic pursuit of great aims

existed. Why was Athens so engaged? Why did it drop the Ionic love of ornament and sumptuousness for Dorian simplicity? why was marriage treated seriously there when in Ionia it was treated with laxity? why does the Asiatic Ionia raise the idea of what is luxuriant and overflowing in taste and language, while Attica raises the idea of neatness, measure, and the purgation of superfluities? Why had Athens politicians and leaders of the people like Aristides and Pericles — men with a strong admixture of Dorian severity in their character, while in Ionia men of this seriousness occur only as recluse students and thinkers?

It was because Athens had felt the Delphic discipline. For Apollo was not only the nourisher of genius, he was also the author of every higher moral effort; he was the prophet of his father Zeus, in the highest view of Zeus, as the source of the ideas of moral order and of right. These ideas are in human nature, but they had "especially been a treasure in the possession of the less gay and more solitary tribes in the mountains of northern Greece." [26] These tribes were Delphi's first pupils, and Delphi did its best to develop those ideas which gave it a hold upon them. Thus the graver view of life, and the thoughts which deepen man's consciousness, became connected with Delphi; and there the Athenians imbibed influences of character and *Halt* which for a long time balanced in the happiest way their native vivacity and mobility, and blended with it.

The main element in our nature conquers at last; the steady, according to Aristotle's profound remark, becomes stupid, and the brilliant becomes non-sane. Dorian Sparta died in the end of dulness; Ionian Athens perished in the end for want of ballast. But their history is in their resistance to the natural excess of their own tendencies, and it is the signal merit of the volume of which we have been treating that it makes manifest the source from which this power of resistance proceeded.

CURTIUS'S *HISTORY OF GREECE* [II]

We return to this interesting history, which grows faster than we can follow it. The fourth volume of Mr. Ward's translation has appeared, and we are only at the third. Nay, in some sort we are still only at the second; for the last chapter of the second volume belongs to the history of Greece after the Persian War, and our last notice stopped at the Persian War. For after the Persian War begins a new period, having its unity in the mounting and declining fortunes of Athens; and with this period, which at the end of the third volume comes to its close in the conclusion of the Peloponnesian War and the surrender of Athens to Lysander, we desire to deal to-day.

Dr. Curtius himself says of Herodotus, that he sought "a general view of the varied multiplicity of human affairs which might enable him to *recognize the invisible connection pervading the course of their development.*"[27] This quest betokens the genuine historian, and in one of our preceding notices we pointed it out as characterizing Dr. Curtius. In the history of Greece he seeks for the essential connection, the vital development; and his work thus gains a seriousness and unity which more than make amends for certain sides of talent which are wanting. A more picturesque narrative, a more masterly handling of military matters, a more vivacious and sympathetic following of political struggles, it would be easy to find in other historians. But while some of these historians leave in the mind a mere hubbub of pictures and words, and others leave a distinct impression of but parts and moments in the subject of their history, Dr. Curtius leaves, and it is his signal merit, the impression of a whole. His translator, though his English is still blemished by such expressions as "*surexcited,*" and "states of *secondary and tertiary* rank," well maintains in his serious and solid translation this impression of a whole. And that whole, in the present case, is the course and meaning of the most important period in the life of the most important factor in the world's intellectual history — Athens. We shall try to exhibit these after Dr. Curtius, and in his own words. If we do not always quite agree with him, yet it is his grouping and handling of the facts that we have to thank for the light which makes us see them differently.

We start with B.C. 479, the days that follow Salamis and Plataea. "The victory over the Persians was at the same time a victory of democracy over aristocracy — a victory of Athens, whose constitution had fully proved itself a victory-giving power."[28] We end with B.C. 405, the days that precede the surrender of Athens to Lysander: —

> Such was the state of matters within the walls of the unhappy city. On the one side, the impetuosity of a savage demagogue, whose senseless obstinacy cut off all remaining means of preservation; on the other, the crafty leaders of the Lacedaemonian party who looked with heartless satisfaction upon the troubles rising to a height around them; while those citizens who loved their native city and her laws constituted too decided a minority for their patriotism to prove of any use. The great multitude was under the absolute influence of terror and want, and lay as an instrument, with no will of its own, in the hands of discordant and raging partisans.[29]

As we look on this picture and on that we cannot but inquire with keen interest for the causes which in less than three-quarters of a century led the "victory-giving power" of democracy from that height of triumph to this depth of ruin; more especially when we have the same "victory-giving power" at work all round us, in various stages of success, in the politics of our own day. To convince ourselves of the likeness of situation we have only to read in Dr. Curtius a passage such as the following: —

The splendour of the rise of the young Athenian State necessarily became a stumbling block for all those who considered the welfare of the States to be founded upon the cautious conduct of affairs by the members of ancient families, and who hated nothing more deeply than a political revolution which brought the multitude into power and which allowed the latter in tumultuous meetings in the market-place to decide the destinies of States. The new generation which was unfolding its forces with incredible activity would no longer have anything to do with privileged classes, but demanded that all things should be within the reach of all men. Meanwhile, in the midst of this free competition of all forces, the ancient families saw their whole authority endangered; and their fall was regarded by the adherents of the old times as the ruin of Hellenic polity and of a higher system of manners and morals.[30]

In fact, as we have already seen in the earlier part of Dr. Curtius's work, what differentiates Ionian Athens from Asiatic Ionia, is the gravity, the steadiness, the centripetal influence tending to a common Hellenism, to religious fixity, and to conservative habits, which Athens imbibed from the discipline of Delphi. This steadiness, or *Halt*, as Goethe calls it, for a long time balanced in the Athenians their native vivacity and mobility. But this conservative period ends with the Persian War, and the pure democratic development of Athens then begins; though Cimon still represented the old spirit in politics, and on domestic life and ways of thinking it still had a strong hold. "It would indeed be a natural conclusion," says Dr. Curtius, "that the mobility and love of change innate in the Attic people offered only a slight pledge for the preservation of ancient usage; but the attachment which the families of worthy citizens felt towards everything handed down to them by their fathers, and the quiet power of tradition, supported by religion and by various remnants of primitive institutions, were strong enough to hold fast the people on the given foundations." [31] Yes, but the question is *how long;* and, once you are fairly launched on the democratic incline, does the check offered by "the quiet power of tradition, supported by religion and by various remnants of primitive institutions" long endure; if it fails, where do you find a check and what is it; or can you do without one? There is much to be said for launching frankly on the democratic incline, as Athens did; Pericles felt this and Dr. Curtius feels it: —

Pericles recognized in democracy the only constitution which could count on a lasting life at Athens; it constituted her real strength, which, considering the smallness of the State and the difficulty of the tasks incumbent upon it, *lay in the free and independent participation of all in the affairs of the commonwealth, which may count upon the readiness of all to make sacrifices on its behalf, because to all is opened, by means of it, the path to equal honours and equal influence.*[32]

There cannot be a better statement of the democratic theory, and nothing can sound more promising; every individual is developed, stimulated, improved to the uttermost, because every individual feels that he is alive, that he *counts;* masses are not sacrificed, as they are apt to be when government is what M. Renan calls "an aristocratic work." How then was "the party of Progress," to use the words of Dr. Curtius, "to proceed, in order to call the democracy, in the full sense of the word, into life?" [33] —

The primary motive (of the party of reform) was the necessity of breaking the power of wealth, in order to make possible the free development of the constitution; for the liberality practised by wealthy citizens brought the poor into a condition of dependence, and served as a support for the efforts of the aristocratic party, at the same time confusing the political consciousness of the nation. To free the citizens from the operation of influences of this kind, the State moneys were employed to enable the poor to procure sources of enjoyment, without on that account feeling themselves under an obligation to single individuals among their fellow-citizens.[34]

In short: —

The power of the party of movement was based upon the multitude of the poorer citizens, and it was desired that the lower classes should be prevented neither by timidity nor by poverty from taking part in public affairs.[35]

And well may Dr. Curtius say that "the means employed for this end were of an extremely effective character!" —

The public treasury continued more and more to be used for the purpose of freeing the poorer citizens from the influence which might be exercised upon them by the munificence of the rich; of gaining their favour by means of presents and distributions of corn; and by compensation in money inducing them more and more generally to take part in public affairs. For upon the multitude of the poorer citizens was based the power of the party of reform.[36]

And this policy, Dr. Curtius thinks, was but fair: —

Since in all States the power of the ruler is surrounded by a certain splendour of life which also redounds to the credit of the entire State, in a democracy the Demos is, as a matter of fairness, entitled to share in this privilege of rulers.[37]

Not only was it fair in itself, but the condition of things which it redressed was unjust: —

Harsh contrasts in social life are an evil in the case of any and every State; but in a democracy, which is based on the joyous participation of all its citizens in the common-wealth, such contrasts are most keenly felt and amount to dissonances contravening the spirit of the constitution. In a democratic State, no class of men ought to be treated as inferior to the rest, or to feel itself hurt by the social position of the rich; no fermenting matter ought to be left in the State, and the peace of public life ought to be endangered by no feelings of envy, jealousy and distrust between the different classes of the citizens.[38]

Thus democracy was "completely established;" and we hardly require to be told further that the Athenians, thus democratized, were "a difficult people to govern; for every man wished to inquire and judge for himself, democracy being in general disinclined to have anything to do with men who lay claim to obedience." [39] Pericles, however, and the party of reform, had made their Frankenstein; what was to be done with him? Singularly enough, the greatness of Pericles seems to consist in his having provided the democracy with a dictator: —

The sovereign power belonged to the Demos. But no man could be more fully persuaded than Pericles of the incapacity of the multitude to govern itself. Every popular body must be governed, its steps guided, and its interests pointed out to it, unless the well-being of the State is to be given up to accident and unreason.[40]

Pericles, however, having destroyed the permanent conservative influences of the Athenian State, the influences of family, property, and office, did undoubtedly substitute for them, in his own personality, a governing influence even stronger, while it lasted. By the force of his personality he was permanent Commander-in-Chief, Minister of Finance, Minister of Public Works: —

No official class existed to oppose him, because all officials on the expiration of their term of office returned immediately into private life. Pericles alone, invested with a continuous official authority which commanded all the various branches of public life, stood in solitary grandeur firm and calm above the surging State.[41]

But what, then, becomes of the essential idea of democracy — *the free and independent participation of all in the affairs of the commonwealth?* Dr. Curtius himself tells us, in describing the government of Pericles: —

Thus a consistent and firm Government was made possible, such as all reasonable citizens must have desired to live under in times of danger; *though, on the other hand, it is true that all the principles of democracy were virtually abolished* — viz, the constant change and distribution of official power, and even the responsibility attaching to it, and forming the strongest guarantee of the sovereignty of the people.[42]

The idea in the mind of Pericles, therefore, was "a combination of democracy and monocracy;" and in order to realize this idea, "Pericles became a party man, and combined with Ephialtes and the other leaders of the party of progress" to democratize Athens as we have seen. But then the anchor-chains by which the ship of State held — the anchor-chains of the influence of family and property, and of the old institutions which made government "an aristocratic work" — were cut, not in order that the people by free development and by the practical school of public life might become a set of individuals able each to think and act wisely for himself, but "in order that the people *might unconditionally give itself up to the guidance of the orator in possession of its confidence.*"[43] This is much less than the other; but Pericles, it seems, was "fully persuaded of the incapacity of the multitude to govern itself,"[44] and that it should be taught and enabled "to give its confidence to the right man," instead of to the often blind superiorities of family, property, and office, was something. Dr. Curtius says; "The Attic Demos was beyond a doubt superior to all other civic communities in this respect, that its happy natural gifts supplied it with a sure tact and correct judgment in the choice of its leaders, and that it knew how to follow these leaders when chosen, if they with superior intelligence indicated to it its true interests."[45] No doubt it redounds to the credit of the Athenian people that it followed Pericles. But how long did it follow him? Fifteen years, and at the end of that time very imperfectly. And afterwards it followed Cleon and Cleophon. Something must have interfered, then, with the natural effects of the beneficent revolutions wrought by the party of progress. Dr. Curtius finds this interference mainly in two disturbing causes: the plague and the clubs. Of the plague he says: —

> During the whole course of the war no more fatal event happened than the Attic pestilence . . . for, although the position of Athens towards foreign States remained for a time the same, yet the city had at home undergone essential changes. The flower of the citizens had perished; many families in which ancient discipline and usage had maintained themselves had died out, and thus the living connections with the age of Aristides and Cimon had come to an end.[46]

That is to say, as long as some remains were left of that non-democratic order which the party of progress was for eradicating, the Athenian State had still something to hold it together, had elements of permanence and stability; when they were gone and democracy was left to itself, the pulverizing and dissolving forces in it worked fully. It is to exaggerate the effect of the plague to say that it *caused* this: it only quickened a little the disappearance of checks which were already condemned and failing. The true check had been the personality of Pericles, the dictatorship of Pericles; this could not outlast his life, and even before he died it had been manifest how things were tending: —

> The moral change which had befallen the Attic community had, it is true, even during the lifetime of Pericles, manifested itself by means of sufficiently clear premonitory signs; but Pericles had, notwithstanding, up to the days of his last illness, remained the centre of the State; the people had again and

again returned to him, and *by subordinating themselves to the personal author-ity of Pericles* had succeeded in recovering the demeanour which befitted them. But now the voice was hushed which had been able to sway the unruly citizens even against their will. *No other authority was in existence* — no aristocracy, no official class, no board of experienced statesmen — nothing, in fact, to which the citizens might have looked for guidance and control. *The multitude had recovered absolute independence.*[47]

And now, as men of the stamp of Pericles are rare, it got another sort of leaders: —

Pericles stood *above* the multitude. He ruled by arousing the noble and active impulses in the minds of the citizens, who by the earnestness marking his treatment of them, and by the moral demands which he made upon them, *were raised above their own level;* they were ashamed to give voice in his hear-ing to their weaknesses and low cravings. His successors were obliged to adopt other means; in order to acquire influence they took advantage not so much of the strong as of the weak points in the character of the citizens, and achieved popularity by flattering their inclinations and endeavouring to satisfy the cravings of their baser nature. Thus the demagogues, who had formerly been the leaders and solemn counsellors of the people, now became its servants and flatterers.[48]

And thus, also, accordingly: —

In a short space of time the civic community of Athens became an unsteady multitude which allowed itself to be swayed by uncertain feelings, a multitude which vacillated between arrogance and cowardice, between infidelity and superstitious excitement.[49]

The other main cause which spoiled the fair experiment of democracy at Athens was, according to Dr. Curtius, the clubs: —

These clubs differed in all respects from the political associations of earlier times. They were for the most part composed of members of ancient families with innate oligarchical tendencies — passionate and excited young men of loose habits of life, who found no sphere for their ambition in the Athens of the day, who had received a sophistic education and were full of unintelligible political theories, which obscured in them the plain perception of law and sense of duty; who were accordingly vain and devoid of conscientiousness, con-temners of law and usage, and scorners of the multitude and its rule. In propor-tion as the foreign policy of the State became democratic, the aristocratic clubs grew into associations of anti-patriotic conspirators.[50]

It is well to remember what one of the great men of the Renaissance, Gemistus, says to the philosopher: that he should always suppose there is some fault in himself when he cannot bring people to his way of thinking. Surely it is of the very essence of *country,* of *constitution,* if they are worth anything, to be attaching; to inspire respect and affection. Then they are not threatened by intriguers; or, if they are threatened, they easily get the better of them. But what blame to the young Barbarians of Athens if they were "scorners of the multitude and its rule," when this multitude "vacillated between arrogance and cowardice, between infidelity and superstitious excitement"? They felt that this multitude had no right to be in power, that it had upset an old state of things which was better than its own rule; they intrigued against it, and their intrigues produced confusion because what they intrigued against had too little worth and dignity to be a firm rallying-point. So we are brought to the end of the period with which we to-day deal, to the crowning defeat of Aegos-potami and to the spectacle presented by the Athenians there: —

Opposed to a well-trained and well-supplied force, which unconditionally obeyed the will of a commander as sagacious as he was enterprising, this the last fleet which Athens was able to send out was *discordant in itself and split up into parties; its strangely mixed crews lacking all discipline, coherence, and moral bearing, and being commanded by six generals who severally pursued utterly different aims.*[51]

To this end has come the great work of the party of progress — "to call the democracy, in the full sense of the word, into life."

Dr. Curtius, like modern Liberals generally, considers this work a good and wise one; like them, he is disposed to throw the blame of its not succeeding anywhere rather than on the work itself. We have let him show, in his own words, the nature and history of the work; they are so interesting that one is tempted, in defiance of Mr. Cobden, to think that "all the works of Thucydides" may be nearly as good reading as the *Times,*[52] at any rate in the Whitsuntide recess. For us, the moral we draw is not that the aim of the party of progress was bad, but that it was inadequate. To give to a whole people entire freedom and the practical school of public life is well; but entire freedom and the practical school of public life are not enough; even joined, as at Athens, to high natural intelligence they are not enough; they are not self-acting for a people's salvation; by themselves, they even bring it not to salvation but to ruin. What Athens lived upon, in her brilliant Periclean period, was the stores of *Halt* and character accumulated through less seen and less heard generations, these stores being moved and used by the new, vigorous force of democracy, by a whole gifted people with the fresh sense of being alive and astir. They were used, and used up, and then came the end; here is our moral. It may be said, indeed, that nothing lasts, and that we may well be satisfied with a nation if it has produced a Periclean period, and done no more. Something of this sort Dr. Curtius urges on behalf of Pericles, as head of the party of reform: "He was aware that the true greatness of an epoch is not dependent on the time of its endurance; he knew that the realization of the loftiest ideal of a Hellenic community in Athens would be a possession for ever. Accordingly, notwithstanding the sadness of his own end, the work of his life was crowned with immortal success." [53] This is nobly said, but it does not quite satisfy the aspirations of a good citizen, who demands of the builders of his State to make it stand permanently, not in spirit only, but in palpable body. And though to permanence of this kind human things can but approximate, yet these aspirations of a good citizen are, we cannot but think, natural and just; the true builder of a State should and will procure for them satisfaction.

CURTIUS'S *HISTORY OF GREECE* [III]

We have got into the ungracious habit of remarking on the spots which blemish Mr. Ward's solid and sensible translation of this useful history, and to be faithful to that habit we will begin by saying that in the volume now before us we find "a city *befallen* by its great calamity," and "that all those *were pried on* who had stood in any relations with the oligarchs." But in general the translator seems to us to show in this volume a style much improved by increasing practice; the English is more easy and idiomatic than in his earlier volumes, and sometimes, as in the account of Socrates, or in the final estimate of Epaminondas, rises into real impressiveness and power.

The volume now before us continues the history of Greece from the surrender of Athens down to the battle of Mantinea, a period of about forty years. This period exhibits the reign of Sparta and her mistakes, the partial recovery by Athens of her old position, the rise of Thebes to be a great Power. That the narrow and stationary policy of Sparta could not work out the salvation of Hellas we need not say, for Dr. Curtius is never weary of saying it. We prefer to continue to point out, from Dr. Curtius's own history, the insufficiency of the anti-Spartan policy — the democratic policy, the policy of movement — to found anything. We think that Dr. Curtius is too much inclined to stamp this policy as right, whereas events prove it wrong, or at least inadequate. Absolute freedom, the independent participation of all in the affairs of the commonwealth, the abolition of the permanent conservative influences in the State, influences of family, property, and office — this, we have seen, was the democratic programme. Those who praise it say that it makes *all* live and *all* count, and rescues the masses from being sacrificed; those who blame it call it, with Aeschylus, merely "an unblest escape from all restraint." We prefer to neither praise nor blame it, but to call it *inadequate*. Unlimited freedom and the practical school of public life are not enough by themselves, are not self-acting for a people's salvation — this is what we say, and what Greek history, and all history, seems to us to prove. The power to respect, the power to obey, are at least as needful for man as unlimited freedom and the practical school of public life; give him these last alone, teach him to rely on these last alone, and you give him forces which but wear out both him and themselves. When first they appear they find present a store of habits of respect and obedience accumulated from old times of discipline, old institutions; the new forces are highly stimulative, undoubtedly, and they create a new life; instead of accepting its chief as hereditary, a Hippias or Hipparchus, the people now choose him as the best, a Pericles. For it has still the *habit* to respect and obey, but its one *doctrine* now is to be free and independent, and the doctrine is at variance with the habit and beats it, and the people will soon have a Cleon who does not make them respect and obey, but lets them feel free and independent; and so a society goes to pieces. And even when circumstances give it a chance to recover itself it cannot; it has no *Halt,* nothing to bind and brace it.

The faults of Sparta, the necessities of Persia, the successes of Conon, gave Athens a chance again after her crushing defeat by Lysander; her walls were rebuilt, her maritime influence revived, Greek States looked to her to lead, she seemed likely to become once more a great Power with a great policy. She could not; national virtue was gone out of her, she could produce henceforth only great individuals, not a great people. Dr. Curtius shall show us that this was so; shall show us how great a change both within and without had come over the Athens of Aristides and Pericles. First for the change within: —

Poetic art at Athens maintained itself for a season at its full height even after the symmetry of public life had been destroyed; but only in the works of Sophocles, who continued to live in the spirit of the Periclean age. After his death poetry, like music, was *seized by the same current which dissolved the foundations of the people's life,* and which swept away the soil wherein the emotions of the classical period had been rooted. Accordingly, in these times of general oscillation, poetry was unable to supply a moral anchorage; the old perished, but the modern age, with all its readiness in thought and speech, was incapable of creating a new art as a support to its children. In the same way the faith of former generations had been cast aside like antiquated household gear, but without any other assurance of morality, without any other impulse towards the virtues indispensable for the life of the community having been obtained in its stead. The need of a regeneration was acknowledged; serious endeavours were made to introduce improvements and order; but political reforms could not heal such wounds as these, or furnish a new basis for the commonweal.[54]

And now for the change without, the political incapacity which always accompany such inward disease: —

The appearance of Conon suddenly changed everything for the better. But neither was the influence of Conon enduring. His task could only be that of freeing Athens from the ban under which she had lain, of restoring to her freedom of movement, obtaining for her allies, and, as it were, opening the portal for a new era in her history. The rest depended on the conduct of the Athenians themselves; it was imperative that they should in a spirit of self-sacrifice recover their manly vigour, and by their own exertions continue the construction of the edifice on the basis offered to them. *But no such sustained onward effort ensued.*[55]

And therefore see what happened at the peace of Antalcidas: —

Thus it came to pass that, in spite of the various particular successes obtained by Athens in this war, she upon the whole lost more in it than she gained. At its close she was more thoroughly disintegrated than before; she had lost all her allies, had found her best men untrustworthy, and had anew recognized the insufficiency of her own resources; and was in the end forced under the pressure of necessity to conclude a peace which deeply injured the honour of the city and by no means corresponded to the original purpose of the war.[56]

So it was, too, after the successes of Timotheus ten years later: —

Athens herself was no longer what she had been of old. The citizens were no longer joyously ready to make all necessary sacrifices, no longer energetically determined to stake everything upon the restoration of their power. The most splendid successes of Timotheus failed to call forth any lasting ardour.[57]

So it was, again, when Leuctra had given to Athens another splendid chance, and she actually summoned the Peloponnesian States to send deputies to Athens, and made as though she were assuming the leadership which they, on their part, were willing and eager to confer on her. *"It soon, however, became manifest that the Athenians were incapable of taking the direction of Peloponnesian affairs into their hands."* [58]

Therefore the lead came to Thebes, whose guiding spirit, Epaminondas, is brought before us by Dr. Curtius with much feeling and power. There at last had come at Thebes the same change which at Athens we have seen come earlier; the old traditional institutions, the aristocratical organization of the State, broke up; a democratic development prevailed. As at Athens, the new force working with what the old force bequeathed to it produced a time of high energy and a great man to wield that energy. The analogy between Epaminondas and Pericles is striking; "indeed it would be difficult to find in the entire course of Greek history any two great statesmen who in spite of differences of character and of outward conditions of life resembled one another so greatly and were men so truly the peers of one another as Pericles and Epaminondas." [59] The nature of the Boeotian race was grosser than that of the Athenian, the Theban aristocracy during its rule had been more brutal than the Athenian, the democracy was less spiritually gifted; the action of Epaminondas upon his people was more moral, less intellectual, than that of Pericles. The

Christian world resorts to Greece for mental stimulus, not moral; our gaze, therefore, is fixed on Pericles rather than Epaminondas. With the Pagan world, whose sources of moral inspiration were more scanty, it was different; to them Epaminondas was a figure of incomparable interest, and his character has indeed a rare beauty, and with him the acceptance of the programme of the "party of movement" shows many more reserves, much more resolution not to be forced beyond what he thought right, to act, when necessary, against the mechanical policy of his party, than with Pericles. He certainly, as he showed in Achaia, "had a loftier end in view than a democratic propaganda, and desired not to excite party passions but to appease them." [60] The propaganda, however, remained, and was the one idea of the many, the one policy the party of movement in general thought saving; that in all cases where a democratic power got the upper hand, "the entire political system of the community should be radically changed, the ancient families driven into exile, their possessions confiscated, legal proceedings instituted against all the members of the wealthier classes as pretended friends of Sparta, property belonging to the temples seized, and a multitude of new citizens admitted into the civic body." [61] While Epaminondas lived he in great measure imposed his own will on the Theban democracy; like Pericles, he was a dictator; but "no sooner had his influence been impaired than they fell back into their own faults; and to such intervals belong those actions which brought shame and failure to the Thebans." [62] Therefore, his work upon Thebes ended with his own life; "like Pericles, Epaminondas left no successor behind him, and his death also was the close of a historical epoch which could never again return." [63] When he was dying on the field of Mantinea, when his policy was victorious at all points, when the fruit for which he had toiled waited only to be gathered, he felt that there was no one to gather it; before he drew out the spear, he recommended his country *to make peace.* "He lived to acknowledge that the goal for which he had striven had not been reached and could not be reached." [64] How indeed could it be, by the virtue of no better forces than were contained in the democratic programme: *Unlimited freedom, absolute independence, strict extirpation of all institutions with an aristocratic taint, constant participation of every citizen in the management of public affairs?* It could not; and after Mantinea, no less than after Leuctra, the political situation is truly summed up in these words: — "In spite of these successes the result was small. The old system had been destroyed, the overbearing power of Sparta had been annihilated; but instead of a new and fixed order of relations, there was perceptible among the Hellenic tribes nothing but an increase of agitation and confusion." [65]

Accordingly Socrates, who assuredly was no mere conservative, who introduced a stream of thought so fresh, bold, and transforming that it frightened "respectable" people and was the cause of his death, Socrates was never weary of recalling the Hellenic mind to the old-fashioned maxims of righteousness, temperance, and self-knowledge engraved on the temple at Delphi. The democratic programme and the teaching of the Sophists possessed the thoughts and affections of the most living communities in the Hellenic family; and the gospel of both these liberalisms came pretty much to the same thing — *freedom and movement.* Where you move to, and how you use your freedom, are left out of the account; and the ground-idea of the working of Socrates and Plato may really be said to be this: *the insufficiency of the liberal programme for salvation.* Modern Liberals do not enough consider that although then, as now, Liberalism could point to its continual advance and its victories of the day and hour, yet the long run, the full development of things, proved Socrates and Plato right.

Of Socrates Dr. Curtius treats in his chapter on "Athens after Her Restoration;" and the whole of this chapter, with its account of the change in religion, poetry, music, and thought in general, is most interesting, and shows to great advantage the author's fulness of knowledge and powers of criticism. Particularly we recommend the pages on Euripides, that "lifelong sufferer from the unsolved conflict between speculation and art," [66] who yet was able by the force and versatility of his genius to make good his place by the side of "Aeschylus the soldier of Marathon, and Sophocles the witness of the Periclean age." [67] It is not difficult to do justice to Euripides in respect of "all his natural gifts and all the acquisitions of his experience and culture; the quick sensibility of his disposition; his brilliant gift of finding the right word for every phase of feeling; his accurate knowledge of all the impulses moving his generation; and his sophistic training, which enabled him incisively to illustrate and account for all standpoints of human opinion." [68] But in general the critic is wont to satisfy himself with passing from this praise to an unfavourable verdict on Euripides, as lacking the "inner contentment, the inner illumination of mind, which mark out the born poet." [69] He did lack them; but the critic, to be complete, should add, like Dr. Curtius, this commentary: —

Euripides, as a poet not less than as a man, was a true martyr to Sophistry. It possessed without satisfying him; he employed it in order to bestow a new interest upon art; he contended for the right of every individual to approach in inquiring meditation all things human and divine; *but at the same time he was not blind to the dangers of this tendency. He openly declared them, uttered warnings and pronounced invectives against it, and at last wrote an entire tragedy* ("The Bacchae") *with no other object than that of representing the miserable end of a man who opposes his reason to the system of the gods.*[70]

The author of "Archelaus" reminds us of Macedon. We hear that Dr. Curtius intends to give us but one volume more: to bring us to the establishment of the Macedonian supremacy by "that dishonest victory" of Chaeronea, and there to leave us. We hope he will be induced to reconsider his intention. We can ill spare the account of Alexander and his Asiatic conquests; and we shall be glad to persuade Dr. Curtius that there is at any rate enough which is Hellenic in Macedon to make it right that the political history of ancient Greece should end with the fall of the Macedonian power, not its rise; with the last Philip, and his son, not the first.

CURTIUS'S *HISTORY OF GREECE* [IV]

With real regret we say to ourselves, on closing the volume now before us, that here we have the last instalment of Mr. Ward's sound and substantial translation of this excellent history. As we read the volume, however, we become convinced that Dr. Curtius has done right in ending here, and in not carrying on the history — as in our review of his fourth volume we expressed our wish to see him carry it — to the death of Alexander. The characteristic political life of the Hellenic people ceased, as Dr. Curtius clearly shows, with the battle of Chaeronea and the supremacy of Philip of Macedon; and a history of ancient Greece fitly ends with the extinction of the characteristic political life of the Hellenic people. Macedonia had many Hellenic elements, but its political life and system were in no wise those of a true Greek State. Its conquests, therefore, though they spread wide the Greek language and culture, and made them cosmopolitan, did nothing to spread the type of a genuine Greek State, like the States where this culture had had its rise. And, this type disappearing, it was no longer Greece itself which was charged with the continued development of Greek culture, but the world.

The present volume affords to Dr. Curtius, before he parts with us, the opportunity of once more showing his strength in all the points where he is strong. His vivid account of the mountain and river system of Macedonia recalls the admirable geographical touch which charmed us in the former volumes. The moral and philosophical interest arising from the development of national character, and from the growth, sure and fatal, of its faults, reappear strikingly in the continuation and close of the life of independent Athens. Finally, the personal and dramatic interest, which Dr. Curtius has so often aroused by his mode of treating his personages, returns with all its force in his presentation of Demosthenes.

But Dr. Curtius shall himself show us his quality as a geographer, as a philosophical moralist, and as a delineator of men. What can be more delightful than this sketch of Aegae or Edessa, the primitive capital of the royal race of the founders of Macedonia, the Argive Temenidae: —

In all Macedonia there is no more excellent situation. As the traveller coming from Salonica ascends the gradually narrowing plain, his attention is already from afar enchained by the glittering silver streak which reaches vertically down into the valley from the rim of mountain side nearest to the front. It announces the waterfalls of Vodena, which lies on the site of ancient Aegae, on a well-wooded declivity turned straight to the east, while in the background rises in solemn grandeur the lofty mountain range. The waterfalls, which at this day mark out the place and give it a striking resemblance to Tibur, were not in existence in ancient times. Only gradually, by means of a progressive formation of tufa, the waters have managed to stop up the passages in the rocks, through which they formerly found a subterraneous outlet. But at all times Aegae must have been a spot of exceeding beauty and salubrity, the portal of the highlands and the dominant castle of the plain in the rear of which it lies, like Mycenae or Ilium. The view from the castle extends over the gulf to the hills of the Chalcidice, and at its feet unite all the main rivers of the country. Aegae was the natural capital of the land. With its foundation the history of Macedonia had its beginning; Aegae is the germ out of which the Macedonian Empire grew.[71]

The present volume exhibits the ultimate development of political character in Athens and the other Greek republics. In what condition did Philip find them all? What had they to oppose to his ambitious projects and to his great material force — great, but not greater than what Greece had already repelled at the Persian invasion?

The position of affairs could not have been more promising (for Philip). Thebes had sunk back into her former impotence, and, after the death of Epaminondas, Athens was the solitary State in which the idea of a national policy survived, but it was merely a dreamy reminiscence of the past which her citizens would not bear to renounce, while at the same time they felt themselves possessed of no vital powers for making the idea a reality. . . . When Philip took into consideration this condition of things; when with his keen glance he perceived how the petty States had degenerated, how the still existing forces of population were uselessly consuming themselves in party discord, in war, and in a lawless life of mercenary service, how among the best citizens many were longing for a vigorous leadership without finding the right men for the purpose in their own people; when Philip could convince himself how in the same measure in which the faith in the vitality of the small republics had sunk, the reputation of royal power had risen in the eyes of many of the most intelligent Hellenes; he naturally and necessarily arrived at the conviction that the objects of his personal ambition were also that which was historically necessary and alone rational, and must thus in the end be also acknowledged by the Greeks, in spite of their obstinate local patriotism and of their contempt for the Macedonian people. The national history of the Greeks had lived its life to an end in the orbit of their native country, in the more limited sense of the term, and under the form of Republican Constitutions.[72]

And why this loss of faith among the Greeks themselves in the vitality of their small republics? Take Athens, the chief of them. "The great difference between the new and the old Athens lay in this, that it was now no longer the entire civic community which of one accord desired progress, and that the efforts made had no endurance. Athens betrayed her exhaustion, and when she had made a vigorous advance she soon sank back into an attitude of fatigue, and craved for nothing but a tranquil enjoyment of life, and undisturbed comfort within the limited sphere of her civic life."[73] The aristocratic and the democratic classes were alike enfeebled. "On the one side a wealthy intellectual life, floating in ideal elevation, from the standpoint of which the Attic civic State was regarded as a thing without value; on the other, an indolent existence, swayed by selfishness, lazily sunk in obedience to daily habit, and unwilling to allow its ease to be disturbed by any exertion. It was thus that the Athens of Eubulus drifted on, like a ship without a helmsman, with the current of the age." [74]

The sixteen years of the administration of Eubulus (B.C. 354–338) mark, therefore, a critical time in Athenian history. Eubulus was generally acceptable. He pleased the poor by making the distribution of the festival-moneys, formerly occasional, a regular law-ordained practice, and by doubling and trebling the amount distributed. He pleased the rich by "a peace-policy, which kept at a distance the terror of the property-tax." [75] Eubulus, in short, "knew how to strike chords which found a ready response on all sides; he based his policy upon the low and vulgar inclinations of humanity, and by satisfying these estranged his fellow-citizens from all more serious endeavours. The grandeur and loftiness of Athenian democracy had vanished, while all the germs of perniciousness contained in it were fully developed." [76] Eubulus was able for sixteen years to conduct on these lines the Athens of Pericles, and one can well understand that the deterioration worked by such a leading was fatal. What one asks oneself is, why the faultier side in the Athenian character, the side which made the reign of Eubulus possible, should have finally prevailed rather than the nobler side, the side which made possible the reign of Pericles? One asks oneself whether it is inevitable, then, that the faultier side of a national character should be always the one to prevail finally; and whether, therefore, since every national character has its faultier side, the greatness of no great nation can be permanent. And the answer probably is that the greatness cannot be permanent of any nation which is not great by its mere material numbers as well as by its qualities. Great qualities are balanced by faults, and in any community there will be more individuals with the faults of their nation than with its great qualities. Now, in a small community like Athens, a community counting its members by thousands instead of by millions, there is not a sufficient recruiting-ground from whence to draw ever-fresh supplies of men of the better type, capable of maintaining their country's greatness at a high level permanently, or of bringing it back there after it has for a time retrograded owing to faults or misfortunes.

However, in no State, great or small, is it the business of a good citizen to believe that the decline and fall of his country are inevitable, and to resign himself to that belief. The grandeur of Demosthenes, and his civic superiority to a man, even, so fascinating as Plato, consists in his having refused to allow himself to entertain such a belief, in his having worked as if the restoration of the true Athens were possible, in his having accomplished something towards that restoration, and in his having thus, though he could not save Athens, contributed in no mean degree to save the ideal of national greatness and of true political effort among mankind. Dr. Curtius shall characterize for us both him and Plato — the divine Plato, who indeed "passes far beyond that which was comprehended in the moral consciousness of his nation," and who therefore "stands like a prophet above his times and his people." [77] But, "In proportion as Plato in his ideal demands rose above the data of the circumstances and principles around him, it became impossible to expect that he would exercise a transforming influence upon the great body of the people. He was by his whole nature far more aristocratic than Socrates, the simple man of the people; and his teachings and aims could only become the possession of a circle of elect." [78]

Dear, therefore, as Athens was to Plato, he found himself by nature unable to look for her recovery or to strive for it. Demosthenes, on the contrary, amidst "the dark experiences of his early life, yet acquired confidence in the sound and honest spirit which lived in the better part of the civic community — a confidence which never afterwards deserted him." [79] Towards the followers of Plato, who constituted an intellectual power at Athens, Demosthenes stood in an attitude of direct opposition. For "he could not but be averse from any philosophy which estranged man from his civic duties, and removed him from the sphere of practical efficiency into the realms of ideas." [80] On the other hand, "He closely studied the ideas of Solon, in whose sayings and laws he found the moral mission of the Attic State most perfectly expressed; he drew strength from recalling the great past of his native city, and already for this reason loved Thucydides more than any other author; to him he felt inwardly akin; the work of Thucydides was to him, so to speak, the canonical book of the Attic spirit; he is said to have copied it out eight times with his own hand, and to have known the greater part of it by heart." [81] Demosthenes was in vital sympathy, therefore, with the Athenian democracy; nevertheless,

His talents had not easily and lightly developed themselves by following the prevailing tendencies of the age; on the contrary, he was opposed to all the tendencies of the present, to rhetoric, to sophistry and philosophy, and similarly to the great world and to the political sentiments which ruled the citizens in the times of Eubulus. It was in solitary struggles that he laboured and strove to form himself, and it was thus that he impressed upon his development the perfect stamp of his own individuality. The weight of the seriousness of his life is impressed upon his eloquence; hence his aversion from all the phrase-making and from rhetorical verbiage. His style is short and condensed; he adheres strictly to the subject, seeking to seize it in the most thorough possible way from every side, and to cut off by anticipation all possible objections. With this mastery over the dialectical art are combined a force of moral conviction and a passionate hatred of all that is base, an inflexible courage, and a fervent love for his native city; so that thus the art of the orator becomes the expression of the entire man.[82]

Demosthenes did not succeed, and with the defeat of Chaeronea ends the genuine existence of the Greek republics and of Athens, the pearl of them. We regret to part with Dr. Curtius; but he has convinced us, we repeat, that he does right in ending his history here. In its close, as also throughout its entire course, his history remains faithful to those moral ideas which, however they may be sometimes obscured or denied, are yet in the natural order of things the master-light for men of the Germanic race, for both Germans and Englishmen. And in our common, instinctive appreciation of those ideas lies the true, the indestructible ground of sympathy between Germany and England.

Notes

[1] On Thursday, August 20, 1868, the Irish mail train collided near Abergele, Wales, with a number of detached freight cars one of which was loaded with petroleum. The ensuing explosion and fire killed thirty-three persons, including Lord Farnham and his wife.

[2] This was a moment of singular extravagance in the history of Ritualism. The activities of Father Ignatius (the Reverend Joseph Leycester Lyne, 1837–1908) provoked a riot in Lombard Street on September 18, 1868, which was extensively commented upon in *The Times*. (See also Charles L. Graves, *Mr. Punch's History of Modern England*, 4 vols., [London, 1921–1922,] II, 106–108.) The *Spectator* had lately reported a Ritualist ceremonial at All Saints', Lambeth, on the eve of the nativity of the Virgin, and also a harvest home at Haydock, Lancashire, which included a "choir boy in a violet cassock, bearing on his head a round basket of fruit, vine-leaves, &c," and "a pig's head, decked out with flowers, corn and berries, a large pat of butter stamped with a lamb, two smaller pats of butter, twelve fresh eggs in moss baskets" (September 19, 1868, pp. 1090–91).

[3] Connop Thirlwall, Bishop of St. David's (1797–1875), *A History of Greece*, 8 vols. (London, 1844).

[4] George Grote (1794–1871), *A History of Greece*, 12 vols. (London, 1846–1856).

[5] Theodor Mommsen (1817–1903), *The History of Rome*, trans. W. P. Dickson, 4 vols. (London, 1862–1866).

[6] At the Wesleyan Conference at Liverpool, August 13, 1868, a letter was read

from E. B. Pusey opposing a bill currently in the House of Commons dealing with religious interests at the University of Oxford. *The Times* gave the affair extensive editorial comment, August 15, 1868, p. 10, cols. 5–6.

[7] Mme. Rachel was Sarah Rachel Levison (*née* Russell). One-time keeper of a fried-fish shop in Vere St. Clare Market, she emerged in 1861 in Bond Street as Mme. Rachel, whose beauty culture professed to make women "beautiful for ever." In 1867 she was said to have paid £400 for a box at the opera. On September 25, 1868, she was sentenced to five years' penal servitude for swindling Mrs. Mary Tucker Borradaile, widow of a colonel in the Madras Cavalry, who aspired, with Mme. Rachel's encouragement, to marry Lord Ranelagh. See *The Times*, September 26, 1868, p. 9, cols. 2–5.

[8] Jean Charles Léonard Simonde de Sismondi (1773–1842), *Histoire des Français*, 31 vols. (Paris, 1821–1844).

[9] Henry Fynes Clinton (1781–1852), *Fasti Hellenici. The Civil and Literary Chronology of Greece, from the Earliest Accounts to the Death of Augustus*, 3 vols. (Oxford, 1830–1834).

[10] Arnold is partly quoting, partly paraphrasing *The History of Greece*, I, 39–42.

[11] *Ibid.*, 43–44.

[12] *Ibid.*, 49.

[13] *Ibid.*, 31–32.

[14] *Ibid.*, 66.

[15] *Ibid.*, 88.

[16] *Ibid.*, 93.

[17] *Ibid.*, 94.

[18] *Ibid.*, 31.

[19] *Ibid.*, 113.

[20] *The History of Greece*, II, 170–171.

[21] *Ibid.*, 253–254.

[22] *Ibid.*, 254.

[23] Mr. B. Lucraft, "a working-man, — a very clever working-man, it is said," was elected "at the bottom of the list of returned candidates, for Finsbury to the Metropolitan School Board," *Spectator*, December 3, 1870, p. 1439. At the second meeting of the London School Board, December 21, 1870, Mr. Lucraft entered the debate on the salary for the clerk and secretary to the Board. "Mr. Lucraft said he considered the salary of 800*l*. much too high. From the pile of papers that he had received from intending candidates he observed that there was no lack of able men anxious and willing to accept the office. He would support the payment of a good salary, but not an extravagant one. He believed the Board would get just as good a man for 500*l*. as for 1,000*l*. Many men receiving the former sum were really equal in every way, and sometimes superior, to those who had 1,000*l*. a year, the only difference being that they had not been quite so fortunate. (A laugh.) He had wished that the committee could have gone on the same plan with regard to the salary of the secretary as they had in suggesting that the messenger should receive 25s. a week. They knew perfectly well that they could get any number of messengers at those wages, and he believed they would get a very sufficient clerk for 500*l*. Some of the best men in the country would compete for the post at such a salary, and there was no reason why the Board should give more. He asked them to consider the rate-payers in the matter. In his canvass he made no promises as to economy, but for all that he went in for being economical. (A laugh.) He was a rate-payer himself, and he admitted that he had something to do to make both ends meet," *The Times*, December 22, 1870, p. 10, cols. 4–5.

[24] *The History of Greece*, II, 445.

[25] *Ibid.*, 205.

[26] *Ibid.*, 83.

[27] *Ibid.*, 502.

[28] *Ibid.*, 315.

[29] *Ibid.*, III, 535.

[30] *Ibid.*, II, 263.
[31] *Ibid.*, 418.
[32] *Ibid.*, 440.
[33] *Ibid.*, 442.
[34] *Ibid.*, 444.
[35] *Ibid.*, 447–448.
[36] *Ibid.*, 445–448. Arnold has condensed here.
[37] *Ibid.*, 444.
[38] *Ibid.*
[39] *Ibid.*, 455.
[40] *Ibid.*, 441.
[41] *Ibid.*, 459.
[42] *Ibid.*, 159.
[43] *Ibid.*, 442.
[44] *Ibid.*, 441.
[45] *Ibid.*, 442.
[46] *Ibid.*, III, 81.
[47] *Ibid.*, 84–85.
[48] *Ibid.*, 85.
[49] *Ibid.*, 84.
[50] *Ibid.*, 316.
[51] *Ibid.*, 518–519.
[52] Richard Cobden (1804–1865), statesman and economist, said in his final speech, at Rochdale, November 23, 1864: "When I was at Athens, I sallied out one summer morning to see the far-famed river, the Ilyssus, and, after walking for some hundred yards up what appeared to be the bed of a winter torrent, I came up to a number of Athenian launderesses, and I found they had dammed up this far-famed classic river, and that they were using every drop of water for their linen and such sanitary purposes. I say, why should not the young gentlemen who are taught all about the geography of the Ilyssus know something about the geography of the Mississippi, the Ohio, the Missouri? There has been of late a good deal of talk about the advantages or disadvantages of classical education. I am a great advocate of culture of every kind; and I say, where you can find men who, in addition to profound classical learning, like Professor Goldwin Smith, or Professor Rogers, of Oxford, have a vast knowledge of modern affairs, and who, as well as scholars, are at the same time thinkers, — these are men I acknowledge to have a vast superiority over me, and I bow to those men with reverence for those superior advantages. But to bring young men from college with no knowledge of the country where the great drama of modern political and national life is being worked out — who are totally ignorant of countries like America, but who, for good or for evil, are exercising and will exercise more influence in this country than any other persons — to take young men, destitute of knowledge about countries like that — their geography, their modern history, their population, and their resources, and to place them in responsible positions in the Government of this country — I say it is imperilling your best interests, and every remonstrance that can be made against such a state of education ought to be made by every public man who values the future welfare of his country." *Speeches on Questions of Public Policy*, ed. John Bright and James E. Thorold Rogers, 2 vols. (London, 1870), II, 364.
[53] *The History of Greece*, III, 80.
[54] *Ibid.*, IV, 115–116.
[55] *Ibid.*, 285.
[56] *Ibid.*, 294–295.
[57] *Ibid.*, 374. Arnold here omits the important words "for war."
[58] *Ibid.*, 415–416.
[59] *Ibid.*, 490.
[60] *Ibid.*, 466.
[61] *Ibid.*, 467.
[62] *Ibid.*, 491.

[63] *Ibid.*, 492.

[64] *Ibid.*, 488.

[65] *Ibid.*, 455. Here Arnold takes the passage out of its context to support his political argument.

[66] *Ibid.*, 90.

[67] *Ibid.*, 84.

[68] *Ibid.*, 91.

[69] *Ibid.*, 98.

[70] *Ibid.*, 97.

[71] *Ibid.*, V, 21–22.

[72] *Ibid.*, 58–59.

[73] *Ibid.*, 78.

[74] *Ibid.*, 212.

[75] *Ibid.*, 139.

[76] *Ibid.*, 138.

[77] *Ibid.*, 164.

[78] *Ibid.*

[79] *Ibid.*, 219.

[80] *Ibid.*, 229.

[81] *Ibid.*, 230.

[82] *Ibid.*, 231–232.

Obermann

Academy
I (October 9, 1869), 1–3

Arnold's short association with the *Academy* began with his review of Etienne Pivert de Senancour's *Obermann*. Dr. Charles E. C. B. Appleton, the editor, gave it the place of honor as the initial article in his first issue. This was in keeping with the high tone which the new periodical took as "a monthly record of literature, learning, science, and art." Arnold is reviewing a new edition of the book: *Obermann. Nouvelle édition, revue et corrigée avec une préface, par George Sand* (Paris: Charpentier, 1863). He calls it the fourth edition, but according to Iris Sells there had been at least six editions of *Obermann* by 1863.[1]

Arnold's renewed interest in Senancour is indicated by his adding in the previous year a long note on Senancour to "Obermann Once More," in the second edition of his *New Poems* (London, 1868). Tinker and Lowry refer to the present review for the *Academy* as the "best and fullest comment" on "Obermann Once More."[2] Nevertheless the review seems somewhat desultory, at least in comparison with the deep meaningfulness that Arnold's Obermann poems show that the book had for him.

The review of *Obermann* has been reprinted in *Essays in Criticism; Third Series* and in the Oxford *Essays;* it appears also as an appendix in Iris Sells, *Matthew Arnold and France*. Arnold's literary relations with Dr. Charles Appleton are discussed in Diderik Roll-Hansen, "Matthew Arnold and the *Academy:* a Note on English Criticism in the Eighteen-Seventies," *PMLA*, LXVIII (June 1953), 384–396.

The most recent edition of *Obermann* lies before me, the date on its title-page being 1863. It is, I believe, the fourth edition which has been published; the book made its first appearance in 1804; three editions, and not large editions, have sufficed for the demand of sixty years. Yet the book has lived, though with but this obscure life, and is not likely to die. Madame George Sand and Monsieur Sainte-Beuve have spoken in prose much and excellently of the book and its author. It may be in the recollection of some who read this that I have spoken of *Obermann* in verse, if not well, at least abundantly. It is to be wished, however, that Obermann should also speak to English readers for himself; and my present design is to take those two or three points where he is most significant and interesting, and to present some of his deliverances on those points in his own words.

It may be convenient, however, that first I should repeat here the short sketch which I have already given elsewhere of the uneventful life of the personage whom we call Obermann. His real name is Senancour. In the book which occupies us, — a volume of letters of which the writer, calling himself Obermann, and writing chiefly from Switzerland, delivers his thoughts about God, nature, and the human soul, — it is Senancour himself who speaks under Obermann's name. Etienne Pivert de Senancour, a Frenchman, although having in his nature much that we are accustomed to consider as by no means French, was born in 1770, was trained for the priesthood, and passed some time in the seminary of St. Sulpice, broke away from his training and country to live some years in Switzerland, where he married, came back to France in middle life, and followed thenceforward the career of a man of letters, but with hardly any fame or success. His marriage was not a happy one. He died an old man in 1846, desiring that on his grave might be placed these words only: "*Eternité, deviens mon asile.*" [3]

Of the letters of Obermann, the writer's profound inwardness, his austere and sad sincerity, and his delicate feeling for nature, are, as I have elsewhere remarked, the distinguishing characteristics. His constant inwardness, his unremitting occupation with that question which haunted St. Bernard — *Bernarde, ad quid venisti?* [4] — distinguish him from Goethe and Wordsworth, whose study of this question is relieved by the thousand distractions of a poetic interest in nature and in man. His severe sincerity distinguishes him from Rousseau, Chateaubriand, or Byron, who in their dealing with this question are so often attitudinising and thinking of the effect of what they say on the public. His exquisite feeling for nature, though always dominated by his inward self-converse and by his melancholy, yet distinguishes him from the men simply absorbed in philosophical or religious concerns, and places him in the rank of men of poetry and imagination. Let me try to show these three main characteristics of Senancour from his own words.

A Frenchman, coming immediately after the eighteenth century and the French Revolution, too clear-headed and austere for any such sentimental Catholic reaction as that with which Chateaubriand cheated himself, and yet, from the very profoundness and meditativeness of his nature, religious, Senancour felt to the uttermost the bare and bleak spiritual atmosphere into which he was born. Neither to a German nor to an Englishman, perhaps, would such a sense of absolute religious denudation have then been possible, or such a plainness and even crudity, therefore, in their way of speaking of it. Only to a Frenchman were these possible; but amid wars, bustle, and the glory of the *grande nation* few Frenchmen had meditativeness and seriousness enough for them. Senancour was of a character to feel his spiritual position, to feel it without dream or illusion, and to feel, also, that in the absence of any real inward basis life was weariness and vanity, and the ordinary considerations so confidently urged to induce a man to master himself and to be busy in it, quite hollow.

"People keep talking," says he," of doing with energy that which ought to be done; but, amidst all this parade of firmness, *tell me, then, what it is that ought to be done.* For my part I do not know; and I venture to suspect that a good many others are in the same state of ignorance."

He was born with a passion for order and harmony, and a belief in them; his being so utterly divested of all conventional beliefs, makes this single elementary belief of his the more weighty and impressive.

"May we not say that the tendency to order forms an essential part of our propensities, our *instinct,* just like the tendency to self-preservation, or to the reproduction of the species? Is it nothing, to live with the calm and the security of the just?" [5]

And therefore, he concludes, "inasmuch as man had this feeling of order planted in him, inasmuch as it was in his nature, the right course would have been to try and make every individual man sensible of it and obedient to it." But what has been done? Since the beginning of the world, instead of having recourse to this innate feeling, the guides of mankind have uniformly sought to control human conduct by means of supernatural hopes, supernatural terrors, thus misleading man's intelligence, and debasing his soul. *"Depuis trente siècles, les résultats sont dignes de la sagesses des moyens."* [6] What are called *the virtues,* "are the laws of nature as necessary to man as the laws of his bodily senses." Instead of teaching men to feel this, instead of developing in them that sentiment of order and that consciousness of the divine which are the native possession of our race, Paganism and Christianity alike have tampered with man's mind and heart, and wrought confusion in them.

"Conquerors, slaves, poets, pagan priests, and nurses, succeeded in disfiguring the traditions of primitive wisdom by dint of mixing races, destroying memorials, explaining allegories and making nonsense of them, abandoning the profound and true meaning in order to discover in them absurd ideas which might inspire wonder and awe, and personifying abstract beings in order to have plenty of objects of worship. The principle of life — that which was intelligence, light, the eternal — became nothing more than the husband of Juno; harmony, fruitfulness, the bond of all living things, became nothing more than the mistress of Adonis; imperishable wisdom came to be distinguished only through her owl; the great ideas of immortality and retribution consisted in the fear of turning a wheel, and the hope of strolling in a green wood. The indivisible divinity was parcelled into a hierarchical multitude torn by miserable passions; the fruit of the genius of primitive mankind, the emblems of the laws of the universe, had degenerated into superstitious usages which the children in great cities turned into ridicule." [7]

Paul at Athens might have set forth, in words not unlike these, the degradation of the Unknown God; now for the religion of which Paul was a minister: —

"A moral belief was wanted, because pure morality was gone out of men's knowledge; dogmas were wanted, which should be profound and perhaps unfathomable, but not by any means dogmas which should be absurd, because intelligence was spreading more and more. All religions being sunk into degradation, there was needed a religion of majesty, and answering to man's effort to elevate his soul by the idea of a God of all things. There were needed religious rites which should be imposing, not too common, objects of desire, mysterious yet simple; rites which seemed to belong to a higher world, and which yet a man's reason should accept as naturally as his heart. There was needed, in short, what only a great genius could institute, and what I can only catch glimpses of.

"But you have fabricated, patched, experimented, altered; renewed I know not what incoherent multitude of trivial ceremonies and dogmas, more fitted to scandalize the weak than to edify them. This dubious mixture you have joined to a morality sometimes false, often exceedingly noble, and almost always austere; the one single point in which you have shown sagacity. You pass some hundreds of years in arranging all this by inspiration; and your slowly built work, industriously repaired, but with a radical fault in your plan, is so made as to last hardly longer than the time during which you have been accomplishing it." [8]

There is a passage to be meditated by the new Oecumenical Council! Not that Senancour has a trace of the Voltairian bitterness against Christianity, or against Catholicism which to him represented Christianity: —

"So far am I from having any prejudice against Christianity, that I deplore, I may say, what the majority of its zealous adherents never themselves think of deploring. I could willingly join them in lamenting the loss of Christianity; but there is this difference between us, that they regret it in the form into which it settled, nay, in the form, even, which it wore a century ago; whereas I cannot consider such a Christianity as that was to be much worthy of regret." [9]

He owns that religion has done much; but, "si la religion a fait des grandes choses, *c'est avec des moyens immenses.*" [10] Disposing of such means, it ought to have done much more. Remark, he says, that for the educated class religion is one of the weakest of the motive-powers they live by; and then ask yourself whether it is not absurd that there should be only a tenth part of our race educated. That religion should be of use as some restraint to the ignorant and brutal mass of mankind, shows, he thinks, not so much the beneficence of religion as the state of utter confusion and misery into which mankind has, in spite of religion, drifted: —

"I admit that the laws of civil society prove to be not restraint enough for this multitude to which we give no training, about which we never trouble our heads, which we bring into the world and then leave to the chance of ignorant passions and of habits of low debauchery. This only proves that there is mere wretchedness and confusion under the apparent calm of vast states; that the science of politics, in the true sense of the term, is a stranger to our world, where diplomacy and financial administration produce prosperity to be sung in poems, and win victories to figure in gazettes." [11]

This concern for the state and prospects of what are called the masses is perpetually recurring with Senancour; it came to him from his singular lucidity and plain-dealing, for it was no commonplace with his time and contemporaries, as it is with ours. "There are men," he says, and he was one of them, "who cannot be happy except among men who are contented; who feel in their own persons all the enjoyment and suffering they witness, and who cannot be satisfied with themselves except they contribute to the order of the world and to man's welfare." [12] "Arrange one's life how one will," he says in another place, "who can answer for its being any happier so long as it is and must be *sans accord avec les choses, et passée au milieu des peuples souffrans*"? [13] This feeling returns again and again: —

"Inequality is in the nature of things; but you have increased it out of all measure, when you ought, on the contrary, to have studied to reduce it. The prodigies of your industry must surely be a baneful work of superfluity, if you have neither time nor faculties for doing so many things which are indispensable. The mass of mankind is brutal, foolish, given over to its passions; *all your ills come from this cause.* Either do not bring men into existence, or, if you do, give them an existence which is human." [14]

But as deep as his sense that the time was out of joint, was the feeling of this Hamlet that he had no power to set it right. *Vos douleurs ont flétri mon âme,* he says: —

"Your miseries have worn out my soul; they are intolerable, because they are objectless. Your pleasures are illusory, fugitive; a day suffices for knowing them and abandoning them. I enquired of myself for happiness, but with my eyes open; I saw that it was not made for the man who was isolated: I proposed it to those who stood round me; they had not leisure to concern themselves with it. I asked the multitude in its wear and tear of misery, and the great of the earth under their load of ennui; they answered me: We are wretched to-day, but we shall enjoy ourselves to-morrow. For my part, I know that the day which is coming will only tread in the footsteps of the day which is gone before." [15]

But a root of failure, powerlessness, and ennui, there certainly was in the constitution of Senancour's own nature; so that, unfavourable as may have been his time, we should err in attributing to any outward circumstances the whole of the discouragement by which he is pervaded. He himself knew this well, and he never seeks to hide it from us. "Il y a dans moi un dérangement," says he; "*c'est le désordre des ennuis*." [16]

"I was born to be not happy. You know those dark days, bordering on the frosts of winter, when mists hang heavily about the very dawn, and day begins only by threatening lines of a lurid light upon the masses of cloud. That glooming veil, those stormy squalls, those uncertain gleams, that whistling of the wind through trees which bend and shiver, those prolonged throes like funeral groans — you see in them the morning of life; at noon, cooler storms and more steadily persistent; at evening, thicker darkness still, and the day of man is brought to an end." [17]

No representation of Senancour can, however, be complete without some of the gleams which relieved this discouragement. Besides the inwardness, besides the sincerity, besides the renouncement, there was the poetic emotion and the deep feeling for nature.

"And I, too, I have my moments of forgetfulness, of strength, of grandeur; I have desires and yearnings that know no limit. But I behold the monuments of effaced generations; I see the flint wrought by the hand of man, and which will subsist a hundred centuries after him. I renounce the care for that which passes away, and the thought of a present which is already gone. I stand still, and marvel; I listen to what subsists yet, I would fain hear what will go on subsisting; in the movement of the forest, in the murmur of the pines, I seek to catch some of the accents of the eternal tongue." [18]

Nature, and the emotion caused by nature, inspire so many beautiful passages in Obermann's letters that one is embarrassed to make a choice among them. The following, with which we will end our extracts, is a morning and night-piece from the north end of the Lake of Neufchâtel, where the river Thiele enters the lake from Bienne, between Saint Blaise and Morat: —

"My window had remained open all night, as is my habit. Towards four o'clock in the morning I was wakened by the dawn, and by the scent of the hay which they had been cutting in the cool early hours by the light of the moon. I expected an ordinary view; but I had a moment of perfect astonishment. The midsummer rains had kept up the waters which the melting snow in the Jura had previously swollen. The space between the lake and the Thiele was almost entirely flooded; the highest spots formed islands of pasture amidst the expanse of waters ruffled with the fresh breeze of morning. The waves of the lake could be made out in the distance, driven by the wind against the half-flooded bank. Some goats and cows, with their herdsman, who made a rustic music with a horn, were passing at the moment over a tongue of land left dry between the flooded plain and the Thiele. Stones set in the parts where it was worst going supported this natural causeway or filled up gaps in it; the pasture to which the docile animals were proceeding was not in sight, and to see their slow and irresolute advance, one would have said they were about to get out into the lake and be lost there. The heights of Anet and the thick woods of Julemont rose out of the waters like a desert island without an inhabitant. The hilly chain of Vuilly edged the lake on the horizon. To the south, this chain stretched away behind the slopes of Montmirail; and farther on than all these objects, sixty leagues of eternal snows stamped the whole country with the inimitable majesty of those bold lines of nature which give to places sublimity." [19]

He dines at the toll-house by the river-bank, and after passing the afternoon there, goes out again late in the evening: —

"The moon had not yet risen; my path lay beside the green waters of the Thiele. I had taken the key of my lodging that I might come in when I liked without being tied to a particular hour. But feeling inclined to muse, and finding the night so warm that there was no hardship in being all night out of doors, I took the road to Saint Blaise. I left it at a little village called Marin, which has the lake to the south of it. I descended a steep bank, and got upon the shore of the lake where its ripple came up and expired. The air was calm; not a sail was to be seen on the lake. Every one was at rest; some in the forgetfulness of their toils, others in the forgetfulness of their sorrows. The moon rose; I remained there hours. Towards morning, the moon shed over earth and waters the ineffable melancholy of her last gleams. Nature seems unspeakably grand, when, plunged in a long reverie, one hears the washing of the waves upon a solitary strand, in the calm of a night still enkindled and luminous with the setting moon.

"Sensibility which no words can express, charm and torment of our vain years! vast consciousness of a nature everywhere greater than we are, and everywhere impenetrable! all-embracing passion, ripened wisdom, delicious self-abandonment, — everything that a mortal heart can contain of life-weariness and yearning, I felt it all, I experienced it all, in this memorable night. I have made an ominous step towards the age of decline; I have swallowed up ten years of life at once. Happy the simple, whose heart is always young!" [20]

There, in one of the hours which were at once the inspiration and the enervation of Senancour's life, we leave him. It is possible that an age, breaking with the past, and inclined to tell it the most naked truths, may take more pleasure than its predecessors in Obermann's bleak frankness, and may even give him a kind of celebrity. Nevertheless, it may be predicted with certainty that his very celebrity, if he gets it, will have, like his life, something maimed, incomplete, and unsuccessful about it; and that his intimate friends will still be but a few, as they have hitherto been. These few will never fail him.

Notes

[1] Iris Sells, *Matthew Arnold and France* (Cambridge, Eng., 1935), p. 259, n. 1.

[2] *The Poetry of Matthew Arnold*, p. 253.

[3] See *Unpublished Letters of Matthew Arnold*, Arnold Whitridge, ed. (New Haven, 1923), p. 68.

[4] Quoted in *Note-Books*, p. 54, from Henri Martin, *Histoire de France* (Paris, 1865).

[5] *Obermann* (Paris, 1882), Letter xliv, p. 188.

[6] *Ibid.*, Letter xliv, p. 190.

[7] *Ibid.*, 190–191.

[8] *Ibid.*, 192.

[9] *Ibid.*, 190.

[10] *Ibid.*, 186.

[11] *Ibid.*, 187.

[12] *Ibid.*, 184.

[13] *Ibid.*, Letter vii, p. 60.

[14] *Ibid.*, Letter, xlv, p. 198.

[15] *Ibid.*, Letter xli, p. 161.

[16] *Ibid.*, Letter xxii, p. 100.

[17] *Ibid.*, Letter xi, p. 72.

[18] *Ibid.*, Letter xlviii, pp. 226–227.

[19] *Ibid.*, Letter iv, pp. 38–39.

[20] *Ibid.*, 39–40.

Sainte-Beuve

Academy
I (November 13, 1869), 31–32

Charles Augustin Sainte-Beuve died on October 13, 1869. Arnold's second contribution to the *Academy* is in effect a eulogy of the great French critic who influenced him pervasively and whom he admired profoundly. The point of departure for Arnold's article is Sainte-Beuve's *Portraits contemporains. Nouvelle édition, revue, corrigée, et très-augmentée.* 5 vols. (Paris: Michel Lévy frères, 1869–1871).

Arnold's longer biographical essay on Sainte-Beuve, written for the ninth edition of the *Encyclopaedia Britannica* (1886), is reprinted in Kenneth Allott, *Five Uncollected Essays of Matthew Arnold* (Liverpool, 1953). For consideration of Sainte-Beuve's influence on Arnold, see Louis Bonnerot, *Matthew Arnold: Poète* (Paris, 1947).

The present review has been reprinted in *Essays in Criticism, Third Series* and in the Oxford *Essays*.

This is neither the time nor the place to attempt any complete account of the remarkable man whose pen, busy to the end, and to the end charming and instructing us, has within the last few weeks dropped from his hand for ever. A few words are all that the occasion allows, and it is hard not to make them words of mere regret and eulogy. Most of what is at this moment written about him is in this strain, and very naturally; the world has some arrears to make up to him, and now, if ever, it feels this. Late, and as it were by accident, he came to his due estimation in France; here in England it is only within the last ten years that he can be said to have been publicly known at all. We who write these lines knew him long and owed him much; something of that debt we will endeavour to pay, not, as we ourselves might be most inclined, by following the impulse of the hour and simply praising him, but, as he himself would have preferred, by recalling what in sum he chiefly was, and what is the essential scope of his effort and working.

Shortly before Sainte-Beuve's death appeared a new edition of his *Portraits Contemporains*, one of his earlier works, of which the contents date from 1832 and 1833, before his method and manner of criticism were finally formed. But the new edition is enriched with notes and retouches added as the volumes were going through the press, and which bring our communications with him down to these very latest months of his life.

Among them is a comment on a letter of Madame George Sand, in which she had spoken of the admiration excited by one of his articles. "I leave this as it stands," says he, "because the sense and the connection of the passage require it; but, *personne ne sait mieux que moi à quoi s'en tenir sur le mérite absolu de ces articles qui sont tout au plus, et même lorsqu'ils réussissent le mieux, des choses sensées dans un genre médiocre. Ce qu'ils ont eu d'alerte et d'à-propos a leur moment suffit à peine à expliquer ces exagérations de l'amitié. Réservons l'admiration pour les oeuvres de poésie et d'art, pour les compositions élevées; la plus grande gloire du critique est dans l'approbation et dans l'estime des bons esprits.*" [1]

This comment, which extends to his whole work as a critic, has all the good breeding and delicacy by which Sainte-Beuve's writing was distinguished, and it expresses, too, what was to a great extent, no doubt, his sincere conviction. Like so many who have tried their hand at *oeuvres de poésie et d'art,* his preference, his dream, his ideal, was there; the rest was comparatively journeymen-work, to be done well and estimably rather than ill and discreditably, and with precious rewards of its own, besides, in exercising the faculties and in keeping off ennui; but still work of an inferior order. Yet when one looks at the names on the title-page of the *Portraits Contemporains:* Chateaubriand, Béranger, Lamennais, Lamartine, Victor Hugo, George Sand, — names representing, in our judgment, very different degrees of eminence, but none of which we have the least inclination to disparage, — is it certain that the works of poetry and art to which these names are attached eclipse the work done by Sainte-Beuve? Could Sainte-Beuve have had what was no doubt his will, and in the line of the *Consolations* and *Volupté* have produced works with the power and vogue of Lamartine's works, or Chateaubriand's, or Hugo's, would he have been more interesting to us to-day, — would he have stood permanently higher? We venture to doubt it. Works of poetry and art like Molière's and Milton's eclipse no doubt all productions of the order of the *Causeries du Lundi,* and the highest language of admiration may very properly be reserved for such works alone. Inferior works in the same kind have their moment of vogue when their admirers apply to them this language; there is a moment when a drama of Hugo's finds a public to speak of it as if it were Molière's, and a poem of Lamartine's finds a public to speak of it as if it were Milton's. At no moment will a public be found to speak of work like Sainte-Beuve's *Causeries* in such fashion; and if this alone were regarded, one might allow oneself to leave to his work the humbler rank which he assigns to it. But the esteem inspired by his work remains and grows, while the vogue of all works of poetry and art but the best, and the high-pitched admiration which goes with vogue, diminish and disappear; and this redresses the balance. Five-and-twenty years ago it would have seemed absurd, in France, to place

Sainte-Beuve, as a French author, on a level with Lamartine. Lamartine had at that time still his vogue, and though assuredly no Molière or Milton, had for the time of his vogue the halo which surrounds properly none but great poets like these. To this Sainte-Beuve cannot pretend, but what does Lamartine retain of it now? It would still be absurd to place Sainte-Beuve on a level with Molière or Milton; is it any longer absurd to place him on a level with Lamartine, or even above him? In other words, excellent work in a lower kind counts in the long run above work which is short of excellence in a higher; first-rate criticism has a permanent value greater than that of any but first-rate works of poetry and art.

And Sainte-Beuve's criticism may be called first-rate. His curiosity was unbounded, and he was born a *naturalist*, carrying into letters, so often the mere domain of rhetoric and futile amusement, the ideas and methods of scientific natural inquiry. And this he did while keeping in perfection the ease of movement and charm of touch which belong to letters properly so called, and which give them their unique power of universal penetration and of propagandism. Man, as he is, and as history and the productions of his spirit show him, was the object of his study and interest; he strove to find the real data with which, in dealing with man and his affairs, we have to do. Beyond this study he did not go, — to find the real data. But he was determined they should be the real data, and not fictitious and conventional data, if he could help it. This is what, in our judgment, distinguishes him, and makes his work of singular use and instructiveness. Most of us think that we already possess the data required, and have only to proceed to deal with human affairs in the light of them. This is, as is well known, a thoroughly English persuasion. It is what makes us such keen politicians; it is an honour to an Englishman, we say, to take part in political strife. Solomon says, on the other hand, "It is an honour to a man to cease from strife, but every fool will be meddling;" [2] and Sainte-Beuve held with Solomon. Many of us, again, have principles and connections which are all in all to us, and we arrange data to suit them; — a book, a character, a period of history, we see from a point of view given by our principles and connections, and to the requirements of this point of view we make the book, the character, the period, adjust themselves. Sainte-Beuve never did so, and criticised with unfailing acuteness those who did. *"Tocqueville arrivait avec son moule tout prêt; la réalité n'y répond pas, et les choses ne se prêtent pas à y entrer."* [3]

M. de Tocqueville commands much more sympathy in England than his critic, and the very mention of him will awaken impressions unfavourable to Sainte-Beuve; for the French Liberals honour Tocqueville and at heart dislike Sainte-Beuve; and people in England always take their cue from the French Liberals. For that very reason have we boldly selected for quotation this criticism on him, because the course criticised in Tocqueville is precisely the course with which an Englishman would sympathise, and which he would be apt to take himself; while Sainte-Beuve, in criticising him, shows just the tendency which is his characteristic, and by which he is of use to us. Tocqueville, as is well known, finds in the ancient *régime* all the germs of the centralisation which the French Revolution developed and established. This centralisation is his bugbear, as it is the bugbear of English Liberalism; and directly he finds it, the system where it appears is judged. Disliking, therefore, the French Revolution for its centralisation, and then finding centralisation in the ancient *régime* also, he at once sees in this discovery, "*mille motifs nouveaux de haïr l'ancien régime.*" [4] How entirely does every Englishman abound here, as the French say, in Tocqueville's sense; how faithfully have all Englishmen repeated and re-echoed Tocqueville's book on the ancient *régime* ever since it was published; how incapable are they of supplying, or of imagining the need of supplying, any corrective to it! But hear Sainte-Beuve: —

"Dans son effroi de la centralisation, l'auteur en vient à méconnaitre de grands bienfaits d'équité dus à Richelieu et à Louis XIV. Homme du peuple ou bourgeois, sous Louis XIII., ne valait-il pas mieux avoir affaire à un intendant, à l'homme du roi, qu'à un gouverneur de province, à quelque duc d'Epernon? Ne maudissons pas ceux à qui nous devons les commencements de l'égalité devant la loi, la première ébauche de l'ordremoderne qui nous a affranchis, nous et nos pères, et le tiers-état tout entier, de cette quantité de petits tyrans qui couvraient le sol, grands seigneurs ou hobereaux." [5] The point of view of Sainte-Beuve is as little that of a glowing Revolutionist as it is that of a chagrined Liberal; it is that of a man who seeks the *truth* about the ancient *régime* and its institutions, and who instinctively seeks to correct anything strained and *arranged* in the representation of them. "*Voyons les choses de l'histoire telles qu'elles se sont passées.*"

At the risk of offending the prejudices of English readers we have thus gone for an example of Sainte-Beuve's essential method to a sphere where his application of it makes a keen impression, and created for him, in his lifetime, warm enemies and detractors. In that sphere it is not easily permitted to a man to be a *naturalist,* but a naturalist Sainte-Beuve could not help being always. Accidentally, at the end of his life, he gave delight to the Liberal opinion of his own country and ours by his famous speech in the Senate on behalf of free thought.[6] He did but follow his instinct, however, of opposing, in whatever medium he was, the current of that medium when it seemed excessive and tyrannous. The extraordinary social power of French Catholicism makes itself specially felt in an assembly like the Senate. An elderly Frenchman of the upper class is apt to be, not unfrequently, a man of pleasure, reformed or exhausted, and the deference of such a personage to repression and Cardinals is generally excessive. This was enough to arouse Sainte-Beuve's opposition; but he would have had the same tendency to oppose the heady current of a medium where mere Liberalism reigned, where it was Professor Fawcett,[7] and not the Archbishop of Bordeaux, who took the bit in his teeth.

That Sainte-Beuve stopped short at curiosity, at the desire to know things as they really are, and did not press on with faith and ardour to the various and immense applications of this knowledge which suggest themselves, and of which the accomplishment is reserved for the future, was due in part to his character, but more to his date, his period, his circumstances. Let it be enough for a man to have served well one need of his age; and among politicians and rhetoricians to have been a naturalist, at a time when for any good and lasting work in government and literature our old conventional draught of the nature of things wanted in a thousand directions re-verifying and correcting.

Notes

[1] *Portraits contemporains,* I, 517, n. 1.

[2] Proverbs 20:3.

[3] "Oeuvres et correspondance inédites de M. de Tocqueville" (II), *Causeries du lundi* (Paris, 1862), XV, 116.

[4] "Oeuvres et correspondance inédites de M. de Tocqueville" (I), *Ibid.,* 97.

[5] *Ibid.*

[6] "Discours au Senat, à propos de la loi sur la presse," *Moniteur universel* (Paris), May 8, 1868, pp. 624–625.

[7] Henry Fawcett (1833–1884), political economist and statesman, was a disciple of John Stuart Mill. He served as Postmaster-General in Gladstone's second administration.

A First Requisite for Church Reform

Pall Mall Gazette
May 30, 1870, pp. 2–3

This letter was pseudonymous, but like almost all of Arnold's other letters to the *Gazette*, it was a paid contribution.[1] It is in a lively vein, and although the issue of church reform now seems remote, the letter opens a view into an amusingly Trollopian world of scandal, and shows Arnold proposing concrete practical reform, rather than only abstract counsel.

The use of the pen-name "A Friend to the Church," with which the letter is signed, suggests that Arnold may again, as in the articles signed "A Lover of Light," have hoped to represent a voice of public opinion distinct from his own well established personality.

Arnold acknowledged this letter in his correspondence. In a letter to Lady de Rothschild, dated from Harrow June 1, 1870, he added this postscript: "I hope you read a letter in the *Pall Mall Gazette* the day before yesterday proposing a Minister of Ecclesiastical Affairs. It was mine. The only thing I have written there this year." [2] The letter is listed in T. B. Smart's *Bibliography of Matthew Arnold* (London, 1882) and in the revised bibliography of which Smart contributed to the Edition de Luxe of *The Works of Matthew Arnold* (vol. 15).

To the Editor of the *Pall Mall Gazette.*

Sir, — The letter from a beneficed clergyman on Church reform which you lately published, the proposals on the same subject which some of the London clergy are circulating, Mr. Cross's bill for abolishing the sale of the next presentation to benefices, the Sequestration Bill of the Bishop of Winchester, are excellent signs.[3] They show a lively sense in clergy and laity of the mischiefs which are present in the Church, and a sincere desire to work at their cure. Unfortunately, there is always in this country too much tendency to be afraid of thorough remedies, to try and do things in a complicated manner instead of in a simple manner, by a great many small and side-long operations instead of by one large direct operation. The present dealings with Church reform exhibit this tendency in a signal manner.

The matters wherein reform is called for fall under two heads. They are matters of doctrine or they are matters of discipline. Alterations in matters of doctrine can only come about through a ripening sense, in both clergy and laity, of the inadequacy and injuriousness of this or that part of the formularies fixed for the Church of England; through this sense pervading the nation, and at last getting effect for itself through Parliament. This is a slow process, and it is not to be desired it should be a swift one. It may safely be left to the natural working of men's minds, engaged upon it as they are now engaged upon it, to bring to fulfilment in due time.

Alterations in matters of discipline are of quite another nature. They cannot be left to the natural working of men's minds to bring about, for there are strong interests opposed to them; and yet, when the need of them is once seen, they require to be made promptly and effectively, for their remaining unmade is an occasion to the Church of real scandal and danger. At present there are no means of making them; and what is wanted, therefore, is the means of making them. What is wanted is an effective *centre of disciplinary recourse.*

The real scandals of the Church are disciplinary scandals. In an Established National Church, Church funds are in their nature, every one feels, public funds; a Church clergyman is in his nature a public functionary. He has often been compared to an officer in the army or navy; let us compare him with a civil functionary to whom he has really, by his condition and duties, a closer analogy — to a school inspector. It would be monstrous that he should keep it when he does not half do its duties. It would be monstrous that he should not be dismissed from it if he is found guilty of drunkenness, adultery, or other scandalous offences. It would be monstrous that he should not be superannuated for it when he is seventy or eighty years old. It would be monstrous he should not be checked, and, supposing him incorrigible, superseded, if, through his ill temper or indiscretion, he sets his district in a flame, and hurts the interests of education there instead of serving them. All this nobody will deny. And will anybody deny that a clergyman may now do all these things which a school inspector may not do, and that it is monstrous he should have the power to do them?

No Act of Parliament can sufficiently provide for what is required; there needs an administrative authority. No Act of Parliament can lay down perfectly what is any functionary's work; yet, if a man receives £500 a year of our property set apart in a parish and affected to the common good in maintaining a parson of the parish, and if he performs no other work of a parish parson except to christen, marry, bury, and do the Sunday services, he clearly does not do his work, the public stipend he receives out of the parish is stipend wasted, and there ought to be a power for getting rid of him. At present there is none. No Act of Parliament can determine at what point a functionary's vagaries of temper or self-will become intolerable; yet, if a man receives £500 a year out of a parish as its public religious minister, and then sets the whole parish by the ears and makes his ministry in the parish null and useless, then the purpose for which his office exists is not answered, the public stipend he receives out of the parish is stipend wasted, and there ought to be a power for getting rid of him. At present there is none. Still more evident, when we come to cases of plain vice and immorality, are the abuses which spring from treating the incumbent of a parish as the holder of a private property instead of as the occupant of a public post. Mr. Jackson's case, which was lately in all the newspapers, is said to have been improperly decided against him, and he has appealed against the decision.[4] Very likely the decision was wrong; sincerely must we all hope it was wrong. But supposing the decision to have been right, and Mr. Jackson's guilt to be established, what a sentence was the sentence passed against him! Instead of instant, utter dismissal from his post, a few years' suspension from it! And this is a sentence on a clergyman proved guilty of gross immorality and adultery! Why, Mr. Lowe dismissed a young clerical school inspector for kissing a pupil teacher. And Mr. Lowe did perfectly right; for a cure of schools is, truly enough a sort of cure of manners and morals, and any flagrant impropriety is inconsistent with it. But what, then, is a cure of souls? and how, except for an abusive system transmitted from quite other times, and for that fetish — worship of property which is in the English nature the element the most ignoble and dangerous, making us treat the characters of property as always a sheer blessing, even where they are in truth a bane — and how with a cure of souls is gross vice and publicly proved adultery consistent?

No alterations or relaxations of dogma can avail the Church greatly while her discipline remains, from this vicious system of tenure of her offices, incurably bad. And no half measures or timid patching will avail to cure this vicious system; only an effective disciplinary power can cure it. A centre of disciplinary recourse must be found, with authority to make ordinary public office in the Church, like ordinary public office every-where else, retainable only during useful service and good behaviour. The sole question is, what will the best centre of disciplinary recourse be? It is impossible to use the bishops for such a purpose; they are not suffi-ciently responsible, they have not sufficiently (or are thought not to have sufficiently) the judicial mind, training and temper. The clergy them-selves, if they were set to choose, would not take the bishops. The only centre possible is a Minister of Ecclesiastical Affairs.

To a Minister of State, as intervening in Church discipline, there are, no doubt, objections, as there are objections to a Minister of State intervening in education; all that can be said is that in modern societies, and more and more as the nature of his trust becomes more clearly con-ceived, his agency is the best available, and has advantages which out-weigh the disadvantages. As a Minister of the State — that is, as Burke says, of "the nation in its collective and corporate character" — he has most distinctly and perpetually enforced upon him the duty of being impartial. As for ever in the eye of the whole nation, and exercising his function amid unceasing comment and publicity, he is, above any other executive that can be found, responsible. An authority which shall be thoroughly impartial, and which, to ensure its being impartial, shall be thoroughly responsible, is just what is wanted. There is no need to give such a Minister patronage. Bills like those of Mr. Cross and the Bishop of Winchester will, it may be hoped, multiply, and will in time wholly change the present bad system of patronage in the Church. In the department of a Minister of Ecclesiastical Affairs the present Ecclesiastical Commission would, no doubt, merge; and to him, as to a natural centre, would come all arrangements seeking to give a more public and satisfactory character to Church property and patronage. But meanwhile, even with patronage left as it is, it would for our present purpose be sufficient to give the Crown — which already as summing up in itself the nation is head of the National Church — to give the Queen in Council, acting through a Minister of Ecclesiastical Affairs, the right of nominating on the presentation of the actual patron to all Church appointments, and of revoking its nomination on due cause shown. Then complaints against a clergyman for vice and immorality, for uselessness or hurtfulness, in his parish through habitual defect of temper and discretion, complaints of neglect of duty, of ineffective discharge of duty through age or prolonged illness, would lie to the Minister of Ecclesiastical Affairs as the clergyman's disciplinary superior, who would act administratively and on his own responsibility, but act after conferring with the bishop, and act with the full inquiry and the fair consideration now shown in the case of any public servant incriminated, and which are certainly not apt to be either scanty or insufficient. If the bishops, as the great dignitaries of the Church, were exempted, like the judges, from all authority of the executive, and removable only upon address from both branches of the Legislature — a proceeding tantamount, in fact, to an Act of Parliament — their high office would but receive the honourable distinction which is its due, and they would also have, in truth, all the solidity and security which they have at present.

Two parties may be thought likely to oppose such a reform: the clergy, as losing by it their present irresponsible dependence; the Dissenters, as averse to all State interference with religion. Those of the clergy who think it the highest honour and advantage for them to be petty country gentlemen, a kind of out-work to the landed gentry, holding their property by the same sort of tenure, classed by public opinion in the same sort of category, and regarded by the landed gentry themselves as their appointed auxiliaries and the natural sharers of their prejudices — those of the clergy who think this a benefit and privilege will, no doubt, dislike losing it. But, whatever may be said to the contrary, this close assimilation to the landed gentry is a danger for the clergy, not a benefit to them; and, much as the landed gentry may gain by the assimilation, the Church is a loser by it. What strengthens the Church is the thorough and active performance of her functions, and her close alliance with the landed gentry impedes this rather than furthers it. The best of the clergy, those who desire the strengthening of the Church more than privilege for themselves, who know what the Church loses for want of a power to deal with superannuated incumbents, incumbents of utterly impracticable temper and judgment, will welcome a public and responsible authority for dealing with these mischiefs, and will themselves be just as little affected or meddled with by it as now that it does not exist.

As for the Dissenters, let it be said to their credit that one of their main objections to the State Church has been the existence of abuses such as our centre of disciplinary recourse would remove. And a Minister of Ecclesiastical Affairs has not to meddle with religion. Even in the one case where his proposed functions might seem to come in contact with religious controversy, the case of a parish at internecine war with its incumbent and appealing to the State power, it would be questions purely of temper and of discretion, not of religious controversy, which a Minister would entertain. But ninety-nine cases out of every hundred in which a Minister had to act would be cases in which not even the semblance or suspicion of interference with religious matters could possibly arise. They would be manifestly and unmixedly cases in which he acted in an interest which is as much a Dissenter's interest as it is a Churchman's — to correct an abuse of public funds or an outrage on public decency. — I am, Sir,

your obedient servant,

A FRIEND TO THE CHURCH

Notes

[1] Neiman, "Some Newly Attributed Contributions of Matthew Arnold," p. 86.

[2] *Letters*, II, 30.

[3] The letter from "a beneficed clergyman" was published in the *Pall Mall Gazette*, May 2, 1870, p. 6.

Richard Assheton Cross, Viscount Cross (1823–1914), introduced in the House of Commons on February 22, 1870 a Bill to render void the sale of the next presentation to a Benefice (*Hansard's Parliamentary Debates*, 3rd series, CXCIX, 694–697). Cross's bill was read for the second time on May 11.

The Bishop of Winchester presented in the House of Lords, May 3, 1870, a Bill to abolish Sequestration for Debt, and to provide a more effectual remedy for securing payment of the Debts of Beneficed Clerks. This Bill was referred to a Select Committee on May 17. The Bishop presented on May 27 a Benefices Registration Bill and a Union of Benefices Amendment Bill (*Ibid.,* CCI, 106, 791–809, 1494).

⁴ See "The Case of Mr. Jackson," *Spectator,* XLIII (May 7, 1870), 578–580. The Rev. Mr. J. Jackson, Rector of Ledbury, was suspended for five years on a charge of "systematic indecency, culminating in rape." The judgment of the Dean of Arches was appealed by Jackson, who was declared innocent on November 25, 1870, by the Judicial Committee of the Privy Council, *Spectator,* XLIII (December 3, 1870), 1435.

Endowments

Pall Mall Gazette
November 12, 1870, p. 10

"Endowments" is an unsigned "miscellaneous article" — to use the termi-
nology of the index of the *Gazette*. It has been identified as Arnold's through his
notation *"write Hobhouse"* in his *Note-Books* for 1869.[1]

Arthur Hobhouse,[2] later Lord Hobhouse, was appointed to the Charity
Commission in 1866 to examine the permissive application of obsolete or im-
practical charitable endowments, including, of course, school endowments. On
March 12, 1868, he made an address to the London clergy at Sion College on
"The Character of Charitable Foundations in England." This lecture, which
was published as a pamphlet, seems, like two subsequent addresses of May
1869 and July 1869, to have provoked lively discussion.[3] Related as they were
to the concerns of the Endowed Schools Commission of 1869, Hobhouse's
views interested Arnold. The projected article on Hobhouse was fulfilled, so
far as it was fulfilled, only when Dr. Richard Frederick Littledale's[4] dissenting
lecture, "The Crisis of Disestablishment," prompted "Endowments."

In a paper that well deserved an earlier and independent notice, Mr.
Hobhouse, addressing an assembly of the London clergy at Sion College,
made it his object to define and illustrate the nature of a charitable foundation, to inquire into the right of founders thus to tie up property, and
to trace the causes why settlements to charitable uses stand on a different
footing from all others. Starting from the generally prevailing admission
that charities are working ill, Mr. Hobhouse sought to show that in order
to make them work better it is necessary to do more than to remedy
neglect in their trustees and abuse in their administration; that the main
mischief lies not in the abuse but in the use, not in the administration of
the law but in the law itself. Till people cease, he says, to bend down
before that false idol, "the wise and pious founder;" till they learn that
few founders are pious, that still fewer are wise, and that no founder,
however wise or pious, has a right to dictate to posterity how they shall
employ the property which was his while he lived — our treatment of
charities, though it may introduce some isolated improvements, will never
make reforms on a systematic and sufficiently large scale.

A charitable use is, according to our law, any lawful public use; not
an eleemosynary use necessarily, nor an advantageous use, but simply a
use on which the law has not set its mark as *contra bonos mores,* and in

which a portion of society large and indefinite enough to be called the public is interested. But how comes it, asks Mr. Hobhouse, that a man should have this wide latitude left him for devoting property according to his mere will and caprice for ever?

Not from natural right, for the farther back we go in man's history the more do all traces of a power of will-making disappear. Following Mr. Maine, Mr. Hobhouse points out how, in examining the codes of our German forefathers, one result has invariably disclosed itself — that the ancient nucleus of a code contains no trace of a will. Not from political expediency, because the whole course of legislation has in general gone to abridge the power of testamentary disposition developed by the Romans and communicated from the Roman jurisprudence to our own. The power of disposition both to public and private uses has been limited by the State in spite of strong resistance from classes and individuals interested. The history of our real property law is the history of private owners trying every shift to make their estates inalienable in their own families for ever, and of their being baffled, first by judicial decisions, and finally by legislation. Settlements in favour, not of the testator's own posterity, but of religious bodies, met the same opposing current, and had to undergo the same process of interference and limitation. Statute law and confiscation were both employed against these settlements.

There remain settlements in favour of charities. Why were these not interfered with and limited like settlements in favour of a man's own descendants or in favour of religious bodies? Partly, says Mr. Hobhouse, because of the general reverence and esteem with which almsgiving of every sort was formerly regarded. Partly because of the distress and social embarrassment following the dissolution of the monasteries, and leading, on the one hand, to the institution of a poor law, on the other to the retention of existing eleemosynary foundations and the encouragement of new ones. Dispositions to so-called charitable uses, therefore, were favoured and respected, not out of any deference to the sacredness of the disposer's testamentary rights, to his power to do what he would with his own, but because all dispositions of this particular kind were supposed to be of public advantage. This supposition is now known to be erroneous. Commissions have reported that our charities are at the present day doing more harm than good; there is a general conviction throughout society that they are not working well. The time has come, therefore, says Mr. Hobhouse, to apply to private settlements to public charitable uses the same principle which has been applied to private settlements for keeping land in families, to private settlements in favour of religious bodies — the principle that property is not the property of the dead, but of the living. Private foundations of whatever kind must be made national, and must be administered with regard to real utility and the present needs of society, not with a superstitious regard to the behests of the dead.

Thus, by a sort of historical method, Mr. Hobhouse has arrived at the general conclusion that property is not the property of the dead but of the living, and that endowments should be made national and administered with a view to public utility. Side by side with his reasoning and conclusions it is interesting to place a lecture lately given by Dr. Littledale to the mechanics of Bradford on the "Crisis of Disestablishment." The mechanics of Bradford offered, one would think, but an ungrateful soil for Dr. Littledale to sow, but he sows it vigorously. Dr. Littledale wants to make out that the Church of England has still a right to its endowments, even though it should be disestablished, as it probably, he thinks, will be. "A thoroughly demoralized tone of opinion as to endowments has," says he, "obtained currency in our day to the effect that a mere caprice of Parliament is sufficient justification for diverting funds from their original use to something unlike and even adverse." "A mischievous fallacy has got abroad that Church funds are national funds." But this, says Dr. Littledale, is not so at all. "The revenues of the Church are the aggregate of funds given by private donors — royal, noble, gentle, and simple — for the performance of certain spiritual duties. And so long as the duties are recognized and tolerated as permissible to be done, and are fairly well discharged, the State has less right to meddle with them than with any other property, public or private, in the country." Therefore, of what Dr. Littledale calls "the five wounds of the Church" the very worst is, in his opinion, "Parliamentary meddling." He cannot deny, indeed, that Parliament has the power to meddle, but he denies that it has the moral right. There are only three cases, he says, in which the State may fairly call the holders of a public trust to account, and alter the application of the trust funds. The first case is where the original design has through natural changes ceased to be of any utility. The next is when the intended use of the funds is inherently bad and mischievous. The third and last is where the object is still capable of being carried out and is in itself good, but where the trustees of the funds have neglected their duty. But in all these cases Dr. Littledale prescribes certain precise limits and conditions to the State's moral right of interference; and he asserts that with respect to the State dealing with the Church of England, either the cases do not apply at all, or the limits are recklessly transgressed.

So utterly vain is controversy, and so blinding rather than clearing is dispute, that one may well be tempted, when one meets with a deliverance like this of Dr. Littledale, instead of taking it point by point and attacking it, simply to place it in juxtaposition with a deliverance like that of Mr. Hobhouse, and to leave the truth to work itself out from the contrast and collision of the two. Only for the purpose of facilitating this result, one or two considerations we will press upon Dr. Littledale and his friends. In the first place, what the State has "a moral right" to do and what it has not will never be abstractedly discussed and settled as a preliminary to the State's dealing with Church endowments. In the second place, the State, if it be left to deal with the Church, and to recast, in whatever way, its status and endowments, will never say, or even in the least think, that it is dealing with the Church, as Dr. Littledale says, "arbitrarily," dealing with it "by caprice," dealing with it as its "enemy." The State will assuredly take as its ground of intervention one of those very three grounds which Dr. Littledale himself assigns as fair grounds for State interference with endowments, or a ground very like them. The question will be, whether the object of an endowment shall be taken literally, as assigned or reassigned many years ago; whether an endowment, with its object taken thus literally, has not, in Dr. Littledale's words, "ceased to be on any utility;" whether it does not even become, to use his words again, "inherently bad and mischievous." The inevitable course of events will probably decide this question, so far as Church endowments are concerned, in a sense at variance with the present notions of Dr. Littledale and his friends. But the decision will not come just yet; and before it comes we shall all have time to meditate this sentence — "Die Religion selbst, wie Zeit, wie Leben und Wissen, in stetem Fortschritt und Fortbildung begriffen ist." [5] "Religion itself, like time, like life and knowledge, is engaged in a constant process of advance and evolution."

Notes

[1] Neiman, "Some Newly Attributed Contributions of Matthew Arnold," pp. 88–89.

[2] Arthur Hobhouse, first Baron Hobhouse of Hadspen (1819–1904), judge and legal reformer, advocated reform of the law governing charitable endowments. He served as a member of the commission created by the Endowment Schools Act of 1869.

[3] L. T. Hobhouse and J. L. Hammond, *Lord Hobhouse: A Memoir* (London, 1905), pp. 26–35.

[4] Richard Frederick Littledale (1833–1890), Anglican clergyman and controversialist, was the author of numerous works dealing with Roman Catholicism, which he vigorously opposed, and liturgical matters.

[5] Friedrich Wilhelm Riemer (1774–1845), *Mittheilungen über Goethe*, 2 vols. (Berlin, 1841), I, 130.

University Reform

Pall Mall Gazette
November 30, 1871, p. 10

Like "Endowments," "University Reform" is a miscellaneous article. It was prompted by a letter in the *Daily News* on November 24, 1871, concerning Gladstone's Royal Commission which was making its inquiry into Oxford and Cambridge endowments.

As in the case of other miscellaneous articles in the *Pall Mall Gazette*, "University Reform" is unsigned. Though more neutral in style than most of Arnold's contributions to the *Gazette*, yet some turns of phrase and certain attitudes suggest his authorship. It echoes the skepticism that he expressed in *A French Eton* regarding the value of popular opinion on educational matters, and it anticipates the discussion of university reform in *Higher Schools and Universities in Germany* (London, 1874).[1]

The letter signed "A Fellow of Trinity, Cambridge," in the *Daily News* of Friday last, called attention to what seems to some university reformers a disappointing feature of the Royal Commission proposed, or we may by this time say virtually ordained, by Mr. Gladstone, for the purpose of inquiring into the endowments of Oxford and Cambridge. On the 17th of July last a question was addressed by Lord Edmond Fitzmaurice to the Prime Minister, of which the object was to ascertain explicitly whether, in the opinion of her Majesty's Government, the reform of the great universities had been sufficiently accomplished by the Ministerial measure for the abolition of tests, or whether that measure was merely to be regarded as an initial step towards further and more comprehensive reforms. This object was attained, and the prospect of ulterior measures implied, by the answer in which Mr. Gladstone announced a new Commission. Amid the preoccupations of the session, neither the answer made to this question nor those made to the supplementary questions of Mr. Spencer Walpole and Mr. Beresford Hope attracted much attention. Probably their precise tenor was present to the minds of few, even among those most interested in the subject, when their substance was repeated and confirmed with additions in the official letter addressed to the two Vice-Chancellors on the 2nd of November. The scope of the Commission announced in July, and towards the appointment of which the preliminaries are now taken, is defined, as the correspondent of our contemporary conceives, in such a way as may push far into the future any prospect of legislation. This Commission is to be rigorously bound down to its mandate of simply collecting and presenting, from data to be voluntarily supplied by the authorities, the arithmetical facts relating to endowments, their present and prospective amounts, their distribution and appropriation, in the universities and colleges of Oxford and Cambridge. Arithmetic without note or comment in the first instance — and after? Nothing, imagines the writer of the letter, more expeditious, under the most favourable circumstances and supposing the present Government unmolested in office, than a second Commission charged to recommend upon the data furnished by the first; and years hence, perhaps, a third charged to put in execution the recommendations of the second. Suppose changes of Ministry or other unfavourable circumstances, and we have the cause of the higher education exposed to yet further obstruction from the contingencies of party politics. This view of the facts may probably be exaggerated, so far as the alarm of indefinite practical delay is concerned; the writer's disappointment (in which another correspondent signing himself "Cambridge" has since concurred) is more palpably justified in so far as Mr. Gladstone's scheme does nothing to encourage, during the period of necessary delay, the means for the formation of opinion. The confident reformer who knows what he wants in this matter, and thinks he sees how it might be compassed, may be discontented with Mr. Gladstone's scheme of a Commission forbidden to hear or hold an opinion, because it does not obviously accelerate the possible realization of his own or any other plan. The diffident reformer, who is not sure what is best, and wishes for all the help possible to assist his judgment, may grumble no less, because he is thus offered figures only when he wants conclusions from figures as well, and when conclusions might with apparent convenience have been collected from the same sources and presented at the same time.

Of these two reasons for taking exception to the form of the ministerial scheme, the latter seems to us to carry considerably the greater weight. What is wanted in relation to the chances of a sound reform in the administration of Oxford and Cambridge revenues is not promptness of action for the present; it is sufficient and sufficiently intelligent and disinterested discussion. It can scarcely be contended that a sufficient body of opinion exists, upon the strength of which operation could, with the best intentions, be taken so soon as the bare statistical report now in question is drawn up for guidance in details. It is of course true that books have been written and ideas expressed by persons conversant with the matter, and that evidence in some sort or another bearing upon it has been taken in the tedious course of previous university Commissions. It is also true that ideas of much value will without doubt be found recorded in the forthcoming Report on the Royal Commission, lately sitting under the presidency of the Duke of Devonshire, on Scientific Instruction and the

Advancement of Science. But on previous university Commissions any ideas broached in the direction of general reform were at best incidental to the immediate scope of the inquiry, which was the operation of religious tests at the universities; and on the Commission of Scientific Instruction we believe the point mainly mooted was the mode of endowing university professorships in physical science. We had never until now got so much as within sight of a possibility of practice for ideas of complete and comprehensive reorganization; and what we now want is that views of such reform should be collected, or, in other words, a public opinion promulgated, among reformers face to face with the responsibilities of practice to give solidity to their speculations.

Now opinion, as concerned to any purpose with national university reform, is a very different thing from opinion as concerned with most other matters of legislation. The general postulate of the problem is that the existing endowments have to be reappropriated or differently administered for the promotion among the nation at large, according to the best modes that can be devised, of science in its widest sense, science as a synonym for the higher education. The solution really rests with that comparatively small body of persons whose own intellectual culture is such as to enable them to have the cause of intellectual culture judiciously at heart. As long as the question of tests lay at the threshold of university reform, the whole body of Nonconformist opinion pressed against the door; and university reform, as understood by the abolition of tests and the throwing open of emoluments to Nonconformists, was a political question like any other. The only portion of university reform that can be said to remain a political question in that sense is the abolition of clerical fellowships. For instance, you could make a political point in the House of Commons, or even on the hustings, against the misuse of educational endowments implied by the practice of certain colleges which devote large sums from their annual revenues to augment the stipends of their livings. And clerical fellowships are precisely a thing foredoomed by the common consent of all university reformers (with the conceivable exception of her Majesty's Ministers). Again, there are certain abstract ends, in university reform upon which a numerically diffused public opinion has something to say. A widely diffused social rather than political public opinion has acknowledged, as abstract ends to be contended for, such a reduction of the costs of living at Oxford and Cambridge as should render them accessible to other classes of the community besides the wealthiest, and such a change in their social tone as should convert them from seats of amusement into seats of learning. But the practical steps on the road to these and other ideals? As to them, we have said, the voices that can speak to much purpose are comparatively few; neither will their number be any larger after the publication of the figures ordered by Mr.

Gladstone than before it; they must be limited to the real representatives of the higher education among us, and these are already either themselves engaged in working the imperfect and partly obsolete educational machinery existing at Oxford and Cambridge, or else have had occasion to make themselves perfectly familiar with it. Now the smaller the section of the community with whom the formation of public opinion rests in any given case — the less they are helped by regular political interests such as that of Dissent — the more needful is it that they should organize the expression of their opinions; and organization must be preceded by agreement. Beyond the abolition of clerical restrictions, and, to some degree at any rate, of celibate restrictions also, there are not many practical points upon which competent university reformers have expressed themselves agreed with sufficient emphasis to produce the effect of an organized opinion. Projects have been broached in a state either too inchoate or too mature for practical application, and each projector has been apt to be wedded to his own scheme. A scheme like that propounded by the Rector of Lincoln a few years ago, with all the weight of his authority and experience, is of immense illustrative and suggestive value; value of the same kind, we have said, will doubtless attach to the evidence of individuals upon the late Science Commission. But now is not the time for the scheme or the testimony of any individual; what we want to hear of is a clear and concerted definition, between competent persons, of available practical heads or bases of reform. Abolish clerical fellowships; encourage the career of research and of instruction in that high sense in which instruction ought to be the correlative of research, by enabling the man who devotes himself to such research and such instruction to make his home and rear his children at your seat of learning. Very well; but after this endless differences of opinion begin. How to establish in each branch of learning something like a Faculty coextensive with the university, and so economize some of the resources formerly wasted by the colleges in supporting each a separate staff for teaching an identical branch to small groups of separate learners; how, and to what extent, to develop the professorial or university part of the teaching system, and merge or reduce under it the tutorial or college part of it; how to cut down the cost of living; whether to make residence an absolute condition of emolument; whether, and to what extent, to depress or disendow the colleges in favour of the university; how to reduce the class of ornamental or superfluous officials, and increase the class of working teachers and their rewards; whether to retain the tradition and discipline of the *status pupillaris,* or modify it in favour of liberty after the German pattern; — these are only a very few out of the hundred mutually implicated problems of practical government upon which advanced university reformers have yet to come to an understanding. Sweeping measures once admitted to be possible, one sort of theorists will be for a revolution doing away entirely with the federative system (so to call it) of the colleges, in favour of a centralized or at least unified and complete university system; while others, seeing the admirable work that has been done by their own initiative at such colleges as Trinity, Cambridge, or Balliol and Corpus, Oxford, in developing their teaching resources and extending their utility beyond the college limits, will pray to be saved the uncertainty of revolutions and allowed to go on undisturbed as they have begun. It is to the efforts of the latter class that Mr. Gladstone made pointed and characteristic allusion in the House of Commons when he described himself as "disposed to believe" that certain colleges would be "very much inclined to co-operate" in any proposed measures "by making use of the powers which they possessed, subject to a control of the Privy Council, for the purpose of introducing important reforms into their administration, especially in connection with the tenure and emoluments of fellowships." [2]

Spontaneous Ministerial ideas of reform are probably not altogether to be trusted even were it more likely than the correspondents of the *Daily News* think that the Ministry, amid the already acknowledged and accumulating pressure of questions calling for legislation, could assume the responsibility or difficulty of initiating reform. The public at large is necessarily uninformed and on the whole incurious, especially as to practical particulars; and there are sections of the public which may be attracted by a policy so far ignoring what we have called the postulate of the problem as to propose a diversion of university endowments — emphatically the endowments of the higher education — to alien and non-university purposes. A Commission is for the present to be specially appointed without leave to collect or express opinions; we say that it therefore behoves opinion, among those alone competent to be its mouthpiece, to reconcile and express itself, and that without delay.

Notes

[1] For other grounds on which I assign this essay to Arnold, see my article, "Some Newly Attributed Contributions of Matthew Arnold," 89–90.

In that article I proposed one other item, "Emmanuel Hospital," as by Arnold. This letter to the editor appeared in the *Gazette* April 26, 1871. The considerations that R. H. Super raises are persuasive enough, in the absence of external evidence, to induce me not to repeat the claim in this volume. See R. H. Super, "Arnold's Notebooks and Arnold Bibliography."

[2] Gladstone to the House of Commons, July 17, 1871, *Hansard's Parliamentary Debates*, 3rd series, CCVII, 1874.

La Réforme intellectuelle et morale de la France

Academy
III (February 15, 1872), 61–64

In this final and most substantial of his reviews for the *Academy,* Arnold enlists in his campaign against the encroachments of democracy and mediocrity two writers whom he deeply admired — Edmund Burke and Ernest Renan (1823–1892). Arnold met Renan as early as December 1859, and recognized then "considerable resemblance" between what he called their "line of endeavour." [1] Arnold frequently disagreed with Renan's position, as he does in this review. The nature of the impact upon Arnold of Renan's manifold interests in religion, politics, and race is pointed out by Frederic E. Faverty in *Matthew Arnold the Ethnologist* (Evanston, Illinois, 1952).

The review of *La Réforme intellectuelle et morale de la France* (Paris, 1871) was printed in the *Academy* under the title "Matthew Arnold on M. Renan." It was reprinted in *Every Saturday,* new series I (March 23, 1872), and in *Essays in Criticism; Third Series.*

Burke says, speaking of himself: — "He has never professed himself a friend or an enemy to republics or to monarchies in the abstract. He thought that the circumstances and habits of every country, which it is always perilous and productive of the greatest calamities to force, are to decide upon the form of its government. There is nothing in his nature, his temper, or his faculties, which should make him an enemy to any republic, modern or ancient. Far from it. He has studied the form and spirit of republics very early in life; he has studied them with great attention; and with a mind undisturbed by affection or prejudice. [. . .] But the result in his mind from that investigation has been and is, that neither England nor France, without infinite detriment to them, as well in the event as in the experiment, could be brought into a republican form, but that everything republican which can be introduced with safety into either of them must be built upon a monarchy." [2]

The name of Burke is not mentioned in M. Renan's book, but it is difficult to believe that Burke's publications of eighty years ago on the French Revolution, from which we have quoted the foregoing passage, were not in M. Renan's hands when he wrote his recent work. If it was so, it detracts nothing from M. Renan's originality; a man of his powers cannot but be original in the treatment of his subject, and to have read and agreed with Burke will not make him less so. But the similarity of the point of view strikes the reader in almost every page; and certainly it will be no bad effect of M. Renan's book if it sends us back to those master-pieces of thinking and eloquence, the *Reflections on the Revolution in France*, the *Letter to a Member of the National Assembly*, and the *Appeal from the New to the Old Whigs*. They are far too little read. They need to be received with discrimination and judgment, and to common liberalism they can never be acceptable; yet so rich is their instructiveness that a serious politician could hardly make a better resolve than to read them through once every year.

"You have industriously destroyed all the opinions and prejudices, and, as far as in you lay, all the instincts which support government." "You might, if you pleased, have profited by our example. You had the ele-ments of a constitution very nearly as good as could be wished. You pos-sessed in some parts the walls, and in all the foundations, of a noble and venerable castle. You might have repaired those walls, you might have built on those old foundations. You had all these advantages in your ancient States; but you chose to act as if you had never been moulded into civil society, and had everything to begin anew." "Rouseau was your canon of holy writ." [3]

These sentences are Burke's, and never surely could he have desired a better testimony to his wisdom than for a man like M. Renan to say eighty years afterwards, with the France of the present moment before his eyes:

"If no more had been done at the Revolution than to call together the States-General, to regularise them, to make them annual, all would have been right. But the false policy of Rousseau won the day. It was resolved to make a constitution *à priori*. People failed to remark that England, the most constitutional of countries, has never had a written constitution, drawn out in black and white." [4]

That the rights of its history do more for a society than the rights of man, that the mere will of the majority is an insufficient basis for gov-ernment, that France was made by the Capets, that she ought never to have broken with them entirely, that she would even now do well to restore them, the younger branch of them, if the elder is impracticable, that with the monarchy she ought to form again aristocratic institutions, a second chamber, and, to some extent, a hereditary nobility — this is the main thesis of the new part of M. Renan's volume. If this is not done, France, he thinks, cannot hope to vie with Prussia, which owes its victory to its aristocratic organisation and to the virtues of endurance and dis-cipline which this organisation fosters. France's only hope of revenge must then be in the International. The superficial jacobinism, the vulgar republicanism, the materialism (for by all these names and more does M. Renan call it), which the French Revolution introduced, and which has brought France to her present ruin, has fatal attractions for the crowd everywhere; it has eaten far into the heart and life of England; it has overrun all the Continent except Prussia and Russia. Prussia too is very probably doomed to enter into this "way of all flesh," to be forced into "the whirl of the witches' sabbath of democracy;" and then Prussia's day, too, is over, and France is revenged. At the same time M. Renan suggests certain reforms in French education. These reforms may at any rate, he thinks, go forward, whatever else the future may have in store for us: whether a Capet at Rheims or the International at Potsdam.

All this makes the new part of M. Renan's volume. He has reprinted here, besides, his two letters to Dr. Strauss and several other publications occasioned by the late war; while the volume ends with an essay on Constitutional Monarchy in France, and another on the respective share of the family and the State in the work of education, which appeared before the war began. These two essays may rank with the best things M. Renan has written, and to read them again heightens our admiration of them. The new part of the book abounds with ingenious and striking thoughts, eloquently expressed; yet this part will not entirely satisfy the friends of M. Renan, nor does it quite answer, to say the truth, to the impression left on us by the summary of its contents which we read in the *Times* before the book appeared.[5] It has not the usual consummate roundness of M. Renan's composition, the appearance of having been long and thoroughly prepared in the mind, and of now coming forth in perfect ripeness; there are, or we seem to see, marks here and there of haste, excitement, and chagrin. This was perhaps inevitable.

Our business is not with politics, foreign or domestic; yet on one or two of the political points where M. Renan does not quite satisfy us, we must touch. We will not ask whether France in general has not let the idea of dynastic attachment, as M. Renan calls it, and the remembrance of its historic self before 1789, so completely die out that it is vain to seek now to restore them, although, when Burke wrote, this might still have been possible. But we will observe that this restoration has, in any case, an enemy more serious and more respectable than that vulgar jacobinism, with no higher aim than to content the envy and the materialistic cravings of the masses, which M. Renan assails with such scorn; it has against it the republicanism of men, for instance, like M. Quinet.[6] This republicanism is a reasoned and serious faith, and it grows not out of a stupid insensibility to the historic life and institutions of a nation, nor out of a failure to perceive that in the world's progress, as M. Renan eloquently and profoundly urges, all cannot shine, all cannot be prosperous, some sacrificed lives there must be; but it grows out of the conviction that in

Arnold
PR 4022 .E3 1966
MA's Essays in
Criticism

Arnold . Essays 1954
PR 4021 . N4
Arnold — Complete Prose...
PR 4021 . S8
Arnold
Poetry & criticism
PR 4021 . C8 1961

Books returned after date due are subject to a fine

Date Due

Fairleigh Dickinson University Library
Teaneck, New Jersey

what we call our civilisation this sacrifice is excessive. Our civilisation in the old and famous countries of Europe has truly been, as M. Renan says, in its origin an aristocratic work, the work of a few: its maintenance is the work of a few; "country, honour, duty, are things created and upheld by a small number of men amidst a multitude which, left to itself, lets them fall." [7] Yes, because this multitude are in vice and misery outside them; and surely that they are so is in itself some condemnation of the "aristocratic work." [8] We do not say that the historic life and continuity of a nation are therefore to be violently broken, or its traditional institutions abandoned; but we say that a case has been made out against our mere actual civilisation, and a new work given it to do, which were not so visible when Burke wrote, which would certainly have fixed the regards of Burke now, and which M. Renan too much leaves out of sight.

A mere looker-on may smile to read at p. 153, written before Alsace and Lorraine were ceded and when there was still hope of saving them, that France could not survive their loss, that she is like a building so compact that to pull out one or two large stones makes it tumble down, or like a living being with an organisation so highly centralised that to have an important limb cut off is death; and then to read at p. 58 and other passages, written since peace was made, that the immense resources of France are hardly at all altered or impaired, that she is *à peine entamée*.[9] But of this kind of inconsistency a man of heart and imagination may well be guilty when his country is in question; Burke, assuredly, might have been guilty of it.

Our one serious point of difference with M. Renan, and where we confess he somewhat disappoints us, is in his discussion of the faults of France. The capital fault, the cherished defect of France, is — what does the reader think? — want of faith in science, *le manque de foi à la science*.[10] In the same strain speaks Mdme. Sand in the charming *Letters* she has lately published: *Nous voulons penser et agir à la fois*, she says;[11] and therefore we are beaten. Nay our amiability itself puts us at a disadvantage, she adds, in this bad actual world: *Nous ne sommes pas capables de nous préparer à la guerre pendant vingt ans; nous sommes si incapables de haïr!* [12] It is the head, *la tête*, which is so greatly in fault; the heart, the sentiments are right; *le Français*, says M. Renan, *est bon, étourdi*; yes, *étourdi* he may be, harum-scarum; but he is *bon*.[13] Burke, whom we have so much quoted, says of Charles II.:

"The person given to us by Monk was a man without any sense of his duty as a prince, without any regard to the dignity of his crown, without any love to his people; dissolute, false, venal, and destitute of any positive good quality, whatsoever, except a pleasant temper and the manners of a gentleman." [14] So far he, too, was *bon*: but his goodness had gaps which, though certainly he was also without the scientific temper, would make us hesitate to say that his chief fault was want of faith in science. Of France we may say the same. It seems to us much more true of England than of France that the national defect is want of faith in science. In France the great defect lies, surely, in a much simpler thing — want of faith in *conduct*. M. Renan's chief concern at the failure of the Reformation in France is for what *the head* lost; for the better schools, the reading, the instruction, which the Reformation would have brought with it. But M. Michelet put his finger on the real cause for concern, when he said that the Reformation failed in France because a *moral* reformation France would not have. That sense of personal responsibility which is the foundation of all true religion, which possessed Luther, which possessed also the great saints of Catholicism, but which Luther alone managed to convey to the popular mind, earning thereby — little as we owe him for the theological doctrines he imagined to be his great boon to us — a most true title to our regard; *that* was what the Huguenots had, what the mass of the French nation had not and did not care to have, and what they suffer to this day for not having. One of the gifts and graces which M. Renan finds in France is her enmity to pedantry and overstrictness in these matters:[15] and in the letter to Dr. Strauss he says that, although he himself has been sufficiently near holy orders to think himself bound to a regular life, he should be sorry not to see around him a brilliant and dissipated society.[16] No one feels more than we do the harm which the exaggeration of Hebraism has done in England; but this is Hellenism with a vengeance! Considering what the natural propensions of men are, such language appears to us out of place anywhere, and in France simply fatal. Moral conscience, self-control, seriousness, steadfastness, are not the whole of human life certainly, but they are by far the greatest part of it; without them — and this is the very burden of the Hebrew prophets and a fact of experience as old as the world — nations cannot stand. France does not enough see their importance; and the worst of it is that no man can make another see their importance unless he sees it naturally. For these things, just as for the more brilliant things of art and science, there is a bent, a turn. "He showed his ways unto Moses, his works unto the children of Israel," [17] — to them, and to the heavy Germanic nations whom they have moulded; not, apparently, to the children of Gomer and to Vercingetorix. But this opens a troubled prospect for the children of Gomer.

But perhaps we English, too, shall be as the children of Gomer; for M. Renan has a theory that according to "that great law by which the primitive race of an invaded country always ends by getting the upper hand, England is becoming every day more Celtic and less Germanic;" in the public opinion and policy of England for the last thirty years he sees the *esprit celtique, plus doux, plus sympathique, plus humain*.[18] We imagine our Irish neighbours by no means share his opinion. A more truly Germanic, or, at least, Anglo-Saxon, performance than the abolition of the Irish Church through the power of the Dissenters' antipathy to church-establishments, then telling ourselves in our newspapers we had done it out of a pure love of reason and justice, and then calling solemnly upon the quick-witted Irish, who knew that the Dissenters would have let the Irish Church stand for ever sooner than give a shilling of its funds to the Catholics entitled to them, to believe our claptrap and be properly grateful to us at last, was never witnessed. What we call our Philistinism, to which M. Renan might perhaps apply his favourite epithets of *dur et rogue*, may well bring us into trouble; but hardly, we think, our *doux esprit celtique.*

It seems, indeed, as if, in all that relates to character and conduct strictly so called, M. Renan, whom at other times we follow with so much sympathy, saw things with other eyes than ours. In a parallel between the English Revolution of 1688 and the French Revolution of 1830, he asks himself why the first succeeded and the second failed; and he answers that it cannot have been owing to the difference between William of Orange and Louis-Phillippe, because the second had no faults as a ruler which the first did not show in fully as great a degree. When we read this, we are fairly lost in amazement. Surely the most important point in a ruler is *character;* and William III., whatever were his faults, had a character great and commanding; while Louis-Philippe had, or gave the world the impression of having, a character somewhat (to speak quite frankly) ignoble.

We would fain stop here in our enumeration of matters of difference; for to differ with M. Renan is far less natural to us than to agree with him. But it is impossible not to notice one or two assumptions respecting the French Revolution and the intellectual value of France to the world, because to these assumptions M. Renan, like almost all Frenchmen, seems to challenge the assent of mankind, at least of all mankind except France's *rogue et jaloux* enemy, Prussia.[19] Greece and Judea, he says, have had to pay with the loss of their national existence the honour of having given lessons to all mankind; in like manner — "France at this moment expiates her Revolution; she will perhaps one day reap its fruits in the grateful memory of emancipated nations." [20] Just in the same strain writes Mdme. Sand, in the *Letters* we have already quoted: "Even though Germany should appear to conquer us, we shall remain the *peuple initiateur,* which receives a lesson and does not take one." [21] In prosperity the French are incorrigible, so that a time like the present offers the only opportunity for disabusing them of notions of this kind, so obstructive to improvement; and M. Renan, one would have hoped, was the very man to do it. Greece has given us art and science, Judea has given us the Bible; these are positive achievements. Whoever gives us a just and rational constitution of human society will also confer a great boon on us and effect a great work; but what has the French Revolution accomplished towards this? Nothing. It was an insurrection against the old routine, it furiously destroyed the medieval form of society; this it did, and this was well if anything had come of it; but into what that is new and fruitful has France proceeded to initiate us? A colourless, humdrum, and ill-poised life is a baneful thing, and men would fain change it; but our benefactor and initiator is the poet who brings us a new one, not the drunkard who gets rid of it by breaking the windows and bringing the house about his ears.

There seems to us a like exaggeration in the French estimate of their country's intellectual rank in the world. France is the *plat de sel*, the dish containing the salt without which all the other dishes of the world would be savourless;[22] she is (we will use M. Renan's own words, for a translation might easily do injustice to them) — "la grande maîtresse de l'investigation savante, l'ingénieuse, vive et prompte initiatrice du monde à toute fine et délicate pensée;"[23] she alone has — "une société exquise, charmante et sérieuse à la fois, fine tolérante, aimable, *sachant tout sans avoir rien appris, devinant d'instinct le dernier résultat de toute philosophie.*"[24] We wonder if it ever occurs to these masters *du goût et du tact* that in an Englishman, an Italian, a German, this language provokes a smile. No one feels more than we do, and a few Englishmen feel enough, the good of that amiability, even if it does not go very deep, of that sympathetic side in the French nature, which makes German and Protestant Alsace cling to defeated France, while, mainly for the want of it, prosperous England cannot attach Ireland. No one feels more than we do, few Englishmen feel enough, the good of that desire for lucidity, even apparent, in thought and expression, which has made the French language. But, after all, a nation's intellectual place depends upon its having reached the very highest rank in the very highest lines of spiritual endeavour; this is what in the end makes its ideal; this is what fixes its scale of intellectual judgment, and what it counts by in the world. More than twenty years ago we said, lovers of France as we are, and abundant and brilliant as is her work of a lower order than the very highest:

France, famed in all great arts, *in none supreme* — [25]

and this still seems to us to be the true criticism on her. M. Renan opposes living names, for or against which we will say nothing, to the best living names of Germany; but what is one generation? and what, directly we leave our own generation, are any names but the greatest? And where, throughout all her generations, has France a name like Goethe? where, still more, has she names like Sophocles and Plato, Dante and Raphael,

Shakespeare and Newton? That is the real question for her, when she is esteeming herself the salt of the earth. Probably the incapacity for seriousness in the highest sense, for that the Greeks called τὸ σπουδαῖον, and Virgil calls *virtus verusque labor*,[26] is here too what keeps France back from perfection. For the Greeks and Romans, and a truly Latin race like the Italians, have this seriousness intellectually, as the Hebrews and the Germanic races have it morally; and it may be remarked in passing that this distinction makes the conditions of the future for Latin Italy quite different from those for Celtic France. Only seriousness is constructive; Latin Gaul was a Roman construction, old France was, as M. Renan himself says, a Germanic construction; France has been since 1789 getting rid of all the plan, cramps, and stays of her original builders, and their edifice is in ruins; but is the Celt, by himself, constructive enough to rebuild?

We sincerely believe that France would do well, instead of proclaiming herself the salt of the earth, to ponder these things; and sometimes it is hard to refrain from saying so. M. Renan tempted us; yet we see with regret our space nearly gone. Why could we not have kept to our own generation? and then we might have given ourselves the pleasure of saying how high is M. Renan's place in it. Certainly, we find something of a bathos in his challenge to Germany to produce a living poet to surpass M. Hugo;[27] but in sober seriousness we might challenge Germany, or any other country, to produce a living critic to surpass M. Renan. We have just been reading an American essayist, Mr. Higginson, who says that the United States are to evolve a type of literary talent superior to anything yet seen in the mother country;[28] and this perhaps, when it is ready, will be something to surprise us. But taking things as they now are, where shall we find a living writer who so habitually as M. Renan moves among questions of the deepest interest, presents them so attractively, discusses them with so much feeling, insight, and felicity? Even as to the all-importance of *conduct*, which in his irritation against the "chaste Vandals"[29] who have been overrunning France we have seen him a little disposed just now to underrate, he is far too wise a man not to be perfectly sound at bottom. *Le monde*, we find him saying in 1869, *ne tient debout que par un peu de vertu*.[30] The faults and dangers both of vulgar democracy and of vulgar liberalism there is no one who has seen more clearly or described so well. The vulgar democrat's "happiness of the greatest number" he analyses into what it practically is — a principle *réduisant tout à contenter les volontés matérialistes des foules*,[31] of that "popular mass, growing every day larger, which is destitute of any sort of religious ideal and can recognise no social principle beyond and above the desire of satisfying these materialistic cravings."[32] The *esprit démocratique* of this sort of democracy, *avec sa violence, son ton absolu, sa simplicité décevante d'idées, ses soupçons méticuleux, son ingratitude*,[33] is admirably touched; but touched not less admirably is another very different social type, the cherished ideal of vulgar liberalism, the American type — "fondé essentiellement sur la liberté et la propriété, sans privilèges de classes, sans institutions anciennes, sans histoire, sans société aristocratique, sans cour, sans pouvoir brilliant, sans universités sérieuses ni fortes institutions scientifiques. [. . .] Ces sociétés manquent de distinction, de noblesse; elles ne font guère d'oeuvres originales en fait d'art et de science" [34] — but they can come to be very strong and to produce very good things, and that is enough for our Philistines. What can be better, and in the end more fruitful, than criticism of this force; but what constituency can accept a man guilty of making it? Let M. Renan continue to make it, and let him not fear but that in making it, in bringing thought into the world to oust claptrap, he fulfils a higher duty than by sketching paper constitutions, or by prosecuting electoral campaigns in the Seine-et-Marne. *"The fashion of this world passeth away,"* wrote Goethe from Rome in 1787, "and I would fain occupy myself only with the eternal." [35]

Notes

[1] *Letters*, I, 111–112.

[2] "An Appeal from the New to the Old Whigs," *The Works of Edmund Burke*, 12 vols. (London, 1887), IV, 109–110. Arnold has condensed the extract.

[3] The second of these quotations is from "Reflections on the Revolution in France," *ibid.*, III, 276–277, and the third is from "A Letter to a Member of the National Assembly," *ibid.*, IV, 25. I have not located the first.

[4] *La Réforme intellectuelle et morale de la France* (Paris, 1871), p. 7. Hereafter cited as *La Réforme*.

[5] "M. Renan on the Decay of France," *The Times*, December 12, 1871, p. 4, cols. 1–2.

[6] Edgar Quinet (1803–1875), French historian and man of letters.

[7] *La Réforme*, pp. 67–68.

[8] *Ibid.*, p. 67.

[9] "La Guerre entre la France et l'Allemagne," which forms part of Renan's book appeared in the *Revue des deux mondes*, September 15, 1870. The essay from which the book gets its title was published at the end of 1871.

[10] *La Réforme*, p. 95.

[11] *Journal d'un voyageur pendant la guerre* (Paris, 1871), p. 30.

[12] *Ibid.*, p. 117.

[13] *La Réforme*, pp. 95 and 50.

[14] "A Letter to a Member of the National Assembly," p. 37.

[15] "Lettre à M. Strauss," *La Réforme*, p. 178.

[16] "Nouvelle Lettre à M. Strauss," *ibid.*, pp. 204–205. Arnold's anxiety to make Renan support his thesis seems to have obscured for him Renan's irony. I doubt that the passage will bear the weight Arnold wishes to put upon it.

[17] Psalms 103:7.

[18] *La Réforme*, p. 27.

[19] *Ibid.*, p. 171.

[20] *Ibid.*, p. xiii.

[21] *Journal d'un voyageur pendant la guerre*, p. 31.

[22] *La Réforme*, p. 120.

[23] *Ibid.*, p. 124.

[24] *Ibid.*, p. 179. Arnold's juxtaposition of these passages gives an effect which is not, I think, Renan's. In this last quotation Renan is speaking of the France of the seventeenth and eighteenth centuries as distinct from the superficial impression given in the nineteenth century from "la littérature charlatanesque et misérable qui a chez nous comme partout les succès de la foule" (p. 178).

[25] "To a Republican Friend, 1848. Continued." *The Poetical Works of Matthew Arnold*, ed. C. B. Tinker and H. F. Lowry (London and New York, 1950), p. 7.

[26] *Aeneid*, XII, 435.

[27] *La Réforme*, pp. x–xi.

[28] Thomas Wentworth Higginson (1823–1911), "On an Old Latin Text-Book," *Atlantic Essays* (Boston, 1871), pp. 337–338.

[29] *La Réforme*, p. 159.

[30] "La Part de la famille et de l'état dans l'éducation," *ibid.*, p. 337.

[31] *Ibid.*, p. 293.

[32] *Ibid.*, p. 285.

[33] *Ibid.*, p. 278.

[34] *Ibid.*, pp. 112–113. Abridged by Arnold.

[35] Riemer, *Mittheilungen über Goethe*, II, 281.

Savings Banks in Schools

Pall Mall Gazette
November 22, 1873, p. 12

"Savings Banks in Schools" is the title of a review of *Conférence sur l'épargne* (Brussels, 1873) by the distinguished Belgian jurisconsult and historian, François Laurent (1810–1887). Laurent was a professor at the University of Ghent.

The book may have commended itself to Arnold's attention because of its theme of self-culture. It afforded the occasion for a homily on the need for man to perfect himself and on his duty and his power to do so.

It is too much to say that by legislative enactments little or nothing can be done to better the condition of the working-man. He does not believe this himself, and he will more and more show us that he does not believe it; it may be a pleasant doctrine for certain people to preach, but for him it is a depressing doctrine, and it is not true. Very much may be done, by laws removing what is old and instituting what is new, to create a form of society more favourable to the working-man than the form in which he now lives. Politics and politicians will have to address themselves to work of this kind going deeper and requiring more care and thought than any work with which they are now conversant. Nevertheless, it will always remain true that, though laws may do something for a man, the most that is to be done for him he must do for himself.

This it is which gives its interest to the little book or tract of which we are going to speak. Whatever laws we may for the working-man's benefit make or unmake, his acquiring the personal habit of self-command is what will always do most for his welfare. "Die Hauptsache ist," as Goethe says, "dass man lerne sich selbst zu beherrschen;" "the great matter is to learn to rule oneself;" [1] it is and always will be so. Now, in order to save, the working-man must learn to rule himself; must set himself to this "great matter" of human life and succeed in it. M. Laurent's tract brings out strongly this moral and elevating side of the habit of saving, and by so doing acquires a special value.

A Dr. Guinard left, in 1867, his property to the town of Ghent, on condition that every five years a prize of 10,000 f. should be given "to whoever had produced the best work or the best invention to improve the material or intellectual position of the working class in general, without distinction." Last year the two classes of letters and of sciences in the

Royal Academy of Belgium were asked to draw up, each of them, a list of candidates with claims to such a prize, and the King named a jury of five members (among them the well-known publicist M. Emile de Laveleye)[2] to judge between the claims presented. The jury decided in favour of a *Conférence sur l'épargne*, an address delivered by M. Laurent to the normal school students of Ghent. "Cet ouvrage," says their report, "ne compte qu'un petit nombre de pages; mais l'idée qu'il développe est si juste, si féconde pour l'avenir, et là où elle a été appliquée, notamment à Gand, elle a donné des résultats si remarquables, qu'il a paru réunir toutes les conditions voulues pour mériter les suffrages du jury." For to effect the improvement needed in the working-man's condition, says the report, "il n'y a qu'un moyen, c'est de porter l'ouvrier à l'épargne." Nowhere, it adds, is this more urgent than in Belgium, where saving is so little the habit of the working-class that, whereas Massachusetts has for every 1,000 of its population 200 depositors in savings banks, and England 110, and Switzerland 83, Belgium has only 10. But how to get the working-class to save, where they have so little the habit of it? "L'écrit que nous couronnons," says the report, "montre admirablement, et c'est là son grand mérite, que c'est surtout par l'école qu'on y parviendra." It is vain to preach to the adult workman: he is past the age when habits are formed. To take the child who is still plastic, who has not yet acquired inveterate habits opposed to saving, is the only chance. In his *Conférence* M. Laurent develops and defends a plan for effecting this, which had been with signal success, thanks principally to him, introduced into the elementary schools of Ghent. The jury adjudged the Guinard prize to M. Laurent for this production, which the Government, also, has distributed through all the schools of Belgium.

In October, 1866, the school savings-bank was first instituted in the communal schools of Ghent. The school savings-bank is in connection with the Government savings-banks, which are spread all over the country. These receive deposits of a franc and upwards, and pay interest at the rate of 3 per cent. per annum. Until a school-child's savings amount to one franc they are kept by the teacher, who receives deposits at the beginning of every school-time. They are entered upon a printed form furnished by the Government, of which the child has a duplicate. When they reach a franc they are paid into the nearest savings-bank, and the child has then a savings-bank book inscribed with his name, and treated by the savings-bank like the book of any other depositor; but his deposits are still received and forwarded by the teacher. In short, to receive and enter deposits is as much a part of the regular morning and afternoon business of a public elementary school in Ghent as to mark registers is with us.

In 1866 the work began in two communal schools; a third school came into the plan in 1867, and in 1868 a fourth. The Government approved and recommended the plan, but did not enforce it; M. Laurent had to go about from school to school and from class to class, explaining its benefits. By the end of 1869 it had already so prospered that the Ghent school children had brought up the total number of savings-bank books for their town to 11,334, while for Antwerp, a town of nearly the same population, the number was only 564. In July, 1871, the Ghent schools alone, with 13,330 scholars, had 8,408 savings-bank books. What opposition there is comes from the parents and from the schools for adult workmen. In adult schools in 1871 more than half those who attended them refused to become depositors, while out of 3,787 scholars in the communal schools for boys all were depositors except 741. In the first six months of 1871 the number of fresh savings-bank books issued in the Ghent schools was 1,262. In June, 1872, these schools had altogether 12,420 books, and their deposits amounted to 430,227 f., giving an average of 34 f. 64 c. for each book. In the first six months of 1871 the savings-banks paid to the schools, in money withdrawn, very nearly 27,000 f. M. Laurent has a good right to say with exultation, as he does, "Un jour tout enfant de nos écoles aura un livret à la caisse d'épargne. Et cequi se fait à Gand peut et doit se faire ailleurs. Déjà l'épargne est introduite à l'école dans presque toutes nos grandes villes; elle se répand dans les campagnes. C'est le premier pas fait dans la révolution qui est appelée à transformer les classes ouvrières."

It seems that it is the practice in Belgium for working people to give their children a couple of centimes every Sunday, and in this allowance, which used to be spent in sweet things, M. Laurent found a basis for his operations. Whether there is any such regular allowance to such children in this country or not, they come frequently, no doubt, into the possession of pence and halfpence, of which school savings-banks might get hold. What would probably be the chief obstacle to the institution of such banks is the doubt many of us might entertain as to the wholesomeness of setting children's minds upon acquisition and hoarding. In his address to the normal school students, M. Laurent meets this objection, and meets it well. It is the great merit, as we have said, of his address, and was probably the secret of his success in establishing his plan, that whereas his object is one which might easily be recommended on low and unworthy motives, he recommends it on high and worthy motives, and powerfully enlists the best side of human nature in its favour. Let us take his answer to the objection that the habit of saving is not one to inculcate upon children, that it will make them hard and calculating, and spoil the native generosity of their age. M. Laurent says: —

What illusions and what errors there are in this accusation! We think children are generous, whereas they are really full of themselves, selfish! Here is a child whose parents, though very poor, give him his couple of centimes on

Sunday for his little indulgences. He runs off to buy some sweet thing with it; does he think of sharing this with anybody? He eats up his apple in a moment, and never even thinks that his parents have denied themselves an apple that he might have one. What are called a child's little indulgences are a mere apprenticeship to selfishness. To tell a child that he had better save his centimes is not, then, to give him a lesson in selfishness; it is, on the contrary, a lesson in going without what he likes; and to go without, what is it but the first step towards self-sacrifice, self-renouncement, self-devotion? This is no theory. The child soon gets to understand how his savings are employed; he draws out his money — why? In nine cases out of ten, to help provide for expenses at home; sometimes to bury his father, or to get bread for his widowed mother. Are these lessons of selfishness?

And M. Laurent gives a number of instances in which the savings of children have come into play at a critical moment and with dramatic effect. They generally serve, however, to purchase clothing for the child himself, or for members of his family.

The wealth, or, to use a more modest term, the command of resources, to which the habit of saving finally conducts the adult workman, M. Laurent treats in the same ethical way. He makes this command of resources a duty, as one of the means to man's perfection, and will not suffer the acquisition of money to remain a purposeless mania or a mere step to selfish indulgence. He says: —

We who preach saving, do we make riches an end in themselves? Riches are never more than means — an instrument of moral and intellectual development. There are outlays which are necessary; it requires an outlay to live, and man does not live by bread alone; his intelligence and his soul have also their wants to be satisfied. Here are legitimate calls for outlay, because their result is to make us reach the object of our life, which is intellectual and moral perfection.

This being so, "Why," asks M. Laurent, "are we not bound to train children to economy, just as we train them to obedience?" But what a dismal childhood, say some people, we thus make for the children of the poor!

How often have tender mothers and kind-hearted men reproached me for wanting to make the children miserable! Well, but it is just because I hold so much to human welfare, to giving the children under our care all the happiness of which they are capable, that I insist so much upon the idea of sacrifice, which is at bottom identical with the idea of saving. Yes, it is a sacrifice which I demand; I ask the child to give up what he calls pleasures; but I maintain that my severe morality will make him far happier than he would be in gratifying his desires and fancies.

We are here on evangelical ground: *He that loveth his life shall lose it.*[3]

We have thought that those interested in popular education would be glad to be informed of the attempt which M. Laurent and his friends are making, and in what spirit it is being made. The movement has, as we have seen, had already great success; the one obstacle to its entire success is to be found in the early age at which children leave school. "What does a child of ten years old retain of its duties?" asks M. Laurent; "above all, of a duty so irksome as that of saving? He forgets his lessons of economy just as he forgets everything else that he has been taught. If we can succeed in keeping children at school till the age of fourteen, our cause will have been gained."

And it is hoped that in this, too, the philanthropists of Belgium will be successful. The savings-bank will then become as universal as the infant school is now; and then, perhaps, we shall see accomplished that saying of the economist Rossi,[4] which M. Laurent has taken as the motto for his address: — "Les Salles d'Asile et les Caisses d'Epargne peuvent, à elles seules, changer la face de la société."

Notes

[1] Eckermann, *Gespräche mit Goethe,* March 21, 1830, p. 404.
[2] Emile-Louis-Victor, Baron de Laveleye (1822–1892), Belgian economist and journalist.
[3] Luke 17:33.
[4] Pellegrino Luigi Edoardo Rossi (1787–1848), Italian publicist and statesman.

A Speech in Response to a Toast to "Literature"

The Times
May 3, 1875, p. 9, cols. 1–4

The anniversary banquet given by the President and Council of the Royal Academy at Burlington House on Saturday, May 1, 1875, before the opening of the exhibition was the occasion of this public address. The occasion was a very imposing one. Sir Francis Grant, president of the Royal Academy, presided. The guests included the Prince of Wales, the Duke of Cambridge, Prince Louis of Hesse, Prince Christian, Prince Edward of Saxe-Weimar, Prince Louis of Battenberg, Maharajah Dhuleep Sing, Disraeli, the Archbishop of Canterbury, the Bishop of London, Gladstone, Lord Coleridge, J. E. Millais, G. F. Watts, John Tyndall, and Robert Browning.

The Times carried an account both of the social splendor of the event and a full report of Arnold's response to the toast to "Literature." Arnold's speech was reprinted in J. B. Orrick, "Hebraism and Hellenism," *New Adelphi*, II, new series (September 1928), 50–56.

Sir Francis Grant, your Royal Highness, my Lords, and gentlemen, —

Literature, no doubt, is a great and splendid art, allied to that great and splendid art of which we see around us the handiwork. But, Sir, you do me an undeserved honour, when, as President of the Royal Academy, you desire me to speak in the name of Literature. Whatever I may have once wished or intended, my life is not that of a man of letters, but of an Inspector of Schools (a laugh), and it is with embarrassment that I now stand up in the dreaded presence of my own official chiefs (a laugh), who have lately been turning upon their Inspectors an eye of some suspicion. (A laugh.) Therefore, Sir, I cannot quite with propriety speak here as a literary man and a brother artist; but, since you have called upon me, let me at least quote to you, and apply for my own benefit and that of others, something from an historian of literature. Fauriel, the French literary historian, tells us of a colony of Greeks settled somewhere in Southern Italy, who retained for an extraordinary length of time their Greek language and civilization.[1] However, time and circumstances were at last too strong for them; they began to lose, they felt themselves losing their distinctive Greek character; they grew like all the other people about them. Only, once every year they assembled themselves together at a public festival of their community, and there, in language which the inroads of barbarism were every year more and more debasing, they reminded one another that they were once Greeks. (Cheers and a laugh.) How many of your Guests to-night, Sir, may remind one another of the same thing. (Hear, hear.) The brilliant statesman at the head of Her Majesty's Government, to whom we shall listen with so much admiration by and by, may even boast that he was born in Arcadia. (Cheers and a laugh.) To no people, probably, does it so often happen to have to break in great measure with their vocation and with the Muses, as to the men of letters for whom you have summoned me to speak. (Cheers.) But perhaps there is no man here, however positive and prosaic, who has not at some time or other of his life, and in some form or other, felt something of that desire for the truth and beauty of things which makes the Greek, the artist. (Hear, hear.) The year goes round for us amid other preoccupations; then, with the Spring, arrives your hour. You collect us at this festival; you surround us with enchantment, and call upon us to remember, and in our stammering and imperfect language to confess that we were once Greeks. (Cheers.) If we have not forgotten it, the reminder is delightful; if we have forgotten it, it is salutary. (Hear, hear.) In the common and practical life of this country, in the government, politics, commerce, law, medicine — even in its religion — some compliance with men's conventionality, vulgarity, folly, and ignobleness, a certain dose of claptrap (a laugh) passes almost for a thing of necessity. But in that world to which we have sometimes aspired, in your world of art, Sir, in the Greek world — for so I will call it after the wonderful people who introduced mankind to it — in the Greek world of art and science, claptrap and compliance with the conventional are simply fatal. (Hear, hear.) Let us be grateful to you for recalling it to us; for reminding us that strength and success are possible to find by taking one's law, not from the form and pressure of the passing day, but from the living forces of our genuine nature: —

"Vivitur ingenio; cetera mortis erunt."

(Cheers.)

Note

[1] Claude Charles Fauriel (1772–1844), *Histoire de la poésie provençale,* 3 vols. (Paris, 1847), I, 66.

The Autobiography of Mrs. Fletcher

Pall Mall Gazette
June 10, 1875, p. 12

This is an unsigned review of the *Autobiography of Mrs. Fletcher, with Letters and Other Family Memorials, Edited by the Survivor of Her Family* (Edinburgh, 1875). The *Autobiography* had been privately printed at Carlisle in 1874.

The "survivor" of Mrs. Eliza Dawson Fletcher (1770–1858) was her daughter Mary, wife of Sir John Richardson (1787–1865). Matthew Arnold's brother Thomas attests to the close friendship that existed between their mother and Mrs. Fletcher, as well as her daughters, Lady Richardson and Mrs. John Davy.[1] Mrs. Archibald Fletcher had resided at Rugby when the Arnolds were there, and she passed the last years of her life near the Arnold home at Fox How. The *Autobiography* contains letters to Mrs. Arnold as well as reminiscences of the Arnolds and mutual acquaintances such as Wordsworth, the Quillinans, Harriet Martineau, Henry Crabb Robinson, and Baron C. K. J. Bunsen. Matthew Arnold, too, knew the family. In a letter to his mother written in February 1867, he said: "I have received a printed notice of Sir John Richardson, which I imagine is by Dr. Davy. Will you remember to thank him for it from me, if it is so. I shall take it with me in my hansom as I go to my school at Notting Hill to-morrow, that I may be sure of reading it." [2]

Arnold's interest in both the literary and political figures whom Mrs. Fletcher had known — Scott, Crabbe, Brougham, John Keble, Lord John Russell — may have led him to review the book. It had also a sentimental interest through the friendly recollections of his own family, to which now after the death of his mother he discreetly alludes.

Mrs. Fletcher's *Autobiography* was intended solely for private circulation, but every one who reads it will judge that Lady Richardson has done wisely in presenting it to the public. It is a charming story, told with admirable simplicity, and full of the genial good-natured gossip about persons and things in which most readers delight. Eliza Dawson — for that was Mrs. Fletcher's maiden name — was the daughter of a land surveyor residing at Oxton, near Tadcaster, in Yorkshire. She was brilliantly beautiful, and had, moreover, most winning of manners. From fifteen to about eighteen a succession of admirers furnished Miss Dawson with "serious occupation," for she had nothing of the coquette in her disposition, "though a good deal of the heroine of romance." [3] "I never cared enough for dress," she writes, "to make much impression in a ball-room, neither did I at all excel in dancing. My pleasure was in the conversation of an agreeable partner. I was never gratified by complimentary admiration of my personal attractions; vanity lay in another corner of my heart. I ambitiously desired to be distinguished for mental superiority, and had no objection to a little sentimental flirtation, though I do not remember ever wishing to inspire a passion for the sake of conquest." [4] It was perhaps this love of intellectual excellence which produced an attachment between the village beauty of seventeen and a Scottish advocate of forty-three, who had gained some reputation in Edinburgh by writing upon Borough Reform. He was a man of mark, and maintained, as Lord Jeffrey said many years afterwards, the independence of the Scottish bar with indomitable courage; but disparity of years, as well as narrow means, were insuperable objections to the father of an only daughter, who probably disliked the engagement all the more from the fact that Lord Grantley was smitten by his child's beauty at the same time. This nobleman was even older than Mr. Fletcher; but his rank and wealth were not without influence, and the writer thinks that she was saved by her engagement from sacrificing her happiness to a splendid but miserable fate. Although unable to gain her father's approval of this attachment, she obtained at last his unwilling consent to her marriage, and a happy wedded life of seven-and-thirty years rewarded her fidelity.

Life in Edinburgh at the close of the last century was eminently social, and Mr. and Mrs. Fletcher, being both fervid politicians and having literary tastes, also appear to have been welcomed by the best society of the place. Party feeling, no doubt, ran high, and there were some Tories of the old school who looked upon Mrs. Fletcher as "a ferocious democrat;" [5] but her great beauty, her thorough womanliness, her modesty, her inability to think evil or to speak evil of any one, drew towards her men and women of all classes, and no one who came within her influence could be otherwise than friendly. It is interesting to read Mrs. Fletcher's impressions of persons whose names now belong to history. In the course of her long life she became acquainted or intimate with many of the illustrious men and women of this century and with some who figured in the last. Her earliest memories are of Mason, the biographer of Gray, "a little fat old man, of hard-favoured countenance;" [6] of John Wesley, who died in 1791; and of Crabbe, to whose second son she became godmother, and who — though, like Rogers, he lived far into this century — won the best part of his reputation in the last. In Edinburgh Mrs. Fletcher became intimate with Brougham, Jeffrey, and Horner, and with other writers for the *Edinburgh Review*, the establishment of which in 1802 was to her a matter of the keenest interest. She mentions the "electrical effects" [7] of this *Review* upon the public mind, and in connection with it there is an anecdote too characteristic to be omitted.

Mr. Fletcher, though not himself given to scientific inquiry or interests, had been so much struck with the logical and general ability displayed in an article of the young *Review* on Professor Black's Chemistry, that in the midst of a few guests, of whom Henry Brougham was one, he expressed an opinion (while in entire ignorance as to the authorship) to the effect that the man who wrote that article might do or be anything he pleased. Mr. Brougham, who was seated near me at the table, stretched eagerly forward, and said, "What, Mr. Fletcher, be anything? May he be Lord Chancellor?" On which my husband repeated his words with emphasis, "Yes, Lord Chancellor, or anything he desires." This opinion seems to confirm Lord Cockburn's words in another place concerning the young Henry Brougham of the Speculative Society, that he even then "scented his quarry from afar." [8]

Lord Cockburn, by the way, was himself a warm friend of Mrs. Fletcher's, and when in her extreme old age his *Memorials* were published she observed — "This delightful book has refreshed my spirit, improved my health, and, I verily believe, will continue to cheer and lengthen my life." [9] Another acquaintance of this early period was Thomas Campbell, who never wavered in his friendship, although she often lectured him and made him angry; and about the same time, on her first visit to London in 1801, a friendship was formed with Joanna Baillie, the "gifted Joanna," and with Mrs. Barbauld, an "incomparable woman," whose friendship was regarded by Mrs. Fletcher as one of the greatest privileges of her life. A few years later, on a fine summer evening, when her eyes were red with weeping after reading the last chapters of *Clarissa Harlowe,* and she sauntered out with one of her daughters to talk the book over, whom should they meet but Professor Playfair, his pupil, Lord John Russell, Mrs. Apreece, afterwards Lady Davy, and Miss Mackenzie, a daughter of the "Man of Feeling." Mrs. Apreece had brought a letter of introduction, and thus was commenced the acquaintance with Earl Russell, who afterwards attended the Fletchers' evening parties in Castle-street. More than forty years later they met again and recalled old times under the roof of Mrs. Arnold at Fox How. For Dr. Arnold and his wife Mrs. Fletcher's esteem was great, and she records with pleasure Dr. Chalmer's high estimate of Arnold's Rugby sermons. She was frequently flitting, and wherever she went found fresh friends and new sources of interest in life. Rarely does she "hint a fault" in people with whom she was acquainted. In consequence, however, of his political sentiments, she was but moderately charmed with Sir Walter Scott, and when Allen Cunningham promised her a cast of one of Chantrey's busts, she elected to have one of Sir Samuel Romilly rather than of Sir Walter, who had supported public principles "injurious to the purity, elevation, and dignity of the public character." [10] Miss Edgeworth, also, whom Scott loved so well, did not particularly attract Mrs. Fletcher, who remarked in her "an excess of compliment, of what in Ireland is called 'blarney.' " [11] The warmth of

sentiment expressed by Miss Edgeworth made Mrs. Fletcher silent; but no
one, when occasion called for it, was more ready to give utterance to her
feelings. Chief among the friends of Mrs. Fletcher's later years was the
poet Wordsworth, who found for her and her family a pleasant residence
in the Lake district. She had had discernment enough to detect the advent
of a great poet on the publication of the *Lyrical Ballads,* but there was no
personal intercourse until long afterwards. In the poet's old age it became
close and endearing, and when he died she felt that "there was much
taken out of life that was most worth living for." [12] With Southey, whom
she terms "excellent and desponding," [13] Mrs. Fletcher, as may readily be
supposed, had less sympathy. The little farm of Lancrigg, in Easedale,
where Mrs. Fletcher passed her last years, had been a favourite resort of
Wordsworth in bygone days, and the picture of the life spent in that mountain home is a pleasant one to look at. There were the Wordsworths at
Rydal, and Mrs. Arnold at Fox How, and Miss Martineau, who happily is
still living to connect literature with the Lake Country, and Hartley Coleridge, who often came in to share the early dinner, and "with his gentle
oddity and large range of contemplation over his own thoughts always
added something to our stock of ideas by these wandering visits." [14] Then
there were pleasant visitors like Bunsen and Lord Russell, Margaret
Fuller and Mr. Tennyson, Mr. Henry Taylor and Mrs. Stirling; and family
meetings of daughters and grandchildren, for all of whom Mrs. Fletcher
has loving wishes and kindly words. Few persons ever gained more
happiness of life or understood more thoroughly the blessedness of content. At the age of eighty-four this cheerful-minded woman writes of
spending months of uninterrupted enjoyment, and of the great pleasure
she had in seeking for birds' nests with an intelligent boy of ten, and in
her eighty-eighth year she again writes of passing several months in surprising health and happiness — saying, "My heart is, I think, as young as
ever." [15]

Notes

[1] Thomas Arnold, *Passages in a Wandering Life* (London, 1900), pp. 51–52.
[2] *Letters,* I, 351–352.
[3] *Autobiography,* p. 25.
[4] *Ibid.,* p. 26.
[5] *Ibid.,* p. 86.
[6] *Ibid.,* p. 26.
[7] *Ibid.,* p. 82.
[8] *Ibid.,* pp. 82–83.
[9] *Ibid.,* p. 320. Lord Cockburn was Henry Thomas Cockburn (1779–1854), the
Scottish judge.
[10] *Ibid.,* p. 150.
[11] *Ibid.,* p. 157.
[12] *Ibid.,* p. 282.
[13] *Ibid.,* p. 214.
[14] *Ibid.,* p. 249.
[15] *Ibid.,* p. 323.

German Letters on English Education

Pall Mall Gazette
May 3, 1877, pp. 11–12

Like the other reviews for the *Pall Mall Gazette,* "German Letters on English Education" is unsigned. It was, however, included in T. B. Smart's *Bibliography of Matthew Arnold,* for Arnold mentioned it in a published letter to his wife, dated May 5, 1877. He said, "Wiese will like my having given an account of his book, and that was why I wrote it; then at the end I had a little fling on my own account. The Master of Trinity told me he thought Wiese's view perfectly just, and that Whewell would have thought so also. I saw Greenwood at the opera last night, who was very grateful for the article, and said, what was true, that it is invaluable to have such criticism as Wiese's put resolutely before the public. It gave me a great deal of trouble to write the thing." [1]

Deutsche Briefe über Englische Erziehung by Dr. Ludwig Adolf Wiese (1806–1900) was first published in Berlin, 1851. That volume, which recorded his impressions of 1850 and, included high praise of Dr. Thomas Arnold, was translated by W. D. Arnold as *German Letters on English Education* (London, 1854). A third edition of Wiese's book published in Berlin in 1877 included a second part, with the identical title, that dealt with Dr. Wiese's visit to England in 1876. This is the work that Arnold reviewed. It was later translated by Leonhard Schmitz.

Dr. Wiese's outspoken opposition to the system of "payment by results," his criticism of English hostility to state "interference" and of the English examination system, as well as his regard for Dr. Arnold, must have commended the book highly to Arnold.

Twenty-six years ago — in 1850 — Dr. Wiese, then at the head of one of the great public schools of Berlin, came over here to see our English public schools. On his return home he published a first series of letters on English education. The book was favourably received and was translated into English. Last year Dr. Wiese again visited England, and a second series of letters on English education is the result. Of this second series, too, there is, we believe, or immediately will be, an English translation. [2]

In Germany Dr. Wiese's first book was accused of exhibiting the English schools by their bright side only. In the preface to his present book our author explains how he came to lay himself open to this charge. He was at the head of the largest boarding-school in Berlin; he had experienced the bad influence upon schoolboys of a great city in a disturbed revolutionary time, and he had just read the Life of Dr. Arnold. Full of that book, he came to England. He saw the English public schoolboy "in his happy liberty, growing up healthy and strong;" and attracted by "the poetry of this youthful life," [3] he regarded mainly what was enviable in it, and gave little heed to its imperfections. In 1876 Dr. Wiese's point of view was no longer the same as in 1850. For many years he had been one of the chief permanent officers in the Education Department of Berlin, the secretary charged with the affairs of Prussian secondary schools. His point of view was now, therefore, that of an administrator, not of a teacher. For England herself the question of a national organization of schools may be said to have emerged since Dr. Wiese's visit in 1850, and to have become a question, at present, of the most pressing concern for us. An administrator's view of our school system is the view, therefore, which at this actual moment most interests us.

Dr. Wiese likes and admires England, and to the good points of our schools, schoolmasters, and scholars, he still does justice. But the total result of his observations is far more unfavourable to us than in 1850. It could not but be so. Instead of fixing his eyes upon the work and influence of a single gifted English schoolmaster, Dr. Wiese now surveys English education as a whole. As a whole it is chaotic. It shows that defect which so much of what is done in England shows — defect in power to co-order things in view of a general result. Good bits and strokes of work one sees in abundance; work well and intelligently co-ordered in view of a large general result distinctly conceived, one hardly ever sees. Our architecture — indeed all our art — bears tokens of this weak side in English performance. But nowhere are they more displayed than in our school organization.

The State has been the great bugbear. Englishmen do not want, they say, to have a paternal Government meddling with their schools and directing them. Or, at any rate, if the poor require it, the middle and upper classes do not. These classes will manage their schools for themselves. At last, however, Englishmen open their eyes to see that in this way they have got a few good schools and a multitude of very bad ones. Some norm-giving agency, some common standard for testing the work of schools, some guarantee of their efficiency, are absolutely needed. The State is not to be thought of. So recourse is had to the universities as a norm-giving power, and to examinations as a test and guarantee of school instruction. But in the universities we have chosen, says Dr. Wiese, an agency by its very nature not well fitted for the task assigned to it; and in our examination test, an influence which, instead of promoting good school instruction, impedes it. And at the same time, inadequate as is our procedure to bring forth good educational results, it has an arbitrariness, a meddlesomeness, and an exuberance of routine not to be matched in bureaucratic Prussia.

But we will let Dr. Wiese, as far as possible, speak for himself on these points. What English education wants is above all, says Dr. Wiese, "unity of plan, and a firm guiding hand — 'Einheit des Plans und eine feste leitende Hand.'" [4] There are great resources, innumerable experiments; there is no clearly marked aim, well chosen, steadily and consistently followed. German schools have their faults; but in arranging the system of German schools and in laying out their instructions, an aim, chosen after the best consideration and the most capable advice, is kept clear in view and is steadily followed. Much has still to be done; but Germany has, at any rate, the great advantage of having its schools co-ordered according to a regular, well-devised system, and their instruction laid out according to a regular, well-devised plan.

This we owe to the State, to the Government; we are fully conscious what it is that we get from it. It is above all this unity of procedure, free from arbitrariness, and in general conducted, both at the centre of government and in the provinces, by men who have come to their administrative posts after long practical acquaintance with schools. In all important questions the counsel of experts throughout the country is taken. In the schools themselves the regulations fixed by law are of a nature not to deprive either the head-master or his assistants of free play in the work of teaching.[5]

In England, on the other hand, we find in the same sphere "the direct opposite of an organization. All clear distribution, all assignment of limits to the different sorts of schools, all fixedly given aims, are utterly wanting." There is absolute freedom, with occasionally a vain complaint of the too evident waste of power, of the reign of caprice and chaos. What the English schools need is "a man in whom a clear perception of requirements and needs is united with practical executive capacity and with energetic will. But if such a man were found, how is he to attain in England, to the position of a guiding authority? The English jealousy of interference, of dictation, would make it impossible." [6] And therefore "the sensitive and tenacious self-assertion of the English involves weakness of organization." For the English schools "the very ground lines of an organization have yet to be drawn — 'Die Grundlinien einer Organisation müssen erst noch gezogen werden.'" [7]

In their terror of bureaucracy and authoritative State-guidance, the English have had recourse to the universities and to examinations for the purpose of keeping or of bringing their schools up to the mark. "The question arises: Is it the proper function of a university, as such, to employ itself in visiting and examining schools? In Germany, we think not." [8] But even could the university, without departing from its proper sphere, undertake the inspection and examination of schools, the university has no power to give the schools what they most want — *unity of plan and a firm guiding hand*. Everything is voluntary. The university is free to inspect or not as it likes, the schools are free to submit or treat them with indifference. "We cannot," says Dr. Wiese, "look upon such an arrangement as supplying any effectual substitute for the official objectivity (*die amtliche Objectivität*) which attends the proceedings of a real independent school authority." [9]

Yet our English arrangements, ineffective as they are, show less regard to the due claims of schools and teachers than such an authority would show.

It is intelligible that the schools should prefer a supervision of this nature to a supervision by a State-authority. What is surprising is that so much mistrust in one direction should be accomplished by so much readiness in another to renounce all exercise of independence and co-operation. What could be of more importance to head-masters than to unite together and request the universities to begin by settling, *in conjunction with them, the head-masters*, the objects for instruction and the requirements for examination? Nothing of the kind has been done. The university rules, with all their detailed directions and provisoes, are accepted without further question as regulative, and are spoken of as the edicts of a superior authority. For example: "*We are now allowed* the same latitude in modern languages that we are in classics, and that is an important concession." Those are the words of a head-master. [10]

Dr. Wiese continually notices how the absence of all general direction is accompanied, in the case of the English schools, by a bondage in points of detail such as strikes a foreigner with wonder.

That he should submit to bureaucracy is an intolerable thought to an Englishman. And yet their schools submit to another and far more oppressive dependence in the system of examinations now prevalent. From complaints I have heard, I think it possible that what the English have of bureaucracy and centralization already, and can see at work upon their elementary schools, heightens their dislike to it. For the endowed schools, also, many of the regulations issued are too bureaucratic for our German notions. The Act of 1869 directs, for instance, as regards the teachers: "In every scheme the Commissioners shall provide for the dismissal at pleasure of every teacher and officer, including the principal teacher, with or without a power of appeal, as to the Commissioners may seem expedient." With us, again, the governing body of an institution not in receipt of State-aid would be at liberty to part with a piece of land belonging to it, if their so doing were likely to benefit the institution. In England the governors must first get the consent of the Court of Chancery. [11]

But it is our mania for examinations, and our reliance upon them, which most excite Dr. Wiese's astonishment. He points out how they interfere with good school-work, and thus continues: —

The method of operating through examinations and prizes is looked upon in England as the most effective; the English have, or venture to apply, no other. German school-administrations regard much more the object of assuring the right way to the goal, and providing that it shall be rightly followed. The number of candidates at a German leaving examination who have been privately prepared is a very small proportion of the whole. In England hardly anything is heeded but the demonstrable final result. Like a bell, the sound goes out at intervals through the land: Come and be examined! And they come, boys and girls, the young and the adult, and have scraped together what knowledge they could. How they have come by it, nobody asks; what is the best way, nobody shows them; and yet what work could be more worthy of a university? Results, results! It is characteristic of England, and best explains the present high value set on examinations in school and university.

The apparent grandiosity, the wide sweep of the examination-system by which the same set of printed questions is given out in England and sent all over the world, to Canada, the Mauritius, and so on, has no imposingness for us. Where is the great difference between that and the mechanical French centralization, where the Minister in Paris could look at his watch and tell the foreigner what chapter of Caesar was at that moment being read in every *lycée* in France? We rather consider it a great and unnecessary piece of circumlocution, to have simple elementary questions, such as many of them must be, in grammar, geography, Bible history, &c., printed and sent all over the world. The English have transplanted their examination system to India. A young Hindoo from Calcutta, who was my travelling companion for some time, spoke very unfavourably of the result. The English teachers in their schools simply urged them, he said, to get ready for examination, and they were thus made to cram their memory with unconnected and often but half-comprehended facts, without acquiring any power of thinking independently. It is singular that the English, who attach so much value to the free development of a man's individuality, do not see that this overdoing of examination is all against it.[12]

The exaggerated prize-system of our schools seems to Dr. Wiese as false and un-English as their exaggerated examination system.

This brings me to the *prizes*. Of all the contrasts which the English fashion of thought and life contains within itself, none has, to my mind, more of inner contradiction than that a nation, which accounts the idea of duty so high and sacred, should make no use whatever of that idea in educating the young, but should have adopted the principle, or rather the negation of principle, to employ the lure or reward and distinction as the grand motive to exertion. Even those who are not so severe as to exclude this motive in schools altogether must be displeased with the stress laid upon it in schools in England. In every stage of instruction, from the university down to the elementary school, rewards and prizes are made in England the chief incentives to industry; even in the Sunday school, the English cannot, incredible as it may seem, do without this motive. And not merely for good work are there prizes and medals; there are prizes and medals for good behaviour too. So universal is the habit that every one follows it without scruple; they can conceive no other way of proceeding. The Monthyon Prize for virtue in France is justly considered by English people to be a thing eminently and characteristically French; but in the premium system of the schools of the two countries, England and France are absolutely alike.

Even the College of Preceptors offers prizes, although it stands in no connection with the schools; but it employs the means of prizes in order to induce the schools and scholars to let themselves be examined by it. At a railway-station, when the English schools were breaking up, I heard a father greet his son with the inquiry, How many prizes? and when the boy answered, Three, the father's face seemed to say, Not more? Even girls are urged to the same sort of competition, and are brought forward at the field-days when prizes are distributed.[13]

After all this we shall not be surprised to hear that what distinguishes, in Dr. Wiese's opinion, the German from the English pupil is that the former carries away from his school a sense of the connection of things in what he has studied, the latter a quantity of isolated, unrelated fragments of knowledge — *einzelne, notizen-artige Kenntnisse.*

Our elementary schools are connected with the State, but in their management Dr. Wiese finds just the same faults as in that of our higher schools which are exempt from State control: an absence of well-chosen aims pursued by well-conceived methods. He describes our Education Department as "an extremely complicated machinery, with a vast deal of bureaucratic deskwork and very little free play for personal initiative." [14] It has plenty of routine, he says, plenty of centralization, more than the Prussian department; but this is not the same thing as guidance and furtherance of popular instruction. The famous panacea of "payment by results" finds no favour in his eyes. "The main hindrance to a sound development of the elementary schools lies in the connection now regnant there between schoolwork and money. *Payment by result* is a spur for teachers and scholars; but the impulse comes from without, not from within. It is impossible that a real organization — a formation, that is, which carries within itself the living law of its own growth — should be created on such a system." [15]

Dr. Wiese deserves our gratitude, in spite of the severe things he says of us, for calling our attention to what is, indeed, the great want of English public instruction: careful, intelligent design, with a firm guiding hand. Some day, perhaps, we may have a statesman of genius who will recognize the want and do something to remove it. But he will have to begin by convincing the great English middle class of an unpalatable truth: that what they achieve by their boasted repudiation of State interference is simply, as has been said, to maintain the aristocratic class in its preponderance, and the middle class, their own class, in its vulgarity.

Notes

[1] *Letters,* II, 137–138. The Master of Trinity College, Cambridge, was William Hepworth Thompson (1810–1886). William Whewell (1794–1866) was W. H. Thompson's predecessor as Master of Trinity. Frederick Greenwood (d. 1909) was the editor of the *Pall Mall Gazette.*

[2] An English translation by Leonhard Schmitz, of the third edition of Wiese's book was published as *German Letters on English Education* (London, 1877) and was reviewed in the *Pall Mall Gazette,* September 22, 1877, p. 12.

[3] L. A. Wiese, *Deutsche Briefe über Englische Erziehung,* 3 ed. (Berlin, 1877), p. v. The translations are Arnold's.

[4] *Ibid.,* p. 112.

[5] *Ibid.,* p. 110.

[6] *Ibid.,* p. 113.

[7] *Ibid.,* pp. 332–333.

[8] *Ibid.,* p. 149.

[9] *Ibid.,* p. 151.

[10] *Ibid.,* pp. 152–153.

[11] *Ibid.,* pp. 138–139.

[12] *Ibid.,* pp. 185–187.

[13] *Ibid.,* pp. 230–233 (abridged).

[14] *Ibid.,* p. 324.

[15] *Ibid.,* p. 325.

The Irish University Question

The Times
July 31, 1879, p. 10, cols. 4–5

The Note-Books of Matthew Arnold contain the entry "Universities letter" in the list of writings projected for 1879.[1] Arnold indicated fulfilment of his intention by ruling out the entry. The article was probably "The Irish University Question." Although it is signed, it was not included by T. B. Smart in his bibliography; but Marion Mainwaring called attention to it in her "Notes Toward a Matthew Arnold Bibliography."

The letter exemplifies the close and continuing interest Arnold took not only in the large principles but also in the practical details of Irish social and political affairs, an interest he manifested in the Mixed Essays published in January 1879, and later in Irish Essays and Others (London, 1882).

To the Editor of the Times.

Sir, — Grattan said just before his death, now more than 50 years ago, "England is not one country; it will take a century before she becomes so." [2]

We shall all agree that for the Irish to feel themselves of one country with us is just what is most desirable both for us and for them. But, if it is to come about within a century of Grattan's death, we have no time to lose.

Let us look honestly into whatever keeps us apart: The Irish say that in our treatment of their demand for a Catholic University they have a signal grievance. Some of us maintain that there is no grievance at all. Others think that there is a grievance, but that it is a very slight one.

It happens, Sir, that I have had to make myself acquainted with the provision for University education in a good many countries, and on that ground you will, perhaps, allow me to say something about this disputed Irish grievance. It seems to me that the Irish have a very real grievance. It is a grievance to which I find no parallel elsewhere in Europe. It is a grievance which must perpetually remind Ireland that she is a conquered country. Finally it is a grievance which must be the more irritating from the manner in which it is denied or excused.

First, there is nothing like it, so far as I know, elsewhere in Europe. The established European type of University instruction is instruction where a young man, Protestant or Catholic, may expect, in religion and in debatable matters, such as philosophy or history, to find teachers of his own communion. Minorities have university instruction of this type as well as majorities. Take Catholic France. The Protestants in France are now less, I believe, than a thirty-sixth part of the nation. France has lost Strasburg, the great centre of Protestant instruction. But the Protestants have still the Theological Faculty, as it is called, of Montauban. This faculty has eight chairs. Four of them are in various branches of what we commonly term divinity; but the other four are in philosophy, Hebrew, Greek and advanced Latin, natural sciences. In all the chairs of this faculty the professors are Protestant. They are every one of them appointed by the State and paid by the State.

Take Protestant Prussia. In the Rhine Province there is a large Catholic population. Accordingly, in the University of Bonn there is a Catholic faculty of theology as well as a Protestant; and for philosophy and history there is a system of double chairs; so that in these debatable matters the student, Protestant or Catholic, may find teachers of his own communion. Here, too, the professors are all of them appointed and salaried by the State. The University buildings, collections, and library the students have in common.

Let us come to England. Here we find a University instruction of the same type. Oxford and Cambridge are places where the religious instruction is that of the Church of England, and where it would be impossible to find a Roman Catholic filling one of the chairs of philosophy or history. The Scotch Universities are places where the religious instruction is Presbyterian, and where it would be impossible to find a Roman Catholic filling one of the chairs of philosophy or history. Our University instruction is provided partly by direct State payment of professors, but mainly from old endowments. Endowments, however, may most certainly be called a form of public and national support, inasmuch as the nation assigns, regulates, and in some cases withdraws them.

We cross to Ireland. There the Protestant minority has in Trinity College a place publicly endowed where the religious instruction is Protestant, and where it would be impossible to find a Roman Catholic filling one of the chairs of philosophy or history.

But in Ireland the Catholics are more than three-fourths of the nation; and they desire a University where the religious instruction is Catholic, and where debatable matters, such as philosophy and history, are taught by Catholics. They are offered something quite different, which they will not have. Then they are told that a University of the kind they want they must found and maintain for themselves, if they are to have it at all. But in France the State provides, even for the Protestant minority, a University instruction of the type that the Irish Catholics want. Trinity College is endowed with confiscated Catholic lands and occupies the site of a suppressed monastery. The Catholic majority in Ireland is neither allowed the use of the old endowments to give it a University instruction such as it desires, and such as in England and Scotland we make the old endowments give us, nor is it allowed the aid of State grants.

There is really nothing like it, I repeat, in Europe. To treat the Irish Catholics in this way is really to have one weight and measure for ourselves and another for the Irish. It is, however we may dress the thing up to our own minds, to treat Ireland still as a conquered country. It is a survival from the state of things when no Irish Catholic might own a horse worth more than £5. The Irish cannot but feel it to be so.

The way in which, in order to cheat our consciences, we deny or excuse the wrong inflicted can only make it more irritating to the sufferers. A Scotch member pleads that Scotland stipulated at the Union for the maintenance in the Universities of certain State grants to religion — grants which would not be conceded afresh now. How it must stimulate the feeling for Home Rule to hear of the Scotch nation thus stipulating for what it wanted and preserving it in virtue of such stipulation, while in Ireland the desires of the majority in a like matter are to be overridden now because they have been overridden always! Or we plead that we cannot now aid a Catholic University in Ireland because we have made the English and Scotch Universities and Trinity College, Dublin, undenominational. Perhaps this must be to a Catholic the most irritating plea of all. We have waited until our Universities have become thoroughly of the character that suits us, and then, when the Anglican character of the English Universities, the Presbyterian character of the Scotch Universities, has got thoroughly established and is secure for the next generation or two, at any rate, we throw open our doors, declare tests and subscriptions abolished, pronounce our Universities to be now perfectly undenominational, and say that, having made them so, we are precluded from doing anything for the Irish Catholics. It is as if our proceedings had had for their very first object to give us an arm against the Irish Catholics. But an Irish Catholic may say, "All we want is an undenominational University just like yours. Give us a University where the bulk of the students are Catholic, where the bulk of the teachers are Catholic, and we will undertake to be open to all comers, to accept a conscience clause, to impose no tests, to be 'perfectly undenominational.'" We will not give him the chance.

It is said that the Government Bill is "something more than a full satisfaction of all that is reasonable in the Irish Catholic claims." The Government Bill is like a chameleon; it keeps changing as one gazes at it. It seems admitted that even in the lowest of the Irish Catholic claims it is not an adequate satisfaction of them to give Ireland an Examining Board all to herself, instead of an Examining Board with its headquarters in London. Nor is a system of prizes and competitions what is wanted. Too much of these is even less salutary, probably, for the young Irishman than for the young Englishman. But such a system by itself is plainly insufficient. *The Times* has truly said that some of the best subjects for University training are to be found among those who are taking a creditable degree but not capable of winning University prizes. But it seems that, besides prizes for competition, there will be grants to assist students who can reach a certain standard, and here, perhaps, is an indirect mode for conveying State help to a Catholic University. The student who passes will hand over his grant to the University as the price of instruction for his next year and for another grant. It is not unlikely that in the hope of thus working the Government Bill the Irish Catholics may accept it. They must judge for themselves. My object, Sir, in this letter is not to discuss the Government Bill. My object is simply to bring home to the mind of the English public that in the matter of University education the Irish Catholics have a great and real grievance, and what it is. At present we have one weight and measure for ourselves, another for them. But a spirit of equitableness on this question is visibly growing. Among the country gentlemen on the Ministerial side there is still found, indeed, in larger numbers than one might have expected, a spiritual progeny of Sir Edward Knatchbull.[3] But almost everywhere else, among politicians, among the Dissenters, in the newspapers, in society, there is a manifest and a most encouraging advance in the fairness of mind with which this question is treated. We begin to acknowledge to ourselves that as to their higher education the Irish Catholics are not equitably dealt with and to seek to help them indirectly. More may not at this moment be possible. But some day we shall surely perceive that both they and we should be gainers — both their culture and our influence upon it — by our consenting to help them directly.

I am, Sir, your most obedient servant,

MATTHEW ARNOLD

Notes

[1] *Note-Books*, p. 595.

[2] Henry Grattan (1746–1820), Irish statesman, wrote, "England is not our country, it will take a century before she becomes so." Henry Grattan, *Memoirs of the Life and Times of the Rt. Hon. Henry Grattan*, 5 vols. (London, 1839–1846), V, 543.

[3] Sir Edward Knatchbull (1781–1849) was a Tory statesman and vigorous opponent of corn-law reform and of Catholic emancipation.

De Maistre's Lettres et opuscules inédits

Quarterly Review
CXLVIII (October 1879), 432–452

The Note-Books of Matthew Arnold contain under the list of "Articles to write" in 1879 a cancelled entry — "Joseph de Maistre." [1] The article was this anonymous review of the sixth edition of the *Lettres et opuscules inédits du Comte Joseph de Maistre, précédés d'une notice biographique par son fils le Comte Rodolphe de Maistre,* 2 vols. (Paris, 1873). Internal evidence of authorship is strongly supported by Arnold's acknowledgment, in an unpublished portion of the manuscript notebooks in the Yale University Library, of the receipt in 1879 from the *Quarterly* of the sum of £26/5/—.[2]

The *Lettres et opuscules inédits* was first published in 1851. Sainte-Beuve made it the subject in the same year of a *causerie du lundi.* But the first mention of de Maistre in Arnold's *Note-Books* occurs in 1863, when he is quoted in an extract from Charles Dupont-White's *L'Individu et l'Etat.*[3] Direct references to the *Lettres et opuscules inédits* begin in 1879. The *Note-Books* also contains under a heading "To order — 1874–6" [4] the entry "Joseph de Maistre — Correspondance." One may assume that it was the sixth edition of 1873 that Arnold ordered, and reviewed in 1879.

"Always," says Goethe, contradicting a popular modern tenet, "Always it is the individual that works for progress, not the age. It was the age, which made away with Socrates by poison; it was the age, which burnt Huss at the stake; the ages have always been the same." [5]

We listen to Goethe with respect, yet we cannot help remembering that it has been said, on the other hand: "There is somebody who is cleverer even than Voltaire, cleverer than any man you can name; this somebody is all the world, *tout le monde.*" Nor is that a bad saying, either. But it is not really at variance with the saying of Goethe. Only we must guard it a little, must explain that the *all the world* which is cleverer than the cleverest individual is not the world of his contemporaries, but the world which comes after him, and which he has contributed to form. He was not perfect, he did not see the whole truth; there were at work other eminent individualities besides his; other aspects of the truth were seen besides the aspect which he saw. There was confrontation and collision, and out of the shock came the next age, an *all the world* clearer and cleverer, in many respects, than even the chief individuals of the age preceding. But to these individuals and to their shock it owes all its advance. Individuals emerging from its own life, again, superior to their age, contradicted by it and contradicting it, dissatisfied with its actual gains, in collision with it and with one another, can alone carry it further and make the future.

We must not forget, then, in laying stress with Goethe upon the individual, that the individual is not perfect, and that he works for a future larger and better than himself. Keeping this well in mind, we may admit, as much as ever Goethe pleases, the interest and significance, the overwhelming interest and significance, in human history, of the individual. As his time recedes, he and his strain of thought grow more distinct; his contemporaries and their thoughts grow fainter. They become more and more to us like hollow shadows, saying they know not what: he alone remains among them a living man, who knows what he is saying, and whose words keep a freshness and power. Burke stands thus to us now, as we look back at him among his contemporaries. In the sphere of thought which was his, in politics in the high sense of the word, in what concerns the general influence to be exercised on man's welfare and progress by the means of government and society, Burke's voice is still for us Englishmen a living voice out of the age preceding our own, it is the one living voice left of innumerable voices, the rest are shadowy. A good deal is wanting to Burke's political philosophy; there are many important things which either he cannot see or does not care to see. Whoever followed his teaching simply and absolutely would make shipwreck. Still, such is his weight and power, that while the chatter of a whole wilderness of friends of "the ideas of 1789" is dead and cold, the voice of this great enemy of the Revolution lives, — moves us and makes us think to this day.

Joseph de Maistre is another of those men whose word, like that of Burke, has vitality. In imaginative power he is altogether inferior to Burke. On the other hand his thought moves in closer order than Burke's, more rapidly, more directly; he has fewer superfluities. Burke is a great writer, but Joseph de Maistre's use of the French language is more powerful, more thoroughly satisfactory, than Burke's use of the English. It is masterly; it shows us to perfection of what that admirable instrument, the French language, is capable. Finally, Joseph de Maistre is more European than Burke; his place at the great spectacle of the Revolution is more central for seeing; moreover he outlived Burke considerably, and saw how events turned. But the two men are of one family, having in common their high stamp of individuality, and their enduring vitality and instructiveness. They have in common, too, their fundamental ideas. Their sense of the slowness of the natural growth of things, of their gradual evolution out of small beginnings, is perfectly expressed by Joseph de Maistre's maxim: "Aucune grande chose n'eut de grands commencements" — "Nothing great ever began great." [6] That is entirely in

Burke's spirit, and the maxim has its indubitable and profound truth. Things grow slowly, and in a gradual correspondence with human needs. Phrases are not things, and a Liberal theorist, some revolutionary M. Cherchemot, striking in with his "Tout est à refaire" — "Everything is to be made afresh" — is impertinent and vain.[7] Only, in their aversion to M. Cherchemot and his shallowness, Burke and Joseph de Maistre do not enough consider the amount of misformation, hamper, and stoppage, coming at last to be intolerable, to which human things in their slow process of natural growth are undoubtedly liable. They do not enough consider it; they banish it out of their thoughts altogether. Another trenchant and characteristic maxim of Joseph de Maistre, which Burke, too, might have uttered, is this: "Il faut absolument tuer l'esprit du dix-huitième siècle" — "The spirit of the eighteenth century must be stamped out utterly."[8] One is reminded of Cardinal Newman's antipathy to "Liberalism." And in a serious man a strong sense of the insufficiency of Liberal nostrums, of the charlatanism of Liberal practitioners, as also of the real truth, beauty, power, and conformity to nature of much in the past of which these practitioners are intolerant, is abundantly permissible. Still, when one has granted all that serious men like Joseph de Maistre and Cardinal Newman may fairly say against the eighteenth century and Liberalism, when one has admired the force, the vigour, the acumen, the sentiment, the grace with which it is all said, one inquires innocently for that better thing which they themselves have in store for us, and then comes the disappointment. Joseph de Maistre and Cardinal Newman have nothing but the old, sterile, impossible assumption of their "infallible Church;" at which a plain man can only shake his head and say with Shakespeare, "There is no such thing!"[9]

It cannot be too often repeated: these eminent individualities, men like Burke, or Joseph de Maistre, or Cardinal Newman, are by no means to be taken as guides absolutely. Yet they are full of stimulus and instruction for us. We may find it impossible to accept their main positions. But the resoluteness with which they withstand the prevailing ideas of their time, the certainty with which they predict the apparition of something different, are often a proof of their insight. Whatever we may think of Ritualism, its growth and power prove Cardinal Newman's insight in perceiving that what he called Liberalism, but what we may perhaps better describe to ourselves as the mind of Lord Brougham, was in general, and in the sphere of religion more particularly, quite inadequate, and was not destined to have things for ever its own way. In like manner, whatever we may think of Ultramontanism, its growth and power signally prove Joseph de Maistre's insight. Continental Protestantism, he declared, was going to pieces, Gallicanism was doomed, "the Sovereign pontiff and the French priesthood will embrace one another, and will stifle in that sacred embrace the Gallican maxims." [10] Rome would become a power again; by no other power could the French Revolution, "satanic in principle," [11] be effectually resisted. "If England grants, as she probably will, Catholic emancipation, and if the Catholic religion in Europe comes to speak both French and English, remember what I say, my good hearer, there is nothing which you may not expect." [12] It is enough to make Mr. Whalley turn in his grave.[13] "A great revolution is preparing, to which that which is just ended (as people say) was only the preface. The world is in fermentation, and there will be strange sights seen; the spectacle, it is true, will be neither for you nor for me, but we may well say to one another in taking leave of this insane planet (if it is allowable to recall one's Horace at such a moment): 'Spem bonam certamque domum reporto.'" [14] Ultramontanism is but a stage in this new revolution prophesied by Joseph de Maistre, it is not, as he imagined, the end; but steadily and confidently, all through the first twenty years of our century, to have foreseen and predicted this stage, is no mean proof of insight and originality.

This remarkable man is far less known in England than he deserves to be. We know him chiefly by one of his publications, the *Soirées de Saint-Pétersbourg*, in which the Baconian philosophy is vigorously attacked. Most of us are no further acquainted with the man or his work. Let us run quickly over the main points in their history. He was born at Chambéry in 1754, the eldest of ten children, of a family of ancient descent and austere manners. His father was president of the Senate of Savoy. The young Joseph-Marie de Maistre was educated by the Jesuits, and took vigorously to his studies. As a young man he knew five languages, French, Latin, English, Italian, and Spanish; to which in later life he added two more, Greek and German. He entered the magistrature like his father, and in 1786, at the age of thirty-two, he married. In the fermentation of mind which preceded the French Revolution, he became a member of the Reformed Lodge of Chambéry, avowed himself an enemy of abuses, and was even accused of Jacobinism. But from the moment of the French invasion and occupation of Savoy in 1793, his fidelity to his own sovereign, his hostility to the French Revolution, never faltered. He quitted Savoy in January 1794, the day after the birth of his third and youngest child, his daughter Constance; he never saw her again until 1814. His property was confiscated. For two years he was employed at Lausanne on the business of the Sardinian government, and it was during his stay at Lausanne that he published his *Considérations sur la France*, a work in which his power and his characteristic ideas first revealed themselves. In 1797 he was moved to Turin; Turin was occupied by the French in 1798, the royal family of Sardinia lost all its possessions on the mainland, and the Court of Turin became the Court of Cagliari. Joseph de Maistre was at first employed as chief magistrate of the island of Sardinia, but in 1802 his government sent him as minister plenipotentiary to Russia. At St. Petersburg he remained fifteen years, all through the great struggle with Napoleon. Ill-paid and ill-understood by the petty government of Cagliari, he was esteemed and admired by the Emperor Alexander, by Russian society, and by his diplomatic colleagues; a still better alleviation of the pressure of embarrassment and anxiety he found in study. During his stay at St. Petersburg his principal works were written, but they remained for the time in his portfolio. He was joined in 1806 by his son Rodolphe, then just sixteen years old, to whom the Emperor Alexander gave a commission in the Russian Guards. His wife and his two daughters rejoined him in 1814. In 1817 he left Russia and proceeded by way of Paris to Turin, where he was made Chancellor and Minister of State. He now published the works on which he had been long busy in Russia, his *Du Pape*, his *De L'Église Gallicane*, and the *Soirées de Saint-Pétersbourg*. He died at Turin in February 1821, at the age of sixty-seven.

His Correspondence was published in two volumes by his son, a quarter of a century after his death, and has passed through six or seven editions. Striking and suggestive as are works like his *Considérations* and his *Soirées de Saint-Pétersbourg*, it is his Correspondence which best makes us feel his variety, his attractiveness, his superiority. These two volumes of his Correspondence will live, and will take their place not merely in Catholic libraries, and as part of the polemics of a great Catholic champion, but in general literature. The literary talent of this Savoyard, whose letters, of far weightier contents than the letters of Madame de Sévigné, are not surpassed by even hers in felicity and vivacity, may well make the French adopt him with pride as one of their classics. But for us, for the world at large, what will preserve his letters is the impression given by them of admirable vigour of mind in union with admirable force and purity of character. We should read them; but alas! we do not even read Burke. Our days go by, and the hour with Mr. Yates in the *World* is followed by the hour with Mr. Labouchere in *Truth*;[15] and this fascinating course of reading leaves us with little leisure or taste for anything else. Yet what a pity to be so absorbed by our enchanters as to be unable to feel also the beauty of things like the following, a cry coming from Joseph de Maistre at the end of his hard day, his life of strenuous and grievous travail: —

I know not what the life of a rogue may be — I have never been one — but the life of an honest man is abominable. How few are those whose passage upon this foolish planet [we had *"insane* planet" a little way back] has been marked by actions really good and useful! I bow myself to the earth before him of whom it can be said, *"Pertransivit benefaciendo;"* who has succeeded in instructing, consoling, relieving his fellow-creature; who has made real sacrifices for the sake of doing good; those heroes of silent charity who hide themselves and expect nothing in this world. But what are the common run of men like? and how many of us are there in a thousand who can ask themselves without terror: "What have I done in this world, *wherein have I advanced the general work*, and what is there left of me for good or for evil?" [16]

The great Napoleon, who ill observed his own maxim, was fond of saying: One must know how to set bounds to oneself — "Il faut savoir se borner."[17] The advice is particularly good when one has to speak of a personage so rich in matter of interest, and at the same time so little known to the generality of one's readers, as Joseph de Maistre. The public is prone to demand grand review-articles, but there are subjects which are too large for the limits of a single review-article, even a grand one. Joseph de Maistre is such a subject. He ought to be treated by instalments. And now, when Russia and the Russian people are objects of so much importance to us in this country, we propose to take that portion of Joseph de Maistre's Correspondence which deals with Russia and things Russian; to observe the impression made by Russia and the Russians, during his fifteen years' experience of them, on this independent and powerful spirit, one of those minds which stand out from the crowd, and of which the thoughts are still fresh and living as on the day when they were uttered.

Joseph de Maistre had every reason to speak well of Russia. In spite of his poverty, in spite of the insignificance of his Sovereign, he was received there from the first with kindness; he inspired, as time went on, the most cordial liking and esteem, and was treated with the most flattering distinction. Not only did the Emperor Alexander, as has been already mentioned, give a commission in the guards to the young Rodolphe de Maistre, but he placed Joseph de Maistre's brother Xavier, the well-known writer, at the head of the library and museum of the Russian Admiralty. The society of St. Petersburg was as favourable as the Czar. Joseph de Maistre had in his character, had even in his demeanour and conversation, something impetuous and trenchant. He knew it himself: —

"I have said and done in my life," he writes to Madame de Pont, "things sufficient to ruin a public man five or six times over. People have been provoked; they have talked of me in the way you may have heard; and yet here I am, still on my legs — nay, in spite of all obstacles, I have gone on mounting higher and higher. Every character has its inconveniences. Do you suppose me not to be aware that I yawn when I am bored; that a sort of mechanical smile says sometimes, *'You talk like a fool!'* that in my way of speaking there is something original, something *vibrante*, as the Italians say, something trenchant, which seems, and particularly in moments of heat or inadvertence, to announce a certain imperiousness of opinion to which I have no more right than any other man? I know it perfectly well, madame: *Chassez le naturel, il revient au galop.*" [18]

In spite of this impetuosity, this imperiousness, he pleased. A diplomatist said of him: — "Count de Maistre is a most fortunate person; he says just what he likes, and yet he never comes to grief." [19] Not only did he inspire respect, he inspired warm liking also, he pleased. He was original, full of knowledge, of high honour and integrity; but at the same time he was entirely free from peevishness, narrowness or littleness; he was not in the least a prig or a pedant. "I am very bookish in my own study," he said, "but in the world I try to be as little bookish as possible." [20] Accompanied by simplicity, integrity, good temper, and largeness of mind, his vivacity in conversation warmed and charmed people without offending them, and in the society of St. Petersburg he was a signal success.

His life in Russia had its drawbacks, indeed. The first July after his arrival showed him what the Russian climate was. The warm season is supposed to begin in May, and in July every one who can get out of St. Petersburg is enjoying the country: —

I spent yesterday with the English ambassador, who is in the country in the direction of Cronstadt. We never left the fire but for a minute or two, to look through his telescope at some vessels in the Gulf. To-day, too, I am obliged to sit by the fire; how long this queer state of things will go on I don't know. People in the country here pave the ground with gold in order to overcome the difficulties of all kinds which nature puts in their way; for climate has to be overcome, and soil also. I have just seen a man spend 10,000 roubles in digging a ditch round a piece of ground which cost 25 roubles. And all this for three months in the very finest years, and for six weeks at the outside in bad years. No outlay seems too great if it will purchase any enjoyment. As I look at all this magnificence, I think of what kind nature does for us by her own unaided power.[21]

Not only of landscape-gardening and of luxuries was the expense in Russia, to a man of moderate means, prohibitory, but of other and more necessary things also: —

A foreigner here who has a daughter cannot possibly get her educated (I mean so far as accomplishments are concerned) unless he be the English ambassador or something of that sort. A young lady's education costs ten thousand francs; you can have no idea what it is. People thus go without masters for their children because they cannot afford them.[22]

Finally even the kindness and hospitality which he met with at St. Petersburg, a capital offering such a contrast to his own "capitale peu fraternelle," as he called Turin, were good so far as they went, and were gratifying, but they were something altogether distinct from the friendship of congenial minds, from the intimacies which elsewhere Joseph de Maistre had formed and enjoyed. In a delightful letter to one of his old friends, Madame Huber, of Lausanne, he says: —

I meet with all manner of kindness in society and at Court, but I stay at home as much as my position will allow me. I have plenty of good books, and I study with might and main; for really one is in duty bound to learn something. As for the supreme pleasures of friendship and of confidential intimacy — a blank. You have often heard people talk of the hospitality of this country, and in one sense what they say is quite true; you are asked to dinner and supper all round, but the foreigner never gets at the heart. I never find myself in full dress amid all the Asiatic pomp here, without thinking of my grey stockings at Lausanne, and of that lantern with which I used to go and visit you at Cour. Oh the delightful drawing-room at Cour! that is what is lacking to me here! After tiring out my horses along these fine streets, if I could but find Friendship in slippers and sit in slippers myself arguing with her, I should be perfectly content. When you have the goodness to say, with your worthy husband, *Quels souvenirs! quels regrets!* listen, and you will hear the echo of the Neva repeating, *Quels souvenirs! quels regrets!* [23]

The touch of Madame de Sévigné herself, in letter-writing, has not more spirit and grace. But we are to concern ourselves with Russia, not with Joseph de Maistre's gifts as a letter-writer. When he had been four or five years in Russia, he describes to the King of Sardinia the state of things there as follows: —

The want of money is extreme; nevertheless luxury runs its course without troubling itself about anything, although its extravagances and its utter thoughtlessness are conducting this country to an inevitable revolution. The nobility throws its money away, but this money falls into the hands of the business class, who have only to cut off their beards and to obtain government posts to become masters of Russia. The town of St. Petersburg will soon belong to trade and commerce entirely. In general the impoverishment and the moral decay of the nobility are the true causes of the revolution which we see in France. That revolution will be repeated here, but with peculiar circumstances. I can venture to assure your Majesty that Russia affords to the observer most abundant matter for interesting reflexion, for it brings back before our eyes the Middle Age, and enables us to see in reality what we had only seen in history. But the native Russian revolution, which may be called natural, combining itself with our eighteenth-century revolution, which is abominable, produces such a complication of things as is not to be understood without the most careful attention.[24]

The Emperor Alexander had his head full of generous projects and reforms for his people: —

There can be no mistake at present about the intentions of his Imperial Majesty. The emperor is tired of his power as handed down to him by his predecessors; and, his youth allowing him to undertake great enterprises, he really means to constitute his people and to raise them to the European level.[25]

Joseph de Maistre, with his distrust of written constitutions, his sense of the slow movement of things and of the extreme actual unripeness of the Russian people, regarded with disfavour these projects of reform from above. The Russians were unripe for them, he said; and he was convinced that a law, though excellent in itself, must prove useless and even mischievous unless the nation were worthy of it and made for it. How else could a law, he asked, have any real sanction? Bestowed by one emperor upon unripe and passive subjects, it might be revoked by another. Had not Paul the First established with every solemnity the Salic Law in Russia? A day or two afterwards, his son abolished it. "Toute nation a le gouvernement qu'elle mérite;" "every nation has the government which it is fit for." [26] As Georgia is to Russia, so is Russia to Western Europe; and as it fared with the introduction of the Russian procedure into Georgia, so it will fare with the introduction of Western constitutionalism into Russia: —

Formerly the Czar of Georgia used to ride out every morning on horseback to do justice; at a slow pace, he made a progress through the streets of Tiflis. Litigants came to him and stated their case. The Czar administered the stick to the party who seemed to deserve it. A Georgian said the other day to my brother, quite seriously: "Well, Sir, it was found that these princes very seldom made a mistake." The Georgians most sincerely regret this bygone street-procedure; and as to the new procedure which the Russians have brought amongst them with its formalities, its delays, its written documents, they cannot abide it, they are sick of it; whoever would give them back their old stick-law would be hailed as a benefactor. There are a thousand subtleties in use amongst our old European nations which I consider to be clean over the heads of the Russians — the Russians as I know them at this moment, at any rate.[27]

Again and again he returns to this actual unripeness of the Russian nation, in every one of the great lines along which the growth of a nation's mental life proceeds: —

People make a mistake when in this country they put 1815; they ought to put 1515, for we are in the sixteenth century. . . . The kind of moral vegetation which gradually leads nations forward out of barbarism into civilization has been suspended in Russia, and, as it were, cut in two, by two great events: the schism of the tenth century and the invasion of the Tartars.[28]

The clergy, which in Western Europe has done so much for knowledge and civilization, has done nothing in Russia: —

Between a Russian pope and an organ-pipe, I see no great difference; both emit sound, and that is all. I have repeatedly asked intelligent Russians whether means might not be found to civilize the clergy, to introduce it into society, to get rid of that disfavour which now more than ever attaches to it, and to make it of use for education, public morality, &c. All people unite with me in desiring this, but they give me no hope of its being accomplished.[29]

The religious knowledge and ideas of the Russian people in general are what might be expected with such a clergy: —

On the matter of religion the Russian knows nothing. His absolute ignorance of the Latin language shuts him out from all the sources of discussion. Of wits he has plenty; but even the best wits can only know what they have learnt, and the Russian has not looked in this direction (I am speaking of the laity). Now that the light of science is beginning to dawn here, it produces its usual effect — that of unsettling the religion of the country; for no sect can hold out against science. The vulgar and unlearned clergy is nothing and counts for nothing; those who have any mind, and who know Latin and French, are all more or less Protestants. In society you hear this denied, either from ignorance, or from inattention, or because people had rather deny it than set it right; but nothing is more certainly true.[30]

In philosophy Russia was as backward as in religion: —

I can hear of no good work on jurisprudence or on philosophy. In these two matters again, as in that of religion, Russia is delivered over, bound hand and foot, to the Germans. The persons who have influence being either art and part in the thing, or else being led by the nose, I see no remedy for it.[31]

The actual demand in Russia for serious reading of any kind was well shown by the state of the book-trade in St. Petersburg: —

A serious work, were it only a hundred pages long, can count here upon but a hundred and fifty purchasers, of whom ten will read it and two will understand it. A publisher, it may well be conceived, prints nothing at his own risk.

And again: —

Pluchart (a bookseller) has assured me, to my great astonishment, that a publisher in this capital, who brings out a philosophical work, however short, can only reckon upon about a hundred and fifty buyers. I quite understand that books are often lent; still, a hundred and fifty is a small number for a town of this size.[32]

Accordingly, Joseph de Maistre was of opinion that the rulers of Russia had better proceed very gradually with their plans of reform and constitution. He doubted whether the Russian people could understand any government except the autocracy of the Czar, or could be held together by it. He prophesied that "those who called for the enfranchisement of the serfs would be found to have been calling for the division of the empire." [33] For the present, he thought, "the reforms of his Imperial Majesty will end in his putting his people back again into the state where he found them, and no great harm either." [34] But what if the Russian nation, unripe as it was, should suddenly shake off its indifference and should take the Emperor's reforms seriously? What if this nation, at its actual stage of development, a nation neither sanguinary nor turbulent by nature (he always did it this justice), but which had suffered enormous losses in money and men from the great war, and was more and more being drawn into contact with the agitations of Western Europe, "should be seized by one of those fits on the brain which have attacked other nations, not more reasonable than Russia is, but more *raisonneuses?*" [35] In this case, Joseph de Maistre foresaw nothing but additional danger and embarrassment from the course now pursued by the emperor: —

If this nation, arriving at the comprehension of our perfidious novelties and acquiring a taste for them, were to conceive the idea of resisting all revocation or alteration of what it might call its *constitutional privileges;* if some university Pougatscheff were to put himself at the head of a party; if once the people got unsettled, and instead of Asiatic expeditions, began a revolution in the European line, I have no words to express the alarm which might well be felt.

"Bella, horrida bella!
Et multo *Nevam* spumentem sanguine cerno." [36]

Pougatscheff was a personage who figured in a revolt against the government of Catherine the Second.

For the present, however, Joseph de Maistre thought that all offers of code and constitution were likely to fall through, by reason of the indifference of the mass of the Russian people to them. In a letter written in October 1815 to Prince Koslowski, he thus sums up the data presented by the actual situation: —

In general I incline to think that you have not sufficiently prepared the people for the code before making the code for the people. I have a grudge against your Peter the Great, who appears to me to have committed the greatest of faults, that of failing in proper respect for his own nation. I never read that Numa made his Romans drop their toga, that he treated them as barbarians, and so on. The Decemvirs certainly went to Greece for laws, but they did not bring Greeks to Rome to make them. At present, the national pride is waking up and feeling indignant; but Peter has placed you in a false position with the foreigner. *"Nec tecum possum vivere, nec sine te"* — that is the motto for you. I do not think that there is to be found at this moment, for the man who knows how to observe, a greater and a finer field than your country, my dear Prince. The good side in you every one can see. You are kind, humane, hospitable, quick, intrepid, enterprising, clever at imitating, not in the least pedantic, with a dislike to all restraint, preferring a pitched battle to a lesson in drill. But on this fine body of yours are established two fistulas which impoverish it — instability and dishonesty. Everything with you is changeable: your laws change like the ribbons in vogue; your opinions like the waistcoats in wear; systems of every kind like the fashions. A man sells his house just as readily as his horse; nothing is constant with you except inconstancy, and nothing is respected, because nothing is ancient — there is your first mischief. Your second is not less serious. Highway robbery is less common here than elsewhere, because you are by nature gentle in as high a degree as you are brave; but the robbery of dishonesty is chronic with you. If one buys a diamond, it is sure to have a flaw; if one buys a match, the brimstone is sure to be bad. This spirit, traversing the channels of business from the highest to the lowest, makes endless ravages. It is against these enemies that your legislators should employ all their wisdom and all their strength. I could go on till to-morrow talking on this subject, *sed de his coram*. All I can now say is, that my interest in you and in all that concerns you is unbounded; your people have treated me with so much kindness, that they have won my heart, and I have no longer any wish to leave you.[37]

To these considerations of the faults, virtues, and condition of the Russian people are to be added considerations of the circumstances of the moment, and of the probable influences of the future: —

Your great country, involved in this enormous shock of the French Revolution, on the point at one time of perishing by it, has, by a rapid turn of events, been saved itself and been made the saviour of others. What will become of it, God only knows! What is certain is, that it cannot remain as it is now. It has had its part in the general commotion; the invasion, in the first place, has not failed to produce a very perceptible effect on the mental state of your peasants; the soldiers who have been in France will be inoculators of a still stronger kind. May God take care of you! [38]

Not codes and constitutions, but the deeper-working and gradual agencies of education and religion, were what Joseph de Maistre placed first in importance for Russia, as he saw and knew Russia. But neither of them was taking a direction which he approved, or which he could witness without disquietude. Of popular education there was no question, the time for it had not yet come. The only education, of which at that time there was any question in Russia, was the education of the middle and upper classes. The Jesuits, expelled in the eighteenth century from the chief Catholic states of Europe, had found a refuge in Russia, and education had come very much into their hands. Simply as schoolmasters, the Jesuits have great merits; an Englishman should never forget Bacon's testimony to the goodness and success of their methods. "Talis cum sis," he says to their Society, applying the words addressed by Agesilaus to Pharnabazus, "talis cum sis, utinam noster esses!" [39] But in the Jesuit schools, letters and literature were preponderant; the cry of the day was already for science, for more of science and less of letters. The Russians, with their appetite for novelty and fresh fashions, joined in the cry eagerly. The worship of science took forms which were not always judicious, the

professors who administered its bread of life were often personages whose
walk and conversation left much to be desired: —

> You mention science and the universities. What a chapter, my dear Prince,
> do we open there! At Wilna they have just been maintaining a thesis that God
> is caloric at the highest stage (*per perfectionem*), that the human spirit is
> caloric at a lower stage, the sun a caloric which organizes, the plant a caloric
> which is organized, &c. An apostate Catholic priest, who has worried two wives
> to death, and is at present the happy owner of a third, is professor of moral
> philosophy in one of your universities. Instruction, with you, is planted the
> wrong end upwards, and bears corruption for you before bearing science.[40]

In a series of letters written in 1810, at the request of Count Rasou-
mowsky, the Russian Minister of Public Instruction, Joseph de Maistre
examines with his usual acuteness the ideas of educational reform which
were prevalent, and discusses their application to the actual state of
Russia. He starts from his favourite, fundamental principle. Just as every
plan of government is a baneful dream, unless it be in harmony with the
character and circumstances of the nation, so it is with education. Before
establishing a scheme of education, the habits, inclinations, and state of
ripeness of the nation for which it is to be designed, are to be considered.
The eighteenth century had promulgated the doctrine that education in
the so-called sciences is the whole of education, whereas it is really, says
Joseph de Maistre, but a part of it; it is also by far the less interesting
part, and one which has no worth at all unless it rests upon moral education. The generation trained according to the new doctrine had made
the French Revolution. Still, in Western Europe education had for centuries been in the hands of the clergy, and it still remained to a great
extent in their hands. The clergy assign to moral training its proper and
prominent place in education. In Western Europe, in spite of the revolutionary propaganda, the schools bear deep traces of the character impressed on them by the clergy, and theories of education are largely
influenced by it. In Russia the clergy, "unhappily cut off from society
and deprived of all civil functions," [41] has never kept school, has created
and sustained no tradition of the indispensableness of moral training as a
part of education. The Russians, lovers of novelty, and peculiarly liable
to be blown about by every breath of vain doctrine, take up with the
new theories of scientific education as if they were a revelation, as if they
were going to do for Russia just what Russia needed. No error could be
greater. The Russians expect from the sciences far more than the sciences
can ever give them, but in the meanwhile Russia is not even ripe for the
sciences at all. The government might found scientific establishments,
but until the nation was ripe for them, and really needed them, they
would get no pupils. They would be like the School of Law, not long ago
instituted by the emperor, which offered to every student board and

lodging free, 300 roubles a year, and a degree; but no students came, and the School had to be closed. And yet, in the times which we call barbarous, the University of Paris could show 4000 students, drawn there from all parts of Europe, and living at their own cost. Everything depends, not on what the government may found, but on what the nation can use: —

Figure to yourself a government which should go to huge expense for the sake of covering with grand inns a country where nobody travelled; there you have the true image of a government which makes a great outlay on scientific establishments before the national genius has shown any turn for the sciences. Learned bodies of European fame, such as the Academy of Paris, the Royal Society of London, the Academy *del Cimento* of Florence, began as free associations of a certain number of individuals united together by their love for the sciences. After a certain time the sovereign, prompted by the public esteem for them, bestowed on them a civil existence by means of letters patent; so arose these great academic bodies. Everywhere they have been established because of the men of science who were there already, not in the hope of getting men of science by their means. It is a silly business to spend immense sums on making a cage for the phoenix, before you know whether the phoenix will come.

"Time," says the Persian proverb, "is the father of miracles." He is the prime minister of all sovereigns: with him they do everything; without him they can do nothing. And yet the Russians hold him in contempt, and will never wait. Time is affronted, and makes sport of them. It is a great misfortune that this famous nation should add to its first error of esteeming the sciences too highly the second error of wanting to become possessed of them all at once, and of feeling humiliated because Russia is more backward than other nations in this respect. Never was there a prejudice more false and more dangerous. The Russians might be the first nation in the universe, and yet have no talent for the natural sciences.[42]

Even if the Russians have no turn for the sciences, they may console themselves, says Joseph de Maistre, by remembering that the Romans, who had none either, nevertheless managed to cut a considerable figure in the world. But the Poles, a Slav people like the Russians, produced three centuries ago a man of science who is one of the ornaments of the human race, the illustrious Copernicus. It is not likely that the water of the Dwina should have some magical property which prevents science from passing. If nature, then, has, as is probable, endowed the Russians with an aptitude for the sciences, a spark will at some favourable moment awaken it, as it has awakened it elsewhere. Public attention will be turned that way, scientific societies and establishments will spring up of themselves, and the Government will only have to give them form and acknowledgment. Until this time of natural fermentation arrives, the mania for teaching science can lead to no good result, and can only do mischief. One kind of mischief Joseph de Maistre points out with especial force: —

A terrible inconvenience springing out of this scientific mania is that the government, having no professors of their own to satisfy it, are obliged to have recourse to foreign nations; and, as men of real attainments and character are not often disposed to leave their own country, where they are recompensed and honoured, it is always merely second-rate men, often it is vicious and damaged adventurers, who come out here to the North Pole offering their pretended science for money. Russia is at the present day covered with a scum of this kind, which political storms have driven from other countries. These runaways bring little with them here except impudence and vices. With no affection or esteem for this country, with no domestic ties civil or religious, they laugh at the undiscerning Russians who entrust them with the most precious of their belongings — their children; their only desire is to make money enough to enable them to go and live as they please elsewhere; and after trying to take in public opinion by performances which in the eyes of all good judges prove their gross ignorance, they depart back again to their own country, and turn Russia into ridicule in worthless books, which Russia is even good enough to buy of these creatures; nay, not unfrequently she translates them.[43]

A nation's beginnings of intellectual activity are naturally in imaginative production and in poetry, and here Joseph de Maistre observed a genuine movement, as genuine as the scientific movement was factitious. Language and letters a nation must begin with; above all, the first stage in its mental progress is the respect for its own language and the employment of it. The predominance of the French language was a real obstacle, in Russia, to the development of the national genius. Joseph de Maistre talks sarcastically of "the St. Petersburg savants who know French perfectly and Russian a little." [44] He speaks of the suppression of the French Theatre, in 1816, as favourable to the improvement of the native drama. In the chief theatre of St. Petersburg the performances were no longer to be in French, but in Russian. We do not know whether this theatrical precedence of the Russian tongue is still perfectly kept up at St. Petersburg. But Dr. Neubauer reported the other day a symptom which is full of promise for Russian literature and life; namely, that in the transactions of the Philosophical Society of St. Petersburg, which used always to be in French and German, the Russian language is now adopted.

Religion, however, was the great agency on which Joseph de Maistre relied for expelling evil where it had reigned and made havoc, and for preventing its entrance into communities hitherto unravaged by it. "The French Revolution is satanic," he used to say; "if the counter-revolution is not divine, it is null." [45] And by this divine counter-revolution he meant "a moral and religious revolution, without which chaos cannot cease and creation begin." But he found in the religious fermentation which surrounded him in Russia a mixture of philosophism, Germanism, Protestantism, and illuminism, which seemed to him to announce a dark future for religion, except so far as this darkness was relieved by numerous conversions to Roman Catholicism. But we ought to let him speak for himself: —

Science, newly arrived here, is commencing its first exploit, which is to take religion by the throat. The conquests of the Protestant spirit, throughout all that portion of the clergy which is acquainted with French and Latin, are incredible. People talk about the Greek Church; the Russian Church is no more Greek than it is Syrian or Armenian; it is an isolated church under a civil head, just like the Church of England. If the patriarch of Constantinople were to dream of giving an order here he would be thought mad; and mad he would indeed be to attempt it. In this state of things, the London Bible Society has come fishing in Russia. This society spent last year 42,000*l*. It was proposed to open a branch here, and the offer was at once accepted, for the Russian is even more greedy of novelties than the Frenchman, with whom he has many points of resemblance. Persons of the highest respectability have become members, and amongst them the Russian and the Catholic archbishops.[46]

To the plan of "sowing Bibles broadcast in the vulgar tongue, without distinction of persons and without explanation," [47] the Catholic Church has always, as is well known, been resolutely opposed. In Russia, says Joseph de Maistre, —

A single ancient version — nay, a few lines only of this version — wrongly interpreted by popular fanaticism, have sufficed to create the Russian *rascolnics* (sectaries), that vast ulcer which eats into the national religion and spreads further every day. What will it be when a simple people, taking things absolutely by the letter, shall possess the Bible in the vulgar tongue in all the variety of the Bible versions?

But it was as "a Protestant enterprise" conducting men towards "*le riénisme Protestant*," [48] Protestant nothingism, that the Bible Society called forth Joseph de Maistre's deepest enmity. The Society was in his eyes, respectable as might be many of its members and excellent as might be their intentions, in real truth nothing more nor less than "a Socinian machine for the overthrow of all ecclesiastical authority." [49] As a Protestant enterprise, he maintained, it moved infallibly towards the sure goal of Protestantism, towards Socinianism or Deism, as people then called it; — in other words, dogmatic decay. With penetrating eye, with the acuteness of a trained observer and the joy of a bitter enemy, Joseph de Maistre saw the ruin, the certain and ever-increasing ruin, upon the Continent, of dogmatic and orthodox Protestantism. Protestantism was no longer a religion, he said, it was become a mere negation: — [50]

There is not a point of Christian faith which Protestantism has not attacked and destroyed in the minds of its partizans. What was sure to happen has happened; this unblessed system has allied itself with philosophism, which is indebted to it for its most dangerous weapons; and these two enemies of all religious belief have exercised so fatal an influence, that those fair regions of Europe where they prevail may be said to have no longer any religion at all.[51]

And therefore the Russian Church, which was fast imbibing "the venom of Germanism and Protestantism," [52] and bidding fair to become professedly Protestant, would probably announce itself Protestant at a time when there were no Protestants left anywhere else.

In his keen, bold, unsparing criticism of continental Protestantism Joseph de Maistre is wonderfully successful. What we must never forget is that his own Catholicism, by virtue of which he thinks himself entitled to treat Protestantism thus disdainfully, and on which he affects to stand as on a rock, is an hypothesis arbitrary, artificial, and unavailing. Always therefore, in watching Joseph de Maistre attack and rout his adversaries, a good critic will have the feeling, that the ultimate fate of the day is not yet by any means fully visible, that the battle is not really won. It is as with Joseph de Maistre's haughty airs of defiance and contempt of middle-class and popular opinion. "What is a nation, my good friend? The sovereign and the aristocracy. We must weigh voices, not count them. A hundred shopkeepers of Genoa would go for less with me, as to what is to be judged expedient or inexpedient for the community, than the family of Brignola alone." [53] The mind of the hundred shopkeepers may be indeed but, as Bacon says, "a poor and shrunken thing";[59] but whoever shall imperiously substitute for it the mind of the House of Brignola, will find the resource artificial and insufficient.

The tendency to Protestantism was favoured in Russia by another tendency, also Germanic in its origin, and which was powerfully influential in the highest quarters — illuminism. Illuminism, says Joseph de Maistre, has for its ideal a kind of transcendental and universal Christianity; it conceives Christianity to have been transformed and disfigured by priests, and is extremely unfavourable to hierarchies and their claims; it looks upon Christendom as a collection of sects differing on many points, but all of them united at bottom in something good, which is fundamental Christianity. The adherents of this illuminism were very numerous at St. Petersburg and Moscow. The Emperor Alexander himself was profoundly imbued with it. The extraordinary Convention of Paris, in which Austria, Prussia, and Russia, after the defeat of Napoleon, solemnly declared their adherence to a universal Christianity, was a concession to the enthusiasm of Alexander for this ideal. "The Emperor Alexander," writes Joseph de Maistre, "with his universal Christianity, his fundamental dogmas, and his Bible Society, may be sure that he is on the high road to the destruction of Christianity." [55] But the Emperor's subjects seemed much inclined to accompany him, and even the Catholic Archbishop joined, as we have already seen, the Bible Society, and when

Rome expressed disapprobation and insisted on his leaving it, he took no notice. The picture of this Catholic dignitary, the Archbishop of Mohileff, who must indeed have been a curiosity, is in Joseph de Maistre's raciest manner. "The Archbishop of Mohileff is Sestrintzewitz, a man eighty years old; formerly a Protestant, then an officer of hussars, finally a Catholic bishop. It was he who said one day, as he saw the Emperor pass: 'That is *my* Pope!' " [56]

In illuminism, however, and also in the dogmatic decay of Protestantism, there was much out of which Catholicism could make its profit: —

The friends of illuminism swarm at St. Petersburg and Moscow; I know an immense number of them. And you are not to think that everything which they say and write is bad; on the contrary, they have some very sound notions, and, — what will surprise you, perhaps, — they tend towards us Catholics in two ways. First, their own clergy has no influence over their minds; they hold their clergy in utter contempt, and accordingly no longer listen to it; if they do not yet listen to our clergy, at any rate they respect it, and even go so far as to own that it has better retained the primitive spirit. Secondly, the Catholic mystics having much that is in agreement with the ideas which these illuminati have formed concerning internal religion, they have plunged head over ears into the reading of this class of authors. They will read nothing but St. Theresa, St. Francis of Sales, Fénelon, Madame Guyon, &c. Now it is impossible they should steep themselves in influences of this kind without being drawn considerably nearer to us; and in fact a great enemy of the Catholic religion said the other day, "What annoys me is, that all this illuminism will end in Catholicism." [57]

The secret societies, therefore, the centres of illuminism, which in Catholic countries are objectionable, are in non-Catholic countries useful: —

Let them be. They are coming our way, all of them, but by a spiral line resulting from an invisible attraction towards the centre, modified by a strong though less potent action of pride, which continually draws them all it can from their direct course. These societies, besides, are detestable in Catholic communities, because they attack our fundamental principle of authority; but in non-Catholic nations I consider them to be of infinite use, because they keep fresh and alive the religious fibre in man, and preserve his spirit from Protestant nothingism.[58]

Philosophism and Protestantism, on their part, too, serve the Catholic Church: —

From the moment that science makes its entry into a non-Catholic country, there is a division in the community; the mass will roll towards Deism, whilst a certain body draw near to us. In all Protestant countries, there is not a man of real intelligence left who is a Protestant; all are Socinians, except that band of persons, more or less numerous, whose conversion to Catholicism makes so much noise at present.[59]

So much noise did it make that Joseph de Maistre quitted Russia in consequence. Amidst the ferment of the new religious movement came a crop of sudden and unexpected conversions to Roman Catholicism. The multiplicity and rapidity of these conversions, principally in the highest rank of society, was, says Joseph de Maistre, an admirable spectacle.[60] They enraged the Minister of Public Worship, Prince Alexander Gallitzin; they greatly disturbed the Emperor himself, to whose autocracy the unbending attitude of the Church of Rome was unfamiliar and unpleasant, while its high doctrine of "Extra ecclesiam nulla salus" went clean contrary to his notions of a universal Christianity. The Jesuits, whose connection with these conversions was evident, were in 1816 by imperial ukase expelled from St. Petersburg, and their schools were closed. Joseph de Maistre's intimacy with the Jesuits made him suspected of complicity, and the Emperor commissioned one of his ministers to request an explanation from him upon the subject. Joseph de Maistre replied that he had never induced one of his Imperial Majesty's subjects to change his religion, but that, if any of them had happened to confide to him their intention to change it, he could not in honour and conscience have told them that they were wrong. The Emperor received the explanation with acquiescence, and continued to treat the Sardinian Envoy with the same courtesy and distinction as before. But Joseph de Maistre felt that his position at St. Petersburg could no longer be quite what it had been — perfectly free from all constraint and perfectly agreeable; and he made up his mind to quit a place which had become dear to him, and where he at one time thought of ending his days. He requested his government to recall him, and in 1817 he returned, as has been mentioned, to pass the last years of his life at Turin.

He left amongst his papers the sketch of a conclusion to be added to his *Soirées de Saint-Pétersbourg,* and with a passage from this conclusion we may fitly end our record of his comments on Russia and the Russian people: —

To my dying day I shall never cease to bear Russia in memory and to pray for her welfare. Her welfare will be a constant object of my thoughts. What will become of you amidst the general unsettlement of men's minds? and how will you manage to blend so many diverse elements which within a short space of time have collected amongst you? Blind faith, grossly superstitious ceremonies, philosophical doctrines, illuminism, the spirit of liberty, passive obedience, the hut and the palace, the refinements of luxury and the rudeness of savage life — what will come out of all these elements set in motion by that turn for novelty which is perhaps the most striking trait in your character, and which, urging you incessantly in the pursuit of new objects, makes you disgusted with what you possess? You dislike living in any house but one that you have just bought. From laws down to ribbons, everything has to follow the untiring wheel of your changes. Nevertheless consider the nations which cover the globe; it is the contrary system which has made them famous. In the tenacious Englishman you have a proof of it; his sovereigns still take pride in bearing the titles which they received from the Popes, so hard is it to detach this people from its old institutions. And yet what people surpasses the English in might, in unity, in national glory? Do you wish to be as great as you are powerful? follow, then, this example given you by England, set yourselves steadily against the rage you have for novelty and change, alike in the smallest things and in the greatest. You say, "My father died in this house, therefore I must sell it." Say rather: "He died here, therefore sell it I cannot." Have done with all your ignoble lath and plaster; God has given you granite and iron; use these gifts of God, and build for eternity. One looks in vain for monuments amongst you; one would say that you had an aversion to them. If you do nothing for time, what is time likely to do for you? As for the sciences, they will come if they are to come; are you made for them? we shall see. Meanwhile, you start, like all the nations of the world, with poetry and letters; your fine language is capable of anything; let your talents ripen without impatience. Your case is but that of all other nations; your warriors and statesmen have come before your scientific era. Strogonoff, who gave you Siberia; Suwarow, who made your arms famous throughout the world, were of no academy; better have no academy than have to fill it with foreigners. Your time if it is really to come, will come naturally and without efforts. [61]

If only, until the time of Russia is fully come, we could have relays of note-takers like Joseph de Maistre, to report progress every quarter or half century!

Notes

[1] *Note-Books*, p. 595.
[2] See Fraser Neiman, "Matthew Arnold's Review of the *Lettres et opuscules inédits* by Joseph de Maistre," *Modern Language Notes*, LXXIV (June 1959), 492–494, and R. H. Super, "Arnold's Notebooks and Arnold Bibliography."
[3] *Note-Books*, pp. 20–21.
[4] *Ibid.*, p. 589.
[5] "Maximen und Reflexionen," *Goethes Sämtliche Werke*, IV, 219.
[6] De Maistre, *Lettres*, II, 494.
[7] "Discours du citoyen Cherchemot, commissaire du pouvoir exécutif près l'administration centrale du M . . . ," *ibid.*, 222.
[8] *Ibid.*, I, 382.
[9] *Macbeth*, II, i, 47.
[10] De Maistre, *Lettres*, I, 508.
[11] *Ibid.*, 381.
[12] *Ibid.*, 508.
[13] George Hammond Whalley (1813–1878), English politician, gained notoriety by his ardent attacks on Jesuits, as well as by his advocacy of the cause of Arthur Orton, the celebrated Tichborne claimant.
[14] De Maistre, *Lettres*, I, 452. Cf. I, 363.
[15] Edmund Yates (1831–1894), novelist and journalist, in 1874 founded the *World: a Journal for Men and Women*. Henry du Pré Labouchere (1831–1912), Liberal M.P. and journalist, was one of the original staff of the *World*. He began to

publish his own weekly, *Truth*, in January 1877. Labouchere's personal column printed information about the royal family that made him *persona non grata* to Queen Victoria.

¹⁶ De Maistre, *Lettres*, I, 450–451. The bracketed comment is Arnold's.
¹⁷ Arnold uses this quotation in his letters. See *Letters*, I, 193, 318.
¹⁸ De Maistre, *Lettres*, I, 86–87.
¹⁹ *Ibid.*, 86.
²⁰ *Ibid.*, 269.
²¹ *Ibid.*, 50–51.
²² *Ibid.*, 114–115.
²³ *Ibid.*, 115–116.
²⁴ *Ibid.*, 220–221.
²⁵ *Ibid.*, 260.
²⁶ *Ibid.*, 264. See also II, 281–282.
²⁷ *Ibid.*, I, 264–265.
²⁸ The first of these sentences is from *Ibid.*, I, 352; the second from II, 286.
²⁹ *Ibid.*, 405–406.
³⁰ *Ibid.*, 362–363.
³¹ *Ibid.*, 405.
³² *Ibid.*, 311.
³³ *Ibid.*, 352.
³⁴ *Ibid.*, 266–267.
³⁵ *Ibid.*, 325.
³⁶ *Ibid.*, 266–267.
³⁷ *Ibid.*, 367–368.
³⁸ *Ibid.*, 366.
³⁹ *Ibid.*, II, 312.
⁴⁰ *Ibid.*, I, 366.
⁴¹ *Ibid.*, II, 283.
⁴² *Ibid.*, 284–285.
⁴³ *Ibid.*, 287–288.
⁴⁴ *Ibid.*, I, 455.
⁴⁵ *Ibid.*, 359.
⁴⁶ *Ibid.*, 352-353.
⁴⁷ *Ibid.*, 253.
⁴⁸ *Ibid.*, 322.
⁴⁹ *Ibid.*, 353. Cf. p. 406.
⁵⁰ *Ibid.*, 361.
⁵¹ *Ibid.*, II, 370–371.
⁵² *Ibid.*, I, 392.
⁵³ *Ibid.*, 448.
⁵⁴ "Of Truth," *Essays* (The World's Classics, Oxford, 1902), p. 2.
⁵⁵ De Maistre, *Lettres*, II, 394.
⁵⁶ *Ibid.*, I, 421. Also I, 445.
⁵⁷ *Ibid.*, 392–393.
⁵⁸ *Ibid.*, 322.
⁵⁹ *Ibid.*, 386.
⁶⁰ *Ibid.*, 418. See also pp. 363, 386, 390.
⁶¹ *Ibid.*, II, 340–342.

Introduction to Poetry: Poets, Dramatists, Novelists

The Hundred Greatest Men,
8 vols. (London, 1880), vol. I

Although it has not been previously reprinted, this essay has, in part, achieved a certain celebrity; for the sentences of the final paragraph, transposed and altered, make the familiar opening of "The Study of Poetry," [1] an essay that originally served as the General Introduction to *The English Poets*, edited by T. H. Ward (London, 1880). The present essay was the Introduction to the first volume of a pretentious work published by Sampson Low, Marston, Searle, and Rivington, the full title of which was *The Hunded Greatest Men: Portraits of the One Hundred Greatest Men of History Reproduced from Fine and Rare Steel Engravings*. Ralph Waldo Emerson wrote a General Introduction to the whole work.

The men who are the flower and glory of our race are to pass here before us, the highest manifestations, whether on this line or on that, of the force which stirs in every one of us — the chief poets, artists, religious founders, philosophers, historians, scholars, orators, warriors, statesmen, voyagers, leaders in mechanical invention and industry, who have appeared amongst mankind. And the poets are to pass first. Why? Because, of the various modes of manifestation through which the human spirit pours its force, theirs is the most adequate and happy.

The fact of this superior adequacy of poetry is very widely felt; and whether distinctly seized or no, is the root of poetry's boundless popularity and power. The reason for the fact has again and again been made an object of inquiry. Partial explanations of it have been produced. Aristotle declared poetry to be more philosophical and of more serious worth than history, because poetry deals with generals, history with particulars. Aristotle's idea is expanded by Bacon, after his own fashion, who extols poetry as "submitting the shews of things to the desires of the mind," to the desires for "a more ample greatness, a more exact goodness, and a more absolute variety, than can be found in the nature of things." [2] No man, however, can fully draw out the reasons why the human spirit feels itself to attain to a more adequate and satisfying expression in poetry than in any other of its modes of activity. For to draw them out fully we should have to go behind our own nature itself, and that we can none of us do.

Portions of them we may seize, but not more; Aristotle and Bacon themselves have not succeeded in seizing more than portions of them. And at one time, probably, and to one set of observers, one ground of the primordial and incontestable fact before us comes clearest into light; at another, and to other observers, another.

For us to-day, what ground of the superiority of poetry is the most evident, the most notable? Surely its solidity. Already we have seen Aristotle prefer it to history on this very ground. Poetry has, says he, a higher wisdom and a more serious worth than history. Compare poetry with other efforts of the human spirit besides history. Compare it with art. It is more intellectual than art, more interpretative. Along with the plastic representation it utters the idea, it thinks. Poetry is often called art, and poets are classed with painters and sculptors as artists. But Goethe has with profound truth insisted on the difference between them. "Poetry is held to be art," he says, "and yet it is not, as art is, mechanism, mechanical. I deny poetry to be an art. Neither is it a science. Poetry is to be called neither art nor science, but genius." [3] Poetry is less artistic than the arts, but in closer correspondence with the intelligential nature of man, who is defined, as we know, to be "a thinking animal;" poetry thinks, and the arts do not.

But it thinks emotionally, and herein it differs from science, and is more of a stay to us. Poetry gives the idea, but it gives it touched with beauty, heightened by emotion. This is what we feel to be interpretative for us, to satisfy us — thought, but thought invested with beauty, with emotion. Science thinks, but not emotionally. It adds thought to thought, accumulates the elements of a synthesis which will never be complete until it is touched with beauty and emotion; and when it is touched with these, it has passed out of the sphere of science, it has felt the fashioning hand of the poet. So true is this, that the more the follower of science is a complete man, the more he will feel the refreshment of poetry as giving him a satisfaction which our nature is always desiring, but to which his science can never bring him. And the more an artist, on the other hand, is a complete man, the higher he will appreciate the reach and effectualness which poetry gains by being, in Goethe's words, not art but genius; by being from its very nature forbidden to limit itself to the sphere of plastic representation, by being forced to talk and to think.

Poetry, then, is more of a stay to us than art or science. It is more explicative than art, and it has the emotion which to science is wanting. But the grand sources of explication and emotion, in the popular opinion, are philosophy and religion. Philosophy — the love of wisdom — is indeed a noble and immortal aspiration in man. But the philosophies, the constructions of systematic thought which have arisen in the endeavour to satisfy this aspiration, are so perishable that to call up the memory of them is to pass in review man's failures. We have mentioned Goethe, the poet of that land of philosophies, Germany. What a series of philosophic systems has Germany seen since the birth of Goethe! and what sort of a stay is any one of them compared with the poetry of Germany's one great poet. So necessary, indeed, and so often shown by experience, is the want of solidity in constructions of this kind, that it argues, one may say, a dash of the pedant in a man to approach them, except perhaps in the ardour of extreme youth, with any confidence. And the one philosopher who has known how to give to such constructions, not indeed solidity, but charm, is Plato, the poet among philosophers, who produces his abstractions like the rest, but produces them more than half in play and with a smile.

And religion? The reign of religion as morality touched with emotion is indeed indestructible. But religion as men commonly conceive it — religion depending on the historicalness of certain supposed facts, on the authority of certain received traditions, on the validity of certain accredited dogmas — how much of this religion can be deemed unalterably secure? Not a dogma that does not threaten to dissolve, not a tradition that is not shaken, not a fact which has its historical character free from question. Compare the stability of Shakespeare with the stability of the Thirty-Nine Articles! Our religion has materialised itself in the fact — the supposed fact; it has attached its emotion to the fact. For poetry the idea is everything; the rest is its world of illusion, of divine illusion; it attaches its emotion to the idea, the idea *is* the fact. The strongest part of our religion to-day is its unconscious poetry. The future of poetry is immense, because in conscious poetry, where it is worthy of its high destinies, our race, as time goes on, will find an ever surer and surer stay.

Notes

[1] *Essays in Criticism, Second Series,* 1 ed. (London, 1888).
[2] Francis Bacon, "The Advancement of Learning," in *Works,* ed. J. Spedding, R. L. Ellis, and D. D. Heath, 14 vols. (London, 1857–1874), III, 343.
[3] "Maximen und Reflexionen," *Goethes Sämtliche Werke,* XXXVIII, 277.

A Genevese Judge

Pall Mall Gazette
July 13, 1881, pp. 11–12

This unsigned review of Eugène Colladon, *Etudes et fragments littéraires, précédés d'une notice par Edouard Humbert* (Geneva, 1881) gives one more evidence of Arnold's willingness to write, even at the height of his prestige, on books that a less modest author might have thought inconsiderable.[1] But the book afforded him an opportunity to encourage the cosmopolitanism of intellectual life and the pursuit of perfection that steadily remained among his objectives. Arnold's praise of Colladon in the opening paragraph of the essay as socially delightful might suggest personal knowledge of him; but of such acquaintance there appears to be no published record. Perhaps it was sufficient to arouse Arnold's interest that Colladon was a grandson of Mallet du Pan, to whose Mémoires Sainte-Beuve gave two *causeries,* and whom Arnold commends in the opening paragraph along with those other opponents of Jacobinism, de Maistre and Burke.

On the 10th of May, 1800, Mallet du Pan died of consumption at Richmond.[2] He and Joseph de Maistre are the chief intellectual figures of the emigration. Both of them have intellectual and spiritual affinities with Burke — Mallet du Pan with Burke at his best, Joseph de Maistre with Burke, brilliant, indeed, but warped, yielding himself to exaggeration, paradox, self-will. M. Taine, in his history of the Revolution, recalls attention to Mallet du Pan and to his thought; it would be well if he and they were better known to us in England. At present, however, it is not of Mallet du Pan that we wish to speak, but of Mallet du Pan's grandson, Eugène Colladon, who died last year at the age of seventy-five. For forty-one years M. Colladon was a member of the magistrature of the republic of Geneva — he became Procureur-Général, and afterwards the President of the High Court. He was an excellent magistrate, an excellent citizen, and socially he was delightful. He was also a lover of letters, and a contributor to the well-known Swiss review, the *Bibliothèque Universelle de Genève.* Since his death his family have published a small volume of extracts and fragments from these review articles. Sainte-Beuve would not unfrequently ask, when a new work of literature appeared, "Qu'en pense M. Eugène Colladon?" and the memorial volume of him well deserves a word of notice. One might desire more variety in the extracts; and to us, at any rate, the discretion which withholds M. Colladon's criticisms on the poetry of M. Victor Hugo because they contain "des pages dont plus d'une pourrait paraître assez mordante aux lecteurs de 1881" — in other words, because they are at variance with the deification since effected and the legend now dominant — appears excessive. Still, the extracts as they stand are remarkable — remarkable both for their own merit and also as bringing before us a type of culture which is probably passing away, but which will not easily find a successor of equal value to replace it.

Eugène Colladon's training was obtained from the Greek and Latin classics — the Latin very much more than the Greek — and from the French literature of the seventeenth and eighteenth centuries. For a man of intelligence, character, and practical occupations in life, this training appears to have had an extraordinary value. Eugène Colladon was neither a genius nor a professional author. He was a magistrate and a judge, with the intelligence and integrity which are the due outfit for that honourable position. From the ancient classics he drew the elevation which they have been so generally found to give; from the French literature of the seventeenth century he drew the sense for style, and for style not in a remote and dead language, but in his mother tongue; from that of the eighteenth century he drew its quick and strong mental movement, its straightforwardness and lucidity of thinking. This combination produced, as its result, a stamp of something widely human, European and central, in comparison with which the intellectual modes of other nations appeared provincial and arbitrary, and in which lies the secret of the strong attraction exercised by the French language and culture. Its characteristic is that it is impressed on society rather than that it is impressed on isolated thinkers and men of letters. Colladon, a functionary and a man of affairs, is strikingly marked with it, and it is better studied in such a man than in Voltaire.

Many of us remember Châtelard near Montreux. Colladon speaks of a visit to its owner, M. Marquis, and of a conversation "by the fireside of the immense salon." He says: — "I remember that I was struck by the turn that Marquis speedily gave, without effort and without the least pedantry, to a conversation that would otherwise have very cheerfully been allowed to stop at vineyard prospects and family gossip. In his busy solitude he thought much, he loved ideas, and he had ideas of his own."

There is one of the signs of the culture we have been speaking of, its ardour! It presses its possessor to extend his interest beyond his vines and his crops, to "love ideas," and to "have them of his own." But *ideas* is a wide term; to love what sort of ideas, to have what sort of ideas of his own? Well, Colladon writes to a friend that he has been reading Quinet's *History of the Revolution,* in which he finds much to admire; we have not space for the whole of the letter, but here is the conclusion of it: —

No doubt Quinet's general point of view is chimerical; for he thinks that, in order to be profitable to the advent and the durability of freedom, the political revolution which came to pass at the end of the last century ought to have been accompanied by a religious revolution that should have been equally profound and equally destructive of the past; in a word, that, in order to remain a free, liberal, strong, and great republic, France ought before all else to become Protestant. This is perhaps true; but as nobody thought of it, as the need has been nowhere felt, and as France would rather have gone over to Mahommedanism than have dreamed for an instant of turning Protestant, it is only a sort of retrospective romance, a play of imagination, to summon from the bowels of fiction a Protestant France, for the sake of endowing it with every kind of virtue, of greatness, and of liberties.

If Lord Selborne[3] and Lord Cairns[4] will allow us to use them as an illustration, we will say that we can perfectly imagine their occupying themselves in their leisure with other things than their vines and their crops; can imagine them reading with interest a grave history and writing letters about it, but that we cannot by any possibility imagine either of them writing such a letter about it as Colladon's. What distinguishes Colladon's letter is the central point of view, the lucidity, what our neighbours call the *coup d'oeil;* it is the letter of a man who has, in Sainte-Beuve's words, "une intelligence ouverte et traversée." And yet Colladon is not a philosopher by profession, not a Niebuhr or Burke, neither historical philosopher nor political philosopher; he is a man in the daily exercise of a profession full of practical detail, full of routine. But he has had a culture which keeps his thinking quick and large and fresh and lucid, and which makes thinking of this sort a necessity to him. It is not for nothing that his spirit, nourished first on the Latin classics and on the French classics of the seventeenth century, has then felt the electric shock of the French genius of the eighteenth century, of its free thought, its bold and clear literature, its incomparable *art de causer.*

How charming an art, how worthy of our liveliest regrets — the art of conversation! Its tradition grows weaker every day, perhaps because we have become more serious, perhaps because family life has taken so great a place in the interests of all of us, but perhaps, too, because egotism has grown stronger, because the love of money and of material pleasures has been so lamentably developed. And then, especially, politics, having fallen into the domain of everybody, people fling themselves on that easy food for talk, accessible as it is to every sort of intelligence; for on this ground nobody is without ability enough to contribute to conversation his contingent of commonplaces, of insipid stalenesses, of inane conjectures, and futile hypotheses. Whereas real *causerie,* made up of ideas, the stimulation of mind by mind, the study in common of the historic and literary past, the spontaneous association of various intelligences for the purpose of analyzing some work of thought, of art, of poetry, of philosophy, and all this with life, with pleasant eagerness, without pretention, among people of subtle and delicate minds — is it not a fine and a lawful source of enjoyment? And especially when this intellectual tournament is directed by the hand of a woman who to all the grace of her sex joins a real depth of thought, surely it doubles in value.

The extract is long, and in the columns of a newspaper we ought to pay due regard to the claims of politics, and of readers anxious to "se ruer sur cette facile pâture." Still, though long, it describes so finely and accurately a phase of culture never to be forgotten that we have not the heart to abridge it. It is worthy of Mdlle. de Lespinasse herself, or of some other heroine of the "art charmant et vivement regrettable — celui de causer." [5] The France of the present day, the France of M. Zola, is in its intellectual habits and aims very far removed from the France of Mdlle. de Lespinasse, which so much influenced M. Colladon. M. Colladon has noted the actual tendencies of the French literature of to-day, tendencies with which he was by no means in sympathy. "Real life in our time is so full of events, so full of storms, that the public will have nothing to say to a book in which there are not to be found ferocious passions and sanguinary crimes — all that the imagination can contain of horror and delirium. But a man of genius would soar above this passing extravagance of humour, and, instead of giving way before the torrent, he would do his best, by force of talent, to restore his generation to nature and good taste."

Pending the arrival of this man of genius, we will remark that the old French culture, with all its limitations, bore excellent fruits, and that in M. Colladon they are exhibited in singular perfection. We may say of him what Voltaire said of one of his visitors: that there are few people to be met with "qui aient l'esprit plus juste, plus net, plus cultivé, et plus éclairé."

Notes

[1] Neiman, "Some Newly Attributed Contributions of Matthew Arnold," pp. 91–92.
[2] Jacques Mallet du Pan (1749–1800) was a Swiss journalist and ardent monarchist. He was the subject of two *causeries* of Sainte-Beuve.
[3] Roundell Palmer, first Earl of Selborne (1812–1895) was Lord Chancellor (1872–1874). He was an eminent lawyer and Rector of the University of St. Andrews. Throughout his life he pursued hobbies in natural history, especially botany. A devout member of the Church of England, he taught a Sunday school class for many years.
[4] Hugh McCalmont Cairns, first Earl Cairns (1819–1885), for many years Solicitor-General, Conservative leader in the House of Lords, and Lord-Chancellor in Disraeli's government after the elections of 1874. He was a "frequent chairman of meetings at Exeter Hall and of missionary meetings" and is said to have "looked askance on the stage" (*DNB*). His zealous evangelicalism lends point to Arnold's derision.
[5] Julie de Lespinasse (1732–1776), French letter writer.

A French Worthy

Pall Mall Gazette
November 8, 1882, pp. 1–2

On October 24, 1882, Arnold wrote to John Morley, later Viscount Morley (1838–1923), who had on May 3, 1880, superseded the now strongly conservative Frederick Greenwood as editor of the *Pall Mall Gazette*,[1] suggesting a notice on the death of Jean Jacques Rapet (1805–1882). He said to Morley: "Rapet, an old French Inspector, has just died in Paris, and the French *Journal des Instituteurs* has had a long article on him. He had 'morality,' so you will not be surprised to hear that I knew him; Guizot sent me to him as the man who could best tell me about popular education in France. Shall I write a page or a page and a half about him for you?"[2]

Morley must have responded favorably at once, for "A French Worthy" appeared as a leading article in the *Pall Mall Gazette*. Although unsigned, it was included in T. B. Smart's *Bibliography of Matthew Arnold*.

We will permit ourselves to distinguish three types of Frenchmen. The Frenchman of one type is the Frenchman of our received notions, gay and free and bold of spirit, positive (as the phrase is), social, sensual. This is the common Gaulish, or rather Gallo-Roman type. Then there is the type of Frenchman grave and austere, self-introspective, meditative, spiritual. We have only to think of Port Royal. Finally, there is again the type with nothing Puritan, but yet with a genuine and serious bent for a well-ordered life, for morality; and of this type we may take personages so various as Mdme. de Sévigné, the Chancellor Daguesseau, Vauvenargues, Joubert, Littré, as representative.[3] It will seem strange that one should speak of Mdme. de Sévigné as having anything very serious about her. But whoever will closely follow the life and nature of this famous woman, both in general contrast with that of the world in which she moved, and in particular contrast with the eminently Gaulish life and nature of her cousin Bussy-Rabutin,[4] will convince himself that strongly characterizing Mdme. de Sévigné, with all her gaiety, all her wit, all her lightness, is an antipathy to moral disorder. The other personages named along with her have the same antipathy; Port Royal, of course, has it;[5] and it points to a strain of race more serious than the Gaulish. It points probably to a German strain brought in by the Franks and appearing in the French people. French personages characterized by this strain are not of the Gaulish type; of what type shall we call them? To talk of a Frankish type sounds pedantic, to talk of an old-French type suggests something superannuated and obsolete: let us say that the French personages of whom we are speaking are morally, by contrast with the Gaulish type of the majority around them, of a Germanic type.

Of this type was an old functionary of primary instruction who died in France this year, and of whom the *Journal des Instituteurs* has recently published a notice — M. Rapet. A less showy life than M. Rapet's, and a more laborious one, can hardly be imagined. He was born in 1805, in the Department of the Ain; his father was a bookseller. He went to school at the Lycée Louis-le-Grand, in Paris; turned his attention to the natural sciences, the modern languages, and education; travelled in Switzerland and Germany, and became acquainted with the Père Girard, Pestalozzi, and Fellenberg.[6] He attracted the notice at Lyons of the Baron Degerando, at that time prominent as an economist and philanthropist.[7] On his recommendation M. Rapet was appointed, after the passing of M. Guizot's school law in 1833, director of the primary normal school at Périgueux.[8] He remained there thirteen years. In 1847 he was made an inspector of primary schools in Paris, in 1861 an inspector-general. In the latter years of his life he had retired from active service, but was continually employed on commissions dealing with popular education.

All questions connected with popular education interested M. Rapet. Normal schools in France, school-management, teachers' conferences, teachers' newspapers, all of them owe him much. He was one of the founders of the *Bulletin de l'Instruction Primaire*, now the *Journal des Instituteurs*. His *Cours d'études des écoles primaires* is or was in the hands of nearly all the primary schoolmasters of France.[9] He was a man of detail, a man of painful labour, often working sixteen and eighteen hours out of the twenty-four. His papers on the condition of the labouring classes and on Pestalozzi were crowned by the Institute. Its prize of 10,000 f. was given to his *Manuel de morale et d'économie politique* for the use of workpeople. M. Cousin[10] told the Commission which had to award the Prix Halphen, a prize founded to reward signal services to popular education, that they had no need to go looking about for the proper prizeman: "Il est tout trouvé, et chacun le nomme: c'est M. Rapet." M. Guizot had previously pointed him out as the man whose practical acquaintance with primary schools was greater and more valuable than that of anyone else in France.

But it is above all on account of his type of character that we wish to call attention to him. He is well described as follows by the writer of the notice in the *Journal des Instituteurs*, an old friend and colleague: "Alike as a public and as a private man he had *un même culte du vrai et de l'être, une même horreur du fictif et du paraître.*" There was something brusque in his manner, there was at times even something harsh: it came from his horror of phrase, of vanity deluding itself and others, of unsoundness and turpitude cloaked under *tant de qualités charmantes,* and from his impatience at meeting them continually. "How true is what you say," he writes to M. Ambroise Rendu[11] from Périgueux, "that *seriousness* in thought and action is our want almost everywhere! It is so in the highest spheres, and it is so in what surrounds me in this place. People pose and make professions; they are men of outside seeming and of apparent success; but men of reality and of duty, no. Provided they can *seem,* they do not care to *be.* And in education this is just what is fatal." Brusque as he was, and at times harsh, the students who passed through M. Rapet's hands at Périgueux, the teachers who came in contact with him as inspector, were conscious, many of them, of finding in this man a virtue which they found nowhere else, and could never forget what they owed to him.

M. Rapet was uneasy at the secularization of popular instruction which accompanies in France its present rapid extension. "I give them ten years," he said a few months before his death, "to show what they will make of it." That there is ground for anxiety his adversaries themselves admit. We have a striking testimony from another inspector-general, who has been an able promoter of the recent changes, a strong advocate of "education compulsory, secular, and free." He says: "We must admit that we are in presence of a vast gap which I here point out merely; dogmatic religion withdraws from our schools, and there is nothing at present to take its place. . . . If our democracy is not to be, what its detractors call it, a régime of mediocrity of soul and of vulgarity of character — that is to say, of decadence — there is no time to lose; we must find a way of uniting, as at this moment we do not unite, *education* with *instruction.*"

M. Rapet was for retaining the usual religious instruction in schools, and for continuing to charge the teacher with the duty of giving it. His biographer remarks that his language on this subject, though in agreement with that of Royer-Collard, Guizot, Cousin, Villemain, Salvandy, is now absolutely *démodé,* gone out of fashion.[12] The difficulty of doing as M. Rapet wished has indeed become in France almost insuperable. The state of things there in regard to religion is entirely unlike the state of things in this country. We know what is the general character of the religious instruction now given in schools. M. Renan tells us in his latest volume that "the negation of the supernatural has become an established article of faith with every cultivated mind," and he adds that even among the uncultivated the same negation is daily coming more and more to prevail. As to France, he is probably in great measure right. As to England and America, the truth is very far indeed from being as he says. These countries may have their difficulties in store for them in the future; that is another matter. But meanwhile the actual condition of things in France is such that to retain the usual religious instruction in French schools seems impossible. To attempt it would probably only heighten animosities and thicken confusion. The "immense gap" exists, indeed; but it will hardly now be filled as M. Rapet wished. How it is to be filled is a question involving the whole future of France, but by no means easy of solution. Only one may predict that it will not be solved by the Frenchman of the Gaulish type, as we have called it, affirming himself more and more, and filling the gap with his new religion of "patriotism and civic virtue." The more numerous type tends to crowd out the less numerous and to efface it. The gifts and graces of her Gaulish type of character France may be pretty sure of having always with her; the type of Germanic character once intermingled with it she cannot be so sure of retaining. Yet few things can be more certain than that her best hope for the future lies in the persistence and multiplication of this type; lies in her producing greater numbers of Frenchmen equipped not only with *qualités charmantes,* but with the seriousness, conscience, and sense of duty which were so admirable in M. Rapet.

Notes

[1] F. W. Hirst, *Early Life & Letters of John Morley,* 2 vols. (London, 1927), II, 91.

[2] *Letters,* II, 207. See also *The Letters of Matthew Arnold to Arthur Hugh Clough,* ed. H. F. Lowry (London and New York, 1932), p. 156.

[3] Marie de Rabutin-Chantal, Marquise de Sévigné (1626–1696), French letter writer.

Henri François d'Aguesseau (1688–1751), magistrate and Chancellor.

Luc de Clapiers, Marquis de Vauvenargues (1715–1747), French moralist whom, as *The Note-Books of Matthew Arnold* show, Arnold was reading at this time.

Joseph Joubert (1754–1824), French moralist, and the subject of an essay in Arnold's *Essays in Criticism* [First Series.]

Maximilien Paul Emile Littré (1801–1881), French lexicographer and philosopher.

[4] Roger de Rabutin, Comte de Bussy (1618–1693), French soldier and writer.

[5] Originally a Cistercian abbey near Chevreuse, founded 1204, Port Royal became in the seventeenth century a celebrated Jansenist school.

[6] Jean Baptiste Girard, in his religious life Père Grégoire Girard (1765–1850), Swiss educator.

Jean Henri Pestalozzi (1746–1827), Swiss educator.

Philippe Emmanuel Fellenberg (1771–1844), Swiss agronomist.

[7] Joseph Marie, Baron de Gerando (1772–1842), French philosopher and public administrator.

[8] François Pierre Guillaume Guizot (1787–1874), French historian and statesman.

[9] Rapet's *Manuel populaire de morale et d'économie politique* was published in 1858; his *Cours d'études des écoles primaires* in 1862.

[10] Victor Cousin (1792–1867), French philosopher. He was assistant to P. P. Royer-Collard 1815–1816 in the chair of the history of modern philosophy at the Ecole Normale. He later became Director of the Ecole Normale, and in 1840 Minister of Public Instruction.

[11] Ambroise A. E. C. M. Rendu (1820–1864), jurisconsult, writer on public education, business law, and patents.

[12] Pierre Paul Royer-Collard (1763–1845), French philosopher and statesman, was at one time Dean of the Faculty of Letters at the University of Paris.

Abel François Villemain (1790–1870), French professor and Minister of Public Instruction.

Narcisse Achille, Comte de Salvandy (1795–1856), French statesman and man of letters.

Address to the Wordsworth Society

Transactions of the
Wordsworth Society, No. 5
(n. p., n. d.)

The Wordsworth Society held its meeting for 1883 on May 2 in the College Hall, Westminster. As Arnold points out in the Address, he had been elected President, although he was not a member, in the preceding year. He discharged the honor so thrust upon him with becoming humor and graciousness. The address was published in *Macmillan's Magazine*, XLVIII (June 1883), 154–155, and in the "Report of Meeting Held on May 2, 1883," *Transactions of the Wordsworth Society, No. 5,* edited by William Knight, who was the secretary of the Society. Knight printed the speech again in *Wordsworthiana: A Selection from Papers Read to the Wordsworth Society* (London, 1889). The text is given here as it appears in the *Transactions*.

At your last year's meeting you did me the honour, although I was not a member of your Society, to elect me your President for this year. I had declined to join the Wordsworth Society for the same reason that I decline to join other societies — not from any disrespect to their objects or to their promoters, but because, being very busy and growing old, I endeavour to avoid fresh engagements and distractions, and to keep what little leisure I can for reflexion and amendment before the inevitable close. When your election of me came, however, I felt that it would be ungracious to decline it; and, as generally happens, having decided to accept it and to join you, I soon began to find out a number of excellent reasons for doing what I had resolved to do. In former days, you know, people who had in near view that inevitable close of which I just now spoke, people who had had their fill of life's business and were tired of its labour and contemplation, used to enter a monastery. In my opinion they did a very sensible thing. I said to myself: Times and circumstances have changed; you cannot well enter a monastery; but you can enter the Wordsworth Society. The two things are not so very different. A monastery is under the rules of poverty, chastity, and obedience. Well, and he who comes under the discipline of Wordsworth, comes under those same rules. Wordsworth constantly both preached and practised them. He was "frugal and severe";[1] he ever calls us to "plain living and high thinking." [2] There you have the rule of poverty. His chosen hero and exemplar, the Pedlar of *The Excursion,* was formed and fashioned by the Scottish Church having held upon him in his youth, with a power which endured all his life long, "the strong hand of her purity." [3] There you have the rule of her chastity. Finally, in an immortal ode, Wordsworth tells us how he made it his heart's desire and prayer to live the "bondman of duty in the light of truth." [4] There you have the rule of obedience. We live in a world which sometimes in our morose moments, if we have any, may almost seem to us, perhaps, to have set itself to be as little poor as possible, and as little obedient as possible. Whoever is oppressed with thoughts of this kind, let him seek refuge in the Wordsworth Society.

As your President, it is my duty not to occupy too much of your time myself, but to announce the papers which are to be read to you, and to introduce their readers. It was hoped that a paper would have been read by Lord Coleridge.[5] There was an additional reason for joining your Society! But the paper has had to be put off, alas, till next year. There is a reason for continuing to belong to you! Mr. Stopford Brooke — whose published remarks on Wordsworth, as on other great English writers, we all know, and excellent they are — Mr. Stopford Brooke, I am glad to say, will read us a paper.[6] Mr. Aubrey de Vere — who has given us more interesting and trustworthy reports of Wordsworth in his old age than any one except Miss Fenwick — Mr. Aubrey de Vere has prepared a paper, which will be read by our Secretary — if he is not more properly to be called the author of our being — Professor Knight.[7] If Professor Knight's work in founding us (I may say in passing) had even had no other result than the production of those photographs of Wordsworth which appear in the Society's Transactions of last year, that result alone would have been a sufficient justification of his work.[8] Other matters, besides the papers which I have mentioned, will come before you, and I must leave way for them. But suffer me, before I sit down, to say seriously and sincerely what pleasure I find in the testimony afforded by the prosperity of your Society, and by the numbers present here to-day, to the influence of Wordsworth. His imperfections, the mixture of prose with his poetry, I am probably more disposed than some members of this Society to admit freely. But I doubt whether any one admires Wordsworth more than I do. I admire him, first of all, for the very simple and solid reason that he is such an exceedingly great poet. One puts him after Shakespeare and Milton. Shakespeare is out of comparison. Milton was, of course, a far greater artist; probably, also, a greater force. But the spiritual passion of Wordsworth, his spiritual passion when, as in the magnificent sonnet of farewell to the River Duddon, for instance, he is at his highest, and "sees into the life of things," [9] cannot be matched from Milton. I will not say it is beyond Milton, but he has never shown it. To match it, one must go to the ocean of Shakespeare. A second invaluable merit which I find in Wordsworth is this: he has something to say. Perhaps one prizes this merit the more as one grows old, and has less time left for trifling. Goethe got so sick of the fuss about form and technical details, without due care for adequate contents, that he said if he were younger he should take pleasure in setting the so-called art of the new school of poets at nought, and in trusting for his whole effect to his having something important to say.* Dealing with no wide, varied, and brilliant world, dealing with the common world close to him, and using few materials, Wordsworth, like his great contemporary the Italian poet Leopardi, who also deals with a bounded world and uses few materials — Wordsworth, like Leopardi, is yet so profoundly impressive, because he has really something to say.[11] And the mention of Leopardi, that saddest of poets, brings me, finally, to what is perhaps Wordsworth's most distinctive virtue of all — his power of happiness and hope, his "deep power of joy." [12] What a sadness is in those brilliant poets of Italy — what a sadness in even the sweetest of them all, the one whom Wordsworth specially loved, the pious and tender Virgil!

> Optima quaeque dies miseris mortalibus aevi
> Prima fugit —

"the best days of life for us poor mortals flee first away;" *subeunt morbi,* "then come diseases, and old age, and labour, and sorrow; and the severity of unrelenting death hurries us away." *Et durae rapit inclementia mortis.*† From the ineffable, the dissolving melancholy of those lovely lines, let us turn our thoughts to the great poet in whose name we are met together to-day; to our Westmoreland singer of "the sublime attractions of the grave," [13] and to the treasure of happiness and hope —

> Of hope, the paramount *duty* which heaven lays,
> For its own honour, on man's suffering heart — [14]

which is in him. We are drawn to him because we feel these things; and we believe that the number of those who feel them will continue to increase more and more, long after we are gone.

---

* See Eckermann, *Gespräche mit Goethe,* ii., 260–2: "Es ist immer ein Zeichen einer unproductiven Zeit, wenn die so ins Kleinliche des Technischen geht, und eben so ist es ein Zeichen eines unproductiven Individuums, wenn es sich mit dergleichen befasst. . . . Wäre ich noch jung und verwegen genug, so würde ich absichtlich gegen all solche technische Grillen verstossen . . . aber ich würde auf die Hauptsache losgehen, und so gute Dinge zu sagen suchen, dass jeder gereizt werden sollte, es zu lesen und auswendig zu lernen." [10]

† Optima quaeque dies miseris mortalibus aevi
  Prima fugit; subeunt morbi, tristisque senectus
  Et labor; et durae rapit inclementia mortis.
       Virgil, *Georgics,* iii, 66–8.

Notes

[1] "To the Memory of Raisley Calvert," line 6.

[2] "Written in London. September, 1802," line 11.

[3] *The Excursion,* I, 399.

[4] "Ode to Duty," line 56.

[5] John Duke Coleridge, first Baron Coleridge (1820–1894), Lord Chief Justice of England, was a personal friend of Arnold, who was his contemporary at Oxford. He was president of the Wordsworth Society in 1882.

[6] Stopford A. Brooke (1832–1916), clergyman, first Anglican and then Unitarian, and literary critic. Arnold reviewed his *English Literature* (London, 1877) in the *Nineteenth Century,* December 1877. The review was reprinted in *Mixed Essays* (1879) with the title "A Guide to English Literature."

[7] Aubrey de Vere (1814–1902), poet and critic. Several of his essays on Wordsworth are collected in his *Essays, Chiefly on Poetry,* 2 vols. (London and New York, 1887).

Miss Isabella Fenwick (d. 1856) was a close friend of the Wordsworths at Rydal Mount.

[8] William A. Knight (1836–1916), the Wordsworthian Scholar, was for many years professor of moral philosophy at the University of St. Andrews. The photographs to which Arnold alludes are those of the following portraits: a miniature profile on ivory by Margaret Gillies (1841), Wordsworth upon Helvellyn, by B. R. Haydon (1842), a portrait by Henry Inman (1844), a bust by Angus Fletcher (1844), the statue by Frederick Thrupp (1852). Angus Fletcher was a brother of Lady Richardson of Lancrigg, an original member of the Society and daughter of the Mrs. Archibald Fletcher, whose *Autobiography* she edited and which Arnold reviewed in the *Pall Mall Gazette* in 1875.

[9] "Lines Composed a Few Miles above Tintern Abbey," line 49.

[10] Arnold has here combined passages from the conversations of February 9, 1831, and February 11, 1831.

[11] The name of Giacomo Leopardi (1798–1837) appears frequently from 1877 on in Arnold's lists of intended reading in the *Note-Books.*

[12] "Lines Composed a Few Miles above Tintern Abbey," line 48.

[13] *The Excursion,* IV, 238.

[14] "Here Pause: A Poet Claims at Least This Praise," lines 5–6.

An Address at the Authors Club

The Critic and Good Literature
I (n.s., March 8, 1884), 113

The Authors Club was organized in New York on October 21, 1882, by Noah Brooks, Edward Eggleston, Richard Watson Gilder, Lawrence Hutton, Charles de Kay, Brander Matthews, and Edmund Clarence Stedman. On October 24, 1883, Matthew Arnold was elected the first honorary member of the club. A reception was held in his honor on Thursday evening, February 28, 1884, at the Hotel Dam on East 15th Street. Macmillan and Company presented the Club with a set of Arnold's works on the same day. See Duffield Osborne, *The Authors Club, An Historical Sketch* (New York, 1913). Professor Charlton Thomas Lewis (1834–1904) presided on this occasion. Arnold's address, in reply to his welcome, was printed under the heading, "Mr. Arnold and the Literary Class."

A somewhat contrasted response to Mr. Arnold's visit to the United States is provided by the article from *Life* (New York), II (December 20, 1883) reprinted in this book on p. 385. An interesting account of this first visit, though it is written in support of a most dubious thesis, may be read in E. P. Lawrence, "An Apostle's Progress: Matthew Arnold in America," *Philological Quarterly*, X (January, 1931), 62–79.

Gentlemen: I have been received in this country with unbounded kindness. Much of that kindness, though it has gratified me, has also surprised me, I was so little prepared for it. But for your kindness, gentlemen, and for the kindness of the Club of Authors, I feel better prepared, on account of the kindness I have experienced from the literary class at home. Gentlemen, I owe everything to the literary class — to the class of writers. Here in this Club of Authors and in the privacy of the family circle I will make a confession to you, and reveal to you the insecurity of my position. [Laughter.] If it were not for the literary class having given me its support the great public would never have attended to me at all, and at this moment if the literary class withdrew its support from me, the public would entirely cease to attend to me. [Several voices "No! No!"] Yes, gentlemen, it would cease to attend to me, and it would give itself up to charmers such as the Rev. Joseph Cook[1] [Laughter.] Now to what do I owe this support — this generous support of the literary class? I owe it, I believe, to their finding in me that which pleased Gil Blas in the road to Merida when he cried, "*Le coeur au métier.*" [2] Put your heart into your business. I believe that I have "*le coeur au métier,*" and that it is on that

account the class has been favourable to me. We all know what has been
said with more or less truth, of the irritability, the envy and the jealousy
of the literary class; but I believe that they recognize when a man pursues
the profession of literature with his heart in his work and takes it seriously
and with conscience, and that they feel a favor toward him in consequence. If they do not recognize it and do not feel a favor toward him in
consequence, who will? I make no distinction between the literary class in
England and that here. Here, as in England, I believe that there is very
much against any one who pursues literature seriously and with conscience. Society will always try to impose its decisions and its preferences
upon a man of letters; the crowd will always try to impose its decisions
and preferences upon him; journalism, which is not quite the same as literature, will always try to impose its decisions and impressions upon him.
Unless, gentlemen, we ourselves take our work seriously the case is lost.
[Applause.] Gentlemen, in thanking you cordially as I do, and in taking
a grateful leave of you, and of this country, from which I am about to sail
almost immediately, suffer me to leave with you these words, *"Le coeur au
métier."*

Notes

[1] Flavius Josephus Cook (1838–1901) delivered at Tremont Temple an immensely
popular series of Boston Monday Lectures. His published lectures include *Biology,
with Preludes on Current Events* (1879), *Conscience, with Preludes on Current
Events* (1879), *Transcendentalism, with Preludes on Current Events* (1878), *Marriage, with Preludes on Current Events* (1879), and *Socialism, with Preludes on Current Events* (1880).

[2] Alain René Le Sage (1668–1747), *Gil Blas de Santillane*, Book V, ch. i.

A Speech at the Unveiling of a Mosaic

The Times
December 1, 1884, p. 10, cols. 3–4

Among the addresses which Arnold more frequently gave, either publicly or privately, in his later years and into which he permits personal feeling to enter, is this speech which he made on the occasion of the unveiling of a mosaic at St. Jude's Church, Whitechapel, on November 29, 1884. The address was printed under the heading "Mr. Matthew Arnold in Whitechapel" in *The Times*. It was likewise printed in full in the *Pall Mall Gazette* on December 1, 1884, under the title "A Lay Sermon by Mr. Matthew Arnold." Except for an extract given in Tinker and Lowry, *The Poetry of Matthew Arnold,* the speech has not been reprinted.

The mosaic, a copy of George Frederick Watts's "Time, Death, and Judgment," was made by Antonio Salviati (1816–1890), whose work also is in St. Paul's in London and the Opera in Paris. The mosaic was placed at St. Jude's, Commercial Street, Whitechapel, as a tribute to the work of the Reverend Samuel Augustus Barnett (1844–1913), the vicar of the parish, who brought yearly exhibitions of paintings to Whitechapel. Barnett, who later became Canon of Westminster, was the first warden of the university settlement, Toynbee Hall, which was founded in 1884.

After the unveiling a meeting was held at Toynbee Hall at which Arnold delivered his address. The chairman was Leonard Courtney, afterwards Lord Courtney (1832–1918). At the time Courtney was a Liberal M. P. for Liskeard, and Gladstone's Secretary of the Treasury, an office he resigned in December 1884. He had been a leader writer for *The Times* from 1864–1877.

According to Mrs. Barnett, Arnold unveiled the mosaic.[1] While Arnold does not appear to have had any close connection with Canon Barnett, he did have an interest in the East End of London both through his having inspected schools there and through his sympathy for the Reverend William Tyler (1812–1890), pastor of the Congregational Church in Hanbury St., Spitalfields, to whom he refers in this address. But the chief ground of his coming to speak on this occasion seems to have been, as he says at the start, the wish of G. F. Watts, and *The Times* reports him as having said again in response to E. T. Cook's thanks for his address, that he came "in deference to a summons from Mr. Watts." Watts had painted Arnold's portrait in 1880.

I come here to-day in deference to a summons I could not resist, a summons from Mr. Watts himself, the author of the beautiful work of art which has just been unveiled on St. Jude's Church.[2] In former times, as

Mr. Courtney has mentioned, I was tolerably acquainted with the East-end of London from inspecting the schools here. But for a long time my work has lain elsewhere, and in my leisure I have not come here. I will tell you the reason. If we go from here westward we come to the City and there we see a possessing class spending and enjoying, and we see a trading class desiring nothing better than to possess and enjoy too; and these are the before-the-scenes, as one may say, of our national world. They produce what is called the national fabric of British civilization, the marvellous work and wonders of British enterprise. Then at the East-end we have what may be called the "behind-the-scenes" of English civilization. You know that behind the scenes at a theatre you see a number of men in their shirt-sleeves, dusty boards and benches, and odds and ends of things, and that always has seemed to me to be a representation of what the east of London is by comparison with the brilliant spectacle which is seen further west. And not only is there this "behind-the-scenes" to be seen in the east of London, but there may also be conceived here as presented to our view a great receptacle and limbo in which the people who have failed and fallen or been hurt and wounded, and whom the excess of production and competition which the trading classes carry on have turned out — in which it may be conceived as a great receptacle and limbo in which these poor people exist as well as they can. When English people speak of English life and of our national civilization they naturally think chiefly of the spectacle which is to be seen westward, in the City and at the West-end, and this spectacle everybody is struck with and very many — the majority, perhaps, — praise and admire. As to the life of the spending and enjoying class we are told that luxury is good for trade. As for the trade and the trading classes, though occasionally there are murmurs and complaints of over-production, over-competition, and depression, there comes an authority, a great authority, such as Mr. Giffen — who, no doubt, is a friend of the chairman's (laughter and "Hear, hear") — a political economist who tells in imposing letters to *The Times,* which *The Times* prints in imposing type, that all is for the best and that the more competition the more prosperity.[3] And so with the spectacle of our civilization most people are well satisfied. But there are two sorts of people who have always been, or generally been, dissatisfied and malcontents — the poets and the saints. (Laughter.) It happens that I was brought up under the influence of a poet who was very much dissatisfied with the proceedings of the middle and upper classes among us, and who, indeed, called them idolatry. This poet convinced me, and therefore I have spent most of my leisure time in preaching in my feeble way to these classes, and in telling them that their idolatrous work could not stand, and that already one began to hear formidable cracks in it, and to see it beginning to sway ominously to and fro. Some there are, however, who came to the East-end, though I did not — some from those classes who possess and enjoy and from the class that is aspiring to possess and enjoy. They, dissatisfied with merely living the life of those classes, came to the East-end, and such men are the true saviours of society. (Cheers.) Their names pass, everything passes, but that matters little — their names are written in the Book of Life. There is written a name, which, perhaps, by this time is beginning to wax faint in the memories of men, because he has now been dead some years — the name is Denison.[4] There is another name which the chairman has already mentioned — the name of the admirable young man whose memory will be preserved by this hall in which I speak — the name of Toynbee.[5] I cannot forbear to say that I myself knew, when I inspected schools here, one of those men — a man fruitful in good works, cheerful, devoted, indefatigable. That man I have never seen since, and I do not know whether he is alive or not; some here will perhaps know him by name — William Tyler.[6] Then there is a man whom we are met to-day to honour, who has been here 12 years — Mr. Barnett. (Cheers.) The first means which people think of in coming to help a neighbourhood of this kind is naturally religion. We have just had here a great attempt to move this neighbourhood by means of an agency of this kind — a mission to the East-end. Religion, when used in this way, is naturally presented under the preternatural and miraculous aspect which popular Christianity assumes. People are told to give a hearty assent to Christianity in this preternatural and miraculous aspect. They are told also — and this we must never forget — to be sober, patient, charitable, kind; and then they are told that after this life they will wake up in a world as little like Whitechapel as possible. (Hear.) An aspect of the Christian Gospel, which in the past has been a stay to millions, and which is still a stay to many, shall never be spoken of by me with hostility; but I have long been convinced that for very many, and above all for very many of those whom you have to reach here, Christianity thus presented appeared something neither solid nor verifiable. There is, no doubt, a profounder, and at present little recognized, aspect of the Christian religion in which it is solid and verifiable. But to seize this aspect the standard of life in religion must be raised, and it cannot be seized until the domestic affections and the social impulses have been cultivated and verified, until the sense of duty has been quickened, until the pleasures of art have been laid open. Some have come here with a wish to cultivate and appeal to the social sympathies. Mr. Barnett's work has been, besides his labours as a parish clergyman, an appeal to the sense of duty, and he has desired in the words of the scroll placed on the wall of the church, "to make the lives of his neighbours brighter by bringing within their reach the influence of beauty." He has, therefore, set on foot these art exhibitions which have attracted so much attention outside the limits of

the East-end, which have already given an access to art to hundreds who
had none before, and which will, no doubt, produce still greater influence
in the future. Nevertheless, that saying remains true — "Whosoever
drinketh of this water shall thirst again." No doubt the social sympathies,
the feeling for beauty, the pleasure of art, if left merely by themselves, if
untouched by what is the deepest thing in human life — religion — are
apt to become ineffectual and superficial. The art which Mr. Barnett has
done his best to make known to the people here, the art of men like Mr.
Watts, the art manifested in works such as that which has just been unveiled, this art has a deep and powerful connexion with religion. You have
seen in coming here the mosaic on the walls of St. Jude's Church, and
you have read, perhaps, the scroll which explains it. There is a figure of
Time — a strong young man full of hope, energy, daring, adventure, moving on to take possession of life; and beside him there is that beautiful
figure of Death, representing the breakings off, the cuttings short, the
baffling disappointments, the heart-piercing separations from which the
fullest life and the most fiery energy cannot exempt us. Look at that
strong and bold young man; that mournful figure must go hand in hand
with him for ever; and those two figures, let us admit if you like, belong to
art. Who is the third figure with the weighing scales and the sword of
fire? We are told on a scroll. It is thus printed — "The Eternal is a God
of Judgment; blessed are they that wait for Him." The figure is that of
Judgment, and that figure, I say, belongs to religion. The text which explains the figure is taken from one of the Hebrew prophets. But an even
more striking text is furnished us from the sayings of the founder of Christianity, when he was about to leave the world and to leave behind him
his disciples, who, so long as He lived, had Him to come to and had
Him to do, as one may say, all their thinking for them. He told them that
when He was gone they should find a new source of thought and feeling
open itself within them; that this new source of thought and feeling
should be a comforter to them, and that it should convince the world of
many things. Among other things, he said it should convince the world of
judgment, because "the Prince of this world is judged." That is a text
which we shall do well to lay to heart and consider along with the text
from the Prophets which is printed beside it. More and more it has become manifest that the Prince of this world is really judged — that the
Prince of this world, which is the perpetual ideal of selfishly possessing
and enjoying, and the worlds fashioned under the inspiration of this ideal,
are judged. One world and another has gone to pieces because it was
fashioned to the inspiration of this ideal, and that is a consoling and edifying thought. Above all, it is a consoling and edifying thought for these
classes, which — in comparison with the great possessing and trading
classes, which may be described as the fortunate classes — may be called

the sacrificed classes. True, if the sacrificed classes merely in their turn, under the influence of hatred or cupidity, desire to change and destroy in order to possess and enjoy, their work too will be idolatrous; the old work will continue to stand for the present, but at any rate their new work will not take its place. In the old world fashioned as we have said much of human nature has entered, and that may often make it pardonable and even lovable; but still, considering how much it has left undone and how much positive ill it has done, we may be allowed to be satisfied when the time comes for its departing. There will always be an infinite charm in the ideal presented by the Christian religion of the new world to rise after the Prince of this world and this idolatrous world are judged. There will always be an infinite charm in such expressions as "The consolation of Israel," "The restoration of all things," "A new Heaven and a new earth," "The Kingdom of God." But I say, however great might be that charm for the man of soul, that charm is perhaps greatest for the sacrificed classes, and it is good for them to have this ideal before them, to have before their eyes in a crowded street like this a monument which recalls it to them. People are always tempted to ask when they entertain ideals of this kind, "Will the change come soon; will the renovation be in our own time?" There are seasons, and this in which we live is perhaps one of them, when the crackings which we hear, and the swayings and the rockings which we see, and the signs and warnings on every side seem to say that the change cannot be very far off. But we must remember at the same time how short our time is, and what the philosopher so well said, that men are always impatient and for precipitating things. We must remember what contradiction the course of events perpetually offers to such an ideal as that of the Kingdom of God. We must remember the delays and adjournments which it is certain to meet with. We must remember the obstacles which not only the base and selfish among mankind but also the fear of the grave and the folly of the world are perpetually offering. Let us therefore beware of expecting that any renovation upon which we have set our hearts will come immediately, but let us also be thankful to be reminded that whether it comes late or soon the Prince of this world is judged, and that that renovation will surely come sooner or later. This it is which makes faith and hope to be among the primal virtues, because they keep alive in us confidence in our ideal when events might otherwise shake it. Faith and hope would not be virtues if the exercise of them was easy. It is because the exercise of them is hard that they become virtues, and that they are a beauty and a merit. (Cheers.)

> And oh, if nature sinks, as oft she may,
> 'Neath long-lived pressure of obscure distress,
> Still to be strenuous for the bright reward,
> Still in the soul to admit of no decay,

Brook no continuance of weakmindedness,
Great is the glory, for the strife is hard.[7]

(Cheers.)

Notes

[1] Henrietta Octavia Rowland Barnett, *Canon Barnett: His Life, Work, and Friends*, 2 vols. (London, 1918) II, 170.

[2] A color-scheme for St. Jude's, which appears to have been carried out, was proposed by William Morris. *Ibid.*, I, 218.

[3] Sir Robert Giffen (1837–1910), political economist, was a defender of laissez-faire. His most recent letter to *The Times* was printed November 27, 1884, p. 8, cols. 1–2.

[4] Edward Denison (1840–1882), philanthropist.

[5] Arnold Toynbee (1852–1883), social philosopher and economist, was the founder of Toynbee Hall, the first university settlement.

[6] See note before speech; also Tinker and Lowry, *The Poetry of Matthew Arnold*, pp. 141–142.

[7] Wordsworth, "To B. R. Haydon," lines 9–14.

The Nadir of Liberalism

Nineteenth Century
XIX (May 1886), 645–663

Arnold's association with the *Nineteenth Century,* whose editor was Sir James Knowles (1831–1907), began with the publication in March 1877 of the essay "Falkland," later included in the *Mixed Essays* (1879). He continued to be a contributor during the next eleven years. Among the earlier contributions were some of Arnold's essays on Irish affairs, "The Future of Liberalism" (July 1880) and the two parts of "The Incompatibles" (April and June 1881). On August 5, 1885, Gladstone, who had lost the premiership in June, wrote to Knowles to encourage him to publish a series of articles on the Irish question.[1] Knowles seems to have responded quickly, for a large number of essays on the subject were published representing a wide range of opinion. James Bryce, W. E. H. Lecky, E. L. Godkin, R. Barry O'Brien as well as Arnold were among the contributors.[2]

Arnold was watching the political changes of 1885 with great interest. He wrote to his sister from Dresden on December 4, 1885, "I hope that Lord J. Manners will get in for Leicestershire, and the Tory for Westmorland, though I should never myself vote for a Tory; but for the present I wish Lord Salisbury to stay in, the Liberals being so unripe."[3] Again on December 21, four days after Gladstone made his statement of his Home Rule policy, he wrote, "What a move is this of Gladstone's in the Irish matter! and what apprehensions it gives me!"[4] Within two months Lord Salisbury resigned his office and Gladstone was returned to power. On April 8 he introduced his Home Rule Bill proposing an Irish parliament and executive in Dublin. By April 21 Arnold was ready with "The Nadir of Liberalism" and Knowles, he wrote to his wife, had telegraphed to him that it was "magnificent."[5]

Immediate events seem to have precipitated the writing of the article, but Arnold had had the leading idea in mind for some time. He wrote his sister Fan on January 11, 1886, "If I had time I would write a last political article with the title of *The Nadir of Liberalism.* For all I have ever said of the Liberals calling *successes* not things which really succeed, but things which take with their friends, unite their party, embarrass their adversaries, and are carried — and how very, very far this is, in politics, from true success, has proved itself to a degree beyond which we shall not, it may be hoped, pass."[6] Rather than being the last political article it was the first of seven, if one may include the two letters to the editor of *The Times,* to which Arnold addressed his energy and enthusiasm, apart from the literary criticism that also commanded his attention, in his last two years.

The point of departure for Arnold in approaching the Irish question was essentially that of Burke. In "The Incompatibles" Arnold had observed, "Burke thought, as every sane man must think, 'connection between Great Britain and Ireland essential to the welfare of both.' " [7] Like Burke he disliked both "Jacobinism" and the Protestant ascendancy. Like Burke he felt that whatever measures were taken to resolve the problems they must be "healing." [8] John Morley (1838–1923) wrote of Arnold in his *Recollections,* "In truth, his insight into the roots of the Irish case, and the strong persistence with which he pressed that case upon unwilling ears, were in some ways the most remarkable instance of his many-sided and penetrating vision." [9]

"Demas hath forsaken me" — so the deserted and dejected Muse of Literature may say — "Demas hath forsaken me, having loved this present world, and hath betaken himself to this or that constituency." It is now more than fifteen years since I exhorted my young literary and intellectual friends, the lights of Liberalism, not to be rushing into the arena of politics themselves, but rather to work inwardly upon the predominant force in our politics — the great middle class — and to cure its spirit. From their Parliamentary mind, I said, there is little hope; it is in getting at their real mind, and making it work honestly, that all our hope lies. For from the boundedness and backwardness of their spirit, I urged, came the inadequacy of our politics; and by no Parliamentary action, but by an inward working only, could this spirit and our politics be made better. My exhortations were as fruitless as good advice usually is. The great Parliamentary machine has gone creaking and grinding on, grinding to much the same result as formerly. But instead of keeping aloof, and trying to set up an inward working on the middle-class spirit, more and more of one's promising young friends of former days have been tempted to put their hands to the machine; and there one sees them now, helping to grind — all of them zealous, all of them intelligent, some of them brilliant and leading.

What has been ground, what has been produced with their help? Really very much the same sort of thing which was produced without it. Certainly our situation has not improved, has not become more solid and prosperous, since I addressed to my friends, fifteen years ago, that well-meant but unavailing advice to work inwardly on the great Philistine middle class, the master-force in our politics, and to cure its spirit. At that time I had recently been abroad, and the criticism which I heard abroad on England's politics and prospects was what I took for my text in the first political essay with which I ventured to approach my friends and the public. The middle class and its Parliament were then in their glory. Liberal newspapers heaped praise on the middle-class mind, "which penetrates through sophisms, ignores commonplaces, and gives to conventional illusions their true value;" ministers of State heaped praise on "the great, the heroic work" performed by the middle-class Parliament.

But the foreigners made light of our middle-class mind, and, instead of finding our political performance admirable and successful, declared that it seemed to them, on the other hand, that the era for which we had possessed the secret was over, and that a new era, for which we had not the secret, was beginning. Just now I have again been abroad, and under present circumstances I found that the estimate of England's action and success under a Liberal Government had, not unnaturally, sunk lower still. The hesitancy, imbecility, and failure of England's action abroad, it was said, have become such as to delight all her enemies, and to throw all her friends into consternation. England's foreign policy, said some clever man, reminds me of nothing so much as that of Retz's character of the Duke of Orleans, brother to Louis the Thirteenth: "There was a wide distance, with him, between wishing and willing, between willing and resolving, between resolving and the choice of means, between the choice of means and the putting them in execution. But what was most wonderful of all, it frequently happened that *he came to a sudden stop even in the midst of the putting into execution.*" [10] There, said the speaker, is a perfect prophecy of England in Egypt! At home we had Ireland; to name Ireland is enough. We had the obstructed and paralysed House of Commons. Then, finally, came the news one morning of the London street-mobs and street-riots, heightening yet further the impression of our impotence and disarray. The recent trial and acquittal of the mob-orators will probably complete it. [11]

With very many of those who thus spoke, with all the best and most important of them at any rate, malicious pleasure in our misfortunes, and gratified envy, were not the uppermost feelings; indeed, they were not their feelings at all. Do not think, they earnestly said, that we rejoice at the confusion and disablement of England; there may be some, no doubt, who do; perhaps there are many. We do not. England has been to us a cynosure; a tower, a pride, a consolation; we rejoiced in her strength; we rested much of our hope for the Continent upon her weight and influence there. The decline of her weight and influence we feel as a personal loss and sorrow. That they have declined, have well-nigh disappeared, no one who uses his eyes can doubt. And now, in addition, what are we to think of the posture of your affairs at home? What is it all coming to? It seems as if you were more and more getting among the breakers, drifting towards the shoals and the rocks. Can it really be so? and is the great and noble ship going to break to pieces?

No, I answered; it is not going to break to pieces. There are sources, I trust, of deliverance and safety which you do not perceive. I agree with you, however, that our foreign policy has been that of people who fumble because they cannot make up their mind, and who cannot make up their mind because they do not know what to be after. I have said so, and I have said why it is and must be so: because this policy reflects the dispositions of middle-class Liberalism, with its likes and dislikes, its effusion and confusion, its hot and cold fits, its want of dignity and of the steadfastness which comes from dignity, its want of ideas and of the steadfastness which comes from ideas. I agree, too, that the House of Commons is a scandal, and Ireland a crying danger. I agree that monster processions and monster meetings in the public streets and parks are the letting out of anarchy, and that our weak dealing with them is deplorable. I myself think all this, and have often, too often, said it. But the mass of our Liberals of the middle and lower classes do not see it at all. Their range of vision and of knowledge is too bounded. They are hardly even conscious that the House of Commons is a scandal or that Ireland is a crying danger. If it suited their favourite minister to tell them that neither the one nor the other allegation is true, they would believe him. As to foreign policy, of course it does suit him to tell them that the allegation that England has lost weight and influence is not true. And when the minister, or when one of his ardent young officials on their promotion, more dauntless than the minister himself, boldly assures them that England has not at all lost weight and influence abroad, and that our foreign policy has been sagacious, consistent, and successful, they joyfully believe him. Or when one of their minister's colleagues assures them that the late disturbances were of no importance, a mere accident which will never happen again, and that monster processions and monster meetings in the public streets and parks are proper and necessary things, which neither can be prohibited nor ought to be prohibited, they joyfully believe him. And with us in England, although not in the great world outside of England, those who thus think or say that all is well are the majority. They may say it, replied the speaker already mentioned, who has a turn for quotation; they may say it. But the answer for them is the answer made by Sainte-Beuve to M. Rouher asserting that all was well with the Second Empire in its closing years: "He may say so if he pleases, but he deceives himself, and he thinks contrary to the general opinion." [12]

Yet surely there must be something to give ground to our prevalent notion of Mr. Gladstone as a great and successful minister. Not only the rank and file, the unthinking multitude, of the Liberal party, have it and proclaim it, but the leaders, the intelligent and educated men, embrace it just as confidently. Lord Ripon speaks of "the policy we might expect from the glorious antecedents of Mr. Gladstone." Professor Thorold Rogers calls him "that veteran statesman with fifty years of victory behind him." Mr. Reginald Brett says that any scheme for Ireland which he produces will be "a scheme based on his unrivalled experience of the art of government." Mr. John Morley says that "in his great abilities and human sympathy will be found the only means capable of solving the great Irish question." Sir Horace Davey "will not hesitate to say that he has confidence in Mr. Gladstone, and that he believes the country also has confidence in Mr. Gladstone. The Liberals of England would not soon withdraw their confidence from that illustrious statesman, who had so often led them to victory." [13] Surely there must be some foundation or other for this chorus of eulogy and confidence. Surely there must have been great success of some kind, surely there must have been victory.

Most certainly there has been victory. But has there been success? The two things are often confounded together, and in the popular estimate of Mr. Gladstone we have a signal instance of the confusion. He has been victorious, true; he has conquered, he has carried his measure. But he has not been successful. For what is success for a statesman; is it merely carrying his measures? The vulgar may think so, but a moment's reflection will tell us that the vulgar are wrong; that success for a statesman is succeeding in what his measures are designed to do.

This is the test of a statesman's success, and the great and successful statesmen are those whose work will bear trying by it. Cavour and Prince Bismarck are statesmen of our own time who are really great, because their work did what it was meant to do. Cavour's design was to make a united Italy, Prince Bismarck's to make a strong Germany; and they made it. No minor success, no success of vanity, no success of which the issue is still problematical and which requires other successes for its accomplishment, will suffice to assure this title of *successful* to a statesman. To some people Prince Bismarck seems great because he can snub all the world, and has even been enabled, by an incredible good fortune, to snub the proudest of countries and the one country against which, above all others, he was powerless — England. These successes of vanity are nothing. Neither is he to be called a successful statesman because he carried the May laws, for it is as yet uncertain whether the end which those laws were designed to attain they will accomplish. But let us see, then, what it is which does indeed make Prince Bismarck a great and successful statesman, a statesman whose "antecedents," to take Lord Ripon's phrase, are indeed "glorious." He is successful because, finding his country with certain dangers and certain needs, he has laboured for forty years, at first as a subordinate, but for the greater part of the time as principal, to remove the one and to satisfy the other.

Germany had needs, she found impediments or she found perils to her national life, on the side of Denmark, Austria, Russia, France. First her needs on the side of Denmark were satisfied, in spite of the opposition of France and England. Graver difficulties had to be faced next. A strong Germany was impossible without a strong Prussia. But Prussia seemed to be one of the Great Powers only in name; Austria, thwarting and supercilious, checked her movements at every turn, frustrated all efforts to

consolidate Germany. Except by Prussia's beating Austria, the consolida-
tion of Germany could not go forward; but a war with Austria — what
a difficult war was that for a Prussian minister to make! Prince Bismarck
made it, and the victory of Sadowa gave Prussia free action in Germany.
But except free action in Germany, Prince Bismarck demanded nothing
from Austria; no territory, no indemnity — not a village, not a shilling.[14]

Russia had saved Austria from the Hungarians, why did she not save
her from the Prussians? Because the Prussian Government, foreseeing the
future, foreseeing the inevitable struggle with Austria, had refused to take
part with the Western Powers in the Crimean War — a foolish and prejudicial war for England, but which would have been still more foolish
and prejudicial for Prussia. Austria had in a half-hearted way taken part
with the Western Powers; Russia's neutrality in Austria's war with Prussia
was Prussia's reward for the past and Austria's punishment.

Meanwhile at Prussia's success France looked on, palpitating with
anger and jealousy. A strong Germany was a defiance to all French traditions, and the inevitable collision soon came. France was defeated, and
the provinces required to give military security to Germany were taken
from her. Why had not Austria now sought to wreak her revenge on
Prussia by siding with France? She had Russia to still reckon with in
attempting to do so. But what was of yet more avail to stay her hand was
that Prince Bismarck, as has been already mentioned, had with admirable
wisdom entirely forborne to amerce and humiliate her after Sadowa, and
had thus made it possible for the feelings of German Austria to tend to
his side.

For the last fifteen years he has constantly developed and increased
friendly relations with Austria and Russia. As regards France, whose
friendship was impossible, he has kept Germany watchful and strong.
Those legitimate needs and that security of Germany, which thirty years
ago seemed unattainable for her, he has attained. Germany, which thirty
years ago was hampered, weak, and in low esteem, is now esteemed,
strong, and with her powers all at command. It was a great object, and
the great *Reichskanzler* has attained it. Such are Prince Bismarck's victories.

I observe that Mr. John Morley, like many people in this country,
speaks of the work of Prince Bismarck as something extremely precarious,
and likely to crumble away and vanish as soon as the Emperor William
dies. "When the disappearance of Kaiser Wilhelm dissolves the fabric
of the Triple Alliance, new light will be thrown on the stability of governments which are anti-democratic." In my opinion, Mr. Morley deceives
himself. Advanced Liberals are always apt to think that a condition of
things where the people cannot hold whatever meetings and processions
they like, and wherever they like, is an unnatural condition and likely to

dissolve. But I see no signs which show that Prince Bismarck and his policy will disappear with the Emperor William. The Crown Prince is too judicious a man to desire it; even if he desired it, I doubt whether he could bring it about. The state of Germany is, unless I am much mistaken, more solid than our own. Prince Bismarck commits errors, the German character has faults, German life has deficiencies; but the situation there is a great deal more solid, and Prince Bismarck far more fixed in the national affections, than our Radicals suppose.

But now let us come to the victories of Mr. Gladstone. Are they not victories only, but successes? that is, have they really satisfied vital needs and removed vital dangers of the nation? Sir Robert Peel's abolition of the Corn Laws may be said to have removed a risk of social revolt. But the general development of Free Trade cannot absolutely, as we are all coming to see, be said to have satisfied vital needs and removed vital dangers of the nation; free trade is not, it is now evident, a machinery making us by its own sole operation prosperous and safe; it requires, in order to do this, many things to supplement it, many conditions to accompany it. The general development of free trade we cannot, therefore, reckon to Mr. Gladstone as a success of the sort which stamps a statesman as gloriously successful. The case was one not admitting of a success of the kind. On foreign affairs I shall not touch; his best friends will not allege his successes there. But at home for a success of the kind wanted, a true and splendid success, Mr. Gladstone has had three great opportunities. He had them in dealing with the Irish Church, with the Irish land question, with obstruction in Parliament. In each case he won a victory. But did he achieve not only a victory, but that which is the only real and true success for a stateman? did he, by his victory, satisfy vital needs and remove vital dangers of his country? Did he in the case of the Irish Church? The object there for a statesman was to conciliate the Catholic sentiment of Ireland; did his measure do this? The Liberal party affirmed that it did, the Liberal newspapers proclaimed it "a great and genial policy of conciliation," and one of Mr. Gladstone's colleagues told us that the Ministry had "resolved to knit the hearts of the empire into one harmonious concord, and knitted they were accordingly." True, there were voices (mine was one of them) which said differently. "It is fatal to the English nation," I wrote in *Culture and Anarchy*, "to be told by its flatterers, and to believe, that it is abolishing the Irish Church through reason and justice when it is really abolishing it through the Nonconformists' antipathy to establishments; fatal to expect the fruits of reason and justice from anything but the spirit of reason and justice." This was unpopular language from an insignificant person, and was not listened to. But who doubts now that the Catholic sentiment of Ireland was not in the very least conciliated by the measure of 1868, and that the reason why it was not and could not be conciliated by it was that the measure was of the nature above described?

The Irish Land Act, in like manner, was a victory but not a success. It was carried, it was applauded; the Liberal party duly extolled it as "a scheme based on Mr. Gladstone's unrivalled experience in the art of government." But did it satisfy vital needs and remove vital dangers? Evidently not; the legislation now proposed for Ireland is impregnable proof of it. Did the victory, again, achieved in the reform of procedure, achieved by Mr. Gladstone wielding a great majority and spending the time of Parliament without any stint, did this victory succeed? Did it satisfy the nation's needs and remove the nation's dangers as regards obstruction in the House of Commons? Why, the Conservatives have had to devise a fresh scheme, and the Liberal Government has had to adopt it from them and is at this moment working in concert with them to mature it!

Well then, "our veteran statesman with his fifty years of victory behind him," with his "glorious antecedents," with his "unrivalled experience in the art of government," turns out, in the three crucial instances by which we can test him, not to have succeeded as a statesman at all, but on the contrary to have failed. "Let me try again," he is now saying. And Mr. Morley assures us that in "Mr. Gladstone's great abilities and human sympathy will be found the only means capable of solving the great Irish problem." The mass of Liberal voices chime eagerly in with Mr. Morley. I do not deny the great abilities and the human sympathy; I admit them to the fullest extent. I do not even say that Mr. Gladstone is to be blamed for not having succeeded. But succeeded, in the true sense of the word, he has not; his work as a statesman has hitherto failed to satisfy the country's vital needs, to remove the country's vital dangers. When, therefore, he proposes, in a most critical condition of things, to fall to work again on a bigger scale than ever, we may well feel anxious. We may well ask ourselves what are the causes which have kept him back from a statesman's true success hitherto, and whether they will not also keep him back from it in what he purposes to do now.

The reason why Mr. Gladstone has not succeeded hitherto in the real and high work of a statesman is that he is in truth not a statesman, properly so called, at all, but an unrivalled parliamentary leader and manager. A little development is needed to bring out clearly what I mean.

Mr. Gladstone is the minister of a party in a period of expansion, the minister of the Liberals — the Liberals whose work it should be to bring about the modern development of English society. He has many requisites for that leadership. Everybody will admit that in effectiveness as a public speaker and debater he cannot be surpassed, can hardly be equalled. Philosophers may prefer coolness and brevity to his heat and copiousness; but the many are not philosophers, and his heat and copiousness are just what is needed for popular assemblies. His heat and copiousness, moreover, are joined with powers and accomplishments, with qualities of mind and character, as admirable as they are rare. The absence in him of aristocratical exclusiveness is one of the causes of his popularity. But not only is he free from *morgue,* he has also that rarest and crowning charm in a man who has triumphed as he has, been praised as he has: he is genuinely modest. Every one should read in proof of this a beautiful and touching letter from him in Hope Scott's Life, a letter so deeply modest, and yet breathing, at the same time, the very spirit of sincerity.[15] If one could be astonished at anything in political partisans, I should be astonished at the insensibility of his opponents to the charm of Mr. Gladstone. I think him an unsuccessful, a dangerous minister; but he is a captivating, a fascinating personality.

Why then, with all these gifts and graces, does he fail as a statesman? Probably because, having to be the minister of the modern development of English society, he was born in 1809. The minister of a period of concentration, resistance, and war, may be spiritually rooted in the past; not so the minister of a work of civil development in a modern age. I once ventured to say to Lord Salisbury, before he became the leading personage he is now, that he interested me because, though a Conservative, he was reared in a post-Philistine epoch and influenced by it. I meant that his training had fallen on a time when a man of his powers and cultivation must needs get a sense of how the world is really going, a sense which the old time of routine and fictions was without. Lord Salisbury is a Conservative leader; his business is to procure stability and prominence for that which already exists, much of it undeniably precious. He may have a sense in his own inner mind of what is mere survival of routine and fiction from the past and of how the modern world is really going, but that knowledge has not to be the grand spring and motor of his public action. A Liberal leader here in England is, on the other hand, a man of movement and change, called expressly to the task of bringing about a modern organisation of society. To do this, he should see clearly how the world is going, what our modern tendencies and needs really are, and what is routine and fiction in that which we have inherited from the past. But of how few men of Mr. Gladstone's age can it be said that they see this! Certainly not of Mr. Gladstone. Some of whom it cannot be said may be more interesting figures than those of whom it can; Cardinal Newman is a more interesting figure, Mr. Gladstone himself is a more interesting figure, than John Stuart Mill. But a Liberal leader of whom it cannot be said that he sees how the world is really going is in a false situation. And Mr. Gladstone's perception and criticism of modern tendencies is fantastic and unsound, as his criticism of Homer is fantastic and unsound, or his criticism of Genesis. But he loves liberty, expansion; with his wonderful gifts for parliamentary and public life he has naturally an irresistible bent to political leadership; he will lead the Liberal party. And he will lead it, he will lead this great party of movement and change, by watching their mind, adapting his programme to it, and relying on their support and his own inexhaustible resources of energy, eloquence, and management, to give him the victory.

But the task of providing light and leading is thus shifted upon men yet more incompetent for it than Mr. Gladstone. It is thrown upon the middle class in English society, the class where lay the strength of the Liberal party until the other day, and upon the working class, which conjointly with the middle class makes its strength now. Both are singularly bounded, our working class reproducing, in a way unusual in other countries, the boundedness of the middle. Both have invaluable qualities, closely allied, as generally happens, with their defects. The sense for conduct in our middle class is worth far more than the superior intellectual lucidity to be found in divorce from that sense among middle classes elsewhere; the English workman, as a great Swiss employer of labour testified to me the other day, is still the best in the world; the English peasant is patient, faithful, respectful, kindly, as no other. But range of mind, large and clear views, insight — we must not go to our middle and lower classes for these. Yet it is on our middle and lower class that the task is really thrown, Mr. Gladstone's gifts and deficiencies being what they are, of determining the programme of Liberal movement for our community, and indeed of determining the programme of our foreign policy also; while Mr. Gladstone finds the management and talents for insuring victory to the programmes so determined. Thus it is that our foreign policy has been what we have seen it; thus it came about that the Irish Church was abolished by the power of the Dissenters' antipathy to Church Establishments. And so we find that precisely the reverse happens of what Mr. Frederic Harrison bids us expect; the minister, says he, initiates, the untrained elector simply finds a good minister. "Now very plain men know how to find the set of ministers who wish them well and will bring them good." But we see that in fact our Liberal electorate has the task thrown upon it not only of choosing a good minister, but also of determining what the good shall be which this minister is to bring us.

Such, then, is our situation. A captivating Liberal leader, generous and earnest, full of eloquence, ingenuity, and resource, and a consummate parliamentary manager — but without insight, and who as a statesman has hitherto not succeeded, but failed. A Liberal party, of which the strength and substance is furnished by two great classes, with sterling merits and of good intentions, but bounded and backward. A third factor in our situation must not be unnoticed — an element of Jacobinism. It is small, but it is active and visible. It is a sinister apparition. We know its works from having seen them so abundantly in France; it has the temper of hatred and the aim of destruction. There are two varieties of Jacobin, the hysterical Jacobin and the pedantic Jacobin; we possess both, and both are dangerous.

At such a moment Ireland sends eighty-five Home Rulers to the House of Commons; and the Irish question, which had previously given to Mr. Gladstone so much occasion for showing how he can conquer without succeeding, must be dealt with seriously at last. What grand scope is here offered for the talents of the great Parliamentary manager! The thing is, to have the eighty-five Home Rulers voting solid with the Liberal party. How is it to be effected? The generous and ardent feelings of Mr. Gladstone rush to his aid. Ireland has been abominably governed! True. Ireland desires autonomy more hotly than any other part of these islands desires it! Very naturally. Why then should we not give to the Irish what they so hotly desire? Why not indeed? responds the Liberal party. Only there must be no endowment of religion, no endowment, above all, of Popish superstition! There shall be none, says Mr. Gladstone. In that case, replies his Liberal following, go on and prosper! Let the Irish have what the majority of them like. It is the great blessedness for man to do as he likes; if men very much wish for a thing, we ought to give it them if possible. This is the cardinal principle of Liberalism; Mr. Fox proclaimed it.

Yes, Mr. Fox proclaimed it — the brilliant and generous schoolboy! But what would Burke have said to it? Nay, even a sagacious woman, who had closely watched a time of civil trouble, knew better.[16] "Quand les hommes se révoltent, ils sont poussés par des causes qu'ils ignorent; *et, pour l'ordinaire, ce qu'ils demandent n'est pas ce qu'il faut pour les apaiser."* Men are driven to revolt by causes not clearly known to them; and in general the thing they call for is not the thing requisite to content them. The observation is profoundly just and true.

The project of giving a separate Parliament to Ireland has every fault which a project of State can have. It takes one's breath away to find an English statesman propounding it. With islands so closely and inextricably connected together by nature as these islands of ours, to go back in the at least formal political connection attained, to make the political tie not closer but much laxer, almost to undo it — what statesmanship! And when, estranged from us in feeling as Celtic Ireland unhappily is, we had yet in Ulster a bit of Great Britain, we had a friend there, you propose to merge Ulster in Celtic Ireland! you propose to efface and expunge your friend! Was there ever such madness heard of?

Those Irishmen, who may happen to know anything about so unimportant a person as I am, will know that I am no enemy of Ireland. They will therefore, I hope, have patience with me while I tell them the truth. The more intensely the Irish desire a separate Parliament, the more it proves that they ought not to have one. If they cry out for a separate Irish Parliament when Scotland and Wales do not cry out for a Scotch or Welsh Parliament, that is not a reason for giving such a Parliament to Ireland rather than to Scotland or Wales, but just the contrary. The Irish desire it so much because they are so exasperated against us. The exasperation is good neither for us nor for themselves. The thing is to do away with the sense of exasperation by removing its causes, to make them friends. The causes of the exasperation are not in our political tie with them, but in our behaviour and treatment. Amend the behaviour and treatment by all means. But simply to cut the Irish adrift in their present state of feeling, to send them away with the sense of exasperation rankling, with the memory of our behaviour and treatment fresh in their minds, what is it but to leave the sense of exasperation to last for ever, and to give them more full and free scope for indulging it? No gratitude for a measure which its supporters are already recommending by the ignoblest appeals to our fears will prevent this. To our fears the measure will be imputed; and to our fears or our foolishness, and to no more worthy or winning motive, will it indeed be due. Every guarantee we take, every limit we impose, will be an occasion for fret and friction. The temptation to the Irish legislature *ampliare jurisdictionem,* to extend and enlarge its range of action, will be irresistible; the very brilliancy and verve of Irishmen necessitate it. The proper public field for an Irishman of signal ability is the Imperial Parliament. There his faculties will find their right and healthful scope; he is good for us there, and we for him. But he will find scope for his faculties in an Irish Parliament only by making it what it was not meant to be, and what it cannot be without danger. It will be a sensation Parliament — a Parliament of shocks and surprises.

Ask those "thoughtful Americans" who in conjunction with his own terrors are the mighty persuaders of Mr. Whitbread's mind, ask them what they would think of a proposal to make the South one homogeneous political body distinct from the North, and with a separate Congress in Richmond.[17] They will laugh. The South, they will say, is certainly much inferior in strength and population to the North. But such a Congress would inevitably come to regard itself as a rival to the Congress at Washington, the Southern States which are in sympathy with the North would be swamped by those which are not; it would be a perpetual stimulus to secession. And then let Mr. Whitbread, if his tremors have left him any voice, ask his "thoughtful Americans" what is it which they are so thoughtfully and kindly exhorting him to do in Ireland!

This brings me to the challenge constantly thrown out to those who condemn Mr. Gladstone's plan of an Irish Parliament, to produce an alternative policy of their own. Why, really such a policy, in its main lines, which are all the state of the case at present requires, produces itself! Let us give to our South, not a single central Congress, but provincial legislatures. Local government is the great need for us just now throughout these islands; the House of Commons is far too large a body, and is weighted with much work which it ought not to have. But in Great Britain we have this difficult: the counties would give us local legislatures too numerous, and not strong enough; and we have no provinces. The difficulty may be overcome, but a difficulty it is. But in Ireland it does not present itself; Ireland had four provinces. Ireland's strong desire for local government is no good reason for giving Ireland an Irish Parliament; but it is a good reason for seizing as promptly as possible any fit means for organising local government there, and for so organising it even before we organise it in Great Britain; and such means the Irish provinces supply. Munster and Connaught may probably be considered as of one character, and some of western Ulster, as being of the same character, might go naturally with them. But we have at least three divisions in Ireland, each of them with a distinct stamp and character of its own, and affording, each of them, materials for a separate provincial assembly: Ulster proper, or British Ireland; Leinster, or metropolitan Ireland; Munster and Connaught, or Celtic Ireland. Evidently the assembly representing British Ireland would be one thing, the assembly representing Celtic Ireland quite another. Perhaps Leinster, the old seat of the capital and of metropolitan life, would give us an assembly different in character from either. So much the better. Each real and distinct part of Ireland would have its own legislature, and would govern its own local affairs; each part would be independent of the others, neither of them would be swamped by the others. The common centre would be the imperial Parliament at Westminster. There the foremost Irishmen would represent Ireland, while for the notables of each province the provincial legislatures would afford a field.

It is deemed enough to say, in condemnation of any scheme of this kind, that it is not what the majority of the Irish are demanding, and that the eighty-five members who follow Mr. Parnell would not accept it. But carry it, and what would happen? Would not Ulster accept it? It is just what Ulster desires, while a general Irish Parliament is just what Ulster fears. Would Leinster, Munster, and Connaught, metropolitan and Celtic Ireland, refuse to accept? How would they carry their refusal into effect? They could only do so by the majority abstaining from the election of members for the provincial legislatures. But this would leave those assemblies to be elected by the minority, who would assuredly elect them gladly enough, but how would that suit the majority? No, the Home Rulers may say that nothing less than an Irish Parliament will they accept, and no wonder that, with Mr. Gladstone's offer before them, they should say so; but once carry a plan for establishing provincial legislatures, and they will come into it before long.

And indeed one cannot but at first feel astonishment that Mr. Gladstone should have preferred to such a plan his plan for an Irish Parliament. Last year I was often and often inclined to say as to Egypt: With one tenth of the ingenuity and pains which Mr. Gladstone spends to prove, what neither he nor any one else ever *can* prove, that his Egyptian policy has been sagacious, consistent, and successful, he might have produced an Egyptian policy sagacious, consistent, and successful. So one may say now as to Ireland: With one tenth of the ingenuity and pains which Mr. Gladstone is expending upon a bad and dangerous measure for Ireland, he might have produced a good and safe one. But alas, he is above all a great Parliamentary manager! Probably he is of the same opinion with Cardinal de Retz, who has been already mentioned; he thinks "that it takes higher qualities to make a good party-leader than to make a good emperor of the universe." [18] The eighty-five Parnellite members added to the Liberal majority, and enabling him, as he hopes, to defy opposition and to carry his measure victoriously, are irresistible to him. To the difficult work of a statesman he prefers the work for which he has such a matchless talent — the seemingly facile but really dangerous strokes of the Parliamentary tactician and party manager.

Not that he himself foresees danger from it. No, that is the grave thing. He does not foresee danger. Statesmen foresee, Mr. Gladstone does not. He no more foresees danger from his Irish Parliament than he foresaw that his abolition of the Irish Church would not conciliate Catholic sentiment in Ireland, or that his Land Act would not conciliate the Irish peasant. He has no foresight because he has no insight. With all his admirable gifts he has little more real insight than the rank and file of his Liberal majority, people who think that if men very much want a thing they ought to have it, and that Mr. Fox's dictum makes this certain. It is this confiding majority under this unforeseeing leader which makes me tremble. Will anything ever awaken either the leader or the followers to a sense of danger? When the vessel of State is actually grinding on the rocks, will Mr. Gladstone be still cheerfully devising fresh strokes of management; and, when not engaged in applauding him, will Mr. Illingworth be still prattling about disestablishment and Mr. Stansfeld about contagious disease? [19]

I have long been urging "that the performance of our Liberals was far less valuable than they supposed, that their doings wanted more of simple and sincere thought to direct them, and that by their actual practice, however prosperous they might fancy themselves, they could not really succeed." But now they do really seem to have done what the puzzled foreigners imagine England altogether has done — to have reached the nadir. They have shown us about the worst that a party of movement can do, when that party is bounded and backward and without insight, and is led by a manager of astounding skill and energy, but himself without insight likewise. The danger of our situation is so grave that it can hardly be exaggerated. People are shocked at even the mention of the contingency of civil war. But the danger of civil war inevitably arises whenever two impossible parties, full of hatred and contempt for each other, with no mediating power of reason to reconcile them, are in presence. So the English civil war arose when, facing and scornfully hating one another, were two impossibilities: the prerogative of the King and the license of the Cavaliers on the one side, the hideousness and immense *ennui* of the Puritans on the other. The Vendean war arose out of a like collision between two implacable impossibilities: the old *régime* and Jacobinism. Here lies the danger of civil war in Ireland, if the situation cannot find rational treatment; Protestant ascendency is impossible, but the Ulster men will not let bunglers, in removing it, drag them down to a lower civilisation without a struggle. Nay, the like danger exists for England itself. Change we must; but if a Liberal party with no insight, led by a victorious manager who is no statesman, brings us to failure and chaos, the existing England will not let itself be ruined without a struggle.

Therefore at the present time that need for us, on which I have so often and so vainly insisted, to let our minds have free and fair play, no longer to deceive ourselves, to brush aside the claptrap and fictions of our public and party life, to be lucid, to get at the plain simple truth, to see things as they really are, becomes more urgent, more the one thing needful for us, than ever. That sentence of Butler, which I have more than once quoted in past times, acquires now a heightened, an almost awful significance. *"Things are what they are, and the consequences of them will be what they will be; why then should we desire to be deceived?"* [20] The laws which govern the course of human affairs, which make this thing salutary to a nation and that thing pernicious, are not of our making or under our power. Our wishing and asserting can avail nothing against them. Lord Ripon's calling Mr. Gladstone's antecedents glorious cannot make them other than what they are — Parliamentary victories, but a statesman's failures. Mr. Morley's "great triumph" in the election of "330 Liberal members, more or less, who without excessive arrogance may be taken to be the best men in the way of intelligence and honesty that the Liberal party can produce," cannot make the Liberal party, both in and out of Parliament, other than what it is — a party of bounded and backward mind, without insight. Deluders and deluded, the utterers of these phrases may fancy them solid while they utter them, the hearers while they hear them. But solid they cannot make them;

and it is not on the thing being asserted and believed, but on its being really true or false, that our welfare turns.

Whatever may be the faults of the Liberal party, "the Conservative party at any rate," says Mr. Bradlaugh, "is blind;" [21] and here, too, of course, there is danger. The Conservative party is the party of stability and permanence, the party of resistance to change; and when the Liberal party, the party of movement, moves unwise and dangerous changes, recourse will naturally be had, by sensible men, to the Conservative party. After all, our country as it is, as the past has made it, as it stands there before us, is something; it is precious, it shall not lightly be imperilled by the bungling work of rash hands. Burke from such a motive threw himself on the Conservative forces in this country to resist Jacobinism. But no solution of the problems of national life is to be reached by resting on those forces absolutely. Burke would have been far more edifying for us to-day if he had rested on them less absolutely. What has been said of the urgent need of seeing things as they really are is of general application, and applies to Conservative action as well as Liberal. If Conservative action is blind, we are undone. True, for the moment our pressing danger is just now from the Liberal party and its leader. If they cannot be stopped and defeated, the thing is over, and we need not trouble ourselves about the Conservative party and its blindness. But supposing them defeated, the Conservative programme requires to be treated just like the Liberal, to be surveyed with a resolutely clear and fair mind.

Now there is always a likelihood that this programme will be just to maintain things as they are, and nothing further. Already there are symptoms of danger in the exhortations, earnestly made and often repeated, to keep faith with the Irish proprietor to whose security England, it is said, has pledged herself; to secure the Irish landowners and to prevent the scandal and peril of Catholic supremacy in Ireland.

As to Catholicism, it has been the great stone of stumbling to us in Ireland, and so it will continue to be while we treat it inequitably. Mr. Gladstone's Bill treats it inequitably. His Bill withholds from the Irish the power to endow or establish Catholicism. That, he well knows, is the one exception which his Liberal followers make to their rule, borrowed from Mr. Fox, that if men very much wish to do a thing we should let them do it. To endow Catholicism they must not be permitted, however much they may wish it. That provision alone would be fatal to any sincere and lasting gratitude in Ireland for Mr. Gladstone's measure. If his measure is defeated it would be fatal to repeat his mistake. Why should not the majority in Ireland be suffered to endow and establish its religion just as much as in England or Scotland? It is precisely one of those cases where the provincial legislatures should have the power to do as they think proper. Mr. Whitbread's "thoughtful Americans" will tell him that in the United States there is this power, although to the notions and practice of America, sprung out of the loins of Nonconformity, religious establishments are unfamiliar. But even in this century, I think Connecticut had an established Congregational Church, and it might have an Established Church again to-morrow if it chose. Ulster would most certainly not establish Catholicism. If it chose to establish Presbyterianism it should be free to do so. If the Celtic and Catholic provinces chose to establish Catholicism, they should be free to do so. So long as we have two sets of weights and measures in this matter, one for Great Britain and another for Ireland, there can never be concord.

The land question presents most grave and formidable difficulties, but undoubtedly they are not to be got rid of by holding ourselves pledged to make the present Irish landlords' tenure and rents as secure as those of a landlord in England. We ought not to do it if we could, and in the long run we could not do it if we would. How greatly is a clear and fair mind needed here! and perhaps such a mind on such a subject the Conservatives, the landed party, do not easily attain. We have always meant and endeavoured to give the Irish landlord the same security that the English has. But the thing is impossible. Why? Because at bottom the acquiescence of the community makes the security of property. The land-system of England has, in my opinion, grave disadvantages; but it has this acquiescence. It has it partly from the moderation of the people, but more from the general conduct and moderation of the landlords. If many English landlords had borne such a reputation as that which the first Lord Lonsdale, for instance, acquired for himself in the north, the English landed system would not have had this acquiescence. In Scotland it has it in a less degree, and is therefore less secure; and, whatever the Duke of Argyll may think, deservedly. Let him consult the Tory Johnson for the past, and weigh, as to the present, the fact that Mr. Winans is possible.[22] But it has it in a considerable degree, though in a lower degree than England. Ireland has it in the degree to be expected from its history of confiscation, penal laws, absenteeism — that is to say, hardly at all. And we are bound in good faith, we are pledged to obtain, by force if necessary, for the Irish landlord the acquiescence and security which in England come naturally! We are bound to do it for a landed system where the landowners have been a class with whom, in Burke's words, "the melancholy and invidious title of grantees of confiscation was a favourite;" who "would not let Time draw his oblivious veil over the unpleasant means by which their domains were acquired;" who "abandoned all pretext of the general good of the community"![23] But there has been great improvement, you say: the present landowners give in general little cause for complaint. Absenteeism has continued, but ah! even if the improvement had been ten times greater than it has, Butler's memorable and stern sentence would still be true: "Real reformation is in many cases of no avail at all towards preventing the miseries annexed to folly *exceeding a certain degree.* There is a certain bound to misbehaviour, which being transgressed, there remains no place for repentance in the natural course of things." [24] But a class of altogether new and innocent owners has arisen. Alas! every one who has bought land in Ireland has bought it with a lien of Nemesis upon it. It is of no use deceiving ourselves. To make the landowner in the Celtic and Catholic parts of Ireland secure as the English landowner is impossible for us.

What is possible is to bear our part in his loss; for loss he must incur. He must incur loss for folly and misbehaviour, whether on his own part or on that of his predecessors, *exceeding a certain degree.* But most certainly we ought to share his loss with him. For when complaints were addressed to England, "the double name of the complainants," says Burke, "Irish and Papist (it would be hard to say which singly was the more odious), shut up the hearts of every one against them." [25] All classes in Great Britain are guilty in this matter; perhaps the middle class, the stronghold of Protestant prejudice, most. And, therefore, though the Irish landlords can, I think, be now no more maintained than were the planters, yet to some extent this country is bound to indemnify them as it did the planters. They must choose between making their own terms with their own community, or making them with the Imperial Parliament. In the latter case, part of their indemnity should be contributed by Ireland, part, most certainly, by ourselves. Loss they must, however, expect to suffer, the landowners of the Celtic and Catholic provinces at any rate. To this the English Conservatives, whatever natural sympathy and compassion they entertain for them, must clearly make up their minds.

On the reasonableness of the Conservative party our best hope at present depends. In that nadir of Liberalism which we seem to have reached, there are not wanting some signs and promise of better things to come. Lord Rosebery, with his freshness, spirit, and intelligence, one cannot but with pleasure see at the Foreign Office.[26] Then the action of Lord Hartington and Mr. Trevelyan inspires hope: that of Mr. Chamberlain inspired high hope at first, but presently his attitude seemed to become equivocal.[27] He has, however, instincts of government — what M. Guizot used to call "the governmental mind." But the mass of the great Liberal party has no such instincts; it is crude and without insight. Yet for the modern development of our society, great changes are required, changes not certainly finding a place in the programme of our Conservatives, but not in that of our Liberals either. Because I firmly believe in the need of such changes, I have often called myself a Liberal of the future. They must come gradually, however; we are not ripe for them yet. What we are ripe for, what ought to be the work of the next few years, is the development of a complete and rational system of local government for these islands. And in this work all reasonable Conservatives may heartily bear part with all reasonable Liberals. That is the work for the immediate future, and besides its own great importance, it offers us a respite from burning questions which we are not ripe to treat, and a basis of union for all good men. The development of the working class amongst us follows the development of the middle. But development for our bounded and backward middle class can be gained only by their improved education and by the practice of a rational, large, and elevating system of local government. The reasonableness and co-operation of the Conservatives are needed to attain this system. By reasonableness, by co-operation with reasonable Liberals, they have it in their power to do two good things: they can keep off many dangers in the present, and they will be helping to rear up a Liberalism of more insight for the future.

But is it possible, and is there time? Will not the great Parliamentary manager, with his crude Liberal party of the present, sweep everything before him now? The omens are not good. At Munich a few weeks ago I had the honour to converse with a wise and famous man, as pleasing as he is learned, Dr. Döllinger.[28] He is an old friend of Mr. Gladstone. We talked of Mr. Gladstone, with the interest and admiration which he deserves, but with misgiving. His letter to Lord de Vesci had just then appeared. "Does it not remind you," Dr. Döllinger asked me, "of that unfortunate French ministry on the eve of the Revolution, applying to the nation for criticisms and suggestions?" Certainly the omens are not good. However, that best of all omens, as Homer calls it, ourselves to do our part for our country, is in our own power. The circumstances are such that desponding and melancholy thoughts cannot be banished entirely. After all, we may sometimes be tempted to say mournfully to ourselves, nations do not go on for ever. In the immense procession of ages, what countless communities have arisen and sunk unknown, and even the most famous nation, perhaps, is only for its day. Human nature will have in dark hours its haunting apprehensions of this kind. But till the fall has actually come, no firm English mind will consent to believe of the fall that it is inevitable, and of "the ancient and inbred integrity, piety, good-nature, and good-humour of the English people," [29] that their place in the world will know them no more.

Notes

[1] J. L. Hammond, *Gladstone and the Irish Nation* (London, 1938), p. 410.
[2] According to J. L. Hammond, *ibid.*, p. 519, Gladstone "prompted Knowles to let Barry O'Brien put the case for Home Rule in the *Nineteenth Century.*"
[3] *Letters*, II, 304.
[4] *Ibid.*, 312–313.
[5] *Ibid.*, 326.

[6] *Ibid.*, 316.

[7] *Mixed Essays, Irish Essays and Others* (New York, 1883), p. 287.

[8] "Two Letters to Gentlemen in the City of Bristol," *The Works of Edmund Burke*, II, 251.

[9] 2 vols. (New York, 1917), I, 129.

[10] The quotation may be found in Sainte-Beuve, "Le Cardinal de Retz" (II), *Causeries du lundi*, V, 200. I do not know who Arnold's "clever man" is who made the comparison, though it is quite possible it is Arnold.

[11] On February 8, 1886, a demonstration in London, reportedly instigated by members of the Social Democratic Federation, precipitated three days of unrest, culminating in panic in the West End on February 10. H. M. Hyndman, John Burns, H. H. Champion, and Jack Williams were charged with inciting the crowd to riot. They were tried, but acquitted on April 10. See R. C. K. Ensor, *England, 1870–1914* (Oxford, 1936), pp. 100–101, and the *Annual Register* for 1886.

[12] Sainte-Beuve's "Discours au Senat, à propos de la loi sur la presse," in which he replied to M. Rouher's speech on that law, was printed in the *Moniteur universel* (Paris), May 8, 1868, pp. 624–625. I have not been able to locate the phrase Arnold translates.

[13] George F. S. Robinson, the Marquess of Ripon (1826–1909), was the First Lord of the Admiralty in Gladstone's cabinet of 1886. J. E. Thorold Rogers (1803–1890), economist and politician, was a Liberal M.P. and strong supporter of Gladstone. (See his speech at Bermondsey reported in *The Times*, March 27, 1886, p. 12, col. 3.) Reginald Baliol Brett, second Viscount Esher (1852–1930), was a rising politician and writer. John Morley, afterwards Viscount Morley of Blackburn (1838–1923), was Gladstone's Chief Secretary for Ireland in 1886. Sir Horace Davey (1833–1907), judge and Liberal M.P. for Christchurch (1880–1885), became Solicitor-general on February 16, 1886.

[14] For Arnold's admiration for Bismarck, whom he heard in a debate in the Reichstag, see *Letters*, II, 354–355, and 362–364.

[15] Robert Ornsby, *Memoirs of James Robert Hope-Scott of Abbotsford*, 2 vols. (London, 1884), II, 273–287.

[16] Marie de Rabutin-Chantal, Marquise de Sévigné (1626–1695).

[17] Samuel Whitbread, M.P. for Bedford, Speech on the Government of Ireland Bill, House of Commons, April 12, 1886, *Hansard's Parliamentary Debates*, 3d series, CCCIV (1886), 1399.

[18] Quoted in Sainte-Beuve, "Le Cardinal de Retz" (I), *Causeries du lundi*, V, 42.

[19] Probably Alfred Illingworth (1827–1907), an active Nonconformist and Liberal M. P. for Bradford (1880–1885) and W. Bradford (1885–1895).

James Stansfeld (1820–1898), a Dissenter and a friend of Mazzini, agitated for the repeal of the Contagious Diseases Acts, which licensed prostitution in several garrison or dockyard towns, from 1874 to 1886. He entered Gladstone's first ministry in 1871 as President of the Poor Law Board. In 1886 he was President of the Local Government Board. See Ensor, *England, 1870–1914*, p. 23 n. 2 and passim.

[20] "Sermon VII: Upon the Character of Balaam," *Fifteen Sermons*, in *The Works of Joseph Butler*, ed. W. E. Gladstone, 2 vols. (Oxford, 1896), II, 134. Bishop Butler wrote, "Things and actions are what they are," etc. Arnold cites the passage in "Bishop Butler and the Zeit-Geist," *Last Essays on Church and Religion, Works*, IX, 261, 330, 336.

[21] See Charles Bradlaugh (1833–1891), M.P. for Northampton, on the government of Ireland bill, House of Commons, April 12, 1886, *Hansard's Parliamentary Debates*, 3rd series, CCCIV (1886), 1380.

[22] James Lowther, Lord Lonsdale (1736–1802), Tory politician, known as the "bad earl," was unscrupulous in his dealings. He controlled nine seats in the House of Commons.

Douglas George Campbell, eighth Duke of Argyll (1823–1900), resigned from Gladstone's cabinet as Lord Privy Seal in 1881 in protest against the Irish Land Bill.

Mr. Winans was an American millionaire who leased extensive deer forests in Inverness. He appears to have dealt arrogantly with the local populace, in one instance endeavoring to interdict a Murdoch Macrae from grazing a lamb at the roadside. See *The Times,* October 21, 1885, p. 7, col. 3; October 27, 1885, p. 10, col. 6; January 23, 1886, p. 10, col. 3. Mr. Winans also appears in "A Word More about America" (1885) in Kenneth Allott, *Five Uncollected Essays of Matthew Arnold* (Liverpool, 1953), p. 30. Mr. J. G. D. Paul of Baltimore, Maryland, has kindly identified him for me as Walter Winans (1852–1920), grandson of Ross Winans and son of William Louis Winans, who represented the family's important railroad interests in Russia. See *New York Times,* August 13, 1920, p. 9, col. 5, and Albert Parry, *Whistler's Father* (Indianapolis and New York, 1939), p. 157.

[23] "Letter to Richard Burke, Esq., on Protestant Ascendency in Ireland," *The Works of Edmund Burke* (1887), VI, 406.

[24] Adapted from *The Analogy of Religion,* in *The Works of Joseph Butler,* I, 58.

[25] "A Letter to Sir Hercules Langrishe, Bart., M.P., on the Subject of the Roman Catholics of Ireland," *The Works of Edmund Burke,* IV, 275.

[26] Archibald Philip Primrose, fifth Earl of Rosebery (1847–1929), generally supported Gladstone's Irish policy. He accepted the foreign secretaryship in Gladstone's cabinet in 1886. He married Hannah de Rothschild, the only daughter of Baron Meyer de Rothschild and niece of Arnold's friend, Lady de Rothschild (née Louisa Montefiore), wife of Sir Anthony de Rothschild).

[27] Spencer Compton Cavendish, Marquis of Hartington and eighth Duke of Devonshire (1833–1908), was a leader of the Liberal party after 1875. Lord Hartington was Secretary for India in Gladstone's cabinet in 1880. In 1862 he became Secretary for War. He supported Gladstone in favor of the disestablishment of the Irish Church in 1868. He opposed Home Rule and pressed for the suppression of agrarian crime in Ireland, where his brother Lord Frederick had been a victim in the Phoenix Park murders of 1882. He declined to accept office in Gladstone's government in February 1886. On April 14 he made a platform appearance with the conservative Lord Salisbury at the Opera House in the Haymarket, and on May 10 he moved rejection of Gladstone's Home Rule Bill, which was defeated June 7, 1886. See John Morley, *The Life of William Ewart Gladstone,* 3 vols. (London, 1904), III, 292, 329.

Sir George Otto Trevelyan (1838–1928), Macaulay's nephew and biographer, was Chief Secretary for Ireland (1882–1884) in Gladstone's second cabinet and Secretary for Scotland in his third ministry, as well as in his last in 1892. He resigned over the Home Rule Bill March 26, 1886, but returned to Gladstone's support in 1887.

Joseph Chamberlain (1836–1914) supported a modified form of local government for Ireland, but he vigorously opposed Gladstone's conception of Home Rule. He said after the general election of December 1885, "My view is that Mr. G's Irish scheme is death and damnation" (*DNB*).

[28] Dr. Johann J. I. von Döllinger (1799–1890), theologian and church historian, and noted Roman Catholic intellectual, was excommunicated in 1871 for his public refusal to accept the recently decreed doctrine of papal infallibility. Gladstone was among his English friends. See *Letters,* II, 320–321.

[29] "A Letter to a Noble Lord," *The Works of Edmund Burke,* V, 204–205.

Two Letters on Home Rule

The Times
May 22, 1886, p. 15, col. 6
August 6, 1886, p. 12, cols. 1–2

Arnold's intense interest in the question of Home Rule which was expressed in "The Nadir of Liberalism" continued as Gladstone's bill was debated for sixteen days in the House of Commons before its ultimate defeat by 30 votes on June 8, 1886. As he was preparing to leave England on his second visit to the United States, he wrote the first of two letters on Home Rule to the editor of *The Times*. The first of these was printed under the heading "Mr. Matthew Arnold on the Political Crisis," on May 22, 1886.

On June 9, 1886, the day following the defeat of the Home Rule Bill on its second reading, Arnold wrote from Germantown, Pennsylvania, "And the papers have long accounts of what passed — all coloured by favour to the Irish, but still very interesting. They had made up their minds here that Gladstone was going to win; from the first I had thought he would lose, but I was not prepared for so good a majority. A load is taken off my spirit, but unless Lord Hartington and Goschen bestir themselves and seize the occasion, it will pass from them, and the Home Rulers, pure and simple, will win. Of course I have not seen the comments of the English papers on my letter to the *Times*, but on this side the water it has done good by drawing the distinction between giving to the Irish legislative control over their own local affairs, and giving to them *a single national legislative body* to exercise such control." [1]

Gladstone resigned office July 20, and Lord Salisbury began his second ministry on the 26th. Arnold's second letter, published with the heading "After the Elections," appeared in *The Times* on August 6, 1886. Arnold was at Laurel Cottage, Stockbridge, Massachusetts, during the greater part of July 1886. He followed with keen interest the news of Gladstone's difficulties, and with distress the exaggerated reporting and misunderstanding that he thought characterized the American press.[2] On July 11 he wrote to his sister Fan, "I shall perhaps write another letter to the *Times*, as now comes the critical moment. Lord Salisbury and Lord Hartington have an opportunity offered to them, and if they miss it now, it will never return; and the worst of it is that the English do not know how much more than other people — than the French, the Germans, the Swiss, the Americans — they are without any system of local government of an effective kind themselves, and what they lose by being without it, so they can the less understand the necessity of granting something of the kind to the Irish, though they see in a dim way what a necessity there is." [3]

Twenty-five copies of these two letters were privately reprinted in a pamphlet *On Home Rule for Ireland* (London, 1891), with a brief prefatory note. Arnold's letter of May 22 was of sufficient interest to be quoted in part in the New York *Nation,* XLII (May 27, 1886), 439.

MR. MATTHEW ARNOLD ON THE

POLITICAL CRISIS

To the Editor of the *Times.*

Sir, — All next week, while the moment for the great vote draws near, I shall be on the sea, going to visit our American kinsmen, who abstained from setting up a Southern Parliament themselves, but are so anxious, it seems, that we should set up an Irish one.

Suffer me to say, before I depart, that the mind of the country, which is slowly but surely waking up on this Irish question, will not be satisfied unless the vote is taken on a clear issue and accompanied by a distinct engagement.

The vote is not taken on a clear issue if it is taken on any question but that of a separate national Parliament for Ireland. Mr. Chamberlain and Mr. Trevelyan may be so committed that they prefer to have the vote taken on some other issue than this. They deserve every consideration. They had the merit of opening their eyes when they saw where Mr. Gladstone was going, instead of shutting them tighter and tighter like Mr. Campbell-Bannerman. An indirect issue may suit the convenience of other members also. But a clear, direct issue is what will alone suit the mind of the country.

A separate Parliament for Ireland is Mr. Gladstone's irreducible *minimum.* Ireland is a nation, says Mr. Parnell menacingly, Mr. Stansfeld gushingly; a nation should have its national Parliament.

Ireland has been a nation, a most unhappy one. Wales too, and Scotland, have been nations. But politically they are now nations no longer, any one of them. This country could not have risen to its present greatness if they had been. Give them separate Parliaments, and you begin, no doubt, to make them again nations politically. But you begin also to undo what has made this country great.

Do not let us be preposterously alarmist. Perhaps, if it suits Mr. Gladstone's purposes, Scotland, Wales, and Ireland may all of them, to Mr. Stansfeld's delight, become politically nations again, and yet this country, such is its force, may still, by new and untried ways, continue great. But it will be a plunge into the unknown, and surely such a plunge is a dangerous thing, not to be risked without absolute necessity.

In the case of Austria-Hungary there was such necessity. Hungary was the bigger of the two. But what was done there was a plunge into the unknown and a very grave one. Who will say that the Austria of to-day is as strong and solid a Power as the Austria of the end of last century, or that by the end of next century Austria's German provinces will not have gravitated to Germany?

But the necessity for making Ireland a separate nation some people find in our ill-treatment of her, and in the failure of coercion. We have let Scotland have her schools and Church to her mind, says Sir Lyon Playfair, we have not let Ireland; therefore we must make Ireland a separate nation! [4] The Northern States could not go on ruling the South by coercion, says Mr. Bryce; therefore we must make Ireland a separate nation! [5] But the North did not give the South a national Parliament; Scotland has not a national Parliament. The course taken has not been to make them separate nations. Scotland had the just and due control of her own affairs left to her; the South was suffered to resume such control. This, then, is what the analogy requires for Ireland, this and this only; the just and due control of her own affairs.

Why should a national Parliament be the only possible cure for Irish discontent? Read Madame de Sévigné's letters from Brittany in 1675. Four thousand soldiers were quartered on the province, the Parliament had been banished, men were broken on the wheel and hanged by scores; the population was seething with turbulence and hatred. What has changed Brittany — separate institutions? No, but a rational and equitable system of government.

Twenty years after Madame de Sévigné wrote, Duke Hamilton was praising Scotland to William III., and the King answered him, "My lord, I only wish it was a hundred thousand miles off, and that you was King of it!" [6] What has changed Scotland — a separate Parliament? No, but a rational and equitable system of government.

And this is what the awakening mind of the country demands for Ireland. Not that we should give her a separate Parliament, but that we should seriously engage and set ourselves to give her a rational and equitable system of government. Lord Salisbury's bad and arbitrary temper (I mean, of course, as a politician, a home politician)[7] is as great a misfortune to the country as Lord Randolph Churchill's intriguing.[8] A separate Parliament for Ireland is a dangerous plunge into the unknown, and not necessary; but not necessary on condition only that we do really at last give Ireland a rational and equitable system of government; and Lord Salisbury can talk of nothing but coercion. Let us refuse a separate Parliament for Ireland with all firmness; but with equal firmness let us insist on the condition which alone justifies our refusal. Lord Hartington has a good temper (I mean, again, as a politician) and is no intriguer; Mr. Goschen has made local government his special study.[9] They may be trusted, I hope, to make the necessary refusal firmly, and the necessary engagement emphatically. Nothing less will satisfy that which it is indispensable to satisfy, the mind of the country.

The passionate supporters of Mr. Gladstone in his operations are the political Dissenters and the Radical workmen in the great towns. I agree with Mr. Labouchere that aristocracies are not, in general, the best of guides in politics.[10] But I have too much respect for his undoubted lucidity to believe him capable of really thinking the political Dissenters and the Radical working men to be on a question like that of Ireland any better guides, or even so good. They know little and prize little beyond the one their dissent, the other their union for trade or politics. In the past they would have applauded Cromwell's dealings with Ireland, or William the Third's, as they applaud Mr. Gladstone's now. It is on the country as a whole, and on the mind of the country, that we must rely.

I am, Sir, your obedient servant,
Matthew Arnold

After the Elections

To the Editor of the *Times.*

Sir, — When I was leaving England two months ago you printed a letter from me on the Irish question. In my letter I expressed the conviction that the country was minded to reject Mr. Gladstone's Irish policy, but also to give the Irish the due control of their own affairs.

I write now from the United States, where the conviction that Mr. Gladstone would be victorious has been universal. Everything favourable to him has been current here; nothing unfavourable. However, my faith in the country which, with all its shortcomings, has yet more of solid political sense than any other country has been justified. Mr. Gladstone is defeated. The American newspapers are now crying out that the defeat is but momentary; that his speedy and complete success is certain. Mr. T. P. Gill writes to them that "the situation looks first-rate;" Mr. John Morley predicts that "within a year Mr. Gladstone's Irish proposals will carry with them Parliament and the country;" Mr. Gladstone exults that he has "the civilised world" with him.

All this confidence would be more impressive if its entertainers had not been equally confident of Mr. Gladstone's success in his late appeal to the country. They were wrong in their confidence then; why should they be right in their confidence now? But in a matter of this gravity one cannot be too prudent. Let us see, then, how the case really stands now that the elections are over.

And, first, as to the unanimity of the civilized world in Mr. Gladstone's favour. This would be important if true. I suppose in no country is the unanimity in his favour stronger than in the United States. And yet, even here, if you weigh opinions instead of counting them, the balance of opinion is against Mr. Gladstone's Irish policy. High intelligence and wide knowledge are rare everywhere; they are rare in America. Moreover, it is notorious that in no country do the newspapers so little represent the best mind of the country as they do here. But yet, even here, whenever you meet with a man of high intelligence and wide knowledge, you will almost certainly find him a disbeliever in the wisdom of Mr. Gladstone's Irish policy. "I admire Mr. Gladstone," he will probably say, "but I think he is making a mistake in Ireland." I have myself found but one stanch supporter here of Mr. Gladstone's Irish policy whom I should call a man of high intelligence and wide knowledge — Mr. Godkin, the well-known editor of the *Evening Post* and the *Nation*. And Mr. Godkin is an Irishman.[11]

The general American public knows that over here the several States have the control of their own affairs, and that Ireland has been badly governed. It hears that Mr. Gladstone proposes to give to Ireland Home Rule. It inquires no further, but says, — "Mr. Gladstone is right; by all means let Ireland have Home Rule." The Americans are glad to be able safely to do a pleasure to the Irish, who live among them in large numbers and have great influence on elections and journalism. This is the main motive. Some ill will there may be in the masses, some pleasure in abetting embarrassments to a country which unaccountably goes on attracting more of the world's attention and interest than "the greatest nation on earth." But the main motive is the temptation to do the Irish a pleasure safely. The weighty opinion is not that of the general public who yield to this temptation; it is that of men who resist it and who look deeper into the matter. Of these serious people in America the opinion is, I repeat, against Mr. Gladstone, and I strongly suspect that the same thing is true of the rest of "the civilized world" also.

Nevertheless, the Americans do sincerely think, one and all, that the Irish ought to have the control of their own local affairs. They cannot understand its being disputed. The same feeling prevails on the Continent of Europe. And, therefore, I return to the second point of my former letter — that the English nation is now minded, at the same time that it rejects Mr. Gladstone's policy, to give the Irish the due control of their own affairs.

The newspapers here keep repeating Mr. Gladstone's declaration that his principle is "to give Ireland an effective government by Irishmen." But this is, I believe, as much the principle of the English nation as of Mr. Gladstone. The question is, how can it be properly done? Mr. Gladstone says, "By establishing a legislative body in Ireland for the management of exclusively Irish affairs." Change one word in this, for "body" read "machinery," and you pass from what is supremely dangerous to what is supremely expedient. A legislative body in Ireland means a national Irish Parliament. With the history of Ireland, and the character and bent of

Irishmen before our eyes, any prudent man can see the dangers from such a Parliament. Place what restrictions upon it you will, it will, by the law of its nature, be for ever striving to pose as an independent Parliament; to make Ireland count as an independent nation. The case is precisely parallel with that of the South over here. If a Southern Congress had been conceded, you might have guarded your concession by what restrictions you pleased, but it would still have been a perpetual source of danger. The remembrance of past enmity, the traditions of the political talents and weight of men like Clay and Calhoun, would inevitably have made a Southern Congress always seek to pose as an independent Parliament, to erect the South into an independent nation.

What the Americans did, therefore, was not to establish in the South a legislative body for the management of local affairs, but a legislative machinery. They let the localities manage their own affairs. In this there was great advantage and no danger. And this is what we have to do in Ireland.

A legislative machinery by which the localities can manage their own affairs is as much wanting in Great Britain as in Ireland. Even that basis of all local government, a municipal machinery, is wanting. We have isolated municipalities in towns; but the country as a whole in regard to municipal government is in the condition of France before the Revolution. This is because our people, being conservative, and both they and our aristocracy moderate in temper, the existing state of things has worked on without our feeling its defects to be intolerable. Local government culminates in local Legislatures. But our Parliament at Westminster has had to act both for the localities and for the nation; it is, to use the American terms, Congress and State Legislatures in one. On the whole, Parliament has done, both in England and in Scotland, what the majority wanted. Its size is now unwieldy, its work is unwieldy; moreover, we are without a safeguard and an education which organized local government affords to those who possess it; there is great need to organize it for us also.

But the need to organize it in Ireland is most urgent of all. For undoubtedly the Parliament at Westminster has not been that tolerable though imperfect substitute to Ireland for local Legislatures which it has been to England and Scotland. It has not done what the majority in Ireland wanted, it has done what either the minority in Ireland wanted, or the British Philistine. The situation is only made hopeless by denying this or by shutting our eyes to it. Ireland is treated, say many, precisely like England and Scotland. And they say this with the Established Churches of England and Scotland before their eyes; with the Universities of Oxford and Cambridge before their eyes, Edinburgh and Glasgow. Of all details of local government, where what takes place in Ireland differs widely from what takes place in Great Britain, they may be ignorant; but what is done in Church and education cannot surely be invisible to them. The allegation that Ireland is treated just like England and Scotland must to Irishmen be almost maddening. And therefore I have never inveighed against Mr. Parnell and his followers, irritating as much in their language and proceedings is, bad for Ireland as I think their policy, firmly as I would resist it, rigorously as I would suppress, if necessary, their seditious meetings and incendiary newspapers. What they do is often most evil and dangerous, but I consider the provocation they have received. To have Parliament treating the local affairs of Ireland as the Irish minority or the British Philistine desire, and then to be told that Ireland is on the same footing as England and Scotland! It needs an Irishman of Burke's calibre to be a reasonable politician under such circumstances.

The dangers of this state of things are nearly as great as those of Mr. Gladstone's proposed plan of dealing with it. Of this the country is becoming conscious. It rejects Mr. Gladstone's plan, but it would give the Irish the control of their own local affairs. If the Conservatives cannot see this, if they think they have only to keep order in Ireland, if they let things drift, then the present great opportunity is lost and we are given over to Cleon and his democracy.

If, on the contrary, the Conservatives do as the country wishes and produce a suitable plan of local self-government, for Ireland first, then for Great Britain also, the situation, to borrow Mr. T. P. Gill's phrase, "looks first-rate." To establish such a plan the Unionists can work in perfect concert with Lord Salisbury. It matters little whether their leaders enter the Government or not, though the leaders of one contingent of them should certainly not enter it without the leaders of the other. What is important is that the Unionists should not allow themselves to be divided, that they should determine resolutely to postpone all other questions to those of procedure and local government, and that on these, and till these are settled, they should act with Lord Salisbury. The future will shape itself, will take care of itself. Sufficient for the day are the needs thereof.

Lord Salisbury may perfectly well frame a good plan of local self-government. But he must weigh his words as well as his measures. He complains of those who say that he has nothing to propose but coercion. He ought, on the contrary, to be grateful to them. When he said that what Ireland required was governing he did not mean, he tells us, that all she required was a firm hand over her; he meant that she needed good government of all kinds. Be it so. But his mode of expressing himself was unfortunate, and he ought to thank those who by seizing on his expression, call his attention to what is his side of weakness and danger. Perhaps all public men have such a side, and we critics, were we in public life, should show ours fast enough. Lord Hartington's is some want of flexibility and fertility, Mr. Goschen's some want of sympathy with men's instinct of expansion. Mr. Chamberlain's some want of respect for the past. Lord Salisbury's is an imperious and scornful treatment of popular wishes. *Beati mansueti*. There never was a moment which tried tempers more than the present moment, or where more was to be gained by controlling them. What is the use of being irritated by exaggeration, violence, and hatred of the Irish members, or by the lively nonsense of Mr. Labouchere? To good temper, good sense, and honesty all things are possible — to negotiate with the Irish members without intriguing with them or surrendering to them, and to make Mr. Labouchere laugh at his own nonsense. Do not let us assume that the Liberals of the nadir must of necessity find a lower nadir still, or that Mr. Gladstone must become more and more of a Cleon. Of Mr. Gladstone's recent performances it is indeed difficult to speak without grave and stern reprobation. The desperado burning his ship, the gambler doubling and trebling his stakes and mortgaging the future as luck goes against him, are the images which come irresistibly to one's mind. This Prime Minister's passionate tirades against a social fabric intrusted to his charge and against a union which it is his duty to maintain, have centupled the difficulties of mending either the one or the other. But wisdom, we are told, is justified of her children, and I suppose unwisdom must needs be justified of hers also. Yet of one with such gifts and graces as Mr. Gladstone I, for my part, will never despair. If Lord Salisbury produces a good scheme of local government for Ireland I should not be surprised if Mr. Gladstone supported it. The important thing is that Lord Salisbury should do as the country wishes and produce it.

> I am, Sir, your obedient servant,
> MATTHEW ARNOLD

July 24.

Notes

1. *Letters*, II, 330–331.
2. *Ibid.*, 335.
3. *Ibid.*, 337.
4. Lyon Playfair, afterwards Baron Playfair of St. Andrews (1818–1898) was Vice-President of the Council in Gladstone's ministry in 1886.
5. James Bryce, afterwards Viscount (1838–1922), jurist and historian, was Gladstone's Under-Secretary for Foreign Affairs in 1886.
6. William Douglas, third Duke of Hamilton (1635–1694). Arnold introduces the anecdote in his *Note-Books* (p. 423) from Horace Walpole's *Letters,* ed. Peter Cunningham, 9 vols. (London, 1857–59), I, 385.
7. Robert A. T. G. Cecil, third Marquis of Salisbury (1830–1903), Conservative Prime Minister. A week before Arnold's letter appeared, Lord Salisbury had urged for Ireland "twenty years of resolute government," declaring that some races, like the Hottentots and the Hindus, were unfit for self-government (*DNB*).
8. Lord Randolph Churchill (1849–1895) was Secretary for India when Lord

Salisbury's first cabinet was formed in June 1885. In July Churchill sided with the Irish prisoners on trial for the Maamtrasna murders and disparaged the coercion policy of Lord John Spencer, who was Gladstone's Irish viceroy from 1882 to 1885. He did not join the outcry against Parnell's strong statements for Irish independence in August 1885; and in a speech at Birmingham, November 20, following conversations with Lord Carnarvon, then Viceroy in Dublin, said that Irish crimes and outrages were diminishing. In the spring of 1886, Parnell revealed that he had had private conversations with Lord Carnarvon during the preceding summer. John Morley reports that a Liberal member of parliament addressed to Lord Churchill on January 28, 1886, this reproach: "Nobody should so often as the politician say the prayer not to be led into temptation. Remember your doings last summer" (*The Life of William Ewart Gladstone*, III, 289). Sir Winston Churchill defends his father's integrity against the charge of appeasing Irish nationalist feeling to win power for the Conservatives in *Lord Randolph Churchill*, 2 vols. (London, 1906), I, 436–443.

⁹ George Joachim Goschen (1831–1907), created Viscount in 1901, served as vice-president of the Board of Trade. A speaker at the Opera House meeting, he supported Lord Hartington whom he aided in forming the liberal unionist party. He too declined to enter Gladstone's cabinet.

For Lord Hartington, see p. 281, n. 27.

¹⁰ Henry du Pré Labouchere, the radical politician, here the object of Arnold's irony, was engaged early in 1886 in trying to harmonize the views of Gladstone, Joseph Chamberlain, and the Irish nationalists.

¹¹ Edwin Lawrence Godkin (1831–1902) was born in Ireland, but of English stock. He came to the United States in 1856. Godkin rejected Arnold's designation of him as an Irishman in "American Opinion on the Irish Question," *Nineteenth Century*, XXII (August 1887), 285–292.

Common Schools Abroad*

Century Magazine
XXXII (October 1886), 893–900

On May 22, 1886, Arnold sailed from Liverpool on his second visit to America to join his wife and to visit his daughter Lucy, who had married Frederick W. Whitridge of New York. Arnold proceeded to Philadelphia where on the afternoon of June 8 he read to a crowded audience of more than six hundred his address on Foreign Education, as it was announced in Dr. William Pepper's cordial introduction.[1] Dr. Pepper (1843–1898) was both Provost of the University of Pennsylvania and professor of the theory and practice of medicine. The day after the lecture Arnold wrote to his sister Fan that it had been "quite a success." [2] The satisfaction seems to have been mutual. Dr. Pepper noted, as Arnold's auditors frequently did, his poor delivery, but he remarked also in his diary, "What a good fellow — frank and easy in manner— strong fine figure, strong face." [3] The University sent him a check for one hundred dollars for the engagement. Perhaps the pleasure that Arnold's letter to his sister reflects was in part due to his having found at length men "serious and cultivated enough to understand the Irish question;" [4] for Arnold's deepest concern at the time was in that issue.

The address, which was signed, was published with some changes in the *Century Magazine*.[5] The original manuscript was given to the University of Pennsylvania in 1907. The address itself, though interesting, contained, as Dr. Pepper noted in his diary, nothing new. Arnold based it on points he had broached in *Schools and Universities on the Continent* as long before as 1868, and that he had again treated very recently in his Education Department *Special Report on Certain Points Connected with Elementary Education in Germany, Switzerland, and France* (London 1886).

I think I have mentioned somewhere or other how much I was struck with a remark made to me more than twenty years ago at Rome by Cardinal Antonelli.[6] I was visiting popular schools on the continent. "So you have come to see our schools," he said, "our popular schools; and many people would tell you that our popular education is nothing at all, or next to nothing, and that you will not be able to find anything worth reporting to your government about it. But you may tell your government this," continued the Cardinal: "that illiterate as the Italian population is said to be, and I suppose is, yet, if you mix with the people at any festival and listen to their criticism of what they see, — *è brutto, è bello* (that's ugly, that's

---

*Address delivered before the University of Pennsylvania.

fine!), — you will find their criticism to be almost invariably right. And a people," he concluded, "of whom that can be said must surely be allowed to have a certain sort of education."

I thought of the stolid insensibility to ugliness, the inability to discern between good and evil where the beautiful is concerned, which so easily besets our Anglo-Saxon race, and I acquiesced in what the Cardinal said. And at the same moment there rose to my memory the admirable sentence of a Moravian school-master in the seventeenth century, John Comenius, fixing the universal scope and aim for education. "The aim is," says Comenius, "to train generally all who are born men to all which is human." [7] Surely, to be offended by ugliness, to be delighted and refreshed by beauty, is eminently human; just as, on the other hand, it is a proof that our humanity is raw and undeveloped if we confound the two together or are indifferent to them. For we are then "in bondage," as Goethe says, "to the common and inferior"; out of that bondage we have to rise, and to know that, however general it may be around us, it is not less a bondage and an evil.

Almost immediately after my arrival the other day in this country, I happened to come across a speech by one of your politicians, whom I hope I may venture to call a friend of mine, Senator Hawley of Connecticut.[8] He was praising the system of government of the United States, and he praised it as being "a government of, by, and for the average man." I will not dispute whether or no in politics this is a benefit; but remember that in our education and culture it is precisely the slough of "the common and average and inferior thing," *das Gemeine,* as Goethe calls it, which we have to cast off and rise out from.[9] The common and average thing is our danger; it is comparatively easy of attainment, but no true friend of education will be satisfied so long as this is attained and nothing more.

In popular education, at present, "the common and average thing" is the ability to read, write, and calculate, and the possession of a certain amount of what is called useful knowledge. This is what, in progressive nations, we nowadays expect the whole population to attain, and what they do attain. If we ask for the educative result of this, we shall find it to be, in the main, that the whole population learns to read the newspapers, is formed by the newspapers. This is what modern popular education really leads up to, and many of us are apt to congratulate ourselves when this result has been achieved, and to think that here we have indeed a triumph of progress and civilization.

But then, Cardinal Antonelli points to an illiterate people able to discern much more justly than the English, and probably than the Americans either, between beauty and ugliness, and suggests how far distant, therefore, the popular education of our progressive nations still is from

Comenius's ideal of a training of all to all which is human. And when our attention has once been called to the matter we may go further, and consider how entirely the popular education actually now given, in England at any rate, often fails to awaken and train not only the sense of beauty, but the soul and feelings generally. Therefore, what interests me in popular training abroad, which I have formerly had opportunities of studying, and have again been studying very recently, is especially to ascertain how far it succeeds in doing more than impart a certain amount of useful knowledge, how far it reaches the soul and feelings, and trains its pupils to that which is really human.

I am not sure to what extent your common schools in America resemble ours in their deficiencies; but I hope you will listen to me while I mention some points in which the common schools of Germany and France seem to me to succeed better than common schools in England in training their pupils to what is really human. You will then be able to judge for yourselves whether your common schools in America are more in the case of our English schools, or in that of the schools of France and Germany.

I will take first what is certainly a main agent in touching man's soul and feelings — religion. In England, religion is excluded from the official programme of the popular schools. If it is taught, it is taught outside of the official school-hours, and subject to private and local regulation. Religious liberty, it is said, requires this. If religion is taught at the public expense, what religion is it to be? If it is the religion of the majority, the minority are aggrieved. Religion, therefore, must not be a prescribed school matter at all.

Well, in Germany they no more hesitate to make the religion approved by the majority a school matter for fear the minority should object, in the name of religious liberty, to its being taught, than they hesitate to make the literature approved by the majority a school matter, for fear the minority should object, in the name of intellectual liberty, to its being taught. In German countries — for German Switzerland is much the same as Germany in this respect — religion stands as one of the foremost subjects of instruction in the popular school. Instead of being, as in England, a subject not laid out or noticed in official programmes, a subject which inspectors and official people are told to avoid, it is a subject laid out with the greatest care, and in which inspectors examine with special diligence and interest.

In general, one may say that three religious denominations, and no more, are recognized in German schools, — the Evangelical or Protestant, the Catholic, and the Jewish. Between Catholics and Protestants the public authority deals, both in theory and in practice, with absolute fairness. There is no persecution and no proselytism. So fair is the action of the administration, so complete is the confidence of the people in its fairness, that in the lower classes of Evangelical or Catholic schools you not unfrequently find the Evangelical or the Catholic minority taking the religious instruction, by the parents' consent, along with the majority. In the upper classes, the law requires the minority in these mixed schools to be separated, and to receive religious instruction from teachers of their own communion.

With us the difficulty of including religion in the school programme is caused by the sects of Protestantism. Everybody knows how our Protestantism breaks into sects. There is an instructive list of them in *Whitaker's Almanack*. One might say that amongst our Anglo-Saxon race a new sect often arose from the mere pleasure of making one. And these sects in England would cry out against a religious instruction based on the formularies of the established church, or in America, where you have no established church, of any one great body of Protestants; but throughout Protestant Germany the religious instruction in Protestant schools is based on the Lutheran catechism, the Evangelical hymn-book, and the Bible, and all denominations are expected to follow it. With us, the individual judges what degree of diversity among religionists renders separate religious instruction necessary; in Germany, the law.

I do not think that in Germany, where the spirit of sect has been less carefully cultivated than amongst ourselves, Protestants in general feel the obligatory religious instruction of the public school to be any hardship. I could not hear of any complaints on the subject. But I was very curious to learn how the working classes in the German cities, who are said to be greatly estranged from the Christian religion, took the obligatory religious instruction of their children. In the capital of Saxony, the country which is reported to be the stronghold of socialism, I asked an inspector what proportion of the working classes he thought were socialist and opposed to the established religion. "At least two-thirds," he answered. "Well, then," said I, "how do they like all this Lutheran religion for their children?" "They do not like it at all," he replied, "but they have to submit to it." He added that the religious instruction did the children good; that the mothers in general could perceive this, and some even of the secularist fathers.

I spoke on the same subject, when I was at Berlin, with a man whose name will be received with respect in any university, — Professor Mommsen, the celebrated historian.[10] I told him how surprised I had been to find, after all I had heard of the decay of religion in Protestant Germany, how important a place it still held in the programme of the public schools. He agreed that it did so, and he, too, thought that this was a good thing. He said that the actual religious instruction given was too dogmatic, and that it was a fault of the persons in power that they made it more and more strictly so. But in general, he thought the school instruction in religion a good thing. He quoted to me words of Goethe which I remembered: "He who has art and science, has religion." But he quoted them with an addition which I had forgotten: "He who has not art and science, let him have religion." The popular school is for those, he said, who have not art or science; to leave religion out of its programme would therefore be a great mistake.

Imagine, in a country where government is, as Senator Hawley declares, of, by, and for the average man, imagine recommending that a religious instruction should be imposed upon the common school because the classes frequenting it, not having art or science, require religion! Every term in the proposition is to the average man either unmeaning or else offensive. But I doubt whether the religious feeling of England would not be as much shocked as the democratic feeling of America by the notion of teaching religion in the popular schools as a thing which uncultivated people require, though cultivated people do not. And therefore, while the spirit of sect makes it in one way impracticable to introduce religion into the programme of our popular schools in England, the spirit of religion makes it impracticable in another.

Nevertheless, I wish to report things as I have actually found them, and as they are. The religious instruction in the popular schools of German countries seems to me one of the best and most effective parts of the school work. I have had a long experience of school-teachers and school-children, but seldom have I seen teachers and children to more advantage than once when in a Saxon school I heard them dealing with a theological problem raised in the Lutheran catechism, — the question in what sense men can be said to be tempted of God. In spite of the necessary ambiguity of terms which attends all such questions, in spite of their perhaps necessary insolubleness, they are eternally interesting when handled with thought and earnestness; and so they were handled in this instance.

But if one might have doubts as to the profitable effect, in the common school, of these theological questions, one could have none as to the good effect of what is, after all, the chief and the best part of the religious instruction in German schools: the learning by heart of Bible sayings and parables, and of the Evangelical hymns. I lay stress on the hymns in particular, because such hymns are a form of literature of which I keenly feel the defects, and of which I have more than once spoken disparagingly. The German hymns, however, are better than ours; and no one who watched the serious and touched expression which often came over a child's face at a moving verse, could doubt that here the soul and feelings were reached in a way of which we get no experience with the secular programme and with the useful knowledge of our own common schools.

It is said that the alienation of the working classes in Germany from the Christian religion proves that all the religious instruction of the popular schools is of very little use. I believe that the alienation is exaggerated. But even admitting it to be as great as anyone chooses to suppose, I feel sure that on the religious German nature sentiments and impulses raised by the religious instruction of school often and often continue to work, even though from positive Christianity a man may have become quite estranged.

Well, then, in the religious instruction of the German schools I find an educative force of much value, which in our English common schools is wanting and perhaps impossible. You will know whether it is wanting in your schools also.

But curiously enough I unexpectedly found in France likewise, in a public school, a type of religious instruction which seemed to me of high interest and value, and which also would be in the public schools of England quite impossible.

Not that religion holds the place in the programmes of the French public schools which it holds in those of Germany. Twenty years ago, when I had last seen the French schools, it did, but it does so no longer. The chaplains are gone from the public schools, and religion is gone from their programmes; it may no longer be taught in the public school-rooms out of school hours even. True, moral and civic instruction has a place in the school programmes, and regulations and high functionaries say that the schools are to teach the existence of a God, "in accordance with that spiritualist philosophy which is the glory of Descartes and of France." But in Paris, the center of that great development of popular education which undoubtedly is now going forward in France, in Paris the municipality, which provides and maintains the popular schools, will not have the name of God introduced in their teaching, and has even sanctioned a school manual altogether hostile to religion and contemptuous of it. It has not been possible, indeed, to bring the book into use; but the action of the Paris municipality, in regard to religion, is undoubtedly violent and blameworthy. That municipality has a sincere zeal for instructing the people, and from jobbery and corruption it is, I am told, perfectly free. But it has pushed forward school establishment so fast, and on such a scale as to expense, that the complaints of its extravagance are loud; and so intemperately as to religion, that it outruns the wishes of even that not very religious population, the population of Paris. The religious teaching orders, banished from the public schools, have been enabled, wonderful to relate, to give to their own schools — which are now maintained by private contributions only, and that in a country where voluntary effort is supposed not to flourish — an immense development, so that these orders now actually educate, in private schools, one-third of the school-children of Paris.

As to the moral and civic instruction of the French schools, it seemed to me to be poor stuff, and I saw no signs of its touching the soul or mind of anybody receiving it. Moral teaching for young people, except when it is indirectly conveyed in stories, as in Miss Edgeworth's immortal *Parents' Assistant*, is in general dull;[11] and when it is conveyed in stories, the story may interest, but the moral is apt to be lost sight of. As to civic teaching, the most remarkable specimen of it which I met with I will mention, for it is worth mentioning. "Who gives you," said the questioner to the children, "all the benefits you are enjoying: these fine school-buildings with all their appliances, your instructors, this beautiful city where you live, everything in which the comfort and security of your life consists?" I was attentive, for I said to myself: Surely the child must be going to answer what children have from time immemorial been taught to answer to the like question, "God gives me all this"; and yet the name of God must not be used in a school of the Paris municipality. But the civic instruction proved equal to the occasion, and a legitimate answer came from the child: "It is our country gives us all this." *Eh bien, c'est le pays!* The force of civic instruction, I think, could hardly go further.

All this seems futile enough; but I am bound to record, too, that in a French training college I found, in connection with the teaching of pedagogy, what was really a religious instruction of the most serious and effective kind. I am disposed to say that I should call it, in view of our modern situation and needs, the best religious instruction which I have ever yet heard. The college is at Fontenay-aux-Roses, a few miles out of Paris. It was instituted a year or two ago by the French government in order to train directresses and teachers for the normal colleges for lay school-mistresses, which are now to be established throughout France. At the head of it was placed a man between sixty and seventy years old, who was originally a Protestant pastor and afterwards an inspector-general of primary schools, M. Pécaut.[12] The choice was indeed an admirable one. M. Pécaut has the very gifts requisite for the delicate and difficult post to which he has been called. Whoever wishes to find a success achieved in the teaching of that much-talked-of but in general most unsatisfactory thing, undogmatic religion, should go to Fontenay and hear M. Pécaut in his morning hour with his students. He is fortunate in their quality; the Frenchwoman, under good teaching, makes one of the best students and school-mistresses in the world: so quick is she, so clear, with such perfect presence of mind, such a keen and true sense for excellence. Most of the girls at Fontenay are Catholics, and attend Catholic service on Sundays. But I heard them taking with their director, paragraph by paragraph, Bishop Dupanloup's book on school, *L'Ecole*, a book in which all sorts of questions of religion in connection with education are raised;[13] and really these girls were led to treat them in the same large and free, but at the same time tolerant, sympathetic, and pious, spirit, in which M. Pécaut treated them himself. A German expert in schools, who has lately been reporting to his government on female education in France, is as much struck with admiration at Fontenay and its inmates as I am.

Now here again we have a success which in England would hardly be possible. A government setting up a training college like Fontenay, with a man like M. Pécaut at the head of it, and with a religious instruction like that given by M. Pécaut, would run the risk of being accused of wishing to start a new religion of its own; and no English government in our day would ever, I suppose, run such a risk as that!

I pass on now to other matters of teaching. Here too I had, of course, our English popular schools constantly in my mind while I was observing the foreign schools, and the comparison thus established was highly instructive. In general I thought the methods of teaching better in the foreign schools than with us, and the results of the teaching better. And they are better because the teachers are better trained.

To take the scientific branches of instruction first. Anybody can construct a pretentious and showy school programme. Such a programme is the habitual instrument of unsound schools and superficial teachers. The limitations of a programme are often a proof of wisdom. In arithmetic and mathematics a hasty observer might at first, perhaps, be disposed to wonder that the common schools abroad, and particularly in Germany, do not go further and faster than they do. But in my opinion they prove the goodness of their methods just by not going too far and too fast, by directing their efforts above all to making sure that the average learner shall master every step of the process which he is following. I take myself to have been barely an average learner in arithmetic and mathematics, and I have the most distinct recollection that in these matters I was taken too far and too fast. Either the rule was propounded to us as a kind of trick, and then we had to bring sums right by following it, whereby we got no real insight into arithmetical principles at all; or else the principle of the rule was explained, but not sufficiently developed and dwelt upon for the average learner, who was too rapidly hurried forward before he had fully grasped it.

Again, the use of the blackboard and of oral teaching for arithmetic will often in German schools strike an English observer as excessive. It seems as if a German child in his school-time was never to be left to work sums quietly on his slate by himself; but the sum is put on the blackboard and one child after another is called up to bear part in working it, with continual questioning as to his reasons for what he does. This certainly takes time; but the teacher's aim and endeavor is, not to make his pupil bring sums right (as the phrase is) in as many rules as possible, but to train him to understand the principles of arithmetic.

In teaching natural science and physics, the Germans show a like care not to outrun their scholar, to insure his comprehending all that is said and shown to him. I heard a lesson on electricity given to a class of girls in a Berlin school. I should call it an ambitious lesson in one sense; namely, that it went much beyond anything that I have known attempted in a popular school for girls in England. But what I felt, as I listened to it, was how thoroughly the lesson was within the girls' comprehension, and how I myself, if I had been taught in this fashion, could have been interested in electricity, though I have no bent for studies of this kind. The answering of the class proved how the girls were interested by their teacher's treatment of his subject, and how intelligently they followed it.

But the literary branches of the instruction were what interested me most. These are eminently the humanities, these are what train us to all which is human; and I find occurring frequently in my notes on the foreign schools this entry: *the children human.* I can best explain what I meant by saying frankly what is the impression generally made upon me by the literary performances — reading, reciting, foreign languages, literary history and criticism — in popular or common schools. Often I have to praise the performance as good; but I feel almost always bound in conscience to add secretly to myself: good, considering the class from which the children come, considering that they come from the uncultivated class.

In fact, for the production of good reading and reciting, really good reading and reciting, reading and reciting with proper intonation, pronunciation, and expression, it seems requisite generally to have been brought up in a certain atmosphere of refinement, in the company of people whose speech has these characters. Of course, raw people may call their own speech proper if they choose, but the good judges will not go with them, and this is a case which turns on what "the judicious," as Aristotle says, would decide.

For foreign languages, again, some advantage of travel, of mixing with foreigners, is in general necessary, if proficiency is to be attained; and this advantage can seldom fall to the lot of those from whom the common schools are mostly recruited.

For conversance, once more, of any genuine sort with literary history or criticism, to have lived with cultivated people and to have heard their talk and their judgments seems in general necessary. There may be individuals of genius who have such astonishing natural aptitudes for declamation, or languages, or literature, that they seem to be self-made; but in general, good reading and reciting, and proficiency in foreign languages, and conversance with literary history and criticism, are produced as I have said, or, if they are produced in a class of learners otherwise, then we conclude that there must have been very superior teaching.

I repeat, therefore, that when I call the reading, or the declaiming, or the French, or the literature in a common school *good,* I usually mean good when all due allowances have been made, good considering that the children come from an uncultivated class. And I can hardly remember a case where I have not had to make such a secret reservation in praising these matters in English common schools, except now and then when I have found myself in presence of an eminent and charming natural gift for declamation.

But in popular schools on the continent of Europe, I have found whole classes whose reading and reciting might be called good without any such allowance or reservation whatever, called good just as absolutely as we can call reading and reciting of children of the cultivated classes good; reading and reciting with proper intonation, pronunciation, and expression, and which it was a pleasure to listen to. I recall particularly the reading and reciting of Lamartine's poetry by a class of girls in a primary school in Paris, and the reading of Schiller's *Wilhelm Tell* by a class of boys in a primary school at Lucerne.

Foreign languages are not in general obligatory matters in popular schools abroad, and it is not judicious, I think, in schools of that kind to make them obligatory. But in the popular schools in Hamburg English is obligatory, owing probably to the commercial intercourse of Hamburg with England; and in the popular schools of German Switzerland French is obligatory, because Switzerland is a bilingual nation. In Hamburg one could praise the performance of an English class, in Zurich that of a French class, without any mental reservation, just as one might praise the performance of a French class in a good and expensive school for young ladies in England. The performance was not limited to a few pages of vocabulary and exercises, as in an elementary school in England; the class turned English or French fluently into German, and German fluently into English or French; they knew the grammar of their foreign language, and the way to pronounce it.

Finally, in literary history and criticism, I found in the common schools abroad entire classes familiar with the biography of the great authors their countrymen; capable of comparing and discussing their productions, and of indicating the sources whence these productions draw their power to move and delight us. I found classes trained to that which is human — to follow still the formula of Comenius — to this remarkable extent, a thing unexampled, so far as my experience goes, in popular schools at home.

I cannot enable you to hear the reading, or reciting, or the French and English, of these foreign classes, and thus to make a comparison of it with what you have in America. But I can give you two instances to show you, first, what degree of grammatical proficiency in a foreign language I have found in a common school abroad, and next what degree of proficiency in literary history and criticism.

Visiting one day the French class in a school at Zurich, I asked the master what his pupils were doing. He handed to me the book he was using, and went on with his lesson. His subject was the place of the pronominal objects in a French sentence. Many people who think they know French well are not sound on this point, though it is one where no French person will ever make a mistake. In a popular school in England, to deal with such a point at all would be ridiculous. The point is that in an indicative sentence the pronoun of the first or second person, used datively, always precedes the pronoun of the third person used accusatively: *on me le donne.* But if both pronouns are in the third person, the accusative comes first: *on le lui donne.* There are further rules as to the order of the pronouns in imperative sentences, both affirmative and negative. The point is rather a nice one for a foreigner who has not the instinct of custom to guide him; but again and again the Zurich pupils, to my surprise, displayed their firm hold upon the rules in question, and applied them unerringly. This is a matter of detail, but to any one who knows what common schools are, and what modern languages in them are, it will have great significance.

My second instance has a wider range. At Trachenberg, near Dresden, I entered the common school with the inspector, and found the upper class at their reading lesson. The inspector took the book; the children were reading a well-known balled by Goethe, "Der Sänger," and he began to question them about Goethe's life. They answered as no children in a similar school in England would answer about the life of Milton or of Walter Scott. Then the ballad was read, and the children were asked to compare it with a ballad by Schiller which they had been reading lately, "Der Graf von Habsburg." They were asked what gave to each of these ballads its charm; what the Middle Age was, and whence is the attraction it has for us; what chivalry was, what the career of a minstrel, and so on. They answered in a way in which only children of the cultivated class, children who had had all manner of advantageous influences to mold them, would answer in England; and which led me to write in my notebook the remark which I have already mentioned: the children *human.*

You will judge whether you have in your common schools a like soundness of performance in these matters; whether you really have it, I mean, and are not merely said by patriots and newspapers to have it. I do not think it has much to do with the form of government. One learns, as one grows older, to assign causes with more and more caution. I do not see any necessary connection between government of, by, and for the average man, and an educational superiority such as I have been describing.

No, that superiority is due to a more direct and simple cause. That cause has powerfully affected and benefited popular education in Germany for a long time past, and is now showing its power for good in France also. It has expression well given to it by an article in the constitution of Canton Zurich, which declares that "there shall be an *organische Verbindung*, an organic connection, between all the schools of the Canton, from the lowest to the highest." It is this connection, this vital connection of popular with higher instruction, which produces its superiority.

America has been severely blamed by foreigners, — by foreigners I do not mean Englishmen; I never speak of Englishmen as foreigners to America, nor of Americans as foreigners to England, — but by foreigners America has been severely blamed for contenting herself generally with instituting a good public system of common schools, and leaving intermediate and higher instruction to chance. When one sees colleges such as Harvard, and Yale, and Columbia, one may be inclined to say that in America higher instruction seems able to take good care of itself. But the question will still remain: What connection does it hold with popular education, what influence does it exercise upon *that?* In England we inherit from the past splendid seats of higher instruction, where some great branches of knowledge are undeniably taught with high success; but our higher instruction has no relations whatever with our popular instruction. In Germany, France, and Switzerland the case is otherwise.

There the Ministry of Public Instruction represents the community, in its collective and corporate character, dealing with education as one whole. Higher schools and universities are for the most part state institutions. With them the minister is most directly concerned. Often he is himself a personage distinguished in the higher instruction; thus Guizot and Cousin have been education ministers in France, Wilhelm von Humboldt in Prussia.[14] At any rate, he is always surrounded by representatives of the higher instruction, and in close communication with them.

The popular school is naturally and properly a municipal thing. The minister's dealings with it will be less direct than with the higher schools. But he has the supervision of it, he has the responsibility for its being kept efficient and complying with the school-law of the country. Above all, he has under his direct care the training colleges, where the teachers of the popular schools are formed.

Now observe what effect this naturally has upon popular education. The minister is, I say, often a man who himself has borne a leading part in the highest and best instruction of the country, — in that which is most opposed to charlatanism, vulgarity, and unsoundness in learning, least apt to be satisfied with the common and average and inferior thing. At all events, he is surrounded by representatives of that higher instruction, he is constantly feeling their influence, he has them at his disposition to be consulted and used at any moment. In all those questions so important to the popular school, questions as to studies, methods, school-books, examinations, he takes their advice. They are his delegates and commissaries in his dealings with the popular schools. In the training colleges a certain proportion only of the teachers may be taken from the popular school; the rest must be representatives of the higher instruction. The minister can also depute special professors to give important parts of the training-college teaching; in France especially this is done. At Fontenay, which I have already mentioned, and at Auteuil, the training college of Paris for school-masters, I found the young men and women thus coming under some of the very best and most stimulative instruction to be had now in all France.

You can understand how this action of superior instruction upon the teachers of the common schools must affect them; how it must tend to raise their work above that "common and average thing" which the school work of institutions fed from the least cultivated classes, and taught by instructors drawn from those classes, would of itself tend to become. You will understand how it produces results upon the training of the scholars of the common school which again and again moved me, as I have told you, to write in my notes: "The children *human*."

In England things are very different. There no branch of education is publicly administered except popular education. The education minister is charged with one branch of national education only, and that the lowest and simplest, as it is thought. When, moreover, the English Government found itself at last compelled to assume the responsibility for popular education, it approached it from the point of view of the politician rather than that of the knower and lover of education. Popular instruction had to be recognized as a public charge; it must necessarily be costly, and the great thing, therefore, was to satisfy the House of Commons and the public mind that the public had value for its money. Hence our system of *payment by results*, as it is called, — a vicious system educationally. But then our education minister does not see education as a whole; he is not surrounded by representatives of the higher instruction, men who look to the effect on education of plans adopted in schools, not to the effect on the House of Commons. A friend of education, who can merely urge interests of education against a plan for schools which is likely to please the House of Commons and the public mind, must feel that he is listened to with polite inattention. "It is all very fine," the minister is saying in his heart, "but my business is not to satisfy educationists; it is to satisfy the newspapers and the House of Commons."

If we could have for education minister in England a man like Sir James Mackintosh or Mr. Hallam,[15] and surround him with the representatives of all the higher instruction of the country, then we should have a minister living in an atmosphere of what one may call *educational opinion,* and induced to give effect to it when the common schools and their studies are concerned. Such a minister we have never had in England, but in Germany and France they have; and the common schools of those countries have felt the benefit of it in their methods and studies, in the training of their teachers and the humanization of their school-children.

Therefore I say that what is most to be desired for the common school is an *organic connection,* to borrow the phrase of the Zurich Constitution, with higher instruction, — a vivifying relation and contact with it. But for this purpose public instruction must be organized as one whole. We have not yet so organized it in England, and I do not think that in America you have yet done so either, although in your State governments you have the very machinery best suited for the purpose, a machinery which is lacking at present to us in Great Britain no less than in Ireland, where its absence attracts just now universal attention. Intermediate and higher instruction would themselves, in my opinion, be great gainers by such an organization. But the great gainer of all would be popular education. I can conceive no worthier ambition than that of training all who are born in a country like this of yours to all which is human. But it will not be done unless we can impart to popular instruction the contempt for charlatanism and vulgarity, the sound standard of excellence, by which all serious higher instruction is characterized. Bring, therefore, popular instruction in America into organic connection with higher instruction. Universities and higher schools would do a gracious, a patriotic, and a wise thing by advocating this; and let me say that such advocacy could come from no university with more grace and more force than from the university of Franklin.

Notes

[1] The manuscript of the introduction is among the William Pepper Papers, University of Pennsylvania Library.

[2] *Letters,* II, 332.

[3] Neda Westlake, "Matthew Arnold at the University," University of Pennsylvania *Library Chronicle,* XXV (Winter 1959), 43.

[4] *Letters,* II, 332.

[5] Arnold received £100 from the *Century Magazine.* See R. H. Super, "Arnold's Notebooks and Arnold Bibliography."

[6] Cardinal Giacomo Antonelli (1806–1876) was secretary of state to Pope Pius IX. Arnold met the Cardinal in June 1865. See *Letters,* I, 276.

[7] This untraced quotation is entered in the *Note-Books,* p. 350.

[8] Joseph Roswell Hawley (1826–1905). Arnold entered in his notebooks the quotation from Hawley that follows, but, which, again, is untraced — the *Note-Books,* p. 423.

[9] "Epilog zu Schiller's Glocke."

[10] Theodore Mommsen (1817–1903), German historian and archaeologist. The quotation that follows is from Riemer, *Mittheilungen über Goethe,* I, 142.

[11] Maria Edgeworth's *The Parent's Assistant; or, Stories for Children,* which was first published in 1795, went through many editions in the nineteenth century.

[12] Félix Pécaut (1828–1898), French protestant theologian and educator. His book *Christ et la conscience* (Paris, 1859) was a widely controversial work.

[13] Félix Antoine Philibert Dupanloup (1802–1878), Bishop of Orléans, published *De l'éducation* in 1850 and *De la haute éducation intellectuelle* in 1866.

[14] François P. G. Guizot (1787–1874), historian and statesman, complimented Arnold in 1865 on his study of French primary instruction. See *Letters,* I, 256–257.

Victor Cousin (1792–1867), French philosopher.

Karl Wilhelm von Humboldt (1767–1835), philologist and man of letters.

[15] Sir James Mackintosh (1765–1832), the philosopher, and Henry Hallam (1777–1859), the historian, were men of broad and varied intellectual interests.

Arnold's Speech on His Retirement

The Times
November 13, 1886, p. 5, cols. 5–6

On November 12, 1886, the school teachers of the Westminster district honored Matthew Arnold with the presentation of a silver claret jug and a salver at a banquet at St. Peter's Schoolroom, Lower Belgrave Street. The occasion was his retirement after thirty-five years as school inspector. Two hundred and fifty-two teachers contributed to the gift. The salver bore the inscription, "This salver was presented to Mr. Matthew Arnold, M.A., D.C.L., LL.D., on his retirement from the inspectorship of Westminster by the teachers of the district as a token of their regard, and in grateful recognition of the happy relations which have marked his connexion with them, November 12, 1886." E. T. Morgan, headmaster of St. James's School, Westminster, was the chairman.

Arnold's response to the presentation was printed in full on the following day in both the *Pall Mall Gazette* and *The Times*. In the former it was headed "Thirty-five Years of School Inspecting: Mr. Matthew Arnold's Farewell," November 13, 1886, page 6; in the latter "Mr. Matthew Arnold and the Westminster Teachers," November 13, 1886, page 5, columns 5–6. Portions of the speech are printed in G. W. E. Russell's *Matthew Arnold* (New York, 1904). The whole address has not been heretofore reprinted.

Ladies and gentlemen. I thank you with all my heart. I remember many years ago, and perhaps my friend, Mr. Healing, behind me will remember it too, that once, after we had been inspecting a school in the north of London, we were entertained at luncheon by one of the managers, who said so many kind things about me that at last, growing embarrassed, I cut it short by saying, "Nobody can say I am a punctual inspector." (Laughter.) You have praised me so much that I feel almost disposed to say something disparaging of myself now. The truth is my path as an inspector has been made very smooth for me. Everywhere I have found kindness; everywhere I have favours to acknowledge and obligations to express. I hardly know where to begin. I will begin where my obligations are least. To the Government I owe nothing. (Cheers and laughter.) But then I have always remembered that under our Parliamentary system the Government probably takes little interest in such work, whatever it is, as I have been able to do in the public service, and even perhaps knows nothing at all about it. And, ladies and gentlemen, we must take the evils of our system along with the good. Abroad probably a Minister might have known more about my performances. But then abroad I doubt whether I should ever have survived to perform them. (Laughter.) Under the strict bureaucratic system abroad I feel pretty sure I should have been dismissed ten times over for the freedom with which on various occasions I have expressed myself on matters of religion and politics. (Laughter.) Our Government here in England takes a large and liberal view of what it considers a man's private affairs, and so I have been enabled to survive as an inspector for 35 years; and to the Government I at least owe this — to have been allowed to survive for 35 years. When I pass from Governments this somewhat bounded kind of obligation ceases, and my obligation becomes ample and full indeed. As to the permanent officials, past and present, of the Education Department, whether I take the living, Lord Lingen, Sir Francis Sandford (hear, hear), Mr. Cumin, or recall the names of the dead — Chester, Bowstead, Clough — I find only friends and friendliness to remember.[1] Most of them have been my personal friends, at the time of life when friendship has an intimacy and a savour which it can hardly acquire afterwards; but all the officials of the department with whom I have had to do have lightened for me the troubles of an inspector's life instead of aggravating them. I suppose the permanent officials are sometimes found by an inspector to be harsh and trying, but in that case I am like the dairymaid in the rustic poem, who found the dun cow that was vicious to others, gentle to her. (Laughter.) If there is any viciousness in the breasts of permanent officials I never felt it; they have left with me no feelings for them but feelings of gratitude and affection. My colleagues the inspectors I have found always friendly and ready to help; we have had no quarrels nor an approach to one. Often and often I have admired work and qualities of theirs, and I rejoice to see succeeding me in my district one of them, for whom I have a special esteem — Mr. Sharpe. (Cheers.) Then my assistants — how my assistants have smoothed my path for me. I know it is thought at the office that an inspector's path is often too much smoothed for him by his assistant. (Laughter.) My rule was — and I think it is a good one — to let my assistant do whatever he could do as well or better than I could myself. I found that to be a considerable quantity, I confess. But I do not think my assistants felt themselves to be unfairly put upon. (Hear, hear.) At any rate, they did not work for me as if they did. What I owe to the assiduity, good sense, and cheerful good temper of Mr. Healing, whom I have known ever since I apprenticed him, a smooth-headed little boy in the Wesleyan school at Cheltenham, I can never forget, and never tire of acknowledging.[2] Mr. Myhill was with me for a much shorter time, but he, too, has left me full of regard and gratitude for his zeal and trustworthiness. Lastly, I come to the managers and teachers. From the time when the authorities of the Borough-road and the Wesleyan Education Committee acquiesced in my appointment, though it was made, let me tell you, irregularly and with neglect of their right of veto, down to the other day, when Canon Fleming insisted on entertaining from the Conference quite an unreasonably large party of us, the managers, too, have been my kind friends.[3] And the teachers! When I think of their good will, their confidence in me, their alacrity to comply with my wishes — when I think of all this, crowned finally by our meeting to-night and by their beautiful gift — I am indeed disposed to say with Wordsworth that it is the gratitude of man which leaves one mourning. I ask myself with astonishment to what I owe this confidence, this favour. I assure you I am not at all a harsh judge of myself. But I know perfectly well that there have been much better inspectors than I; I could enumerate and I have seen in my colleagues dozens of merits which I do not possess. Whence, then, all this favour and confidence towards me? Well, one cause of it was certainly that I was my father's son (cheers); another cause has been, I think, that I am more or less known to the public as an author (hear, hear), and I have been always touched to see how the teachers — so often reproached with being fault-finders and overweening — are disposed to defer to their inspector on the score of any repute he may have as an author (hear, hear), although, undoubtedly, an author of repute may be a bad inspector. However, I do not mean to say that I think I have been altogether a bad inspector. (Cheers.) I think I have had two qualifications for the post. One is that of having a serious sense of the nature and function of criticism. I from the first sought to see the schools as they really were. Thus it was soon felt that I was fair (hear, hear), and that the teachers had not to apprehend from me crotchets, pedantries, humours, favouritism, and prejudices. (Cheers.) That was one qualification. Another was that I got the habit, very early in my time, of trying to put myself in the place of the teachers whom I was inspecting. I will tell you how that came about. Though I am a schoolmaster's son I confess that school teaching or school inspecting is not the line of life I should naturally have chosen. I adopted it in order to marry a lady who is here to-night, and who feels the kindness as warmly and gratefully as I do. (Cheers.) My wife and I had a wandering life of it at first. There were but three inspectors for all England. My district went right across from Pembroke Dock to Great Yarmouth. We had no home; one of our children was born in a lodging at Derby, with a workhouse, if I recollect right, behind and a penitentiary in front. (Laughter.) But the irksomeness of my new duties was what I felt most, and during the first year or so this was sometimes almost insupportable. But I met daily in the schools with men and women discharging duties akin to mine, duties as irksome as mine, duties less well paid than mine, and I asked myself, Are they on roses? Would not they by nature prefer, many of them, to go where they liked and do what they liked, instead of being shut up in school? I saw them making the best of it; I saw the cheerfulness and efficiency with which they did their work, and I asked myself again, How do they do it? Gradually it grew into a habit with me to put myself into their places, to try and enter into their feelings, to represent to myself their life, and I assure you I got many lessons from them. This placed me in sympathy with them. Seeing people once a year is not much, but when you have come into sympathy with them they do not fade from your mind, and I find myself able to recall, and almost daily recalling, names and faces and circumstances of teachers whom I have not seen for years. That is because I have been in sympathy with them. I will not accept all the praise you have given me, but I will accept this — I have been fair and I have been sympathetic. (Cheers.) And now, my kind friends of many years, before we come to the word which, as Byron tells us, must be and hath been, although it makes us linger, the word farewell, let me say that I had hoped to come round and take leave of you all in your schools before meeting you here. I have not been able to accomplish this yet, but those of you whom I have not already visited at your schools I hope to visit there shortly. (Cheers.) And before we now part I wish to give a counsel and to make a reflection. First, the counsel. You have a very strong association, the Elementary Teachers' Union. Some people would say it was too strong. I do not think so (hear, hear); but I wish it would concentrate its strength in one object in the first place, and let other objects be until this one is gained. Insist on having a Minister for Education. (Cheers.) I know the Duke of Richmond told the House of Lords that, as Lord President, he was Minister of Education (laughter); but really the Duke of Richmond's sense of humour must have been slumbering when he told the House of Lords that.[4] A man is not Minister of Education by taking the names, but by doing the functions. (Cheers.) To do the functions he must put his mind to the subject of education; and so long as Lord Presidents are what they are, and education is what it is, a Lord President will not be a man who puts his mind to the subject of education. A Vice-President is not on the Lord President's own showing — and cannot be, Minister for Education; he cannot, therefore, be made responsible for mistakes and neglects. Now, what we want in a Minister for Education is this — a centre where we can fix the responsibility. Insist, therefore — as you, the chief sufferers by mistakes and neglects in the management of education have a right to insist — insist on having a Minister for Education. There is my counsel; now for my reflection. My reflection is one to comfort and cheer myself, and I hope others, at this our parting. We are entering upon new times, where many influences, once potent to guide and restrain, are failing. Some people think the prospect of the reign of democracy, as they call it, very gloomy. This is unwise, but no one can regard it quite without anxiety. It is nearly 150 years since the wisest of English clergymen told the Lord Mayor and Sheriffs of London in a hospital sermon that the poor are very much what the rich make them.[5] (Hear, hear.) That is profoundly true, though perhaps it rather startles us to hear it. On the other hand, it is almost a commonplace that children are very much what their teachers make them. I will not ask what our masses are likely to be if the rich have the making of them. I prefer to ask what they are likely to be so far as the teachers have the making of them. And on the whole — and here is the consoling reflection with which I shall end — though the teachers have, of course, their faults as individuals, though they have also their faults as a class, yet, on the whole, their action is, I do think and believe, powerful for good. (Hear, hear.) And not in England only, but in other countries as well, countries where the teachers have been much spoken against, I have found it so. I find plenty of deleterious and detestable influences at work, but they are influences of journalism in one place, in another influences of politicians, in some places both the one and the other; they are not the influences of teachers. The influence of the elementary teacher, so far as my observation extends, is for good; it helps morality and virtue. I do not give the teacher too much praise for this; the child in his hands so appeals to his conscience, his responsibility is so direct and palpable. But the fact is none the less consoling, and the fact is, I believe, as I have stated it. Burke speaks of the ancient and inbred integrity and piety of the English people;[6] where should this influence of the teachers for good be so strong and sustained as here? Thus, in conclusion, we are carried beyond and above the question of my personal gratitude, although that, too, is very deep and real. I love to think of the elementary teachers, to whom I owe so much and am so grateful, as more and more proving themselves to deserve, and more and more coming to possess, in the days which are now at hand for us, the esteem and gratitude of the entire country. (Cheers.)

Notes

[1] Ralph Robert Wheeler Lingen, Baron Lingen (1819–1905), was Secretary of the Education Department from 1849–1869.

Francis R. J. Sandford, Lord Sandford (1824–1893), was Secretary of the Education Department from 1870 to 1884. He collected Matthew Arnold's *Reports on Elementary Schools, 1852–1882* (London and New York, 1889).

Patrick Cumin was Secretary of the Education Department from 1884–1890.

[2] Thomas Healing. See W. F. Connell, *The Educational Thought and Influence of Matthew Arnold* (London, 1950), pp. 231–232.

[3] Canon James Fleming (1830–1908), Canon of York.

4 Charles Henry Gordon-Lennox, sixth Duke of Richmond (1818–1903), was Lord President of the Council in Disraeli's second Cabinet (1874–1880). He strongly opposed the theories on endowments of Arthur Hobhouse, member of the Endowed Schools Commission (see above the essay on "Endowments"). For reference to "Minister of Education," see *Hansard's Parliamentary Debates,* August 3, 1874, 3rd series, CCXXI, 1122.

5 Bishop Butler, "Six Sermons Preached upon Public Occasions: Sermon II," *The Works of Joseph Butler,* II, 305.

6 "A Letter to a Noble Lord," *The Works of Edmund Burke,* V, 204–205.

The Zenith of Conservatism

Nineteenth Century
XXI (January 1887), 148–164

"The Nadir of Liberalism" drew upon itself the adverse comment of the *Saturday Review,* which, in an article entitled "Off the Platform" (May 1, 1886), attacked Arnold's comment as "critical" rather than constructive, and "belated." The *Saturday Review* also took note, with better humor, of "The Zenith of Conservatism" in "Matthew Arnold on the Situation" (January 1, 1887). The *Saturday Review* said: "Fortified by a dictum of Ptolemy the astronomer, Matthew Arnold comes forward in the current number of the *Nineteenth Century* to discuss the political situation. We are so accustomed to find Mr. Arnold deriving encouragement from unexpected sources that we regard his new counsellor almost without surprise. Better Ptolemy, we are tempted to exclaim, than Bishop Wilson (although a quotation from the worthy Bishop is good-humoredly thrown in for our special behoof); and, if Mr. Arnold requires the incitement of the maxim, 'As you draw near your latter end, redouble your efforts to do good,' in order to move him to political criticism, we are not disposed to grudge it to him. He is always excellent reading whether we agree with him or not."

There was a favourite saying of Ptolemy the astronomer, which Lord Bacon quotes in its Latin version thus: *Quum fini appropinquas, bonum cum augmento operare* — "As you draw near to your latter end, redouble your efforts to do good." From time to time I have ventured to criticise the action of our great political parties. The professional politicians are always apt to be impatient of the intervention in politics of a candid outsider, and he must expect to provoke contempt and resentment in a good many of them. Still the action of the regular politicians continues to be, for the most part, so very far from successful, that the outsider is perpetually tempted to brave their anger and to offer his observations, with the hope of possibly doing some little good by saying what many quiet people are thinking and wishing outside of the strife, phrases, and routine of professional politics. Declining years supply a motive, Ptolemy tells us, to an aged outsider for more than ever trying to do this, and so, at the present moment of crisis, I find myself drawn back to politics. Before the defeat of the Liberals I criticised the performance and situation of the Liberal party under Mr. Gladstone, and said that this great party seemed to have at that moment pretty well reached its *nadir,* or lowest. The other great political party, the party of the Conservatives, might on the contrary before the recent sudden surprise of Lord Randolph Churchill's resignation have been said to stand at its zenith, or highest.[1] Before Parliament meets, and it is decided whether the fortunes of Conservatism shall remain prosperous or shall take a turn to decline and fall, I want to inquire how things look to plain people outside of the rivalry of parties, and on what the standing or falling of the Conservative fortunes seems to depend.

When one thinks of the weakness of the Conservatives in the last Parliament, of the confidence of Mr. Gladstone and his followers that in the elections for the present Parliament they would sweep the Conservatives from the field, and how this confidence proved false and the Conservatives from very weak in Parliament became very strong; when one thinks, next, of the prophesying of the Liberals that the alliance between the Conservatives and the Liberal Unionists would instantly dissolve, and how false, too, this prophesying proved; when one considers, finally, how the Conservatives in their resistance to Mr. Gladstone had and have the mind of the country with them, or at least the mind of England, of the far greatest, most civilised, and most influential part of the country, the part, too, where the mere trade or game of politics least absorbs men, where there is to be found the largest number of people who think coolly and independently — when one considers all this, one must surely own that the Conservatives might until just now have been said to be at their zenith.

Certainly there have been appearances of danger. We heard at one time that Mr. Chamberlain was consenting to an attack on the Home Secretary's seat at Birmingham, at another that Sir George Trevelyan was going himself to contest a Conservative seat at Brighton. Then, too, there was Mr. Gladstone's friendly proposal that the Liberal Unionists should join with him to force the hand of the Conservative leaders at the beginning of this coming session, and to make them at once produce their plans for dealing with Ireland. But these former appearances of danger passed off. Mr. Chamberlain was staunch, Sir George Trevelyan was staunch. Mr. Gladstone's friendly call to co-operation was received by Lord Hartington with a coldness which reminds one irresistibly of the attitude of the prince in *Rasselas:* "His old instructor officiously sought opportunities of conference, which the prince, having long considered him as one whose intellects were exhausted, was not very willing to afford." [2]

Now, however, has come the startling surprise of Lord Randolph Churchill's resignation. Of course, that resignation is a grave event, throwing a very serious responsibility upon Lord Randolph Churchill, a very serious responsibility upon Lord Salisbury. So long, however, as the Liberal Unionists continue staunch, and the majority remains unimpaired, the gravity of the event is ministerial and parliamentary, rather than national. But the attitude of Mr. Chamberlain, agitated by Lord Randolph Churchill's resignation, has become equivocal. More than ever is it important that the mind of the country, the great power of quiet reasonable opinion in England, should make its force felt. Parliaments, parties, and politicians, are more or less discredited; that force is at bottom sound, and affords our best guarantee of national strength and safety. It placed the Conservatives in office, and, if not alienated, it will for the present keep them there. Questions of persons sink into insignificance beside the paramount question, whether Ministers will, by their policy on two or three matters, now of main concern, carry the mind of the country with them. It is favourable to them at present, in spite of Lord Randolph Churchill's defection and of Mr. Chamberlain's signallings to the enemy. It is favourable to them at present, and shows no signs of withdrawing from them its goodwill. But how are they to keep it favourable? How are they to retain the goodwill of that great body of quiet reasonable people, who thought the course attempted by Mr. Gladstone and his Liberals a false and dangerous one, and rejoiced at the success of the Conservatives in stopping it?

Well, what the Conservatives, having been themselves successful, have now above all to do, is to make their country too, in its turn, *succeed*. There can be no doubt that for this good while past our country has not been, in the judgment of any cool-headed person, succeeding; that it has seemed somehow, as has been said, to flounder and to beat the air; to be finding itself stopped on this line and on that, and to be threatened with a sort of standstill. People carried away by party spirit will say anything; they will say that Mr. Gladstone succeeded in Egypt, that he was successful with his Land Act, successful with procedure. But that great body of plain reasonable people, whose goodwill at present makes, I say, the strength of the Conservative Government, know better. Perhaps party writers on the Tory side will say that Lord Salisbury's Government, since it has been in power, has already been succeeding; but dispassionate observers will hardly agree to that either. The Conservatives have done little or nothing hitherto, since they came into power, to make their country *succeed*, to make things go happily for us, any more than the Liberals did. I do not say that the Conservatives are to be blamed for this; perhaps they have not had time, perhaps they have been reserving themselves for the meeting of Parliament. But the fact remains; they have not yet made their country visibly recover itself and succeed, and to make it do this is what is wanted of them. If they are to remain at the zenith, they must do it; and both for their own sake and for the sake of the country it is most important for them, and now since Lord Randolph Churchill's defection more important than ever, to consider by what sort of proceedings when Parliament meets, since they seem to be waiting for the meeting of Parliament, they are likely to do it.

Soon enough will the occasions come to the Conservative Government, the occasions for standing or falling; and in what fashion soever they may meet them they will have plenty of party foes sure to tell them that they do ill, and plenty of party friends to tell them that they do well. But the verdict which will decide whether they and the great Conservative party led by them shall really stand or fall is, I repeat, the great force of fair and reasonable English opinion independent of party. This force is what they must keep in view and seek to satisfy. It will go with them in not permitting questions to be raised which ought to be postponed to matters more urgently pressing now. But with three matters of urgent present importance the Government will, as every one knows, have to deal: procedure, the state of Ireland, local government. It is probable also that some branch or other of the question of Church disestablishment will force itself under the notice of Parliament and compel discussion. On perhaps four matters, therefore, the Government will, we may expect, have to declare itself: procedure, the state of Ireland, local government, Church disestablishment. On these it will have to carry with it, if it is to stand and not to fall, the great body of independent reasonable opinion in England.

Let us take procedure first. Probably no member of Parliament quite knows how scandalous and intolerable the present state of the House of Commons appears to the great body of quiet reasonable people throughout the country. Party men may find their account, one way or another, in that state of things; the excitement of it, and self-importance, may make many members of Parliament blind to the actual truth. But the actual truth is that plain reasonable people outside the House of Commons regard the confusion into which it has fallen, and its apparent helplessness to extricate itself, with ever deepening disgust and shame; it is a relief to them when Parliament is not sitting; they are uneasy and apprehensive as soon as it meets again, for they know that the time for humiliation has returned. A Minister said solemnly, after a scandalous scene: "The country will judge;" the *Times* sounded its eternal warning: "If this sort of thing continues, it will become necessary to apply some very stringent remedy." The country *has* judged, judged and condemned. It has judged that the stringent remedy ought to have been long before now applied, and has condemned the House of Commons of impotence for not applying it. Factious men in the House of Commons may from party interest oppose a stringent reform of procedure, vain men may oppose it in the interest of their own importance; pedants, both inside and outside the House of Commons, may oppose it on the strength of stock phrases which perhaps had force and truth once but which have them no longer. But the body of quiet reasonable opinion throughout the country is in favour of a most stringent reform; and this opinion will heartily approve the Government if it undertakes such a reform and carries it through, will be displeased and alienated if it does not. Plain people will not be impracticable and insist on having closure by a bare majority, if the Government finds that time and labour are saved through accepting closure by a majority of three-fifths, or of two-thirds; but the more stringent a closure the Government can carry, the better will plain people be pleased. I presume it will hardly now be Lord Randolph Churchill who will propose closure; but to imagine that we should have been so stiff as not to accept closure from Lord Randolph Churchill because he of old intemperately inveighed against it, is to think us foolish indeed. The *Saturday Review* objects to my quoting Bishop Wilson, but really I have a maxim of his which fits Lord Randolph Churchill's duty in this matter exactly: "Let us not afflict ourselves with our failings; our perfection consists in opposing them." [3]

The subject of Ireland I will leave to the last, because it requires to be treated at most length. We come next, therefore, to the question of local government. It cannot be said that the opinion which the Conservative Ministry is so concerned to satisfy, the opinion of quiet reasonable people throughout the country, has as yet much addressed itself to this question of local government, or feels a keen interest in it. Such people are indeed bent, as I believe, on giving to the Irish the due control of their own local affairs, just as the Scotch have it, or the English themselves. Through the Parliament at Westminster Scotchmen and Englishmen do in the main get this control, though by an imperfect and inconvenient method; Irishmen, however, fail to get it, and a plan of local government is necessary in order to give it to them. The necessity is recognised; it is known, moreover, that other nations have reformed their system of local government to meet modern needs, whilst ours remains chaotic and inefficient. And the more the advantage of the reforms effected elsewhere comes to be understood, the greater will be the impatience at our unreformed chaos. Difficulties are raised, it is objected that a thorough system of local government, such as we see, for instance, in the United States, implies a federal organisation of the people concerned. But the kingdom of Prussia is not organised federally any more than the kingdom of Great Britain; and in Prussia the Liberals have reformed almost the whole system of the local governments, and established a system new and thorough; it is the one success of the Prussian Liberals. Prussia has thirteen Provinces and four hundred and sixty-nine Circles or Districts, each with its assembly elected by a very simple and wide suffrage; after these come all the municipalities, urban and rural, each of them with its own elective assembly too. The system works well. I have most examined it in connection with the elementary schools. These have far more to do with the district and provincial governments than with the central government. They are gainers thereby, they are managed with less of what we call *red tape,* with much more understanding of local needs. Furthermore, in monarchical Prussia just as in republican and federal America, the district and provincial assemblies afford a wholesome training in public affairs to their members, a training which both informs and raises them, and of which the middle class in our country is destitute. The more that all this comes to be known and considered, the more will the force of quiet reasonable opinion here be engaged in favour of creating a thorough system of local government. At present our people do, as I have already admitted, chiefly think of it as a remedy for the Irish difficulty. Whether as a system for Ireland only, or for the entire kingdom, it is important that it should be built on sufficiently large lines, not too complicated, not fantastic, not hesitating and suspicious, not taking back with one hand what it gives with the other. Why? Because a measure of that kind cannot possibly win general and cordial acceptance, cannot, therefore, really succeed; and *success,* clear and broad success, is what the general sentiment demands from measures produced by the Government. People are become very impatient of seeing their country fumble and fail, the efforts of government turn awry, our affairs go amiss. If Ministers do not see their way to producing a full and frank measure of local government at the present moment, they would surely do well to put off the production of their measure rather than produce a lame one; most especially if, as is rumoured, Ireland is thought to be not in a proper state for the immediate introduction there of any such measure at all.

Next we have the question of Church disestablishment, which is likely to come under discussion in connection with Wales. Here it is above all important that Ministers should not only think of defeating their party opponents and of gratifying their party supporters, but also of carrying with them the mind of the country, the force of quiet reasonable opinion in the nation. Admit reforms they must; but Conservatives are always saying that it is their principle to make needful reforms, only without destroying. I will add that they can afford to disregard entirely their adversaries' reproach of stealing the Liberal reforms. The important reforms which the Liberal party, the party of movement and change, has brought about, are almost entirely reforms demanded — legitimately, I will add, demanded — by the instinct of expansion in our community, reforms among which the extension of the suffrage, with the ballot, may stand as chief. But these are reforms of machinery, requiring not much insight or thought to make them; comparatively easy, and tempting in proportion to their ease. For the more vital and constructive kinds of reform the Liberal party has shown, except in the single and doubtful case of Free Trade, little disposition and no faculty. What is the Liberal policy in Ireland? Throwing up the game there, the virtual abandonment of the Union. What is the Liberal policy with regard to the Church? Mere destruction of a great and old national agency. What with regard to the House of Lords? Very much the same thing. Sir George Trevelyan seems inclined, Unionist though he is, to make the Liberal party his religion, just as the religion of Gambetta, Mr. Frederic Harrison tells us, was France; and I must say that neither the one nor the other object for religion seems to me adequate.[4] When the Liberal party proposes to reform without destroying, its proposals are commonly childish. Take the well-known Liberal proposition to expel the bishops from the House of Lords. One can hardly imagine sensible men planning a Second Chamber which should not include the Archbishop of Canterbury for the time being, or which should include the young gentlemen who now flock to the House of Lords when pigeon-shooting is in question. But our precious Liberal reformers are for retaining the pigeon-shooters and for expelling the Archbishop of Canterbury.

No: if the Conservatives can produce vital and constructive reforms, there is no fear of our finding them to be plagiarisms from the Liberals. But vital and constructive reforms, such as may so properly come from the party of stability and prominence — reforms which possess, as Burke finely says, "all the benefits which may be in change without any of the inconveniences of mutation," these the Conservatives must produce, or must at least show themselves capable of producing; and nowhere more than in Church matters.

Twenty years and more have now gone by, since in a lecture at Oxford I quoted the declaration of a member of Parliament, a friend of mine, that a thing's being an anomaly was in his opinion no objection to it whatever, and I remarked that at any rate, perhaps, the labours of the friends of light might be trusted to prevail so far as this: that in twenty years' time it should be thought, even in England, an objection to a thing that it is absurd.[5] And this is what has really come about. The epoch of concentration has ended for us, the ice has broken up, things are no longer looked upon as a part of the order of creation merely because we find them existing. If they are absurd, this is now a positive objection to them; they become impossible as well, and have to be got rid of. Apply this to Church matters. The American newspapers have all been saying with wonder lately, and our newspapers have repeated it after them, that the present Earl of Lonsdale has forty Church livings in his gift, and nominates their incumbents. Perhaps he has not really so many as forty, but certainly he has a good number. Well, twenty years ago, if a like thing had been mentioned, the stale old hacks in politics and religion, whose business it was to talk plausibly on these topics but to prevent all innovation, would have uttered their decorous platitudes, would have said that the thing was unfortunate, but that it could not possibly be helped, and our society at large would have gravely acquiesced. But now the mention of a thing of this kind startles people, raises their impatience. They feel that Lord Lonsdale's having the presentation to these livings is an absurdity. The body of quiet reasonable people throughout the country, whose goodwill is so essential to the Government, have come, I say, to perceive, when a thing of this kind is brought to their notice, that it is absurd; it is felt to be absurd, and its long continuance henceforth, therefore, becomes impossible. The Government must in questions of Church patronage be in concert with this force of reasonable opinion, not lagging behind it or in conflict with it.

The same as to the maintenance of the Church establishment on its actual footing, under circumstances such as those which we see presenting themselves in Wales. To maintain the establishment in Wales for the sole benefit of a small minority of the population is an absurdity there, just as it was in Ireland. When it comes before the mind of reasonable people, it is felt by them to be an absurdity. The thing being felt to be an absurdity, its long continuance becomes impossible. Does that necessitate disestablishment, secularisation of Church revenues, giving to roads and bridges what was meant for religion? Not by any means. The sterile programme of our actual party Liberalism has no better solution than this to offer, but a better solution may be found, and it is the business of a truly Conservative government to find it. The mind of the country will be heartily with them if they can produce and apply it.

And now I come, lastly, to that which is, after all, both the great opportunity and the great danger for the Conservatives at present — Ireland. If they succeed here, they will be at the zenith beyond all doubt or question, and whatever Lord Randolph Churchill or Mr. Chamberlain may do or say; if they fumble and fail, if their efforts go awry and affairs in Ireland go amiss, then inevitably must come the turn of Cleon and his democracy, who will resume in triumph the game which the country cut short once, but will then reluctantly leave them free to pursue. All that will be left for the Conservatives will be to cry out, like the Abbé Sièyes: *Ruit irrevocabile vulgus.*[6]

Now, however, Ministers have the mind of the country thoroughly with them in resisting Home Rule — Home Rule as Mr. Gladstone and his followers understand it. There prevails, apparently, in the ideas of many people who think and talk about Home Rule, the most astonishing laxity and confusion. Home Rule, for many people, means just the same thing as local government. Whoever is for local government, for giving the Irish people the control of their own local affairs, is for Home Rule, only his opposition to Mr. Gladstone makes him choose a different form of expression! I have seen Sir Redvers Buller called a Home Ruler because he is, or is supposed to be, for putting pressure on harsh and impracticable landlords.[7] But Home Rule has for Mr. Gladstone and his followers a certain definite, fixed meaning, which they have again and again declared to us, and it is this: *A separate Parliament for Ireland, with an Irish executive responsible to that Parliament.* I know they reserve Imperial affairs, and withhold them from the control of the Irish Parliament and Irish executive. But the point is, that by Home Rule they mean one separate Parliament for the Irish, with a separate executive responsible to it. Local government may mean many things, but Home Rule has now come to mean this particular, definite thing, which Mr. Gladstone and his followers declare themselves to understand by it. And the question is, is the thing expedient, or is it dangerous and to be resisted? There can be no doubt that the Conservatives think it dangerous and to be resisted, that the mind of the country has gone with them in their resistance to it hitherto, and still goes with them in resistance to it now.

Treatises might be written — treatises *are* written, treatises very ingenious, very elaborate, and very long — on the dangers of Home Rule as Mr. Gladstone and his followers understand it. But I have here in view the opinion and disposition of the great body of plain reasonable people throughout the country, whose favour has brought the Conservatives to their zenith, and must be retained if they are to stay there. For general use by plain reasonable people the apparatus of argument employed against Home Rule is excessive; it is much too full and too vast. And it is not required; a single apposite and clear illustration brings the state of the case home to their minds better than scores of long speeches and treatises, with all their elaborate apparatus of argument. This is why I have so much insisted on an illustration afforded by the United States of America. Lord Spencer, having apparently, in his strange courses of late, got hold of a formula of Jacobinism by mistake for a formula of Whiggery, asks with earnestness: "Is there not a mandate from the Irish people to the British Parliament to give Home Rule?" — and seems to think that this settles the matter.[8] Ireland could address no stronger mandate to Parliament to give Home Rule than the Southern States addressed to the North to give them a separate Congress and a separate executive. If that mandate ought to have settled the matter for the Americans, then the Irish mandate ought to settle the matter for us. If it would have been the same thing for the United States to grant to the South a separate Southern Congress and executive at Richmond as to grant them provincial governments at Montgomery, Atlanta, and all the rest of the Southern chief towns, then to grant Gladstonian Home Rule to Ireland is the same thing as granting local government to it. If it would have been dangerous to grant a Southern Congress and a Southern executive, then it would be dangerous to grant an Irish Parliament, and an executive responsible to it. If a Southern Congress, with whatever restrictions you might have surrounded it, would have been sure to pose sooner or later as an independent Parliament and to threaten and embarrass the North, so would an Irish Parliament — take what securities now you please, devise and apply every safeguard you can — inevitably act towards Great Britain. It is in the nature of things that it should be so, and in the case of Ireland even more than in the case of the Southern States of America. If these States were left confronting the North, after their bitter conflict, with feelings of irritation and estrangement, what were those feelings compared with the rage, hatred, and scorn with which the Irish, as they themselves are every day telling us, regard Great Britain? To be a thorn in Great Britain's side, to make alliance with its rivals, to turn against it in a crisis of danger, would be more tempting to the Irish by far (I judge them, again, simply from what they themselves say) than a similar conduct towards the Northern States would have been to the South. The abundance of political talent and energy in the South, however, would have of itself been enough, without fierce hatred to help it, to impel a Southern Parliament to make itself independent and formidable. The love for the game of politics, and the talent for it, are as strong in the Irish as in the men of the South; Bishop Berkeley long ago remarked the "general parturiency in Ireland with respect to politics and public counsel." And to make Irishmen extend the scope, importance, and power for mischief of their Parliament, they have all the stimulus of fierce hatred as well.

What has been here said touches only, an Irishman may urge, the interest of Great Britain in the matter. A separate Parliament may still, he will say, be for the advantage of Ireland, and an Irishman may desire it, though it might prove embarrassing to Great Britain. Burke, we now continually hear it alleged, was for retaining the Irish Parliament, and against such a union with Great Britain as was afterwards established. It is most important to have Burke's very words on this matter. Thus he writes in 1792:

> I have heard a discussion concerning such a union amongst all sorts of men ever since I remember anything. For my own part I have never been able to bring my mind to anything clear and decisive upon the subject. There cannot be a more arduous question. As far as I can form an opinion, it would not be for the mutual advantage of the two kingdoms. Persons, however, more able than I am, think otherwise.[9]

Was ever disapprobation more cautious, more candidly doubtful of itself? I have so much respect for Burke's judgment that I am willing to share his doubt whether in 1792 the projected Union may have been advisable. But I am quite sure that to go back upon it in 1886, after it has been established for nearly a hundred years, and to return to a separate Parliament for Ireland, is a retrograde step inexpedient and dangerous, and for Ireland not less than for England; and I am sure that Burke would have thought so too. For in our present circumstances, and with tempers as they are now, a separate Parliament for Ireland would assuredly, as we have seen, of itself supply fresh occasions for conflict between Ireland and Great Britain, and increase the alienation and distrust already too prevalent. And "the closest connection between Great Britain and Ireland is essential," Burke thought, "to the wellbeing, almost to the very being, of the two kingdoms." [10] He thought that "by the separation of Ireland Great Britain, indeed, would be ruined; but as there are degrees even in ruin, it would fall the most heavily on Ireland. By such a separation Ireland would be the most completely undone country in the world, the most wretched, the most distracted, and, in the end, the most desolate part of the habitable globe." [11]

The Irish mandate for Home Rule, therefore, on which Lord Spencer relies, is really a mandate for increased alienation; and increased alienation means increased misery, for Ireland above all. If the Irish have set their affections on this, it is surely a case for telling them, with Shakespeare, that

> . . . your affections are
> A sick man's appetite, who desires most that
> Which would increase his evil; — [12]

for telling them, in the words of the Frenchwoman who observed the troubles of the Fronde, that *ce qu'ils demandent n'est pas ce qu'il faut pour les apaiser,* "what they ask for is not what is wanted to bring them peace." [13] Mr. Gladstone may fail to perceive this, because, with all his wonderful gifts, he yet lacks so signally the crowning gift of wisdom and insight. Mr. Morley may fail to acknowledge it, because he despairs of the English people and Parliament. But the mind of the country at once instinctively perceived it, instinctively felt that the separate Irish Parliament and Irish executive means a lull for an instant, to be followed by increased contention and misery in the near future. Lord Hartington's sound judgment is shown by his having from the first signalised this proposal of Mr. Gladstone as the specially dangerous one, and never wavered in doing so. The Conservative party, as a whole, has staunchly taken and held the same view. The mind of the country is with them in it, the great body of quiet reasonable opinion in England wishes them continued success in their resistance to Gladstonian Home Rule.

But what, now, shall we say of the set and disposition of this great force of opinion, in the questions which arise as to acts of firm government in Ireland? It is entirely favourable to such acts. The language of certain eager and impassioned Liberal newspapers on this topic is such as to show a sheer absence of all instinct of government, and finds no response at all in the mind of plain reasonable Englishmen generally. "What might be a fair rent to pay?" Mr. Sheehy asks an Irish crowd. "A voice responded, '*Nothing!*' followed by a burst of laughter and applause. 'I like your music,' says Mr. Sheehy, 'and I hope that many will learn it.'" "We will march on from victory to victory," says Mr. O'Brien, "until we shall have liberated this land from the two curses of landlordism and English rule." "In the day of our power we will remember the police," says Mr. Dillon.[14] O'Connell was prosecuted in 1824 for saying: "If Parliament will not attend to the Catholic claims, I hope that some Bolivar will arise to vindicate their rights."[15] That was excess on the side of government. But now we have changed all that, and if Mr. Dillon and Mr. O'Brien are prosecuted when they use language such as that which I have just quoted, the *Pall Mall Gazette* exclaims that this is "arbitrary interference with the ordinary liberties of the subject." Surely this is excess on the side of anarchy. It finds, I say, no response in the minds of quiet reasonable Englishmen generally. Rather they are indisposed by what looks like weakness, hesitation and pedantry enfeebling the mind and hand of the executive government, suffering disorder to grow to a height, and the public authority to be scorned and set at naught. Far from thinking that the interference of Government with Irish liberty of speech and action has been excessive, the majority of fair-minded and peaceable Englishmen think that it has been insufficient. It is fatal for the Irish themselves to acquire the habit of setting government and law at defiance. Merely to break down this habit of defiance is not all that we have now to do in Ireland; that is quite true, and most important it is to insist upon it. But the habit of defiance must not be allowed to establish itself, must be quelled when it seeks to establish itself. Whatever fanatics or party politicians may say, the mind of the country is clear and firm on this matter, and will uphold Government in quelling anarchy.

But there must be *success* in quelling it. The executive must not give to the world, and to the Irish themselves, in trying to quell it, the spectacle of fumbling and failure, of efforts going awry, of justice defeated, of authority made ridiculous. Days spent by a sheriff and his men in vainly trying to get possession of a barricaded house, the sheriff's men maltreated and blinded, the crowd jeering and yelling, with a force of police and soldiers looking on and doing nothing — this is not quelling anarchy. Bringing offenders before juries who are delighted to show their enmity to Government by acquitting them, is not quelling anarchy. In general, administrative action is what is now required against anarchy in Ireland,

never hearing what they have to ask or say, doing nothing at all for them, is an absurdity, and therefore cannot now long be maintained. Being felt to be absurd, he is become, or is fast becoming, impossible. That same great force of reasonable opinion in this country which is now favourable to Ministers, and makes their chief force, will not suffer this sort of landlord to be long maintained. True, if his tenants are evicted, they are to be evicted without the spectacle of a siege in which the sheriff's people are maltreated and scalded all day amid the yells of a mob, while the police and soldiers are kept looking on, doing nothing. But that he should be long maintained is impossible.

Ministers should consider that the general opinion is not without sympathy for Mr. Dillon personally, and for much which he thinks and says, although it wishes his defiance of law to be firmly stopped. If Lord Clanricarde's tenants are evicted, it wishes them evicted without rioting; but it has its own thoughts about Lord Clanricarde. Lord Salisbury's figure of the highwayman, Mr. Goschen's of the garrotter, are smart rhetoric rather than sound statesmanship, if the tenants in conflict with Lord Clanricarde do not really at all present themselves to the mind of the country as highwaymen and garrotters, and cannot be made so to present themselves. Samson's pulling down of the court-house of Gaza upon himself and the Philistine lords was a violent, irregular, and unlawful proceeding. But we do not in the least think of Samson as a garrotter and highwayman, nor will quiet people in general think of Lord Clanricarde's tenants under this figure. Garrotters and highwaymen have only to be brought under the strong hand of the law; Lord Clanricarde's tenants have to be firmly stopped, indeed, from rioting, but then something further has to be done for them, some relief afforded. The land question has indeed to be dealt with, and there can be no peace in Ireland until it has been dealt with successfully; that is most true.

The Land Act of 1881 unsettled everything; it introduced or confirmed a divided ownership full of inconvenience, full of elements of dispute. But its chief fault was that whereas the Irish tenant had two grievances, a material grievance and a moral grievance, the Land Act, which dealt after a fashion with the material grievance, left the moral grievance, the grievance of bad landlordism carried to lengths hardly exampled elsewhere and striking at the root of order, wholly untouched. How very great a force moral grievance has in human affairs we all know. But the Land Act recognised no difference whatever between good landlords and bad, between landlords who had always done their duty and landlords who had never done it at all. I insisted, at the time when the Land Act was passing, upon this its capital defect; I urged that the great and passionately felt moral grievance of the Irish peasantry could be met and wiped out best, could be met and wiped out only, by a direct moral satisfaction, by some measure distinguishing between good landlords and bad, and telling on the bad with severity. I said that if we liked to suppose one of our chief judges and one of our chief philanthropists authorised to establish, on due inquiry the distinction demanded, and then a measure of expropriation founded on the distinction so reached, that would give us the sort of equity, the sort of moral satisfaction, which the case needed. By Mr. Gladstone's recent Purchase Bill the landlords were to be bought out; but again no distinction was recognised between good and bad landlords, all were to get the same terms.[21] The Purchase Bill is said to have reconciled Lord Spencer to the Home Rule Bill; the majority of Mr. Gladstone's followers would probably have rejected it after they had carried Home Rule. But the Purchase Bill, like the Land Act before it, left the moral grievance of the Irish tenantry wholly untouched; and it may be confidently affirmed that no bill for buying out the Irish landlords will really *succeed* which does not touch this grievance, does not distinguish between good landlords and bad, does not give better terms to the good landlords, worse to the bad.

The mind and conscience of the country, not only Irish malcontents and their Liberal allies, will demand this, and would be alienated, I most sincerely believe, by the Government's declaring against it. Meanwhile Ministers have promised to put what pressure they can upon bad landlords in order to make them reasonable. Administrative action is here again of extreme value and importance. Sir Michael Hicks-Beach and Sir Redvers Buller have been sharply attacked on the supposition that they were putting pressure on bad landlords. Under present circumstances they perform a high public duty in applying it; and they are, moreover, the very best persons by whom it can be applied. Their own interests are known to be naturally with the landlords; what they do to press them will therefore be done simply for the public safety. It is asked, why may Sir Michael Hicks-Beach put pressure on bad landlords, when Mr. Morley might not?[22] I have often expressed my high esteem for Mr. Morley, and wherever his course may lead him I shall always feel for him regard and affection. But in despair of the good sense and justice of England he has surrendered to Mr. Parnell and his party; and to complain of its being thought unsafe to let Mr. Morley put pressure on the landlords, is like complaining of its being thought unsafe, in the War of Secession, to let Mr. Jefferson Davis put pressure on the abolitionists. The same as to Mr. Dillon and Mr. Parnell. Why not let Mr. Dillon put pressure on bad landlords, since pressure on them is needed? why not have accepted Mr. Parnell's bill for putting it? Why? Because Mr. Parnell and Mr. Dillon are Separatists and Home Rulers, and it is not consistent with public safety to let them usurp the functions of government in Ireland, in the midst of a struggle whether Home Rule and separation are or are not to be conceded. But functionaries who are the strong opponents of Home Rule and separation, and whose interests, too, are naturally with the landlords, are just the people whom we may well trust, if they put pressure upon landlords, to put it so far as the public good imperatively requires, and no further.

May they to that extent put it freely, and may Government uphold them in putting it, as the general opinion of the country most certainly will! May Government also, when it comes to deal by legislation with the land question in Ireland, make good the Land Act's great omission, and regard equity! May the Conservative leaders also produce a good measure of local government, and rescue procedure from chaos; may they likewise be reasonable on Church questions; then the opinion and favour of the country will remain with them, as that opinion is with them now. Let them therefore be strong and of a good courage. A government not brilliant, but with an open mind, and quite honest and quite firm, may serve our present needs much better than a government far more brilliant, but which is not perfectly honest or not perfectly firm. But on no account must Ministers give cause for saying, as Mr. Chamberlain has hastened to say already, that Lord Randolph Churchill's retirement marks the victory, in the Conservative Government, of the stupid and noxious Toryism opposed to all serious improvement. They must "be up and doing, and doing to good purpose;" they must keep friends with the mind of the country. And in the present unripe state of the Liberals of the nadir, we Liberals of the future, who happen to be grown, alas, rather old, shall then probably have to look forward to the Conservative Ministry, whether with or without Lord Randolph Churchill, lasting at least our time, and shall be able to look forward to this without much repining or dissatisfaction.

Notes

[1] Lord Randolph H. S. Churchill (1849–1895) was Chancellor of the Exchequer in Lord Salisbury's cabinet. He resigned December 23, 1886. Arnold wrote to his sister Fan on 27 December 1886, "Of course, it was an awkward circumstance, Lord Randolph's sudden resignation coming when my article was already in type. Then came Chamberlain's speech also, to change the posture of things still further. But I have made everything right, and think the article will do very well, and, I hope, be of use. I am told the pantomime people are in despair" (*Letters*, II, 359).

[2] Dr. Samuel Johnson, *Rasselas*, ch. III. The passage is quoted in Arnold's *Note-Books*, p. 398.

[3] The *Saturday Review* in an editorial, "Mr. Matthew Arnold" (LXII, November 20, 1886, 676), on his retirement speech to the Westminister teachers expressed the hope that he would stick to literary criticism, art, and letters, saying: "Much excellent and stimulating work on these subjects is yet to be had from him, we feel sure, if only he will finally forswear the ambition to settle the Irish question and to recast the Christian religion. We earnestly counsel him to spare no effort to divert his mind, if need be finally, from meditation on these projects." The editorial continued, "A prize might with advantage be offered to any one who could suggest the 'best hundred books for Mr. Matthew Arnold.' We have not got our own list ready, but we have

one or two books in our mind which we should probably, and others which we should certainly, exclude from it. We have our doubts whether we should allow Mr. Arnold to read the Vulgate — except, perhaps, for a few minutes daily as a religious exercise. But of the fate of two books, if we had the disposal of it, we can speak with certainty. We should lock up his Bishop Wilson and his Burke." This amusing suggestion gains point from Arnold's having contributed a letter to "The Best Hundred Books. By the Best Hundred Judges. IV," *Pall Mall Gazette*, January 29, 1886, p. 4.

For the maxim which Arnold quotes from Bishop Thomas Wilson, see the *Note-Books*, p. 405.

[4] For Trevelyan, see p. 281, n. 27. Frederick Harrison (1831–1923) was an essayist, professor of jurisprudence and international law, and a positivist.

[5] "The Function of Criticism at the Present Time" (1864), *Essays in Criticism* [First Series] (New York, 1893), p. 12.

[6] Emmanuel Joseph Sièyes (1748–1836), quoted in C. A. Sainte-Beuve, *Causeries du lundi*, 2 ed. (Paris, 1853), V, 165. Abbé Sièyes' Latin verse is Lucan, *De Bello Civili*, I, 509.

[7] Sir Henry Redvers Buller (1839–1908), British general and Privy Councillor.

[8] John Poyntz Spencer, fifth Earl Spencer (1835–1910), served in all four of Gladstone's cabinets. He was a recent convert to Gladstone's Home Rule policy.

[9] "A Letter to Sir Hercules Langrische," *The Works of Edmund Burke*, V, 296–297.

[10] "A Letter on the Affairs of Ireland" (1797), *ibid.*, VI, 420.

[11] *Ibid.*, 421.

[12] Shakespeare, *Coriolanus*, I, i, 181–183.

[13] Mme. de Sévigné.

[14] William O'Brien (1852–1928), Irish journalist and political leader, founded the militant newspaper *United Ireland*. He held a seat in parliament 1883–1895. John Dillon (1851–1927) was a leader of the Irish Nationalist Party. He was M.P. at Westminster for Tipperary 1880–1883, and for East Mayo 1883–1918.

[15] Daniel O'Connell (1775–1847), the "Liberator," founded the Catholic Association, which was suppressed in 1826. He ardently espoused the cause of Catholic Emancipation.

[16] Sir James Robert George Graham, baronet (1792–1861), statesman, served as First Lord of the Admiralty, 1830–1834 and 1852–1855, and as Home Secretary, 1841–1846.

[17] William Edward Forster (1818–1886) was one time vice-president of the Committee of the Privy Council for Education (1868–1874) and Chief Secretary for Ireland, 1880–1882. He married Arnold's sister Jane in 1850. See *Letters* II, 333, for Arnold's appreciation of his late brother-in-law's views on Home Rule.

[18] John Wilson Croker (1780–1877), *The Croker Papers: The Correspondence and Diaries*, ed. Louis I. Jennings, 2 ed., 3 vols. (London, 1885), III, 259.

[19] *A Sketch of the State of Ireland, Past and Present*, 2 ed. (London, 1808), p. 42. This pamphlet is reprinted as an appendix in the first volume of *The Croker Papers*. Croker wrote, "A landlord is not a mere land merchant."

[20] For the extravagant behavior of Hubert George de Burgh-Canning, second Marquess of Clanricarde (1832–1916), see J. L. Hammond, *Gladstone and the Irish Nation* (London, 1938), pp. 565–566, 572. See also the *DNB*. Lord Clanricarde sat as Baron Somerhill.

At the time of the writing Lord Lonsdale was Hugh Cecil Lowther, fifth Earl Lonsdale (1857–1944). He was the patron of fifty-nine livings.

[21] A draft for a Land Purchase Bill was first introduced for cabinet discussion May 15, 1885. According to John Morley, it was framed with a hope of its being acceptable to Lord Spencer (*The Life of William Ewart Gladstone*, III, 194–195). Widely opposed, it was not brought to a vote when the ministry fell in the summer of 1886.

[22] Sir Michael Hicks Beach, created Viscount St. Aldwyn in 1905 and earl in 1914 (1837–1916), was Chief Secretary for Ireland in Lord Salisbury's cabinet of 1886, succeeding John Morley, who had held the office in Gladstone's third ministry.

A "Friend of God"

Nineteenth Century
XXI (April 1887), 499–506

Arnold wrote to his wife November 27, 1886, that he had "promised Knowles a political article for the beginning of the session, and half a dozen pages on Tauler (whom I was reading at Stockbridge) to help a poor ex-colleague who has translated him." [1] Arnold's review of Johann Tauler's *The Following of Christ*, translated by J. R. Morell (London and New York, 1886), appeared the following April. It has been reprinted in *Essays in Criticism, Third Series*.

Johann Tauler (c. 1300–1361), German mystic, was a Dominican monk. Extracts from his writings in the collection *Choix d'ouvrages mystiques* (Paris, 1843) are entered in Arnold's *Note-Books* as early as 1861.

There has lately been published * a pretty little volume entitled *The Following of Christ, by John Tauler; done into English by J. R. Morell.* It is not certain that the work is by Tauler; the weight of authority and of probability is, it seems to me, against his being its author. The book has many repetitions, and a manner formal and sometimes tiresome of conducting its argument. Mr. Morell's translation is written in an English occasionally slovenly and even inaccurate. Still, this little volume — which is cheap, let me say, as well as pretty — should certainly not be suffered to pass unnoticed. If it does not proceed from Tauler himself, it proceeds from one of that remarkable group of German mystics — "Friends of God," as they called themselves — amongst whom the great Dominican preacher of Strasburg lived and worked. And the contents of the little book, notwithstanding its form and repetitions, are full of value. Therefore we may well say in this case with the *Imitation,* which itself, also, issued from the deep religious movement felt in the Germanic lands along the Rhine in the fourteenth century: — "Ask not who wrote it, but attend to what it says." Mr. Morell's translation, finally, in spite of its occasional inaccuracy and slovenliness, is on the whole a sound and good one, with the signal merit of faithfully reproducing the plain and earnest tone characteristic of the original.

Every one is familiar with the *Imitation,* attributed to Thomas à Kempis. Tauler however, and his immediate group, are to most of us names and nothing more. *Tauler's History and Life and Twenty-five of his*

* By Burns & Oates, London and New York.

Sermons, translated by Miss Winkworth, were published in 1857, with a preface by Charles Kingsley. The book is out of print and can hardly be obtained. Some of the sermons are interesting, but in general the book, even if obtained, will disappoint, I think, those who have been attracted to it by Tauler's reputation, and to reprint it as it stands would be unadvisable. Much more interesting is the *Theologia Germanica*, also translated by Miss Winkworth, a work not by Tauler himself, but by one of his group who shared his spirit. On this short book Luther set the very highest value, and justly. But this book likewise is out of print, and scarcely obtainable.

Its merit is of like kind with that of the book translated by Mr. Morell to which I now wish to call attention. Each of the two is an answer of the sincere and deeply religious German nature to the need felt, by itself and by others, in a time such as was the middle of the fourteenth century, a time "of famine" (to use the words of the prophet Amos) "of hearing of the words of the Eternal." [2] We read in the *Following of Christ*: "It is often said, He who suffereth a man to die of bodily hunger when he might have helped the sufferer, would be guilty of the death of that man. Much more is a man guilty towards souls when he letteth them die of hunger. For just as the soul is much nobler than the body, so much more are you guilty if you allow the soul to suffer hunger." To this hunger and suffering of the soul the *Following of Christ* is a response, but a response with a special character of its own. The *Imitation* is also a response to the same hunger, but a response of a different character. "No way to life and peace but the way of the cross!" that, in sum, is the response of the *Imitation*.[3] Tauler and his group would have sincerely professed that they likewise adopted it; and yet the real and characteristic response of the "Friends of God" and of such works as the *Following of Christ* and the *Theologia Germanica* is far rather this, which I quote from the first-named work: "Sin killeth nature, but nature is abhorrent of death; therefore sin is against nature, therefore sinners can never have a joy." That is the negative side of the response, and its positive side is this: "They who have left sins and come to grace have more delight and joy in one day than all sinners have ever gained."

It is the natural truth of religion and of Christianity which occupies these "Friends of God." The truly natural thing is virtue, Christian virtue; and that it is so is proved by the peace and happiness ensuing from it. "It is much more according to nature to work virtue than vice; for virtue places nature firmly and supports it, while vice displaces it. A thoroughly natural man is a pure man. That which maketh nature impure is a faulty accident of nature and is not the essence of nature." But in order to be "a thoroughly natural man," one who "enters into himself, listens to the eternal word, and has the life full of ecstasy and joy," a man must "set aside all things and follow Christ. Christ is the everlasting aim of all men."

I have mentioned Luther as a lover of the *Theologia Germanica*. Luther too, some hundred and fifty years after our mystics, had to provide for "a famine of the words of the Eternal." Vinet has said with perfect truth that "the reformers did not separate morals from dogma; Calvin, the most dogmatic of them all, is the one who most efficaciously and most constantly preached morals." [4] Undoubtedly the reformers preached morals; undoubtedly, too, Calvin and Luther produced an immeasurably greater effect than Tauler and his group. But how was the effect obtained? After laying down the *Following of Christ*, I took up Luther's famous *Commentary on Galatians*. The Commentary deserves its reputation; it has clearness, force, unction. But on what thought does Luther rest with all his weight, as Tauler rests with all his weight on the thought: "Sin is against nature; they who have left sins have more delight and joy in one day than all sinners have ever gained"? Luther rests with his whole weight on the article of justification, that Gospel doctrine which, he says, is *suavissima et consolationis plenissima*.[5] "All heretics have continually failed in this one point, that they do not rightly understand or know the article of justification; do not see that by none other sacrifice or offering could God's fierce anger be appeased, but by the precious blood of the son of God." [6]

The article of justification has been made arid and obnoxious by formalists; let us take it from the mouth of this man of genious, its earnestly convinced and unrivalled expositor. *Christ has been made a curse for us!* — that is the point; Christ has assumed, in our stead, the guilt and curse of sin from which we could not otherwise be delivered, but are delivered by believing in his having so done. "When the merciful Father saw us to be so crushed under the curse of the law, and so bound by it, that we could never through our own strength get free from it, he sent his only begotten Son into the world and laid on him the sins of all men, saying: 'Be thou that Peter the denier, that Paul the persecutor, that David the adulterer, that sinner who ate the apple in Paradise, that thief on the cross; in a word, be thou the person who has done the sins of all men; consider then how thou mayest pay and make satisfaction for them.' Then comes in the law and says: 'I find him a sinner, and a sinner who has taken unto himself the sins of all men, and I see no sin besides except in him, therefore let him die on the cross!' and so the law falls upon him and slays him. By this transaction the whole world has been purged and purified of all sins, and at the same time, therefore, been set free from death and from all evil." [7] By giving our hearty belief to this transaction we are admitted to its benefits.

Here we have the *Cabala vera*, says Luther,[8] the true mystery of Christianity — here, in the transaction just recorded. I will not now discuss the misunderstanding of St. Paul which Luther's message of comfort involves. I will not discuss its faults as a religious conception. I will admit that it has indeed been a message of comfort to thousands, and has produced much good and much happiness. I will simply point out that it is mythology, and that this is daily becoming more and more evident; as sheer mythology, at bottom, as Saturn's devouring his children or Pallas springing from the head of Zeus. The transaction between the magnified and non-natural man, whom Luther calls "the merciful Father," and his Son, never really took place; or what comes to the same thing, its having taken place can no more be verified, and has no more real probability in its favour, than Saturn's devouring his children or Pallas springing from the head of Zeus. This character of mythology is a disadvantage to Luther's message of comfort now. But it was an advantage to it when the message was delivered. It gave to it an immense superiority in effectiveness over such a message of comfort as Tauler's. The one leavened a group, and individuals; the other created the Protestant Churches.

To the mass of those who seek religion, an element of mythology in it, far from being an objection, has hitherto been a recommendation and attraction; and they hold to this element as long as ever they can. Only, to moral and serious people, such as were the Germanic races who made the Reformation, it must be a moral mythology, and moreover a mythology receivable and approvable by them in the intellectual stage at which they are then arrived. The serious Germanic races, visited by that *soul-hunger* which Tauler describes, could easily be brought to recognise that much of the mythology presented to them by mediaeval religion, with its machinery of Virgin and saints, Pope and priest, was unscriptural and immoral; and that good works in the current conception of them as "fasts, pilgrimages, rosaries, vows" — to adopt Luther's list[9] — were unfruitful. A powerful spirit who went to the Bible and produced from it a new and grave mythology with a new and grave conception of righteousness, was the man for that moment. Luther's doctrine of justification, Calvin's doctrine of election, were far more effective to win crowds and found churches than Tauler's *Following of Christ* just because the doctrines of Calvin and Luther are mythology, while the doctrine of Tauler is not. Luther's doctrine and Calvin's were a mythology appealing directly and solely to the Bible for support, and they professed, also, to deepen men's conception of righteousness; they were therefore acceptable to thousands of serious people in the intellectual and moral stage of that time. They were, however, a mythology. But as such they enlisted in their favour those forces of imagination, wonder, and awe, which men love to feel aroused within them; and they enlisted these in an immeasurably greater degree than Tauler's doctrine of the *Following of Christ*, which is not a mythology at all. Hence their immeasurably greater scale of effect and number of adherents.

And so it has been ever since, up to this day. Let us confine our view to our own country. Hitherto an element of mythology, the stronger and the more turbid the better, has been a help rather than a hindrance to what are called religious causes. To the Calvinists, to the Methodists, to the Revivalists, to the Salvation Army, have been the striking effects and the heavy numbers; to the Latitude Men, to Leighton, to Erskine of Linlathen, as to Tauler and his friends in the fourteenth century, action on a group merely, or on individuals.[10] Men such as Butler, or Wilson of Sodor and Man, who have had far wider influence in our religious world than the mystics, and who yet at the same time were true "Friends of God" at heart, have owed their wide influence not to this character but chiefly to something else. The true grandeur of Butler is in his sacred horror at the thought "of committing the dreadful mistake of leaving the course marked out for us by nature, whatever that nature be;" [11] his reputation is from his embarrassed and unsatisfying apologetic. The true glory of Wilson is his living and abiding sense that "sin is against nature, therefore sinners can never have a joy;" his reputation is as the most exemplary of Anglican Churchmen.

The immense, the epoch-making change of our own day, is that a stage in our intellectual development is now declaring itself when mythology, whether moral or immoral, as a basis for religion is no longer receivable, is no longer an aid to religion but an obstacle. Our own nation is not specially lucid, it is strongly religious, we have witnessed in the Salvation Army the spectacle of one of the crudest and most turbid developments of religion with the element of mythology in full sway;[12] and yet it is certain that, even amongst ourselves, over all which is most vigorous and progressive in our population mythology in religion has lost or is fast losing its power, and that it has no future. The gross mob has ever been apt to show brutality and hostility towards religion, and demonstrations of this spirit we have often enough still. But mingled with the mere ignoble and vicious enmity against any discipline to raise, restrain, and transform, there is also in the common people now a sense of impatience and anger at what they think futile trifling with them on the part of those who offer to them, in their sore need, the old mythological religion — a thing felt to be impossible of reception and going if not quite gone, incapable of either solving the present or founding the future.

This change is creating a situation much more favourable to the mystics. Whole libraries of theology have lost their interest when it is perceived that they make mythology the basis of religion, and that to take seriously this mythology is impossible. But for those groups and individuals, little regarded in their day, whom their heart prompted to rest religion on natural truth rather than on mythology, the hour of hearing and of well-inclined attention has at last come. For a long while it was heavily against them that they merely preached the following of Christ, instead of the article of justification, the article of election; now at last it is in their favour.

Let me be candid. I love the mystics, but what I find best in them is their golden single sentences, not the whole conduct of their argument and result of their work. I should mislead the reader if I led him to suppose that he will find any great body of discourse in the work attributed to Tauler, *The Following of Christ,* which Mr. Morell has translated, of like value with the detached sentences from it which I have quoted above. But the little book is well worth reading if only for the sake of the sentences. The general argument, too, if not complete and satisfying, has an interest of its own from the natural, or, as we nowadays say, the *positive* point of view taken by the author, without regard to mythology, or conventions, or *shams,* in Carlyle's phrase, of any kind.

For instance, the book developes the idea of following Christ, and teaches how for him who would follow Christ, poverty, both inward and outward, is necessary. Christ's is emphatically a *"poor* life." Yet to follow him and his life is really to follow nature, to be happy. And to enter into the kingdom of heaven is really nothing else than this following him, this following nature, this being happy. When Jesus said: "How hardly shall they that have riches enter into the kingdom of heaven," this was, in our mystic's view, but another way of saying: "How hardly shall they that have riches follow me and my life, live naturally, be happy." The life poor in external goods, as Christ's was, is therefore, concludes our mystic, the happy, natural life, the life to be preferred.

But the official and current religion interprets Christ's words, as we all know, in quite another fashion, and makes him in fact say: "If you trust in riches, if you make a bad use of riches, you cannot enter after death into the paradise above the sky." Now I do not at present inquire whether the doctrine of our mystic is right or wrong, adequate or inadequate. But it is well to remark how much nearer, at any rate, he comes to the mind of Christ, how much more sincerely and faithfully he interprets it, than our official religion does. For undoubtedly what Jesus meant by the kingdom of God or of heaven was the reign of saints, the ideal future society on earth. "How hardly shall they that have riches be fit for the society of the future," was what he in fact said. One who is unfit for this ideal society does not follow Christ; he is also in conflict with nature, cannot be happy. This is the doctrine of Jesus, and our mystic has rightly seized it. Jesus threw out the doctrine and left it to bear fruit. It has worked in many and many an individual mind since, and will work more and more. The worldly themselves have to deal with it. They can free themselves from all concern about the paradise above the sky, but from concern about the society of the future they cannot. It will arrive, its beginnings are even now. No one yet, however, has disengaged the doctrine from difficulty, has so set it forth as to make it useable and serviceable; certainly our mystic has not. But to have rightly seized it is something.

Christ's sentence on riches is but a corollary from what we call his *secret:* "He that loveth his life shall lose it, he that will lose his life shall save it." Now the infinite progress possible in Christianity lies in the gradually successful application, to doctrines like this secret of Jesus and the corollary from it, of what we call his *epieikeia,* his temper of sweet reasonableness, consummate balance, unerring felicity. Although the application has here not yet been successfully made, and the mystics have not made it, yet the secret and its corollary are unceasingly felt to have in them something deeply important, and to be full of future; at the same time that mythology, like Luther's article of justification or Calvin's article of election, is felt to be passing quite away and to have no future at all. The mystics, then, have the merit of keeping always before their minds, and endeavouring earnestly to make operative on their lives, just that in Christianity which is not perishable but abiding.

But I ought before I end to let our mystic, whether he be indeed Tauler as Mr. Morell thinks, or another, to speak for himself at more length than I have let him speak hitherto. I have mentioned his insistence on external poverty; let us hear him on internal poverty, poverty of spirit, "a going out of yourself and out of everything earthly." A man "must perceive and listen to the eternal word, and this hearing bringeth him to everlasting life."

Through the outer word that men hear, they attain to the inner word, which God speaketh in the essence of the soul. They who have not come to this should hear preaching, and learn and follow what they hear or read; thus they come to the real truth, and to life, which is God. Even if a man is so advanced that he hear the word in himself, he is yet not at all times prepared for it, for bodily nature cannot bear it, and a man must sometimes turn to his senses and be active; but he ought to direct this work of the senses to the best end. If preaching is useful to him, he can hear it; if an outward virtue is useful to him, he can work it; and he ought to exercise himself in what he recognises as the best. But this by no means hindereth him from hearing the everlasting word, but it furthers him to what is best. And he should drop and drive out with violence all that hindereth him in this. Then he doeth as Jesus did in the Temple, when he drove out buyers and sellers and said: "My house is a house of prayer, but ye have made it a den of thieves." A pure heart is a temple of God; the tradesmen whom Jesus drove out are the worldly furniture and goods that rust in the heart and are hurtful to it. If now the heart keepeth the useless thoughts and tarrieth over them, it is no longer a house of prayer but a den of thieves, for the evil thoughts drive out God from his dwelling and murder him. But the man who resisteth all thoughts that keep him apart from God, receiveth from God living, divine power. This inpouring is God's inspeaking, and that is the life full of ecstasy and joy.

The reader will recognise the strain of homage which from age to age successive generations of mystics have ever loved to uplift to "the eternal word." I will not say that it is entirely satisfying, but at least it is always refreshing, consoling, and ennobling.

Whoever turns to the little volume which Mr. Morell has translated will find plenty in this strain to give him refreshment. But he will find more than this, he will find sentences such as those of which I spoke in beginning, and to which in ending I would return; isolated sentences fitted to abide in the memory, to be a possession for the mind and soul, to form the character. "Sin killeth nature, but nature is abhorrent of death; therefore sin is against nature, therefore sinners can never have a joy." "They who have left sins and come to grace have more delight and joy in one day than all sinners have ever gained."

Notes

[1] *Letters*, II, 354.

[2] Amos 8:11.

[3] Thomas à Kempis (1379?–1471), *The Imitation of Christ,* Bk. II, ch. XII, ii.

[4] Alexandre Rodolphe Vinet (1797–1847) in E. Rambert, *Alexandre Vinet, histoire de sa vie et ses ouvrages* (Lausanne, 1875), p. 93.

[5] Martin Luther, *Commentarium in Epistolam ad Galatas,* ed. Joannes C. Irmischer, 3 vols. (Erlangen, 1843–1844), II, 24.

[6] See *ibid.,* II, 22–23.

[7] *Ibid.,* 18–19.

[8] *Ibid.,* 35.

[9] *Ibid.,* 23.

[10] Robert Leighton (1611–1684), archbishop of Glasgow.

Thomas Erskine of Linlathen (1788–1870), advocate and theologian. Among his friends were Alexandre Vinet and Dean A. P. Stanley, the biographer of Dr. Arnold.

For Arnold's interest in the Latitudinarians see "A Psychological Parallel," *Contemporary Review,* November 1886, reprinted in *Last Essays on Church and Religion* (1877), and Arnold's selections from John Smith, *The Natural Truth of Christianity* (London 1882).

[11] Bishop Joseph Butler, "Upon the Ignorance of Man," *Sermons* (Cambridge, Eng., 1835), pp. 232–233. Thomas Wilson, Bishop of Sodor and Man (1663–1755), was one of the devotional writers whom Arnold most admired.

[12] The Salvation Army was the name given in 1880 to the missionary organization of William Booth (1829–1912), first called the East-End Mission, and then the Christian Mission.

Up to Easter

Nineteenth Century
XXI (May 1887), 629–643

In *Friendship's Garland* Arnold wryly observed, "We are now on the point of commencing what Arminius, with his fatally carping spirit, called our 'Thyestëan banquet of clap-trap;' — we are on the eve of the meeting of Parliament." A decade and a half later he was amused to hold the same view of parliamentary sessions, for in an invitation to dinner he urged John Morley on March 2, 1885, to "snatch two or three hours from the 'Thyestëan banquet' in Palace Yard." [1] He seems himself to have observed the proceedings with pleasure through the first year of Lord Salisbury's second ministry.

"Up to Easter" was published as a lead article and on May 12 Arnold wrote to his sister "K" (Mrs. W. E. Forster), "Lord Emly has been greatly pleased with my article." [2]

Professor Huxley told us in this Review last month, that in his eyes the chief good is, in brief, freedom to say what he pleases, when he pleases. Singular ideal for so clear-sighted a man! [3] It is the ideal of Mr. Dillon, and Mr. W. O'Brien, and apparently of the Gladstonian Liberals generally: if Mr. Dillon and Mr. W. O'Brien please to say "disagreeable things," it is monstrous and intolerable, says Mr. John Morley, that they should be prevented. [4] For my part, as I grow old, and profit, I hope, by the lessons of experience, I think the chief good, that which above all makes life worth living, is *to be of use*. In pursuit of this good, I find myself from time to time brought, as almost every one in the present critical juncture must be brought, to politics. I know the objections to meddling with them; I know and can perfectly understand the impatience and irritation which my intervention in these matters causes to many people. Nothing I should like better than to feel assured that I should never have occasion to write a line on politics again. I write on other subjects with much more pleasure; and it is true, quite true, that there are springs of movement in politics which one must be in the game to perceive and estimate fully — which an outsider, as he is called, cannot duly appreciate.

But on the other hand there is in practical politics a mass of insincerity, of phrase, fiction, and claptrap, which can impose, one would think, on no plain reasonable man outside of politics. This insincerity is found useful for purposes of party or faction; but there are moments when it is expedient for plain reasonable people, who have nothing to gain by it and everything to lose, to say to one another how hollow it all is. There are happily thousands of such people in this country, and they are the greater force here in England because to their plain reasonableness, which is a thing common enough where men have not interest to bind them, they add courage. They want nothing for themselves in politics, they only demand that the politician shall not bring the country into danger and disaster. To them, as one to whom some of them are not ill-disposed to listen, I speak; as one of themselves, as one who wants nothing for himself through politics, who is too old, and of habits and tastes too formed, to wish to enter the House of Commons even if he could; whose one concern with politics is that the politicians should not bring the country into danger and disaster.

The force of which I have been speaking has defeated Mr. Gladstone; but the call upon its activity and watchfulness is not yet over. It is very far from being over, although the prospects of a happy issue, if this great force remains active and watchful, are favourable. From time to time those who compose it should ask themselves how things stand at the moment to which we are come, what has been accomplished; what still remains to be accomplished; what is likely to lead us to success, what to failure: and this, at the short pause brought by Easter, I now propose to do.

When Parliament met there were three questions making evidently the first and chief demand upon its attention: the questions of procedure, Ireland, local government. Procedure has been dealt with. The debate on the Address was proof enough, if any proof had been wanted, how urgent was the need of some power to stop debating prolonged for the purpose of delay and obstruction. The amiable leader of the House of Commons expressed his profound regret at having to propose the creation of such a power; he ought rather to have expressed profound regret at its not having been proposed long ago. Long ago the country had made up its mind that to pretend "discussion" to be the object of such debates as those which have gone on in the House of Commons during the last few years was an absurdity; a conspicuous instance of that inveterate trick of parliamentary insincerity of which one is inclined to ask with Figaro, "Who is being taken in by it?" [5] It matters not what party it is which may seek to profit by such "discussion," whether Conservatives, or Radicals, or Parnellites: it should be made impossible. The state of the House of Commons, since such "discussion" grew to prevail there, had become a scandal and a danger. Mr. Gladstone seems now doomed to live, move, and have his being in that atmosphere of rhetorical and parliamentary insincerity of which I have spoken; to him, therefore, it may be vain to urge that the state of the House of Commons alone was perhaps a change more serious for evil than all his catalogued jubilee-host of Liberal reforms was a change for good. Instinctively, however, the country felt how grave was the danger, and was deeply relieved when the power of closure was carried.

It is a step of incalculable importance; a step restoring to the House of Commons free action, dignity, all that enables it to be a blessing to the country and not a bane. The form in which the power is conferred is a thing of minor importance as compared with the attainment of the power itself. Perhaps closure by a majority of three-fifths would have been a better form than that which has been adopted. That which has been adopted is in itself good and reasonable enough, and no one really doubts that the Speaker's leave will be given or refused with perfect fairness. But parliamentary insincerity is to be reckoned with, which certainly will never hesitate to denounce the Speaker's action as unfair, so often as it finds its own interest in doing so. This, however, is an inconvenience which we must now make up our minds to face, along with the other inconveniences of parliamentary insincerity. The great matter is that we have at last got the desired, the salutary, the indispensable power of closure.[6] May it be applied wisely, but resolutely!

The debates on the Address and on Procedure were full of Ireland, but since those debates ended Ireland occupies the attention of Parliament with hardly an admixture of anything else. There is the Bill for making good certain shortcomings in the Land Act of 1881 which have become apparent, and there is the Crimes Bill. The first of these two Bills need not long detain us. The Act of 1881 may be a bad one, but if it exists and has to be worked, manifest shortcomings in it ought to be repaired. The Crimes Bill — the eighty-seventh Coercion Bill, so its enemies are fond of telling us, the eighty-seventh of our Coercion Bills, and the most savage and odious of them all, — is the important matter in question just now. How is the country likely to take it? how ought the country to take it? I have repeatedly urged that we might need a much more thorough repression of disorder than any we have had hitherto, but that much more thorough remedial measures were needed as well. Lord Spencer, a man who deserves all our respect, tells us that he has come to believe in Home Rule, because he found that "repressive measures, accompanied though they had been by remedial measures, had not succeeded, though they for a time put down crime." [7] But surely the defect may have lain in the remedial measures. If they had been better, they might have succeeded; but unless crime is put down, and if law and government are powerless, your remedial measures, even though thorough and good, cannot have the chance of succeeding. Therefore whoever obstructs the repression of disorder, obstructs remedial measures. Meanwhile, as to the past, it is something to have put down crime, even if your remedial measures have turned out to be not yet what is right and sufficient.

Many Conservative candidates at the last election declared against coercion. They said with Mr. Pitt that they wished the Irish to live under equal laws with the English and Scotch, and they added that they were against all Coercion Bills for the future. If they had confined themselves to the first of their two propositions they would have been on impregnable ground. In truth the real necessity for the Crimes Bill arises from the Irish not being under equal laws with the English and Scotch. If an Englishman or a Scotchman commits murder, or mutilates animals, or cuts off a girl's hair and tars her head, he can with certainty be punished; an Irishman, at present, cannot. It is to make the convictions and sentences of the criminal law reach the Irish criminal as they reach the English or Scotch criminal, that a Crimes Act is at present necessary. If the Conservatives stuck obstinately to their second proposition, they would be making it impossible to give effect to their first. They do well, therefore, to confess that their essential proposition was their first one, and that their second, which they imagined to mean but the same thing as their first, was a mistake. The country did not commit their mistake, and can have no difficulty in concluding that if the Irish ought, as certainly they ought, to live under equal laws with the English and Scotch, and to have impunity for crime no more than we have, a Crimes Act may under the present circumstances be necessary, and to this conclusion the country will, I believe, certainly come.

I myself could have wished that the government had seen its way to act administratively, and by the common law, with much more vigour than it did. My opinion that it was in their power to do so counts for very little, but it is an opinion held also, I know, by men well entitled to judge. How much a government can do administratively, under the common law, in such a state of things as that which prevails in Ireland, has never fairly been tried. It needs resolution to try it, but to try it might have been well, and might have shown government that it had much more strength than it supposed. "The laws," says Burke with his usual wisdom, "reach but a very little way. Constitute government how you please, infinitely the greater part of it must depend upon the exercise of the powers which are left at large to the prudence and uprightness of ministers of state." [8]

Our ministers, however, instead of boldly using the large powers given to them by the common law to prevent crime and outrage, prefer to proceed by statute. Their preference is natural enough. They have Great Britain in view, where the state of affairs and the temper of the people are not revolutionary, and where to proceed regularly by statute gives all the security needful. But the state of affairs and the temper of the people in a large part of Ireland is revolutionary. If we suppose parts of Great Britain in the same state, it would be preferable here also to act with vigour administratively, rather than to proceed by special statute. Administrative action is what certain emergencies require. The French republican government the other day did not prosecute the municipality of Marseilles for glorifying the Commune: it dissolved it.

In certain emergencies, therefore, vigorous administrative action may be required in some parts of one whole country under the same laws, although in other parts it is not required. Does such an emergency present itself in parts of Ireland? Is the state of affairs, the temper of the people, revolutionary there, and the law set at defiance? In Kerry, says Judge O'Brien,[9] "the law has ceased to exist: there is a state of war with authority and with the institutions of civilised life." In other parts, terrorism, we are told, is regnant; there is quiet, because the orders of the League are obeyed without resistance. If resistance is attempted, crime comes swiftly to punish it. "I am not fastidious," says a lieutenant of Mr. Parnell, "as to the methods by which the cause may be advanced: I do not say you should alone use dynamite, or the knife, or the rifle, or parliamentary agitation; but I hold no Irishman true who will not use all and each as the opportunity presents itself." If resistance has made it necessary to "advance the cause" by crime, convictions for crime can no longer be obtained. As to the law's being set at defiance in parts of Ireland, this will surely suffice.

Then as to the temper of revolution, Mr. Parnell declared his programme, with entire candour, some time ago in America. "None of us, whether we are in America or in Ireland or wherever we may be, will be satisfied until we have destroyed the last link that keeps Ireland bound to England." But since then, he and his followers have consented, we are told, to be satisfied with Ireland's having the control of her own local affairs only, and for imperial affairs they will let her remain subject to the Crown and to the Imperial Parliament. And Mr. Godkin is angry with me for not believing them. But only the other day comes another lieutenant of Mr. Parnell and cries: "Ireland a nation! Strike a blow for Home Rule, the Irish nation, and the green flag of our people!" And another lieutenant avows at Chicago — a place very favourable to plain speaking — that it is "the duty of the League to make the government of Ireland by England an impossibility." Another declares that "any person entering Ireland officially commissioned by England to any administrative office *enters it at his peril.*" A priest who refuses to give evidence in a court of justice is brought up for contempt of court, and a Board of Guardians, which has no concern whatever with the matter, publishes the following resolution: "We condemn the brutal and tyrannical action of the authorities in arresting Father Kelleher, the respected and patriotic parish priest of Youghal." Finally Mr. W. O'Brien, elate with his impunity at home, promises to his friends new worlds to conquer ahead: "If Trench dares to lay a robber hand upon any honest man's home, we will hunt Lord Lansdowne with execrations out of Canada."

This is the revolutionary temper and language which Mr. Gladstone formerly described as that of men "marching through rapine to the disintegration of the Empire," but which, since the last election, he and his friends prefer to call "the disorder inevitable while the responsibility for the maintenance of order is withdrawn from the leaders chosen by the majority of the Irish people." With them, with the very holders, therefore, of the language just quoted, are "the influences of moderation and legality" which will give us all that we want, if we do but surrender Ireland to Mr. Parnell and his lieutenants. And I suppose it is in order to enable us to believe this the more readily that Mr. Dillon says: "The magistrates and police know perfectly well that Mr. Parnell will be their master, as he will be the master of this country, within a very short time." One can feel the balmy "influences of moderation" beginning to breathe already. And Mr. Morley is shocked that people should be prevented from saying the "disagreeable" things which have been above quoted. He and Mr. Gladstone are shocked that we should even call them "revolutionary," and talk of repressing them, when they proceed from "the representatives of Ireland." If they proceeded from the representatives of Yorkshire they would alike be revolutionary, alike need repression. I wonder how far Mr. Morley's indulgence would extend. I believe he is kindly disposed to me, as I am sure I am kindly disposed to him; yet I should not like to be brought before him, as president of a Committee of Public Safety, on a charge of *incivism*. I suspect he would be capable of passing a pretty sharp sentence with "sombre acquiscence." At any rate the "disagreeable" sayings and doings which in his Irish friends he cannot bear to check would in any other country of Europe infallibly bring down upon the performers the "state of siege."

For they are really and truly the sayings and doings of revolution, as different as possible from those of lawful political agitation familiar in this country. The latter may be a safety-valve; the former is an incendiary fire. Its kindlers and feeders do not exhale their passion by what they are doing and saying: they heighten it. By holding such furious language as theirs, a man in Great Britain finds that he diminishes his importance, and stops; in Ireland he finds that he increases it, and therefore proceeds more hotly than ever. "What you make it men's interest to do," says Burke, "that they will do." The more they have free play, the more do the sayers of such things as I have been quoting get drunk with rage and hatred themselves, and make their followers drunk with them also.

It is of no use deceiving ourselves, and holding insincere language. I regretted to see Mr. Balfour congratulating himself on the number of meetings which had been held without hindrance.[10] Perhaps he congratulates himself, too, on the Dublin municipality being undissolved, or the *resolving* board of guardians. Perhaps Mr. Forster congratulated himself on *United Ireland* appearing quite regularly. I suppose being in Parliament debauches the mind and makes it lose all sense that make-believe of this kind is not only insincere but absurd. Else Mr. Gladstone would not gravely tell us that such debates as have of late gone on in the House of Commons were "protracted discussion which was required," and that he "can conceive no greater calamity to the House of Commons" than the frequent cutting-short of such debates by the closure. Sir George Trevelyan would not tell us that "the real defect" of the Crimes Bill is that "it is directed against the written and spoken expression of opinion." As if all that chooses to call itself debate and discussion were really such! As if, because in general the expression of opinion should be free, you must allow the expression of *all* opinion, at all times, and under all circumstances! This is adopting Professor Huxley's theory of the *summum bonum* with a vengeance. In the present state of Ireland, is Mr. Parnell's "None of us will be satisfied until we have destroyed the last link that keeps Ireland bound to England;" is Mr. Harris's "If the tenant farmers shot down landlords as partridges are shot down in September, Matt Harris never would say one word against them;" [11] is Mr. W. O'Brien's "If Trench dares to lay a robber hand upon any honest man's home, we will hunt Lord Lansdowne with execrations out of Canada," *expression of opinion* which it is wise to permit, and with which it is *a real defect* in the Government to interfere? A man must surely have deluged his mind with make-believe before he can think or even say so. Anywhere else in Europe, as I have said, such *expression of opinion*, and what is now going on in Ireland, would be met by the state of siege. For the sake of the Irish themselves it is wrong and cruel to let it continue. The whole force of reasonable opinion in this country will go with the Government in stopping it. Whether Government should have proceeded administratively or by special statute may be a question; but the important thing is to stop the state of things and the language now prevailing in parts of Ireland, and as the Government have elected to proceed by statute, they should be supported. And with regard to details of the statute, the end to be attained should be steadily kept in view. A man may dislike, for instance, the change of venue, but he must keep in mind the end to be attained, conviction on clear proof of guilt. Can a conviction for murder, even on clear proof, be now secured without change of venue? If not, the Government ought to be supported in changing it. But the real mind of the country, if the Government will be frank with it and trust it, may be relied upon, I hope, much more than politicians, for not being led off from the real aim by cries and pretexts.

I hope so, and I believe so too; and therefore merely to exhort reasonable people, who are happily a great force in this country, to be steady as they have hitherto been, to brush insincerities aside, to keep in clear view the dangerous features of disorder in Ireland at present, and to support the Government in quelling it, I should not now be writing. It is what is to come after quelling it that has the great interest for me. I am not afraid of a refusal by the reasonable people of this country for the powers necessary to quell disorder; I am only afraid of their not insisting strongly enough on a further thing — how much, after it is quelled, will still require to be done. Not that they do not sincerely desire to give Ireland the due control of her own affairs. I am convinced that the great body of reasonable people in this country do, as I have repeatedly said, sincerely desire and intend two things: one, to defeat Mr. Gladstone's dangerous plan of Home Rule; the other, to remove all just cause of Irish complaint, and to give to the people of Ireland the due control of their own local affairs. But how large and far-reaching are the measures required to do this, I am afraid many of us do not adequately conceive. Yet, if these measures are not forthcoming, Mr. Gladstone's Home Rule will certainly arrive.

The Gladstonian contention is now, as we all know, that for the disordered state of Ireland "no remedy is possible until the national aspirations of the Irish people are gratified." The cry of the Irish people is, "Ireland a nation! Strike a blow for Home Rule, the Irish nation, and the green flag of our people!" The Gladstonian cry is, "A separate Parliament and a separate Executive for Ireland." Both cries lead in the end to the same thing, and a thing full of mischief and danger both for Great Britain and Ireland — a separate Ireland.

To this they lead, as the great body of reasonable people in England perceived instinctively, and as no reasonable person who has not an interest in being sincere with himself can fail to perceive. It would not be possible for Ireland to possess, without using it for getting more, such a vantage-ground as a separate Parliament and Executive would give her, any more than it would have been possible for the Americans of the South to possess, without using it for getting more, such a vantage-ground as a separate Southern Congress and Executive would have supplied. Such is the nature of things. In the case of Ireland we have our warning, not only from the nature of things, but from the express words of the Irish themselves, who when they are free to speak their real mind tell us that they "will not be satisfied until they have destroyed the last link that keeps Ireland bound to England," and that what they want is "Ireland a nation, and the green flag of our people." I can understand Mr. Gladstone shutting his eyes to what is sure to happen, because he can shut or open his eyes to whatever he pleases, and has his mind full of a great piece of parliamentary management which will insure to him the solid Irish vote and seat him firmly again in power. I can understand his partisans shutting their eyes to it, some out of fidelity to his person, some out of fidelity to their party, others from reasons which I will not now stay to draw out. But that any reasonable man, letting his mind have fair play, should doubt that Mr. Gladstone's "separate Parliament and Executive for Ireland" leads by a rapid incline to Mr. W. O'Brien's "Ireland a nation, and the green flag of our people," I cannot understand. Nor can I understand his doubting that this has danger.

We confuse ourselves with analogies from distant and unlike countries, which have no application. Let us take our analogy from close at hand, where the political incorporation has been, and is, the same as that of Ireland and England. Provence was once a nation, the *Nation Provençale*, as down to the end of the last century it was still called. A sagacious lawyer, Portalis, remonstrating in 1798 against a uniform legislation for France, declared that France was a country *composé de divers peuples*, "composed of different peoples," and it was for Provence, in particular, that Portalis spoke.[12] Whatever Ireland had to make her a nation, that Provence had also. Ireland's troubled history can show one beautiful and civilising period in the far past; but Provence founded modern literature. It had its own Estates and Parliament; it had the greatest of French orators, Mirabeau. Well, if Provence were discontented to-day, and demanded back its separate Estates and nationality, what should we think of a French statesman, a French political party, which declared that for the discontent of Provence there was "no remedy possible until the national aspirations of the Provençal people are gratified?" We should say they were lunatics. If they went on to inflame and infuriate the discontent by all the means in their power, calling the incorporation with France "disgraceful," and expatiating on the "infamy and corruption" through which it had been brought about, we should say they were criminal lunatics.

As for Provence being a nation, we should say that she was indeed a nation poetically, but not now politically, and that to make her now a nation politically would be suicide both for France and herself. And if some well-meaning ex-prefect, like Lord Spencer, were to plead as a reason for making Provence a nation politically, that "repressive measures, accompanied though they had been by remedial measures, had not succeeded," and that therefore "they ought to use the Provençal spirit of nationality, having failed in the past from not having sufficiently consulted the wishes of Provence in that respect," what should we say? We should say he was a most extraordinary reasoner. We should say that if his remedial measures had not succeeded, that was probably because they were bad and insufficient; and not till the right remedial measures had been sought and applied far more seriously than hitherto, need France think of committing suicide by erecting Provence, and probably this and that other part of France afterwards, following the example of Provence, into a separate nation again. In fact, means have been found, without "using the Provençal spirit of nationality," to make Provence perfectly contented in her incorporation with France. And so they have to be found, and may be found, for Ireland.

It is a consolation for us in the troublous times through which we are passing, that we have public men who appear to possess, distributed amongst them, the powers requisite for discerning and treating all the capital facts of the situation: one having the powers needed for dealing with one branch of such facts, another of another. Mr. Gladstone is no doubt a source of danger. The historian will some day say of him what was said by the preacher of an eccentric funeral sermon in Mayfair Chapel on Frederick, Prince of Wales: "He had great virtues; indeed they degenerated into vices; he was very generous, but I hear his generosity has ruined a great many people; and then his condescension was such that he kept very bad company." But as a compensation for our dangers from Mr. Gladstone, we have in Lord Hartington a statesman who has shown that he thoroughly grasps the meaning of Gladstonian Home Rule, sees where the proposal to give Ireland a separate Parliament and Executive leads, and is staunch in rejecting it, clear and keen in judging fallacious securities offered with it. Such a security is the retention of the Irish members at Westminister. Their retention, if their brethren wielded the legislature and executive of Ireland, would but double, as Lord Hartington truly saw, our dangers and difficulties.

All Lord Hartington's firmness will be needed. It has suited Mr. Gladstone and his friends to launch their new doctrine that no constraint must be put upon the Irish, and that there is no remedy for the disorder there until the national aspirations of the Irish are gratified. I have said that no reasonable man, who thinks fairly and seriously, can doubt that to gratify these aspirations by reconstituting Ireland as a nation politically, is full of dangers. But we have to consider the new voters, the *democracy*, as people are fond of calling them. They have many merits, but among them is not that of being, in general, reasonable persons who think fairly and seriously. We have had opportunities of observing a new journalism which a clever and energetic man has lately invented. It has much to recommend it; it is full of ability, novelty, variety, sensation, sympathy, generous instincts; its one great fault is that it is *feather-brained*. It throws out assertions at a venture because it wishes them true; does not correct either them or itself, if they are false; and to get at the state of things as they truly are seems to feel no concern whatever. Well, the democracy, with abundance of life, movement, sympathy, good instincts, is disposed to be, like this journalism, feather-brained; just as the upper class is disposed to be selfish in its politics, and the middle class narrow. The many restraints of their life particularly incline the democracy to believe with Mr. Fox that if people very much desire a thing they ought to have it, and that, therefore, the national aspirations of the Irish ought to be gratified. They do not look to the end and forecast consequences. When they are told that if we satisfy the national aspirations of the Irish the Irish will love us, and that all will thenceforth go well, they believe it because they wish to believe it. If they are told that the Bill for dealing with disorder in Ireland is savage and odious beyond precedent, they believe it, because to think this of a restraining measure is agreeable to them. The democracy is by its nature feather-brained; the English nation is not; and the democracy will in England work itself, probably, at last clear. But at present, even here, in England, and above all in those industrial centres where it is most left to itself, and at least in contact with other classes, it is disposed to be feather-brained. This makes the strength of Mr. Gladstone. The great body of reasonable opinion in England is against him on Home Rule, and in Lord Hartington we have a leader convinced and firm; but we must not deceive ourselves. The democracy is being plied with fierce stimulants, and is agitated and chafing. If we cannot remove all just cause of complaint in Ireland, cannot produce, for local government there and for the land, a plan manifestly reasonable and good, the democracy will burst irresistibly in, bearing Mr. Gladstone in triumph back to power, and Home Rule along with him.

Lord Salisbury has declared his belief that "remedial measures, and remedial measures of a very far-reaching tendency, are strongly called for by the condition of things in Ireland." Undoubtedly they are, and to hug ourselves in the belief that they are not, but that all which is required is to put down disorder, is fatal. Some people say Ireland has no more cause of complaint than England or Scotland. One of these gentlemen wrote the other day to a newspaper saying that Ireland had even less, because she has not an established church. This is like congratulating Mr. Gladstone on living under the blessings of a Divorce Act, or Mr. Beresford Hope on having the prospect of soon being allowed to marry his deceased wife's sister.[13]

A man peculiarly well informed on the matter, Mr. Edwin Chadwick, asserts that in several important branches of local government (he mentions the Poor Law system in especial) Ireland has the advantage of England.[14] No doubt he is right. But this advantage is something devised and conferred by superior authority: the question is whether the call of the community itself for a thing desired by it and fairly reasonable, is not more likely to be thwarted in Ireland than in Great Britain. Most certainly it is. Let me take a single instance in illustration: I will be as brief as possible. I believe that public aid was desired for a Catholic training school for elementary teachers in Ireland, and that Lord Spencer thought the desire reasonable, and wished it to be complied with. Denominational training schools, as we call them, have in Great Britain, and have long had, the bulk of their expense supplied from public funds. But the moment the members from northern Ireland got wind of the matter, they were indignant, and protested against the project. Probably the northern members would have had the support of British Nonconformity and secularism: "the Liberal party has emphatically condemned religious endowment." At any rate Lord Spencer foresaw a storm, and the project was not persisted in. But how reasonable and permissible a thing, how entirely a thing within the fair scope of a community's wishes, to have in a part of Ireland, where the vast bulk of the community is Catholic, a Catholic training school with public aid; and how irritating to find that in Great Britain there are denominational training schools with public aid, because the community wishes it; but in Ireland, although the community may wish it, it cannot have them!

I have often said that one has no need to go beyond Church and education to see how completely Great Britain, while talking pompously of "the tolerance of the British Constitution," has had two sets of weights and measures, one for itself and another for Ireland. The tolerance of the British Constitution consists in letting Irish revolutionists say whatever they like; a liberty often extremely bad for them. But in complying with the fair wishes of the Catholic community in Ireland the tolerance of the British Constitution utterly disappears. I feel the more strongly on this matter because of what I have seen abroad, in acquainting myself with the humble but everywhere present public service of popular education. There indeed there is absolute equality of treatment; there indeed there is not a double set of weights and measures; there you will never find a Protestant community indulged with a training school of its own, while a Catholic community is denied one. Goethe used to pray: "God give us clear notions of the consequences of things." [15] If the British Philistine could ever frame such a prayer and have it granted, he would come to understand how completely Archbishop Walsh and Archbishop Croke are the consequences of things of our own doing.[16] No doubt the Vatican disapproves their action; but how must the Vatican at the same time secretly feel that it serves us right!

It is undeniable that a fairly reasonable wish of the community in Ireland is more likely to be thwarted than in England and Scotland. That is a reason against leaving the Imperial Parliament to go on controlling Irish local affairs. But who, with Colonel Saunderson and Mr. Sexton present to his mind, will believe that in the present state of tempers the Catholic Irish in an Irish Parliament would duly entertain reasonable wishes of the Protestants of the north, or the Protestant Irish those of Catholics of the south? [17] This is an objection to Mr. Gladstone's Home Rule not from an imperial point of view any longer, but from a purely Irish one. The fairly reasonable wishes of the community, in the respective parts of Ireland, ought to be made possible of attainment by the community. "Ireland a nation, and the green flag of our people," is not a fairly reasonable wish. But a Catholic training school is.

Whoever has had occasion to learn the course of public business in foreign countries, knows what we lose for want of proper local government in Great Britain. The House of Commons is far too large; a quantity of business comes before it which it should not have to discharge. Of our numerous House of Commons very many men are members, and unfit for such a position, who would be excellently fitted for local assemblies, which do not, however, exist to receive them. The best thing I have observed in New England is the effect of the training in local government upon the average citizen there. With us, little is known of systems of local government, and there is no cry for the thing; to discredit it, to throw out the scoff of *the Heptarchy*, is easy enough. But it is unpatriotic and unwise. Infinitely more unpatriotic and unwise is the neglect of this remedy in Ireland, where the want of it has had special bad consequences which it has not had in Great Britain, and which are full of danger. It should be made as serious, important, and strong there, as possible.

The county is too small a basis to take even in rich and populous England, except in a very few cases. Certainly it is too small a basis to take in Ireland. Every one sees how the province in Ireland affords a larger unit at once convenient and natural. I do not know what arrangements might be the best in the interests simply of local business. But it is important to remark that *politically* there could be no objection to resolving the provincial assemblies of Ireland into two only, one for the Catholic South and another for the Protestant North. The formidable political danger of Mr. Gladstone's one Parliament and Executive for all Ireland is that such a power would most surely be tempted, so far as we can at present foresee, to pose as a separate nation with a policy contrary to that of Great Britain. But an assembly for a part only of Ireland cannot so pose; the assembly and government of the Catholic South will be balanced by those of the Protestant North, which is smaller, indeed, in extent and numbers, but superior in wealth, energy, and organisation. The governments would balance one another politically, and administratively would each do simply their own business, which in the furious conflicts of a joint assembly would often suffer or be left undone. Many men who now have no trade but agitation would become good and useful citizens in the field of activity opened by these assemblies and their business. The flower of the political talent of Ireland would find its place in the Imperial Parliament.

Mr. Reginald Brett[18] says that no other Irish policy is possible than Mr. Gladstone's, "which was *right in principle, but faulty in vital details.*" This is in the sacred language of the practical politicians, to which a plain outsider has not the key. But let us hope that the plan of two assemblies may be sufficiently like Mr. Gladstone's to pass with Mr. Brett as Gladstonian in principle, possible, and desirable.

The reason of the country judged Mr. Gladstone's Home Rule dangerous. It perceives, however, the need of local government for Ireland, and leaves the plan of it to the Government; only let us insist that what is done shall be effectual. Happily we have in Mr. Goschen a statesman as fit for planning local government as Lord Hartington is for combating Gladstonian Home Rule.

Finally, there is the land question. Mr. Gladstone's missionaries are sent out to cry that all the Conservative Government wants is to enable the landlords to extort their unjust rents. Of course some danger there is that the Conservative party may not be stringent enough in dealing with landlords. But evidently something has to be done. It is confessed that the Bill for admitting leaseholders to the benefit of the Act of 1881, and for preventing harsh evictions, is a measure of temporary relief only. The Act of 1881 has failed, as it was likely to fail. I may say so, for I said so in 1881, provoking somewhat, I may add, my friend Mr. John Morley by my want of faith. By that Act, I said, "ownership and tenure will be made quite a different thing in Ireland from that which they are in England, and in countries of our sort of civilisation generally, and this is surely a disadvantage." * An adumbration of dual ownership there was in Irish land-tenure already; such an ownership, with such parties to it, had elements of trouble; the thing was to get rid of it. Instead of getting rid of it, the Act of 1881 developed and strengthened it. What we all now see to be desirable, is to have one owner, and that owner, as far as possible, the cultivator.

The reason of the country supports the Government in quelling revolutionary anarchy in Ireland, and in restoring the rule of law and order there. Here it is as conservative as the Conservative party. But it has no landlord bias, and in its judgment on Irish landlords it is disposed to be severe. "Mere land-merchants," too many of them, says their own friend Croker; "from their neglect of their duties springs their difficulty with their rents, and the general misery and distraction." [19] Often "insolent"

* *Irish Essays*, p. 29.

besides; an offence which the Irish peasant resents more even than oppression. It is a terrible indictment; and there are landlords still against whom it might justly be brought. The Land Purchase Commissioner of the government "has known rack-renting prevail to an extent simply shocking;" Sir Redvers Buller desires "a court with a very strong coercive power on a bad landlord." [20]

Landlordism, as we know it in these islands, has disappeared from most countries. It depends on the consent of the community. In England, as I have often said, it has kept this consent partly through the moderation of the people, but above all through that of the landlords themselves. It has become impossible to maintain by the force of England the system of landlordism where it has not, as in England itself, the consent of the community; and this the reason and conscience of England begin to feel more and more. Mr. Chamberlain, I believe, is the statesman who might be proctor for the real mind of the country on this matter, as Lord Hartington might be proctor for it on the matter of Home Rule, and Mr. Goschen on that of local government. It seems admitted, however, that if we organise local government in Ireland, we yet cannot leave, as would be natural, the community itself to deal with the landlords there: the Government of the Catholic South with the landlords of the South, that of the Protestant North with those of the North. England and its Government are partly accountable for the faults of the landlords and for their present position. The Imperial Parliament must therefore help in solving the land question. But Mr. Gladstone's twenty years' purchase all round is as little pleasing to the mind of the country as his Home Rule. No solution will satisfy the mind and conscience of the country which does not regard equity, discriminate between the good landlord and the bad, and lance the deep imposthume of moral grievance.

Sir George Trevelyan adheres to his passionate love for the Liberal party, his passionate grief at its not being in power.[21] I am too old for these romantic attachments. Sir George Trevelyan himself confesses that "it is impossible for young politicians to have any idea of the half-heartedness of the Liberal politics of the past." I confess that I am not sanguine about those of the near future. Why then should we be so very eager to take up again with "the tabernacle of Moloch," Mr. Gladstone's old umbrella, or "the star of our god Remphan," the genial countenance of Sir William Harcourt,[22] merely in order to pass forty years in the wilderness of the Deceased Wife's Sister? If the Conservative Government will quell anarchy in Ireland, give us a sound plan of local government there, and deal effectually with the land question, we may be well satisfied to allow them the lease of power requisite for this, and I believe the country will let them have it.

Notes

[1] *Letters,* II, 275.

[2] *Ibid.,* 367.

[3] Thomas Henry Huxley (1825–1895) said in "Science and Pseudo-Science," *Nineteenth Century,* XXI (April 1887), 497: "It is a great many years since, at the outset of my career, I had to think seriously what life had to offer that was worth having. I came to the conclusion that the chief good, for me, was freedom to learn, think, and say what I pleased, when I pleased."

[4] John Dillon and William O'Brien promoted in the autumn of 1886 a "Plan of Campaign" to organize tenants in their dealings with landlords. A new series of evictions followed the initial success of their efforts. See Ensor, *England, 1870–1914,* pp. 178–179.

[5] Beaumarchais, *Le Barbier de Séville,* III, xi. Not Figaro, but Don Bazile says, "Qui diable est-ce donc qu'on trompe ici?"

[6] The House of Commons upon reassembling in January 1887 amended their rules of procedure to include the principle of closure. In connection with the word itself Arnold wrote the following letter which was printed among the "Occasional Notes" in the *Pall Mall Gazette,* February 14, 1882, p. 3: "I have just been reading the vigorous article in yesterday's *Daily Telegraph* about 'the French gag' with which the Government are going to stop free debate in England. I notice that the racy and idiomatic writer does not say *bâillon.* May I ask why we all persist in saying *clôture?* Is it for the pleasure of describing the circumflex when we write the word, and of pronouncing the French *u* when we speak? Or is it from the mere English love of whatever is complicated and not simple? We all say *enclosure, disclosure,* every day of our lives. But *closure* itself, also, in its uncompounded state, is a perfectly good English word; a word used by Chaucer, Shakespeare, Boyle, Atterbury, and Pope."

[7] See n. 8 on p. 329. Spencer became Viceroy for Ireland in April 1882. It was on the day of his arrival in Dublin, May 6, that Lord Frederick Cavendish, Chief Secretary for Ireland, who had succeeded Arnold's brother-in-law W. E. Forster, and Thomas Burke, the under-secretary, were murdered by terrorists in Phoenix Park.

[8] "Thoughts on the Cause of the Present Discontents," *The Works of Edmund Burke,* I, 470.

[9] Peter O'Brien, Baron O'Brien (1842–1914), was Attorney General and later Lord Chief Justice of Ireland. He presided at the trial of Thomas Casey in the Maamtrasna murder case.

[10] Arthur James Balfour, afterwards first earl of Balfour (1848–1930), nephew of Lord Salisbury, in March 1887 succeeded Sir Michael Hicks Beach as Chief Secretary for Ireland.

[11] Matthew Harris, M.P. for Galway East, made this remark in 1881 according to G. Locker Lampson, *A Consideration of the State of Ireland in the Nineteenth Century* (London, 1907), p. 381.

[12] Jean Etienne Marie Portalis (1746–1807), French jurist. The phrase Arnold quotes appears in Sainte-Beuve, "Portalis," *Causeries du lundi,* V, 450.

[13] Alexander James Beresford-Hope (1820–1887), independent Conservative M.P. and co-founder with John Douglas Cook of the *Saturday Review,* was a vigorous and continuous opponent of the Deceased Wife's Sister Bill from 1859. Arnold made sport of the Bill frequently, but especially in "Our Liberal Practitioners" in *Culture and Anarchy,* where its sponsor Sir Thomas Chambers (1814–1891) is his particular butt. More recently, in 1882, the Queen in *Iolanthe* had threatened that Strephon, her newly made M.P.:

"shall prick that annual blister,/Marriage with deceased wife's sister."

[14] Sir Edwin Chadwick (1800–1890), sanitary reformer.

[15] Riemer, *Mittheilungen über Goethe,* II, 95.

[16] William J. Walsh, Archbishop of Dublin (1841–1921), a supporter in 1881 of Gladstone's Land Bill, strongly advocated the claim of the Irish tenantry.

Thomas William Croke, Archbishop of Cashel (1824–1902), was an ardent supporter of Charles Stewart Parnell and the Irish Nationalists.

[17] Col. Rt. Hon. Edward James Saunderson (1837–1906), M.P. for County Armagh, N.

Sir Robert Sexton (1814–1901), Alderman of Dublin and, from 1886, Chairman of the South Dublin Board of Guardians.

[18] Reginald Baliol Brett, second Viscount Esher (1852–1930).

[19] See page 329, n. 18.

[20] Sir Henry Redvers Buller (1839–1908), British general and Privy Councillor. John Morley quotes Buller as saying, "You have got a very ignorant poor people, and the law should look after them, instead of which it has only looked after the rich." *Life of William Ewart Gladstone*, III, 372.

[21] For Trevelyan, see p. 281, n. 27.

[22] Sir William G. G. V. Vernon Harcourt (1827–1904), statesman and lawyer, served as Professor of International Law at Cambridge and as Solicitor General.

From Easter to August

Nineteenth Century
XXII (September 1887), 310–324

Arnold continued his commentary on Lord Salisbury's government in 1887 with "From Easter to August." The sense of accomplishment he enjoyed is reflected in a letter from Fox How, Ambleside, dated August 31, 1887, to Charles Eliot Norton in which he said, "I do not know whether I shall do any more poetry, but it is something to be of use in prose, and by coming out from time to time as the organ of 'the body of quiet, reasonable people,' I believe I do some good." [1]

The Session is ending. Whatever we may have wished, whatever we may have conjectured, when the Session began, as to things likely to happen in it, it is ending now, and its facts can speak for themselves. And for any one with his eyes open two facts above all, at the closing of the present Session, stand out clear and undeniable—the disappearance of the Gladstonian plan of Home Rule, the weakening of the Government.

Whether the Liberal Unionists live or die, they have at any rate rendered to their country this signal service — they have compelled the abandonment and disappearance of the Gladstonian plan of Home Rule. The Land Bill which was to be its accompaniment and condition disappeared long ago. But the scheme of a separate national Parliament and a separate national Executive for Ireland remained, and was full of dangers. To give to the people of Ireland the due control of their own local affairs was, as I said a year ago, an object approved by all reasonable people in this country, and professed by every Liberal Unionist, by Mr. Bright and by Mr. Chamberlain as much as by Mr. Gladstone. But what gave to Mr. Gladstone's scheme its essential character was the withdrawal of the Irish members from Westminster and their establishment as a national power in Dublin, with an executive and justice and police of their own. It is now conceded that the Irish members shall be retained at Westminster. Nor is there to be at Dublin any national Parliament or Executive for Ireland. An assembly and executive for the northern province is conceded; and so Ireland will have, at any rate, not a national Parliament and national Executive single, but an assembly and government for northern or British Ireland on the one hand, and an assembly and government for southern or Celtic Ireland on the other. Finally, assurances appear to have been given with respect to the control of justice and police which to Sir George Trevelyan, at all events, are satisfactory.

The Liberal Unionists, I say, may survive or they may be extinguished, but they have saved their country from a great peril, they have converted the Gladstonian scheme of Home Rule from a most dangerous to a comparatively safe one. Not a single Gladstonian candidate who now wins an election wins it as a supporter of Mr. Gladstone's old unconverted plan. The plan converted, or to be converted, is the one he adopts and upholds; and the conversion of the plan has been brought about by the opposition of the Liberal Unionists to the surrender originally offered by Mr. Gladstone.

On the other hand, the Government is weaker than when the Session began. It has been losing, not gaining, in credit and consideration. I speak of home affairs only. The Leader of the House of Commons has qualities which win every one's good word; he has filled his difficult position far better than people in general expected, and on the whole with success. Mr. Balfour, who did not begin happily, has since shown himself to possess great vigour and resource. The Government has carried and applied the closure, which the country, I am convinced, heartily wished to be carried and applied; it has also carried the Crimes Bill, which its adversaries loudly and confidently defied it to carry. Still it is at the present time visibly, I am sorry to say, declined and declining in consideration, credit, and power. True it has actually lost only four seats, but the change indicated by the voting at those and other elections is grave. Nor can the Government show any important gain, except in one constituency, to set on the other side. It is manifest that the democracy, in whose impulses lies the Government's danger, is beginning to move; while, on the other hand, the great body of quiet reasonable people, in whose support lies the Government's strength, are somewhat discouraged and disconcerted.

Let me recall two warnings which I was moved to give (it is so easy to give warnings!), one of them in a letter to the *Times* more than a year ago,[2] the other in this Review just before the present Session began. In the *Times,* after a misunderstood and unfortunate speech by Lord Salisbury, I urged that however necessary restraining measures for Ireland might be, still for the Government to rely on restraining measures merely was to play the game of their adversaries and to deliver us over to Cleon and his democracy. In this Review I urged, when the Session was about to begin, that of fumbling and failure the country has had more than enough, that people are become impatient of seeing the efforts of Government turn awry and our affairs go amiss; that *success,* clear and broad success, is what the general sentiment earnestly demands from the Government and its measures.

Now it is evident that, if the first of these two warnings was sound, the Government could not expect that the Crimes Bill, a purely restraining measure, would be sufficient alone. It might be accepted, and I am convinced it *was* accepted, by the great body of quiet reasonable people as a necessity, and as such approved, but with the understanding that fit remedial measures would follow it. By the democracy, by the new electorate, any Crimes Bill was sure to be regarded with impatience and misgiving. It might be just tolerated, in the hope of better things immediately to follow it; it could not be approved. Everything depended upon what came after. What came after was the Bodyke evictions, a repetition of the scenes enacted at Woodford and Glen Beigh.[3] Mr. Balfour said he "thought it his duty" to enable the Bodyke evictions to take place. Mr. Balfour is a brilliant man, but his "thinking it his duty" to carry into execution, at that juncture, the Bodyke evictions, reminded me painfully of a saying of Goethe's: *The English are pedants!* [4] It was pedantry at that juncture, in a revolutionary state of things, with a bad case, and with a Crimes Bill before Parliament, so to construe his duty. And heavily indeed was Mr. Balfour's stroke of pedantry punished. The evictions were conducted, like the preceding cases of the kind, in a manner to bring ridicule and contempt upon the police and soldiery, and upon the Government which was behind them. Some of the evictions were of a character to raise the temper of the democracy, already impatient and annoyed at the Crimes Bill, to a white heat of indignation. Rude but moving pictures of the harshest passages in the evictions were hawked about through the villages; mob orators used with all their might the opportunity given to them. "It is to perpetuate scenes like this," they kept crying, "that the Government pass a Crimes Bill!" Quiet, reasonable people, out of the reach of mob orators, and well knowing that even in harsh evictions the fault is not always all on the side of the evictors, were yet seriously shocked and disquieted.

In this untoward condition of things, it was of the utmost importance that the next proceeding of the Government should be beyond all question frank, firm, simple, and healing. Success is what is demanded, and the first conditions of success for the measures of a government are frankness and firmness. It was necessary, further, that their proceeding should be simple, because the time was short, and healing, because after the Crimes Bill the turn for a healing measure was come, and was announcing itself imperiously. Under these circumstances the Government appeared with their Land Bill in the House of Commons. The measure was neither frank, firm, simple, nor healing. The promise of a complete Land Bill at the beginning of next Session, and a short bill staying evictions in the meantime, would no doubt have produced a far better and more satisfying effect upon the mind of the country. But to take this course was thought impossible. A course, however, less calculated to weaken the Government than the course actually followed by them might surely have been found. When something healing has to be done, it is surely weak statesmanship to seek to do it by a bill fashioned at first in the House of Lords so as to suit the landlords, then gravely altered in the House of Commons at the instigation of the Liberal Unionists, but with a burning question, that of arrears, left unprovided for; subsequently again altered in the House of Lords in such a manner as to create fresh dissatisfaction and delay. I will not pronounce an opinion upon a single clause of the bill, it is not necessary to do so in order to be convinced that this intended measure of healing has been managed most unhappily. The main alterations made by the House of Lords have finally been adopted, but to the bitter disappointment of the Ulster Unionists and at the cost of much heart-burning and friction; so that, instead of the Government having derived any advantage from this their first attempt at a healing measure, the positive weakening of the Government is, I fear, the capital and serious fact at the close of the Session.

Plainly, then, Conservatism is not now any longer at its zenith. It ought to be added that this is in no degree by the fault of the Conservative party in the House of Commons. That party has behaved itself admirably. Readers of the Fathers, if there are any such readers left, may possibly remember a passage in a homily at the end of St. Cyprian's works: *Incredibilis res est pastores pati posse aliquid a pecore.* The homilist puts it too strongly; the shepherd has sometimes cause to complain of the flock. But certainly of their *pecus,* the Conservative flock in the House of Commons, the Ministerial shepherds have no cause to complain. Never was there a body of followers more steady, more willing, more self-sacrificing. Mr. Courtney[5] has spoken severely of the demeanour of some of their younger members; but Mr. Courtney, like myself, has come to an age when one is liable to attacks of a sort of irritable antipathy towards white waistcoats, and when one has to be on one's guard against the moroseness of old age. From all I have myself seen, or can learn from others, I should say that any impartial observer who recalls the interruptions prevalent and victorious in the House of Commons of former days, and who witnesses the provocation offered by many of the Irish members now, would be inclined to pronounce the parliamentary demeanour of the whole Conservative party at present, young as well as old, almost angelic. At any rate, of the staunchness, fidelity, patience, and reasonableness of this party towards its leaders there can be no doubt. Nor has the staunchness of the Liberal Unionist members been less exemplary. Their course has been that of men sincerely anxious to save the Government from committing errors, to help the Government out of difficulties, not to make capital out of those errors and difficulties for themselves. Their position is in many respects a harassing one, a position to cause restlessness; but only two of them have been unsettled and carried away by restlessness, Mr. Winterbotham and Sir George Trevelyan. The majority behind the Government has, I repeat, done its duty perfectly. But the fortunes of the Government decline, and those of the majority cannot but decline with them.

Before the Session began, I inquired what the Government should do in order to retain the goodwill of that great body of quiet, reasonable people throughout the country, who thought the course attempted by Mr. Gladstone and his followers a false and dangerous one, and had placed the Conservatives in power in order to stop it. And I answered my own inquiry by saying, as I have mentioned above, that what the Government had to do was to take, on the great questions of the Session, a course not dubious, fumbling, and failing, but frank, firm, and successful. At Easter I inquired how things stood at the moment to which we were then come; what had been accomplished, what still remained to be accomplished; what was likely to lead to final success, what to failure. And again I answered my own inquiry, and said that reasonable people were glad to see the closure carried, and would be glad to see the Crimes Bill carried, but that there was perhaps a danger of quiet people not insisting strongly enough upon a further thing: how much, after the Crimes Bill was carried, would still require to be done. I said that I believed them to desire and intend most sincerely both to defeat Mr. Gladstone's dangerous plan of Home Rule, and also to remove all just cause of Irish complaint, but that I feared we did not all of us adequately conceive how large and far-reaching were the measures required in order to effect the latter purpose. I added that it was the more necessary for reasonable people to acquire an adequate conception of this, and to make the Government act upon it, because the democracy, the new voters, were feather-brained, were unapt to understand the dangers of such a plan of Home Rule as Mr. Gladstone's, were by nature inclined to dislike a restraining measure such as the Crimes Bill, were being plied with fierce stimulants by Mr. Gladstone and his followers, were agitated and chafing, and if nothing effective was done for removing cause of complaint in Ireland as well as repressing crime there, were likely to burst irresistibly in, bearing Mr. Gladstone back to power.

What I feared has in great measure come to pass. The democracy has not yet indeed borne Mr. Gladstone back in triumph to power, but in the Northwich division it has broken irresistibly in, carrying in triumph on its shoulders Mr. Brunner, who adopts his leader's watchword of *Masses against classes!* and proclaims his election to be a signal victory in that war.[6] Mr. Gladstone and his followers are superbly elate, they will ply the democracy with fiercer stimulants than ever; if things continue to go as they are now going, the agitation will grow hotter and hotter; at election after election will be raised the cry of *Masses against classes!* and a perpetual series of Mr. Brunners will win by it, until at last there is nothing left for them except to devour one another.

The end of the Session will give us a little breathing time. At Easter I said that the prospects of a final happy issue were favourable, if the great force of quiet reasonable opinion throughout the country — the force which defeated Mr. Gladstone at the last election — remained active and watchful. At the end of the Session, in spite of all that has happened, I still say the same thing. The Government is weaker. But the dangerous parts of the Gladstonian plan of Home Rule have been dropped and abandoned by its authors. To plain people outside of the rivalry of parties it will seem of little matter which party settles the Irish question so long as the settlement is a safe and good one. But it may be said that the passions they have fomented, the tempers they have raised, the feather-brained democracy to which they appeal, may compel Mr. Gladstone and his lieutenants to withdraw concessions which he had been compelled to make, and to recur to a scheme of Home Rule bad and unsafe. And this is no doubt a possible danger. Only in one way can it be averted. Only in one way can either the present weak Government be strengthened so as to endure and so as to achieve a settlement of the Irish question, or Mr. Gladstone be controlled and influenced so as to adhere to his present concessions, and to adopt a settlement of the Irish question, if to him it falls to settle it, safe and reasonable. Either thing can come about only by the force of quiet reasonable opinion in the country continuing active and watchful — nay, increasing its activity and watchfulness. And it is in one direction above all that its activity and watchfulness have to be directed: to secure the full and frank removal, now that power has been taken for quelling disorder, of all just cause of complaint in Ireland; and with this object, to habituate itself to consider, more adequately perhaps than it has yet considered, what large and far-reaching measures are required for that purpose, and to make its insistence on such measures as operative as its approval of a Crimes Bill has been.

Nor, in doing this, need our friends go back in the very slightest degree from their approval of the closure and the Crimes Act. To them, indeed, to brush away the claptrap and insincerities, with which the politician inflames the feather-brained democracy, is not difficult. In "the present deplorable Session, which must make every Englishman blush, or weep, or both," cries Mr. Gladstone, "the closure imposes upon the deliberations of your free Parliament restraints hitherto totally unknown." But in the eyes of reasonable people the present Session is deplorable not because too much restraint has been put upon the barren obstructive talk which Mr. Gladstone is pleased to call deliberation, but because too little has been put upon it. "The liberties of the House of Commons," he cries again, "have been sacrificed to the causeless, wanton, mischievous, insidious coercion of Ireland." But a Judge declares to us that in parts of Ireland "the law has ceased to exist; there is a state of war with authority and with the institutions of civilised life." Mr. Dillon boasts that "there are hundreds of farms in Kerry on which no person dares lay his foot." The *Tuam News* reports: "Hugh Baldwin was summoned to attend the meeting of the Kiltartan branch of the National League, the charge of associating with a notorious anti-Nationalist being brought against him. He assured some members of the Committee before the meeting that he did not know what he was doing, and that it would not happen again." If these things are so, if there is this paralysis of the law, this intimidation and terrorism, and if the offenders either cannot be brought to justice, or if they are brought to justice cannot be convicted, what reasonable quiet man will call it "causeless, wanton, mischievous, invidious coercion" to strengthen the ordinary law so as to enable it to reach them? "No coercion, but a vigorous enforcement of the ordinary law!" cries the feather-brained journalism of the democracy. This is as much as to say, "No enforcement of the law, but a vigorous enforcement of it!" It is because the ordinary law cannot be enforced that it needs strengthening. Every reasonable man must surely see that the strengthening of the power of the ordinary law is here no case for crying out against "causeless, wanton coercion," but rather for applying the excellent Bible: "Do that which is good, and thou shalt not be afraid of the power." [7]

Or, again, when Sir George Trevelyan asserts that "the real defect" of the Crimes Bill is that "it is directed against the written and spoken expression of opinion," and Mr. Labouchere complains that it will "crush out the legitimate expression of opinion in Ireland," and Professor Smart admonishes us that "whatever may be the opinions of any body of persons, it is for the public detriment that those opinions should not be fully expressed," reasonable people will surely take the trouble to ask what is really the sort of *opinion* which all this fine talk is to cover and license. And they will find that it is such opinion as this of Mr. Wm. O'Brien's: "If Trench dares to lay a robber hand upon any honest man's house in Ireland, we will hunt Lord Lansdowne with execrations out of Canada." And reasonable people will surely think that to permit, in the present state of things in Ireland, the free expression of this sort of "opinion," is good neither for Ireland, England, Canada, nor Mr. O'Brien. No one would call this "the legitimate expression of opinion" except a political agitator; and he would himself expect no one except a feather-brained democracy to take him seriously.

The coercion, then, is not causeless in the present instance. Is it mischievous? Reasonable people in this country, if they have no bias, will not think so. The democracy, with a life full of restraints, naturally thinks restraint a curse, and doing as one likes the height of felicity. The Americans in general think so too. Mr. Godkin reports that "go where you will in the United States, you will find that popular feeling, however ignorant about the facts of the case, runs in favour of the Irish."⁸ It runs in their favour because of the opinion, so prevalent in the United States, that "any measures of coercion are not only unjust, but nugatory." Perhaps in a country like America, with society in an early and simple stage, even reasonable people may easily enough come to hold this opinion. I do not say that it does them no harm, but at any rate they have little practical experience of its unsoundness and danger; they have not yet reached that corporate stage when its falsehood is manifest. Senator Riddleberger is thrown into prison in Virginia for some contempt of court.⁹ His friends are indignant, and these plain citizens, in their unsophisticated stage of life, after a repast of fishballs, no doubt, and a drink of iced water, march to the prison with ladders and take Senator Riddleberger out. And what is characteristic of American society in its present stage is, that then the citizens go away, one to his farm, another to his merchandise, and no disturbance follows. But reflecting people in our artificial European world would be inexcusable if they expected here a like termination to a like case. Suppose Mr. Labouchere were unlucky enough to be cast into prison, and that the democracy of Northampton, when the tocsin sounded from all the Nonconformist chapels, could go with ladders and take him out; we all know that here this would mean riot, roughs, drinks, fires, and bloodshed. And Macaulay used to contemplate with sadness, as we know, the sure coming of a time when in America too it would, alas, be the same.

The Irish themselves are the worse, not the better, for the license which they claim for themselves, and of which their friends say it is wrong to deprive them. Democratic journalism reproaches the Conservatives with want of chivalry in not sparing men who are down, as the Irish are. Mr. Parnell's threat that his countrymen will "look to methods outside the Constitution," Mr. O'Brien's threat, "If Trench dares to lay a robber hand upon any honest man's home, we will hunt Lord Lansdowne with execrations out of Canada," is scarcely the language of men who are down. In fact the extraordinary impunity which the Irish enjoy has generated in them a temper of audacity and defiance as mischievous to themselves as it is to England. Misgovernment — for the misgovernment must never be denied or put out of sight — has begotten alienation, impunity in violent language and proceedings has begotten defiance. The Irish have many fine qualities, but they have also qualities which render them prone to be reckless and defiant, and which make excess of this kind peculiarly baneful to them. A penetrating moralist has observed that of ordinary human nature itself "the ground is seditious, insolent, refractory, inclined to contradict and contemn whatever lays claim to rule over it; consequently opposed to order, ungovernable, and negative." Certainly this is no inaccurate description of the temper which has grown up, whosesoever the fault may be, in Ireland, and which at present is in possession of the Irish nature. And it is a fatal temper; the *radicale Böse,* as our moralist goes on to say, of Kant; a temper which makes not only government impossible, but all order, progress, and happiness. Until the Irish are convinced that the law is stronger than they or we, until they have had to renounce and forgo this temper of "insolence, refractoriness, defiance," not only they cannot be governed, they cannot be sane, they cannot be settled, they cannot be happy.

Both Lord Spencer and Sir George Trevelyan have used an argument, intended to embarrass the Unionists, which may usefully be noticed in this connection. They reproach the Unionists with believing and countenancing certain grave charges against Mr. Parnell and others of his party, and they say: "You yourselves propose to bestow on Ireland local government, to give to the Irish, not indeed Mr. Gladstone's Home Rule, but the due control of their own local affairs; and how can you reconcile it with your conscience to put the local government of Ireland into the hands of men against whom such charges as these are admitted by you?" Now of the charges here spoken of I say nothing; I have never relied upon them in the discussion of the Irish question — never, I believe, mentioned them. But this I will say to Lord Spencer and to Sir George Trevelyan: To put the local government of Ireland into the hands of men in whom their present temper of insolence, refractoriness, defiance is rampant, would indeed be to invite failure and misery. Not until their temper has yielded, not until Irishmen have convinced themselves that the law is stronger than they, that it is vain and foolish for them to talk of making the government of Ireland impossible and of driving Lord Lansdowne with execrations out of Canada, not until then can a system of local government work well in Ireland. And surely all reasonable people will see that this is an irrefragable argument for the Crimes Bill.

Whether or no it is expedient to suppress the National League, or any particular branches of it, must depend, reasonable men will think, upon whether or no this refractory temper of outrageous defiance yields or is broken down without such suppression. If not, all reasonable people will wish the League suppressed. But they will wish it suppressed simply to break this malign temper, and not to comply with any clamour or hatred; as, on the other hand, they will wish its not being suppressed, if suppressed it is not, to be because this temper is suppled and reduced, not because the Government is nervous about an election, apprehensive of enraging the democracy. And if any branch of the League is to be suppressed they will wish it suppressed firmly, not in a hesitating and fumbling manner; because proceedings taken in a hesitating and fumbling manner never succeed. Meanwhile all reasonable people must rejoice, I should have thought, that the League has been, at any rate, proclaimed.

I have said that any Crimes Bill will be distasteful to the democracy, because a measure of this kind is a restraining one; and the proclamation of the League is likely to be distasteful for the same reason. But I believe that the new electors, who have a root of the English good sense and moderation in them, and who not only hear Irish stump orators but begin also to read newspapers, and newspapers not all on one side only — I believe that the new electors might have been brought to understand the necessity for a Crimes Bill, and even for the proclamation of the National League. They might be disposed to judge severely men who had told them they would never vote for a Crimes Bill, and then went and voted for one. But neither would this have been decisive with them. What was decisive with them was, I repeat, the evictions, the continuing evictions, the harsh and inhuman evictions of suffering people. The plea that the landlord had no other course left to him; that the same thing is done elsewhere; that the sufferers are much to blame — the kind of unction which the propertied and satisfied classes lay to their soul so readily — had and could have no power upon the democracy at all. These evictions were brought home to their imagination, feeling, senses; they thought them horribly harsh and inhuman, and that was decisive. It cannot be too often repeated: Mr. Balfour's "thinking it his duty" to allow the Bodyke evictions to take place was the crying, fatal fault in the Government's proceedings this Session. It has made it almost impossible for the democracy either to see the Crimes Bill, or to see the proclamation of the League, as reasonable people see it.

Of course the dangers of Mr. Gladstone's plan of Home Rule the democracy was not likely to see; of course the grievances alleged as a reason for it the democracy was likely to see readily, and readily to admit the separatist constitution prescribed as a cure for them. To the mass of mankind nothing can sound more plausibly than a cry for Home Rule; nothing needs more training and reflection than to appreciate rightly the character and tendencies of the Home Rule proposed. Let me ask Mr. Godkin (it is a pleasure to converse with him even in the pages of a Review), whether he has sufficiently understood how small was the number of persons I meant, when I said that all the highly instructed and widely informed people I met in America, except himself, thought Mr. Gladstone's scheme of Home Rule injudicious. Mr. Godkin begins by quoting my words accurately enough; but presently he makes me speak of "intelligent" Americans, as if that were the same thing as "highly instructed and widely informed" Americans. Now the whole American nation may be called "intelligent," that is to say, quick; and certainly

I never meant to dispute that, as Mr. Godkin asserts, "go where you will in the United States, popular feeling is in favour of the Irish demand." I fully admit that this is so, that such is the feeling of the mass of "intelligent Americans" as they are called; only I add, with Mr. Godkin himself, that these intelligent Americans are for the most part "ignorant of the facts of the case." But I said that when I came across highly instructed and widely informed Americans, I found *them* of opinion that Mr. Gladstone's Irish policy was a mistake. I say the same thing still. I say it of the Continent of Europe as well as of the United States of America; I say it of what Mr. Gladstone calls "the civilised world." Mr. Gladstone sometimes appears to think that the civilised world is on his side if it agrees that Ireland has been misgoverned. But what I maintain is, that throughout the civilised world, so far as my experience goes, the highly instructed and widely informed people, while strongly thinking that Ireland has been misgoverned, think at the same time that Mr. Gladstone's plan of Home Rule, with its national Parliament and national Executive for Ireland, was a mistake. But indeed he has now abandoned the plan himself, although apparently without any just conception, even now, of its intrinsic character and of its dangers.

Yet Mr. Gladstone is a highly instructed and widely informed person. So is Mr. John Morley, so is Mr. Godkin. But in each and all of these cases there is a bias. Mr. Gladstone is biassed by his longing to command the eighty-five Parnellite votes, and so to be master of the House of Commons and of power. Mr. John Morley is so convinced of the stupidity and stiffness of the English nation, that he despairs of its ever managing Ireland properly. Mr. Godkin has the alienated feelings of so many of his Irish countrymen. All the three men, having this bias, use arguments, take a line, which without bias such men would never employ.

I always invite Americans, who call out for Irish Home Rule, to consider how they would themselves like to have not a number of Southern States each with its own Legislature and Executive, but one South with a national Southern Congress and a national Southern Executive. No one has ever cried, that I know of, *Alabama a nation!* as the Irish cry, *Ireland a nation, and the green flag of our people!* But there has been in America, as we well know, the cry, *The South a nation, and the flag of the Confederate States!* Would the Americans concede that nationality — would they not recognise its danger? I can myself imagine but one answer from them. Yet I seem to remember that Mr. Godkin, in his zeal to parry the argument against Home Rule which this illustration of mine conveys, was capable of maintaining in his newspaper that if the South had chosen to insist on their own Congress and Executive they might have had it.

Mr. Gladstone too — how, without a bias, could a man of Mr. Gladstone's training and knowledge, who has learnt how hard and slow a labour is the grand work of building a nation, how mischievously the jealousies and pretensions of "our parish" interfere with it — how could such a man go about the country evoking and envenoming provincial discontents everywhere, and thus not only vexing the present, but sowing also, so far as in him lies, the certain seeds of trouble for the future? Without a bias how could Mr. John Morley taunt the Ulstermen with being bad Irishmen if they hold aloof from the national Parliament and Executive in Dublin? As if the height of political virtue for the Irishman was to feel allegiance to his island, not to the Empire! As if a Breton who stood aloof from a separatist movement in Brittany, and said that he placed his pride in being a citizen not of Brittany but of France, was to be called a bad patriot! Yet a Breton is no more a Frank than an Irishman is an Angle.

Reasonable people have no cause to waver in their judgment that Ireland, like Brittany or Wales, is and must be now a nation poetically only, not politically, and that all projects for making it a nation politically are disastrous and pregnant with danger. A project of the kind their firm resistance has baffled. Let them be watchful and zealous to prevent any reappearance either of that project or of a second project fraught with like dangers.

But Home Rule is not the pressing question for the moment; the pressing question for the moment is the question of the land and the landlords. The greatest possible service, which the body of quiet reasonable people in England can now render to their country, is to set their face like a flint against all paltering with this question, to insist on a thorough and equitable settlement of it. I am convinced that they are sincerely bent on doing right as to the land, no less than on quelling disorder. Their body is not aristocratical in its composition; if it were, it would have but a very small part of its present strength. The Conservative Government is aristocratical in its composition, and inevitably contracts weakness from this cause; it leans to the landlords; it imagines solidity where there is none; above all, it has not the popular fibre, the instinct for what will please or offend the feelings and imagination of men in general. The present Conservative Prime Minister, Lord Salisbury, is even conspicuously devoid of this instinct. His Jubilee honours afforded a good measure of his popular fibre. As seriously as if he had been celebrating the Jubilee by assigning to Phidias or to Socrates a public maintenance in the Prytaneum, he celebrated it by investing Mr. Eaton with a purple robe, and lost the Coventry seat for his party in consequence.[10]

The body of quiet reasonable people throughout England is not a feather-brained democracy, but it has popular fibre enough to be shocked by such evictions as some of those which we have seen, to feel the madness of permitting them, to insist on their ceasing. And it does not lean to the landlords. On the contrary, it judges them with entire freedom. As I said in January: "If Lord Clanricarde's tenants are evicted, the general opinion of reasonable people wishes them evicted without rioting; but it has its own thoughts about Lord Clanricarde." [11]

The Irish landlords complain that they are being sacrificed, that they are treated differently from other landlords, that the faults of the past are visited upon them, that no account is taken of their amendment. And indeed their case is peculiar. Everywhere the propertied and satisfied classes have to face an aspect of things which is new and unfamiliar to them; everywhere a change is preparing; everywhere the word *equity* is acquiring a force and an extension hitherto unknown; everywhere it becomes plainer that he who thinks it enough to say, *May I not do what I will with my own?* will no longer be suffered to have the last word. But for the Irish landlords we cannot but see that, above and beyond this general and gradual law of change, an epoch has indeed come, what the Bible calls a *crisis,* the close of a period, of a whole state of things. In such an epoch, even the amendment of individuals and the efforts of their friends are powerless to avert the end which is inevitable. We may and must insist on the morality of a crisis of this sort by calling to mind the faults committed and the warnings given. And that is why it is well to repeat again and again that impressive expostulation of Croker, an Irishman and a Conservative, with the Irish landlords: "A landlord is not a mere land merchant; he has duties to perform as well as rents to receive, and from his neglect of the former springs his difficulty in the latter, and the general misery and distraction." [12] It is well to recall the words of Henry Drummond, an English country gentleman and high Tory: "I much err if the enemies to the happiness of the Irish people are not the Irish gentlemen and nobility; but this is a truth which well-conditioned people dare not utter." [13] Even at the present hour, though amendment there has undoubtedly been, the evictions which have recently caused so much scandal have shown us still existing and powerful for mischief the three types of landlord which have been the bane of Ireland: the insolent landlord, the exacting landlord, the beggared landlord in the hands of mortgagees and attorneys. But we need not dwell on the faults of living individuals, or deny the amendment in the class of Irish landlords. What we have to do is to recognise and acknowledge that great law of human affairs, which makes amendment, after a certain lapse of time and course of conduct, too late, and the crisis and fall inevitable. Butler's profound and solemn sentences utter the stern truth which is fulfilling itself in Ireland to-day: —

Though, after men have been guilty of folly and extravagance *up to a certain degree,* it is often in their power to retrieve their affairs, at least in good measure, yet real reformation is, in many cases, of no avail at all towards preventing the miseries naturally annexed to folly and extravagance *exceeding that degree.**

There is a certain bound to imprudence and misbehaviour, which being transgressed, there remains no place for repentance in the natural course of things. It is further very much to be remarked, that neglects from inconsiderateness, want of attention, not looking about us to see what we have to do, are often attended with consequences altogether as dreadful as any active misbehaviour from the most extravagant passion.

It is by steadily directing their minds to the necessity for great and far-reaching changes in the land system of Ireland that the body of quiet reasonable people will keep abreast of events, and can now be of most service to their country. By bringing the Government to recognise that necessity they will be of service to the Government. For the Government everything now depends upon their producing an adequate Land Bill next Session. I say that everything depends upon this, presuming, of course, that in the meanwhile Mr. Balfour will not "think it his duty" to authorise any more evictions such as those of Bodyke.

Not impossibly, however, we may have to traverse a time when the quiet reasonable people will be swept away, and their influence quenched for the time and annulled; when the Liberals of the nadir and the new democracy will pass over their body. It is not for nothing that a stump orator of Mr. Gladstone's calibre proclaims the divorce between the masses and the classes, and invites every province and platform to consider its wrongs. The masses are stirred, tempers are kindled, a torrent of insincere and envenomed declamation feeds the flame. Mr. Gladstone's powers of self-deception are so inexhaustible that he is never insincere. But how is it possible for Sir William Harcourt or Mr. John Morley, if, as I suppose, they are sincerely desirous to get judicial rents in Ireland revised, to imagine that they further this object by covering the Government with scorn, contumely, and insult for adopting it?

This is probably the last time that I shall speak on these political subjects; certainly, if I follow my own inclination, it will be the last time. In ending, therefore, let me fortify the quiet reasonable people, with whom all along I have supposed myself conversing, by reminding them that even if, as seems not altogether improbably, they should have to traverse bad times, to see their wishes thwarted, and to be for a while powerless, yet the temper of fairness and moderation, which makes their force, is not to be still cultivated by them in the highest degree. In the first place, its time is sure to come again, it will not be powerless always, or even for very long; in the second place, it is its own exceeding reward.

* The italics are Butler's own.[14]

It is hardly possible to exaggerate the comfort and consolation which this temper is capable of producing, even in view of characters and proceedings obnoxious to us. The Irish members are extremely provoking; but the provocation is far less acute when we have the fairness to remember that these men are impulsive natures to start with, pariahs in the House of Commons, with no hand in the regular administration of their country, and that country long and grievously mismanaged; that they are men, finally, maddened by the stolid self-delusion of a number of worthy people in Great Britain that the Irish have nothing to complain of, but are treated just like the English and Scotch. Again, it is painful to see the new democracy inflaming itself by feeding greedily on the declamation of stump orators who to a man of training and reflection are intolerable; but here again it is tranquilising to make oneself consider that here may be the first beginnings, however crude, of a new life and new interests among men full of good stuff, and who are by skill and patience to be brought to listen by-and-by to the counsels of reason and moderation. Mr. Gladstone makes us indignant with his *masses and classes;* but what peace of mind comes from the spirit of mildness and indulgence which makes us own that to lose power after so many years of it is for a public man a sore trial, and the re-acquisition of it through the popular vote a mighty temptation! Mr. John Morley's pessimism, his conviction that his countrymen are too stupid and stiffnecked ever to manage Ireland, shocks us, and we condemn it; but I for my part find a positive satisfaction in forcing myself fairly to admit at the same time, that our countrymen, with a thousand good qualities, are really, perhaps, a good deal wanting in lucidity and flexibility. Therefore let the body of quiet reasonable people take heart and keep up their spirits, even though the line of Mr. Brunners should stretch out to the crack of doom. To be a quiet reasonable person always answers, always makes for happiness; there is always profit in being, as Horace says the poets are, a counter-influence to asperity, envy, and anger —

Asperitatis et invidiae corrector et irae.[15]

Notes

[1] *Letters,* II, 368.

[2] See Arnold's letter to *The Times* of August 6, 1886, in this volume, p. 285.

[3] At Bodyke, County Limerick, on June 3, 1887, an estimated crowd of 5,000 persons protested the eviction of certain tenants, but the evictions were carried out with the assistance of the military and the police. See the *Annual Register* (1887), p. 24.

The Woodford evictions of 1882 involved a number of Lord Clanricarde's tenants. Sir Michael Hicks Beach authorized the use of 500 constabulary to support the evictions, which were opposed by a public demonstration. Seventy-five young men of Woodford were tried and sentenced by a packed jury to terms of imprisonment of twelve to eighteen months. In reprisal for the evictions Lord Clanricarde's agent and his steward were murdered on June 29. See Lord Eversley, *Gladstone and Ireland, The Irish Policy of Parliament from 1850–1894*, pp. 321–324, and Locker-Lampson, *A Consideration of the State of Ireland in the Nineteenth Century*, p. 406.

The Glenveagh evictions occurred on the estate of a Mr. Adair at Derryveagh, Donegal, in 1861. Twenty-eight houses were unroofed or leveled and 244 persons evicted in reprisal for the murder of Adair's manager. See Locker-Lampson, p. 335.

Arthur James Balfour, first Earl of Balfour (1848–1930) succeeded Sir Michael Hicks Beach as Chief Secretary for Ireland upon the latter's resignation in March 1887. Balfour was the nephew of the prime minister, Lord Salisbury. He was instrumental in carrying the Crimes Bill of 1887.

⁴ Eckermann, *Gespräche mit Goethe*, December 20, 1826. See *Note-Books*, p. 529.

⁵ Leonard Henry Courtney, first Baron Courtney (1832–1918). He opposed Gladstone's plan for Home Rule.

⁶ John Tomlinson Brunner (1842–1919), industrialist and philanthropist, was a Liberal M.P. for Cheshire. Elected in 1882, he supported Home Rule and temperance. With Ludwig Mond he established the great alkali works, Brunner, Mond and Co., at Winnington, Cheshire. He was knighted in 1891.

⁷ Romans 13:3.

⁸ E. L. Godkin, "American Opinion on the Irish Question," *Nineteenth Century*, XXII (August 1882), 291.

⁹ Harrison Holt Riddleberger (1844–1890), United States Senator, 1883–1889.

¹⁰ Henry William Eaton (1816–1891), Conservative M.P. for Coventry was created first Baron Cheylesmore as a Jubilee honor on June 21, 1887. His seat was filled by William Henry Walter Ballantine, Liberal and Home Ruler. The *Spectator* commented, "Six new peers have been created, viz.: — Sir John St. Aubyn, Sir W. Armstrong, Sir J. McGarel Hogg, Mr. Sclater-Booth, Mr. E. Fellows, and Mr. Eaton, — and nobody either knows a good reason for choosing any one of these gentlemen, or a good reason for blaming the selection" (June 25, 1887, p. 850).

¹¹ "The Zenith of Conservatism," see above, p. 326.

¹² See above, "The Zenith of Conservatism," note 15.

¹³ Henry Drummond (1786–1860), British statesman, in a letter to John Wilson Croker, February 26, 1825, *Correspondence and Diaries of J. W. Croker*, 3 vols. (London, 1885), I, 284.

¹⁴ Bishop Butler, *The Analogy of Religion*, in *The Works of Joseph Butler*, I, 58.

¹⁵ *Epistles*, II, i, 129.

Disestablishment in Wales

National Review
XI (March 1888), 1–13

The question of the disestablishment of the Church of England in Wales was recurrent in the latter nineteenth century, especially between 1865 and 1890 when relations between non-conformist groups and Anglicans were sensitive.[1] The non-conformist bodies were united, and most of the Welsh members of Parliament were committed to disestablishment. The issue became acute in the later 1880's. A Tithe War began, which was terminated only in 1891 by the Tithe Act. Disestablishment itself was achieved in the twentieth century.

On Christmas Eve, 1887, Arnold wrote to George de Bunsen, "The editor of one of the Conservative reviews has begged me to give him an article on Disestablishment in Wales.[2] A number of the Conservatives are becoming very reasonable, and this editor thinks they will be willing to hear reason about the Establishment in Wales from me. The Liberal party has no idea beyond that of disestablishing the Church and secularizing its funds, the old-fashioned Tories have no idea beyond that of keeping things as they are. I am anxious that the endowments should remain for religion, that the Episcopalians should keep the Cathedrals, since in the cathedral towns the Episcopalians are in a majority, but that the Nonconformists, who are all of the Presbyterian form of worship, should have the churches and endowments, for that Presbyterian form, where they are in majority, as in many of the country districts."[3]

A good while ago I said I would write no more on religion, and up to the present time I have kept my word pretty faithfully. About six months ago I declared that on politics, too, I would write no more; and now here I find myself with a subject where both politics and religion are concerned, and which I cannot treat without doubly breaking my word. A casuist might say that a promise not to write on religion, or a promise not to write on politics, was no promise not to write on a conjunction of the two together. But instead of resorting to casuistry, I will say, what is the truth, that I have been led to depart from my intention by the temper of openness and moderation which is at present visible in so many members of the Conservative Party and in their main organs. To see this temper may well raise the spirits and the hopes of all quiet reasonable people who simply desire the good of their country [;] the wish to turn this happy and wholesome temper to advantage, in a question which especially needs the exercise of such a temper, is my motive for returning, yet this once, to subjects which I had quitted.

I have frequently lamented the narrow aims and the bitter temper of those whom, since they dislike the name of political Dissenters, I will call religious Liberals. Vinet's cry on issuing from a disestablishment debate in Canton Vaud has often risen to my mind as I watched them: *"O religion de Jésus Christ! ô culte en esprit! ô paisible et silencieux asile des âmes!"* [4] The secular Liberals are not narrow; they are free enough. But, they, on the other hand, have spokesmen who always make me think of Voltaire's delicious comment on a young friend who was extolled as as being *libre*, free. *"C'est déjà quelque chose; mais malheureusement cette bonne qualité, quand elle est seule, devient un furieux vice."* [5] Where religion is concerned, their good quality of freedom stands so entirely alone, that it "becomes a furious vice." The difficulty to be feared is, that in confronting the religious and the secular Liberals on questions where religion and the Church are concerned, one may have only a party of impracticable Conservatives. The moment Conservatives show themselves equitable and moderate in temper, open and reasonable in mind, this difficulty vanishes, and a good deal of danger along with it.

In England, an old country full of anomalies, and where the national characteristics, as has often been said, are energy and honesty rather than lucidity and logic, it is not enough recognized that a thing's being absurd is really an objection to it. As long as the political party charged naturally with the interests of conservation and permanence fails to recognize this, so long the party charged with the interests of demolition and change goes on and prospers, sure of succeeding in the end, whatever resistance it may have to overcome, however it may be checked for a time. The guiding spirits of this party do not want to mend, they want to demolish; they think demolishing *is* mending. To suggest to them ways of mending is therefore waste of time. To have suggested, for instance, to the Liberal Party in 1868 ways of mending the Irish Church Establishment would have been waste of time; their desire and resolve was simply to destroy it. And so long as the Conservatives, too, on their side, will not really entertain the notion of mending things, but seek simply to keep them as they are, while their adversaries seek simply to destroy them, it is of no use to suggest ways of mending a thing to Conservatives any more than to Liberals.

The case, however, is quite altered when the minds of the Conservative party open, and that party brings itself to recognize that a thing's absurdity puts the thing in danger, makes it indefensible as it now stands; and that the thing must be, not necessarily destroyed, but certainly altered and mended so as to get rid of this source of danger.

The Stoics, with whom the great matter was adherence to the moral will and purpose, the living, as we commonly express it, *by principle*, used to tell their pupils to say to themselves, whenever they found themselves desiring a thing: "This I desire; *and also to keep my principle.*" And so, too, the Conservatives should learn to say to themselves — and learning to say to themselves they do seem now to be: "We desire government, order and stability; *and also to get rid of what is indefensible and absurd.*" With regard to Ireland they should say: "We desire to see the Crimes Act put resolutely in force; *and also to get rid of Lord Clanricarde.*" [6] With regard to the Church of England they should say: "We desire to keep a National and Established Church; *and also to get rid of Lord Lonsdale.*" [7] I mean, of course, of Lord Lonsdale as the patron of forty English livings, and of Lord Clanricarde as the owner of fifty thousand Irish acres; not of Lord Lonsdale and Lord Clanricarde as men passing their little hour above ground like the rest of us.

The moment the notion of mending an absurd and indefensible thing is fairly entertained, the question arises, how best to mend it. And for arriving at an answer to this question, it is well to know what is done elsewhere in the matters wherein our practice is alleged to be absurd and indefensible. The establishment, as at present existing, of the Anglican Church in Wales is alleged to be absurd and indefensible, and to be a grievance. If it is so, there seems good hope that the Conservative party will now be disposed to correct the absurdity and to remove the grievance. But, in doing this, Conservatives may naturally look for some help from knowing what happens elsewhere, where religion is publicly endowed and established, and yet all religionists are not of one confession. The United States can teach us nothing here, for the United States, founded by Separatists and with separation in their people's blood, have no public endowment and establishment of religion. But on the Continent of Europe the public endowment and establishment of religion is general. What happens there? — so I can imagine a Conservative asking himself when he has to deal with the case of Wales — what happens on the Continent, where there is public endowment for religion, and yet the religionists are of different religious confessions? Now it happens that in going repeatedly about among elementary schools on the Continent, I have seen also a good deal of the provision for churches and ministers there, what it is, and how it works. I could hardly help seeing it, the school system has so many connections with the parish system. Therefore, when I see the case of Wales, I think naturally of what I have seen on the Continent; and Conservatives, too, may perhaps be glad to look there with me, and to see what is there done.

Now the Anglican form was settled and imposed by law, in the belief that all might unite in it. In England the majority did unite in it, and are united in it now; but in Scotland, Ireland, and Wales it has not been so. For Scotland and Ireland other arrangements have been made, but not for Wales; Wales remains with its churches and church property confined to the Anglican form, which has not been accepted by the majority of the inhabitants of the principality. A different religious form is preferred and used by that majority. And it may be said, that never has the preference of the people been regarded in disposing of the churches and church property in Wales, but it was taken for granted that the people would acquiesce in the form chosen for them, and would come to use it; and they have not. I put the thing in the simplest and most informal language I can find, because it is my object, not to seek technicalities on which an argument may be founded, but to present the matter as it really presents itself to plain people. I shall use language of the same kind in describing what happens on the Continent. I will confine myself to countries whose example will most interest us. We shall not find in France or Germany one form of religion chosen by the legislature as suitable to the whole nation, and entitled to the sole possession of the churches and of church property accordingly. We shall find public endowment of religion, but what the law has done is not to select one form of religion and establish it, but to follow the preference of the people; to ascertain the main forms actually existing among the people, and to endow these main forms. Thus in France the Catholic form of Christianity, the Lutheran form, the Calvinistic form, all receive support from public funds. The example of Germany interests us more nearly than that of France, because Germany was the country of the Reformation, and has never been revolutionized. In Germany the settlement of 1648, after the Thirty Years' War — the settlement by the treaties of Westphalia — took for its basis just this fact of the forms of religion actually existing among the German people, and preferred by them. It took a particular year, the year 1624, as an *annus normalis,* and provided that the churches and church property, in German territories, should remain with the religious party which had possessed them on the 1st day of January in that year. These great parties in religion, whom the settlement of 1648 thus established as corporations in possession, were the Catholic, the Lutheran, and the Zwinglian or Reformed, the more Calvinistic Protestant party. And so things remain to this day, except that in Prussia the Lutheran and the Reformed churches were united by a measure due to Frederick William III., in the present century, and are now a united corporation with the name of the Evangelical Church. To one or other corporation the churches belong, and in each parish the church established is maintained from its own property, and from the contributions of its members — contributions supplemented, in cases of necessity, by grants from the State.

The further sects and sub-divisions into which Protestantism is apt to break up are not regarded. There are Baptists, Wesleyans, Plymouth Brethren, Irvingites, found in Lutheran parishes in Germany, and these sects have the free exercise of their worship, but they are not endowed and established. The establishment of the main form of Lutheranism is held to be sufficient. Attempts have been made to establish the old Catholics in some Catholic territories of Germany. But these attempts have not succeeded; the main form of Catholicism holds, as we say now, the field.

People may call it a grievance not to have sects and sub-divisions of religious parties established, as well as the main bodies. And, perhaps the German governments and legislatures are not ready enough and flexible enough to making changes which might more thoroughly adapt the settlement of 1648 to the wants of the present day. But the tendency to multiply sects is a misfortune to Protestantism; it may become a disease; it would not be possible for establishment to follow it into all the varieties it produces, and would not be desirable if even it were possible. Some main forms must be chosen for establishment, if establishment there is to be. In Germany the somewhat unelastic settlement inherited from the seventeenth century does not, so far as I can learn, cause any serious dissatisfaction, although there are many Dissenters for whom it does not provide; no one talks or thinks of altering it.

But the case is different where, as formerly in Ireland and now in Wales, the form of religion established is one which was not that followed in those localities at the outset, and has not been adopted by more than a minority of the people there since. A grievance in this case there certainly is, and it will be felt to be a grievance, will provoke complaints. In Ireland it was removed by disestablishment; the question now is as to the grievance in Wales. People dispute as to the numbers of the majority outside of the Establishment; some say that they are diminishing, and that the established form will win over the majority in time. The Dissenters have prevented hitherto the taking of a religious census; such a census would be of very great convenience, and its refusal is indefensible; it is to be hoped that the Conservative majority will procure its being taken. In its absence no one can say with certainty what are the numbers, in Wales, of the majority outside of the Establishment; but, at any rate, a considerable majority is outside of it. In some districts of Wales almost the whole population is outside of it; in other districts the Establishment has many adherents, and they are increasing in number. But I am talking to Conservatives, and considering what is the line for them, in their present temper of fairness and moderation, to follow as to the Establishment in Wales. Let them take it, then, that the majority outside of the Establishment is certainly considerable; and do not let them be deceived into thinking, that to uphold the Establishment as it is, is the way to win the majority over to the Establishment, and thus to solve the question peaceably and happily. The Church has, in the last thirty or forty years, been much more active than formerly, and has, accordingly, gained much ground, especially in localities where it has circumstances in its favour. But it is not to know human nature to imagine that with the Establishment upheld just as it is the Church will ever absorb dissent in Wales, or the minority be converted into the majority. Above all, this will not happen in times like ours, democratic times when the masses are keen to spy a grievance, to attack a grievance, and when the Welsh Dissenters have leaders whose temper and character are what they are — eager to encourage battle, averse from composing or preventing it.

I feel sure that if the Conservatives enter on the battle with the resolve to uphold in Wales the Establishment just as it is, the Establishment in Wales is lost. The Conservatives are strong now, as they deserve to be strong; they may defeat those who attack the Church in Wales, they may put off the evil day of its disestablishment; but its disestablishment will have been rendered certain, and will soon come. The battle will have been engaged on terms which make impossible any other solution of the question at issue. And, undoubtedly, this will bring the Establishment into some danger in England also. It will be said: "Where there are several forms of religion present, none of them ought to have any support from public funds. It is unfair that one form should have all the support, and no mode of concurrent endowment is found practicable. The case of Wales proves it. It was quite clear that the Church of the minority could not continue to take all the endowments, and the friends of the Church had nothing else to suggest. Disestablishment is the only solution."

It is not the religious argument that Christian Churches suffer spiritually through not being independent of the State, and that Jesus Christ enjoined that independence when he said: "My kingdom is not of this world" — it is not this argument which endangers the Establishment, either in Wales or elsewhere. I see the *Guardian* thinks the strength and prevalence of that argument under-estimated, and the attention of Churchmen not directed to it enough. I know that it is very prevalent among Dissenters at the present day, but I do not think it requires any great attention, because really there is very little in it. Dissenters use it, I admit, with entire sincerity, and believe that it utters a genuine religious conviction with them; but they did not entertain it originally and naturally, they were led to it by circumstances which made it of irresistible convenience to them, and they have given it a firm and central place in their minds because of that convenience. Anyone who reflects seriously will perceive that there is very little in it. An established Church may be unspiritual; so may a free church also. It is neither the freedom nor the establishment which makes the unspirituality. On the other hand, religion exciting the strong affection which it does, religious people, when circumstances favoured, gladly had honour done to their religion by making it a thing of public institution, and this honour they will be reluctant to withdraw from it. And they are right. Who will deny that religion has gained in England through the hold of the Church of England upon the upper and cultivated classes, and that its being *the Church of England* has made this hold stronger? Who will deny that in modern democratic times a great and imposing institution, if it can be had, for the higher spiritual life and culture of the nation, becomes more desirable rather than less. If its friends are grasping and unreasonable, it cannot be had; but if their minds open and their tempers soften, it can. I said not very long ago that Professor Goldwin Smith was too bitter against the Church; in an admirable letter he has told me that against *the Church* he had never meant to be bitter, and that he now no longer urges Disestablishment, but Church Reform.[8] For the times have changed, and the possibilities widened.

Arguments from religious theory against established Churches will not destroy the Establishment in Wales. What will destroy it, if it comes to be destroyed, is the sense of grievance; of grievance not redressed, grievance which the friends of the Church will not attempt to redress, will not recognize. Let the Conservatives put themselves in the place of the dissident majority in Wales. I altogether agree with Lord Selborne in wishing to preserve the Establishment there.[9]

I agree with him that a man who takes land binds himself to pay the tithe upon it just as much as to pay the rent. I am ready to admit that tithe was not imposed on Wales by any English laws; that in Wales, as elsewhere, tithe arose out of a sense of religious propriety. But the grievance is that this tithe, arising out of a sense of religious propriety, is not applied to meet the religious needs acknowledged by those who pay it, but to meet some other sort of religious needs. It is true that the tithe is as much the property of *somebody* as any land which the law secures to an individual, and that this somebody is by law the clergyman; but the hardship is that in Wales, throughout Wales, the clergyman, and the clergyman alone, it should be. And in Wales now, as in Ireland formerly, those who can allege this hardship will very easily bring themselves to dispute and deny the obligation of tithe.

Let the Conservatives beware of plausibilities, of arguments which may well enough do duty for reasons with men who have made up their mind to keep things as they are, but which cannot possibly have the smallest effect in convincing or satisfying the man whom the shoe pinches. I have mentioned Lord Selborne, for whom I entertain a great respect. Lord Selborne adopts an argument, used with effect, it appears, by Mr. Gladstone formerly in the House of Commons; the argument that "there is a complete ecclesiastical, constitutional, legal, and I may add, for every practical purpose, historical identity between the Church in Wales and the rest of England." Well? afterwards? This argument is of that unreal sort so abundantly provided in the House of Commons, and which made me once say that the banquet for the mind there was to any serious taste a banquet of Thyestes.[10] If the Establishment in Wales is on its present footing a grievance, why should it be kept because between the Church in Wales and the rest of England there is complete identity ecclesiastical, constitutional, and so on? If the four Welsh dioceses were suppressed, the Church of England would have four dioceses the less, just as from time to time it acquires dioceses additional; if the dioceses survive, but with the arrangements somewhat altered, the Church of England will have those four dioceses with their arrangements somewhat altered. Is the danger that we may then be called upon to do for other parts of England what we have done for Wales? Well, if in other large well-defined territories, as large and as well defined as Wales, there is inflicted by the actual establishment a grievance similar to the grievance inflicted in Wales, certainly we should act by those territories as we should act by Wales. But in Wales, as formerly in Ireland, the large majority is admittedly dissident. Is there in England any other territory, well-defined and considerable as Wales, where the large majority is admittedly dissident as in Wales? There is none. We have not at present the statistics, for the Dissenters have prevented our getting them; but I believe that in every one of the large divisions of England, except Wales, the adherents of the Church will be found to outnumber the Dissenters. In Wales the contrary is clearly the case, and statistics are not needed to establish it; we will talk about the other large divisions of England when we get the statistics. But let me again say beforehand, that if in any one of these divisions the case was proved to be as in Wales, the Conservatives would be very ill advised in refusing to modify the Establishment there.

The Conservatives cannot maintain the Establishment in Wales on its present footing; of that they may be certain. The Church will not be suffered to try the experiment whether, continuing in sole possession of the churches and church property as at present, it cannot, in the course of another century, absorb the Dissenters. I feel sure it could not, but it will not be suffered to try. I believe the power of attraction in the Church of England, indeed, to be great and increasing; I believe the establishment of the Church adds to its force and efficiency, and I wish it to remain established in Wales, though not established sole; I feel confident that its powers of attraction will continue to operate after it has ceased to be established sole, and to operate more efficaciously than at present because they will no longer have the angry sense of grievance to counteract them. But at any rate the Establishment in Wales will not be long allowed to endure on exactly its present footing; so much, I say, is certain.

Conservatives may perfectly well refuse to enter upon the question of altering the Establishment in Wales during this present Session of Parliament. This Session has its own work already laid out for it, and the Welsh question will gain by being deliberately and fairly thought over before it is approached in the House of Commons. What is important is that the Conservatives should show themselves capable of an equitable treatment of it; that they should recognize the grievance which exists, and should be prepared to do for its redress something which may satisfy the moral feeling in men, something which answers to men's desire for justice, which their conscience can rest upon.

To lay out in detail measures for politicians to adopt is not my business; to attempt such a thing would, in me, be pedantic, officious, and nugatory. But what a man in my position may, perhaps, usefully do, is to indicate the sort of plan which a Government and politicians, bent on a Conservative but equitable solution of this Welsh question, would do well to keep before their mind as desirable, as the kind of solution to be aimed at, because it can satisfy, and may, therefore, succeed.

Now what is done elsewhere, where there is an establishment of religion, may surely afford us some guidance, supposing that this which is done elsewhere works smoothly, as it does, and gives satisfaction to those concerned. Establishment there, instead of dictating a religious form, follows the main religious form prevalent. Now there are districts of Cardiganshire and Caermarthenshire in which, as I suppose no one will deny, almost every soul is a Dissenter; yet the religious establishment there takes no account of this, but offers to the people a religious form not theirs, and that form only. But the people, it will be said, are divided into so many sects! True; but all their important sects follow one form of worship, the Genevan form as it used to be called, but which is now best understood if we speak of it as the Presbyterian form, because we have most of us seen this form in the churches of Presbyterian Scotland, if not here. This all the considerable sects follow; and to this main form of the religious worship of Protestant Dissenters, not to the Anglican and Episcopalian form, the churches and tithe, in such districts as those I just now mentioned, ought surely to be given. The churches and tithe should remain to the Church of England in districts on whose population the Church has laid firm hold; and the Church should, moreover, retain the Cathedrals, which followers of the Episcopalian form prize more and turn to greater account than followers of the Presbyterian form do.

Patronage, in so far as this change is concerned, might remain as it is; only, in Presbyterian districts, ministers of the Presbyterian form must be appointed, and everywhere the parish should have a power which, I think, throughout Protestant Germany the parishes possess — the power of a *suffragium negativum,* or veto. This power would be a safeguard against the appointment of a minister, following the Presbyterian form indeed, but of a sect at variance with the religious persuasion of the majority.

But how are the districts to be adjusted? Why, if once the equity of the case were brought home to people's minds, and there were a disposition and resolve to make things conform to it, an adjustment of the districts might be accomplished with very little difficulty. It is a matter to be referred to fair and intelligent men, of whom, happily, we have plenty whom one could quite trust to carry honestly into effect a distribution of which the principle was understood and accepted by them. The counties I mentioned above are in South Wales. To take, then, South Wales: I have no doubt whatever that if Lord Cawdor and the Bishop of Llandaff on the one part, Lord Aberdare and Mr. Henry Richard on the other, were commissioned to make an equitable division of South Wales into districts of the Presbyterian and of the Anglican form (the Cathedrals being reserved to the Anglicans), so that establishment might follow that division, they could do it admirably and to the full satisfaction of the Principality.[11]

Between this kind of arrangement and disestablishment the Conservatives have at present the option. Keep things just as they are they cannot. The case is in a remarkable degree parallel to that which presents itself to the Conservatives in dealing with Ireland. In Wales, as in Ireland, much that the Conservatives propose to themselves is wrong and dangerous. In Ireland the Conservatives propose to themselves to restore law and order; in Wales to maintain an establishment of religion. Both objects are, in my opinion, excellent. Still, if the Conservatives confine themselves to these objects, if they cannot, in addition, discover and propose, to remedy the state of things now existing, something which may satisfy the moral feeling in men, something which answers to men's desire for justice, something which men's conscience can rest upon, the Conservatives will suffer defeat; the policy proposed by the Liberals, however wrong and dangerous it may be, will prevail.

In Ireland there is, as again and again I have urged, a moral grievance which has never yet been met. The Land Act did not meet it, and that was the great defect of the Land Act, a defect on which I kept insisting so long as the Land Act was under consideration. The Land Act created a condition of intense complication and entanglement; it enabled Mr. Shaw-Lefevre to speak of Lord Clanricarde's tenants as his "co-owners" — a promising and blessed state of things, indeed, for Lord Clanricarde's litigious and discontented tenantry! But the Land Act did not meet the moral grievance which had mainly prevented Ireland's settling down into tranquillity, and which constituted permanent danger to public order — the grievance Ireland had and has in its bad landlords. Lord Clanricarde, at the recent trial in Dublin, showed the world what they can be. The Land Act did not touch that grievance, did not stay disorder. The disorder continued, convictions for crime and outrage could not be obtained, and we had a judge telling us that "the law has ceased to exist," and Mr. Dillon boasting that "there are hundreds of farms on which no man dare set his foot." Mr. Parnell's original declaration, that "none of us will be satisfied until we have destroyed the last link that keeps Ireland bound to England," has been uttered again and again by his followers whenever they had no pressing motive to disguise their real thoughts; it was re-uttered only the other day. The Government passed a Crimes Act, and they did well. Mr. Balfour has won praise for putting it in force with determination and vigour, and he deserved praise. To a sane mind the sayings and doings of that "victim" of the Crimes Act, Mr. William O'Brien, appear, not fine and impressive, but pitiful, ridiculous. Still, the disorder continues.

The Liberals propose remedies certain to secure to them the support of the Irish vote, and which they hope will be approved also by the democracy, feather-headed and passionate, of Great Britain. They propose to repeal the Crimes Act. Lord Rosebery says that Ireland is in a revolutionary state, in a state of what may be called civil war; and Mr. Redmond supplements this by explaining that what exists in Ireland is, more precisely, "a state of rebellion tempered by scarcity of fire-arms." [12] Then Lord Rosebery goes on to ask how we, in England, should like to be deprived of those three grand liberties, liberty of speech, liberty of publishing, liberty of meeting, and complains that from the Irish these liberties are, in part at any rate, withheld. How extraordinary that so clever a man should not perceive that if England were, unfortunately, in "a state of rebellion tempered by scarcity of fire-arms," in a state of civil war, these liberties would most certainly be suspended in England too; perhaps he may even one day see his Radical friends suspending them. Ireland is not in a state of civil war because those liberties are suspended; they are suspended because she is in a state of civil war.

Then the Liberals have the remedy of a national Irish Parliament. Mr. Gladstone talks now constantly of the "national aspirations" of Ireland; he asks if anyone believes that they can long be left ungratified. Mr. John Morley feels himself "deeply moved to see the representatives or cities like Cork and Limerick and Kilkenny still bearing aloft the national flag, and bent on showing that the old national aspiration survives and is cherished by them as warmly as in any past century." This is statesmanship, indeed! When one thinks what an old, highly-organized country, such as France or our own country is, to talk with this satisfaction of the persistence, in such a country, of rival and disintegrating nationalities, to encourage them, to promise them help in establishing themselves more fully! It is as if a French statesman congratulated himself on the persisting "particularism" of La Vendée, and promised to give La Vendée a separate Parliament. The "particularism" may be inflamed and angry, but this is owing to injudicious treatment; it is to be suppled and reduced, not further inflamed. Who would think that a Liberal statesman needed to be taught this? But at this time the Liberal leaders are not serious statesmen. Serious partizans they all are; serious politicians some of them are; but a serious statesman not one of them is.

Nevertheless, because the Liberals insist now on that moral grievance of Ireland, the bad landlords, they will win, as I have repeatedly prophesied, and now prophesy for the last time — they will win, if the Conservatives think it enough to put firmly in force the Crimes Act, and do not touch the moral grievance. The measures proposed by the Liberals are in a high degree unwise and dangerous; but they do insist on that moral grievance, and they appeal to a mass of untrained and ardent minds. A Land Court with power to expropriate bad landlords would be a far more efficacious cure for the grievance than the elaborate Liberal Land Act turning the tenants of all landlords alike, bad and good, into *co-owners;* and a far safer cure than an Irish Parliament. Even safe and much-needed measures of local government for Ireland may quite properly be deferred until the country is less inflamed and disorderly. But some sign of wishing to deal with the moral grievance there must be; there must be some satisfaction given to men's sense of impatience under it. I fear that Mr. Balfour, with all his talents and all his energy and courage, does not see this clearly enough. The Irish agitators and Separatists have never been in such danger of defeat as at the moment when Sir Michael Hicks-Beach firmly drew his line of distinction between evictions which are permissible and aidable, and evictions which are not. His step may have been revolutionary, but Ireland is, as Lord Rosebery truly says, in a revolutionary state. Mr. Balfour damaged the Unionist cause last year by thinking it his duty to support harsh and fair evictions indifferently. If the moral grievance in Ireland continues to find in him without any sense or resource for it, the trouble will not die away, but the satisfaction with his spirit and courage will. He will fail, the Liberals will win, and for a time, at any rate, the Unionist cause will be lost.

Let us come back to Wales. There, also, is found a moral grievance — the moral grievance of the establishment of the minority's Church sole. There, too, the Liberals have only a mischievous remedy to propose, the remedy of Disestablishment. There, too, there is danger of the Conservatives imagining they have nothing to do but to stand on the defensive, and to uphold things as they are. If they do no more than this, the Liberals will win, and disestablishment will arrive. It is a stupid remedy; a mere work of destruction; and abandonment of means and influences very valuable. But the Conservatives cannot prevent it by a mere negative; they can prevent it only by having some satisfaction to offer to the moral feeling and the sense of justice with which the actual arrangement conflicts. Let them be ready with such satisfaction; a good deal is at stake. There is no doubt that disestablishment in Ireland lessened the security of the Church in England, and that disestablishment in Wales would lessen it still more. It would further familiarize people with the idea of disestablishment as inevitable, as the only solution possible wherever there is complaint. By offering a better solution in Wales, the Conservatives will benefit not only Wales, but England. By failing to offer it they will weaken the Church of England, and that they may indeed well be loth to do.

> Who lets so fair a house fall to decay,
> Which husbandry in honour might uphold
> Against the stormy gusts of winter's day,
> And barren rage of death's eternal cold? [13]

Notes

[1] Two articles entitled "Disestablishment in Wales" appeared in the *Saturday Review*, March 19, 1887, pp. 390–391, and April 9, 1887, pp. 498–499. The topic is briefly discussed in S. C. Carpenter, *Church and People, 1789–1889* (London and New York, 1933), pp. 424–425.

[2] The editor in question was Alfred Austin (1835–1913) who had begun the *National Review* in 1883. Austin had a brief correspondence with Arnold between 1880 and 1887, for which see *The Autobiography of Alfred Austin, Poet-Laureate, 1835–1910*, 2 vols. (London, 1911), I, 79–80, 127–128.

[3] *Letters*, II, 370. See also pp. 372–374.

[4] Eugène Rambert, *Alexandre Vinet* (Lausanne, 1875), p. 545.

[5] Letter of September 11, 1735, referring to the young Argens. See *Note-Books*, p. 432.

[6] Hubert George de Burgh-Canning, second Marquess of Clanricarde. See above, p. 329, n. 20.

[7] Which of the Earls of Lonsdale Arnold has in mind for his emblem is immaterial. Henry Cecil Lowther (1790–1876) and St. George Henry Lowther (1855–1882), the third and fourth Earls, were patrons of thirty-three livings, and the fifth Earl of Lonsdale, Hugh Cecil Lowther (1857–1944), was patron of fifty-nine at the time of Arnold's writing.

[8] Goldwin Smith (1823–1910), English educator, historian, and publicist, is criticized for his bitterness in "A Word More about America" (1882), reprinted in Allott, *Five Uncollected Essays of Matthew Arnold*, p. 43. Goldwin Smith, who was a friend of Arnold's, taught at Cornell University from 1866 to 1876. He resided thereafter in Toronto.

[9] Roundell Palmer, first Lord Selborne (1812–1895), was a strong high churchman.

[10] See "Dedicatory Letter," *Culture and Anarchy and Friendship's Garland* (New York, 1910), p. 217.

[11] John Frederick Vaughan Campbell, second Earl Cawdor (1817–1898), was M.P. for Pembrokeshire from 1841 to 1860.

The Rt. Rev. Richard Lewis, ninety-third Bishop of Llandaff (1821–1905).

Henry Austin Bruce, first Baron Aberdare (1815–1895), was an Ecclesiastical Commissioner for England 1869–1874. An Anglican himself, he nevertheless appreciated the strength of the nonconformists in Wales.

Henry Richard (1812–1888), politician, was at one time a Methodist minister. A strong supporter of disestablishment, he seconded Edward Miall's motion in the House of Commons for disestablishment. Thomas Ellis is quoted in the *D.N.B.* as writing of Richard, "He was the first real exponent in the House of Commons of the puritan and progressive life of Wales, and he expounded the principles which nonconformity has breathed into the very heart and life of the Welsh people."

[12] John Edward Redmond (1856–1918), Irish politician. For Lord Rosebery, see p. 281, n. 26.

[18] Shakespeare, Sonnet XIII, lines 9–12.

An American Comment on Arnold

Life (New York)
II (December 20, 1883), 314–315

This satirical article had been long forgotten when Miss Marion Mainwaring called attention to it in her unpublished doctoral dissertation on "Matthew Arnold's Influence and Reputation as a Literary Critic" (Radcliffe College, 1949). The authorship of the text is unknown. Mr. John Gordan of the Berg Collection in the New York Public Library has suggested that the "F. G. A." who did the caricatures, is probably Francis Gilbert Attwood (1856–1900).

Triplicate Philosophy

'Twas Christmas Day; the air was crisp and sparkling. All men's hearts were opened wide by a genial glow. All hearts, but that of England's greatest Philosopher, who sat a melancholy man in his library; his table was heaped with unreceipted bills. "The butcher, the baker, the candle-stick-maker," representative tradesmen, clamored for pay; his son at Oxford, destined for holy orders, sent a penitent letter and a list of debts, while his son John, Cowpuncher in Montana, demoralized by local color, had drawn on his governor at sight. Philosophy had been a drug upon the market that year and the Philosopher's bank account was at its lowest ebb. What should he do? An apostle of sweetness and light could not consistently go through the Bankruptcy Court. Remembering a droll legend of plantation life, a cold smile played over his lips as he murmured, "I must catch that coon; there is no meat in the house."

"A MELANCHOLY MAN IN HIS LIBRARY."

Presently the cold smile developed into a grin, and the Poet and Philosopher sat down at his desk and wrote the following advertisement, which appeared in the morrow's *Times*:

"WANTED.

Three sad-eyed, high-browed, intellectual men, of lean habit; for foreign travel. Light work, large pay."

II.

It is needless to say, that the Philosopher's house next day was overrun with sad-eyed and intellectual men of lean habit. In fact, every kind of a man, out of employment in London, whether bullet-headed or highbrowed, of gross or of lean habit, besieged the door of the Philosopher. He had never before appreciated the efficacy of advertising, excepting upon one occasion, when his best dog ran home of his own accord before the newspaper had printed the offer of a reward for his finding.

Ranging the applicants in a row, the Philosopher winnowed from the mass three men who bore a startling likeness to himself. The disappointed applicants departed, some with umbrellas and others with overcoats of the Philosopher. Left alone with the chosen three, he bade them sit down and having sworn them to secrecy, spoke as follows:

"Gentlemen — for since you strikingly resemble me, I may safely call you gentlemen — I have received flattering offers to lecture in the United States, Australia and India, during the coming season. Research has taught me that I cannot be in three places at once, and worldly wisdom dictates that I should make hay while the sun shines. For a greater Philosopher than I may arise. I have prepared three lectures, which I wrote when I was an undergraduate; the first being upon a subject of which I know very little and the world knows nothing; the second on a subject of which the world knows very little and I know nothing; and the third is upon a subject of which neither I, nor the world know anything whatever. I myself, shall stay at home and get needed exercise by dodging my creditors. I wish one of you to go to the United States and impersonate me; another to Australia and the third to India. Salary, £4 a week and travelling expenses. Do you all agree?"

They all agreed and the next day departed for their respective three quarters of the globe.

III.

[Extract from the "Sydney Boomerang," April 14th, 1883.]

"England's greatest Philosopher read his lecture upon 'Lubricity' last night to a cultivated audience. His evening dress was made striking by

" LUBRICITY."

his wearing, a red cravat and a diamond pin. He delivered his lecture in a quick, nervous manner, from printed notes. We are requested not to publish the lecture; and cheerfully refrain from doing so. After the lecture, the poet went with some other gentlemen to a cock-fight, and in the evening expressed his intention of 'painting the town red.'"

["Calcutta Times," April 14th, 1883.]

"The great Philosopher arrived yesterday. He is a thin man, with side whiskers, and a complexion burned by his voyage. His lecture, last night, was largely attended. The lecture, though full of brilliant ideas, seemed so obscure, that we cannot but think that the leaves had not been numbered and that the lecture had been shuffled wrong. We are told at the hotel, that the Philosopher invariably goes to bed with his boots on, and lunches upon a glass of whiskey and a cigar."

["Boston Herald," April 14th, 1883.]

"Another chance has been offered the citizens of the Modern Athens, to listen to a distinguished son of England. The great Poet, last evening, lectured at the Music Hall, to a cultivated and refined audience. At eight o'clock a light figure, clad in pink tights and a single eye-glass, bounded upon the stage, and spoke a few words in the dialect peculiar to the educated English.

" 'My blooming friends, since I landed in your blasted country, I 'ave 'ad the misfortune to lose the notes of my bloody old lecture. I 'aven't 'ad time to write another, and accordingly 'ave decided to give you an Exhibition of Sleight of Hand or Spiritualism Unmasked!' The Philosopher then proceeded, to the great surprise of the audience, to give an inferior exhibition of magic and cabinet work. It was indeed painful to see England's greatest Philosopher eating glass and swallowing swords."

"THE PHILOSOPHER AT WORK."

IV.

It is Christmas again. The air is crisp and sparkling. The Philosopher's heart is opened wide by a genial glow, as he surveys the gold of three continents heaped upon his library table.

Index

Index